Keynes, the Keynesians and Monetarism

Keynes, the Keynesians and Monetarism

Tim Congdon

Financial Markets Group, London School of Economics, UK

Edward Elgar
Cheltenham, UK • Northampton, MA, USA

Published by
Edward Elgar Publishing Limited
Glensanda House
Montpellier Parade
Cheltenham
Glos GL50 1UA
UK

Edward Elgar Publishing, Inc.
William Pratt House
9 Dewey Court
Northampton
Massachusetts 01060
USA

A catalogue record for this book
is available from the British Library

Library of Congress Control Number: 2006940748

ISBN 978 1 84720 139 3 (cased)

Printed and bound in Great Britain by MPG Books Ltd, Bodmin, Cornwall

Contents

Figures

Tables and boxes

TABLES

BOXES

Preface

Since my first collection of papers and articles, *Reflections on Monetarism*, was published in 1992, I have written several further papers on monetary economics and British economic policy-making. When these papers were being prepared they seemed rather miscellaneous, but they were all related in one way or another to Keynes, the Keynesians and monetarism. This collection brings the new papers together in one volume. I have included three of the pieces from *Reflections on Monetarism*, since they also were concerned with the reputations of Keynes himself and the two schools of thought which have quarrelled about his legacy. The three pieces have been rewritten to bring them up to date.

I would like to make three remarks on presentation. First, in the text of the book the different pieces are called 'essays'. I think this is the best way to characterize them, because the argument of the book is not sufficiently consecutive to justify the use of the word 'chapter'. However, I hope that – with the various changes I have made for this book – there is enough substance and thematic unity for the word 'essay' to be more appropriate than 'paper'. Secondly, as this is a personal collection, a case could be made for using the first person throughout. But I try to avoid the first person in my work, as (in my opinion) resort to the phrase 'in my opinion' is the last refuge of the person who is losing the debate. As far as possible, an argument should be substantiated by an appeal to facts or logic. But relentless use of the third person ('the author said . . .') can sometimes become stilted and clumsy. I have therefore adopted the first person in the Introduction, the short notes which preface the book's different parts, the second part of the exchange on the 1981 Budget with Professor Nickell in Essay 10 and the autobiographical Essay 15. If the result is inconsistency, I apologize. Finally, the essays often refer to the same events or people, and the result is a certain amount of repetition. With harsher editing, the repetition could no doubt have been reduced. Nevertheless, I feel that each essay has something to add, while the excision of passages and phrases in Essay A similar to those in Essay B would impede the flow of the argument in Essay A. So I have left the offending passages and phrases in Essay A. Again, I apologize if the outcome is less than ideal.

In the Introduction to *Reflections on Monetarism* I mentioned a number of people who had helped me in my work over the previous 20 years. The list has not changed much and perhaps I should not embarrass them again by repeating the exercise. But I would like to express my thanks to Sir Alan Budd of Queen's College, Oxford, Professor Vicky Chick of University College London, Professor Charles Goodhart of the London School of Economics, Professor Stephen Nickell of Nuffield College, Oxford, Walter Eltis of Exeter College, Oxford, and Professor Geoffrey Wood of the Cass Business School in the UK, the late Professor Milton Friedman, Professor Thomas Mayer and Professor Allan Meltzer in the USA, and Professor David Laidler in Canada. Their own work has been a stimulus and inspiration to me, as this collection shows. I have often disagreed with them, but they have always taken my work seriously (when many others have not) and exchanged views with me in an open-minded way where the only objective is to establish the truth. In late 2005 Professor Goodhart kindly arranged for me to become a visiting research fellow at the London School of Economics' Financial Markets Group. I am particularly grateful to Professor Nickell for his permission to reprint the exchange on the 1981 Budget (which appears here as Essay 10) and for the courteous way in which the exchange was conducted. I would also like to acknowledge that three of the essays evolved from contributions to Institute of Economic Affairs (IEA) publications, edited by Professor Philip Booth. My thanks are owed to both the IEA and Professor Booth.

Most of the essays here were written while I was working at Lombard Street Research, the research company I founded in July 1989 and have now left. I would like to thank Simon Ward (now at New Star Asset Management) and Stewart Robertson (now at Aviva, the insurance company) for their contribution both to my work and to the success of Lombard Street Research. Professor Gordon Pepper – who bravely took on the chairmanship of Lombard Street Research a few years ago – continues to challenge me in several ways and I must again say 'thank you'. More recently Ed Nelson has questioned my interpretation of various macro-economic developments in these years and I must thank him for spending so much time trying to put me straight.

None of the above is in any way responsible for the judgements and analyses in this book. I alone am to be blamed for all the mistakes and infelicities. I should also be held to account for any unjustified roughness to particular individuals. However, the 20 years to the mid-1990s were a period of bitter controversy among British economists, as well as of macro-economic turmoil that was painful to millions of people. It seems to me that – if the individuals in key positions made mistakes – they deserve to be criticized. (They would have been praised if they had got it right.) I like to think that some of the ideas I injected into the public debate helped in the policy improvement from 1993 onwards, but perhaps I am kidding myself.

Finally, I am grateful to the various editors for permission to reprint the various papers and articles.

Acknowledgements

Essay 1: Revised and updated version of an article 'Are we really all Keynesians now?' in the April 1975 issue of *Encounter*, originally republished with the permission of the editor of *Encounter* in the author's *Reflections on Monetarism* (Aldershot, UK and Brookfield, US: Edward Elgar, 1992).

Essay 2: Revised and expanded version of a book review of the second volume of Skidelsky's biography of Keynes, which appeared in *The Spectator* of 7 November 1992, by kind permission of the publisher of *The Spectator*.

Essay 3: Revised and updated version of a lecture given at Cardiff Business School in November 1990, and first published in the author's *Reflections on Monetarism*.

Essay 4: Reprinted, with minor changes, from the author's 'Did Britain have a Keynesian revolution? Fiscal policy since 1941' in John Maloney (ed.), *Debt and Deficits: An Historical Perspective* (Cheltenham, UK and Lyme, USA: Edward Elgar, 1998), with the copyright held by the author.

Essay 5: Revised version of a paper 'Fashions and continuity in British fiscal policy', which appeared in the March 1999 issue of *Economic Affairs*, by kind permission of the Institute of Economic Affairs.

Essay 6: Revised and updated version of chapter 4 'The philosophical implications' of the author's *Monetarism: An Essay in Definition* (London: Centre for Policy Studies, 1978), by kind permission of the Centre for Policy Studies.

Essay 7: Revised and updated version of a paper 'British and American monetarism compared', given at the 8th Keynes seminar at the University of Kent and published in Roger Hill (ed.), *Keynes, Money and Monetarism* (London: Macmillan, 1989), by kind permission of Palgrave Macmillan.

Essay 8: Revised version of an article 'The futility of deficit financing as a cure for recession' in *The Times* of 23 October 1975, by kind permission of *The Times*.

Essay 9: Reprinted, with minor changes, from the paper 'Why the 1981 Budget mattered: the end of naïve Keynesianism' in Philip Booth (ed.), *Were 364 Economists All Wrong?* (London: Institute of Economic Affairs, 2006), by kind permission of the Institute of Economic Affairs.

Essay 10: Reprinted, with minor changes, from an exchange between the author and Professor Stephen Nickell in the December 2006 issue of *Economic Affairs*, by kind permission of the Institute of Economic Affairs and Professor Stephen Nickell.

Essay 11: Revised and updated version of an article 'Monetarism: success in practice, failure in theory' in the *Times Literary Supplement* of 18 April 1997, by kind permission of the *Times Literary Supplement*.

Essay 12: Revised version of a paper 'Monetarism: a rejoinder' in the July–September 2004 issue of *World Economics* (Henley-on-Thames: NTC Economic and Financial Publishing), in response to an assessment of monetarism by Thomas Mayer and Patrick Minford in the April–June 2004 issue, by kind permission of the editorial board and publisher of *World Economics*.

Essay 13: Revised and updated version of a paper 'The UK's achievement of economic stability: how and why did it happen?' in the October–December 2002 issue of *World Economics* (Henley-on-Thames: NTC Economic and Financial Publishing), by kind permission of the editorial board and publisher of *World Economics*.

Essay 14: Reprinted, with minor changes, from the author's paper 'Money, asset prices and the boom–bust cycles in the UK' in Kent Matthews and Philip Booth (eds), *Issues in Monetary Policy: The Relationship between Money and the Financial Markets* (Chichester: John Wiley and Sons, 2006).

Essay 15: Reprinted, with minor changes, from the author's paper 'The role of money in the British business cycle: a personal perspective' in the third 2004 issue of *The Business Economist*, by kind permission of the editor of *The Business Economist*.

'[I]ncomes and [the] prices [of securities] necessarily change until the aggregate of the amounts of money which individuals choose to hold at the new level of incomes and prices thus brought about has come to equality with the amount of money created by the banking system. This, indeed, is the fundamental proposition of monetary theory.'

(Penultimate paragraph of Chapter 7 of *The General Theory of Employment, Interest and Money* by John Maynard Keynes)

Introduction: what were (and are) the debates all about?

Sharp public debates about money, banking and the business cycle have been a feature of the leading industrial nations for over 200 years. One debate – that between Keynesianism and monetarism – has good claims to be the most protracted and intense of all. It started quietly in the USA in the late 1950s, with the publication of influential academic papers arguing that the quantity of money played an important role in the determination of national income. Its period of most extensive public influence, and also perhaps its greatest notoriety, was in the UK in the late 1970s and early 1980s. A set of ideas widely labelled 'Thatcherite monetarism' was adopted by key figures in the Conservative Party and incorporated in the party's economic policy documents, notably *The Right Approach*. The application of these ideas from the general election of 1979 radically changed not just the direction of British macroeconomic policy, but also the pattern of wider interactions between the state and the economy.

It may be too early to seek a perspective on or even to summarize what was at stake. If the Keynesian–monetarist quarrel were to be compared to a volcano, it would certainly not be an extinct volcano. Instead it would be better described as at the border zone between dormancy and activity, and liable to nasty flare-ups at any time. The purpose of this collection of papers is to present a view of what the debates were about and how they seem to have ended. The phrase 'how they seem to have ended' is more appropriate than 'how they ended', because of the many continuing tensions and uncertainties. In preparing the collection it has sometimes been difficult to decide whether to use the past or present tense. Both Keynesianism and monetarism, or what remains of them, are still evolving.

I

When the debates started, Keynesianism was the incumbent and monetarism the challenger. Policy-makers in the English-speaking world thought that they were practising 'Keynesian macroeconomics', while economists in university departments regarded themselves as predominantly

'Keynesian' in their views. Keynesianism originated in the macroeconomic thought of John Maynard Keynes, an economist from Cambridge, England, who lived through the financial instability and economic turbulence of the inter-war period. His book on *The General Theory of Employment, Interest and Money*, published in 1936, had immense influence on economic thought on both sides of the Atlantic. Its theory of national income determination – in which total spending is a multiple of autonomous demand (or the sum of investment and government spending) – remains standard in macroeconomics textbooks to this day.

Keynes had an extraordinarily wide range of intellectual involvements, and agile, ever-changing responses to the economic and political developments in which he was interested. No summary of either his beliefs or the main tenets of Keynesianism can be altogether definitive. However, in the 1960s and early 1970s Keynesianism was associated in Britain with certain well-defined policy themes. The first, implied by his theory of national income determination, was that government spending and taxation could and should be varied to affect the level of demand in the economy. The second was that demand ought to be maintained by these means (that is, by 'fiscal fine-tuning') at a high level in order to promote 'full employment'. The centrality of full employment as a policy goal could be explained by a strong memory among the policy-making elite of the heavy unemployment of the 1930s. The third was that, if high demand led to inflation, the correct response was direct official control over individual wages and prices or, for short, 'an incomes policy'.[1]

The emphasis on fiscal policy as the best method to sustain full employment and on incomes policy as the correct antidote to inflation left monetary policy with little to do.[2] Keynes's *General Theory* provided some justification for the neglect of monetary policy, as it explored the circumstances in which action by the monetary authorities could not further reduce 'the rate of interest'.[3] If these circumstances applied (that is, in the celebrated 'liquidity trap'), monetary policy could not be used to stimulate demand and reliance had instead to be placed on fiscal measures. Before his death, in 1946, Keynes was unable to identify any real-world example of the liquidity trap. Nevertheless, in the 1950s and 1960s the Keynesians gave the liquidity trap a prominent role in their macroeconomic theorizing. They further argued that – even if the authorities could vary interest rates easily – investment was not particularly responsive to interest rates.[4]

These claims about the 'interest-inelasticity of investment' were part of a wider pessimism (so-called 'elasticity pessimism') about the ability of relative price movements to motivate changes in quantities, including the quantities of demand and output that were relevant to the determination of employment. In general, the Keynesians were sceptical about the efficiency of market mechanisms. Following Keynes's recommendation of 'a somewhat comprehensive socialisation of investment' in *The General Theory*, they supported state ownership of the 'commanding heights' of the economy (meaning, in practice, the energy and transport utilities) and hankered after more state intervention. They thought that changes in public sector investment, if appropriately timed and correctly calibrated, were a better way of keeping the economy on track than variations in interest rates by the Bank of England.[5]

In the first two decades after the Second World War rapid economic growth, low unemployment and moderate inflation were enjoyed in all the industrial nations. The low level of unemployment was widely attributed in the English-speaking countries to the successful deployment of fiscal policy along Keynesian lines. In both the USA and the UK some economists dissented from the mainstream enthusiasm for Keynesian ideas, and the late 1950s even saw an attempt in the UK to control incipient inflation by monetary methods. But the Radcliffe Report of 1959 represented majority opinion among British economists when it repudiated a straightforward link between money growth and inflation. The apogee of Keynesian influence on UK policy-making came in the 1960s and early 1970s, with the Wilson government of 1964–70 appointing many academic economists with Keynesian leanings to official positions in the Treasury and the Department of Economic Affairs. (Nevertheless, it is far from clear that UK fiscal policy was conducted on Keynesian lines over any extended period of years. See Essay 4, pp. 81–111, on 'Did Britain have a "Keynesian revolution"?', for more discussion.)

Ironically, it was at about this time that the good performance of the post-war economy started to break down. The inflation rate touched a post-war low of virtually nil in 1959 and 1960 after squeezes on the growth of bank credit and deposits in the mid-1950s, but it edged up during the 1960s. Each cyclical peak in inflation was higher than the preceding one. A big boom in 1972 and 1973 was accompanied by extreme asset price buoyancy, and was widely attributed to annual growth of the money supply of well over 20 per cent. It was followed in mid-1975 by an inflation rate of above 25 per cent, the highest in Britain's peacetime history. Policy-induced recessions were needed in the late 1960s and mid-1970s to keep inflation under some sort of control, but they led to significant rises in unemployment. Even full employment seemed to be at risk.[6] A further humiliation came in 1976, when the British government sought the help of the International Monetary Fund to deal with a collapse in the pound's exchange rate and an acute lack of foreign confidence in its financial policies. Whereas in the 1950s and 1960s the Keynesians could claim that that their prescriptions had delivered full employment with low inflation, such boasts seemed hollow by the late 1970s.

II

The changed policy environment led to a questioning of Keynesian ortho-doxy and the articulation of an alternative set of beliefs about the func-tioning of the economy. An important part of the original intellectual impetus to monetarism in the UK came from the work of economists in the American Mid-West, notably Professor Milton Friedman of the University of Chicago and a number of less well-known figures at the Federal Reserve Bank of St Louis. Using (what were then) the latest statistical techniques, they demonstrated a long-run link between money supply growth and inflation. This was a vital input to the international macroeconomic debate. But Friedman's papers and the St Louis research findings were mostly directed towards the USA, and in the mid-1970s Friedman had written comparatively little about the UK.[7] British economists with monetarist inclinations therefore had to analyse by themselves the obvious mess in their own country's macroeconomic policies, and to devise answers which respected the UK's own policy traditions and institutions. A 'British mon-etarism' developed which was different in key respects from 'American monetarism' (or from 'standard monetarism', if there is such a thing). This collection of essays is largely about 'British monetarism', and the debates with which it deals are mostly – although not exclusively – those that occurred in the UK between this type of monetarism and a similarly 'British' Keynesianism. (The distinction between American and British monetarism is made in as Essay 7, 'British and American monetarism compared', pp. 146–72.)

One area of contention was far more prominent in the UK than in the USA.[8] As already noted, the Keynesians gave incomes policy a pole pos-ition in their strategy for controlling inflation. Throughout the twentieth century the UK's workforce was more unionized than the USA's, while trade union leaders had great political salience because the Labour Party relied on them for financial support. It was precisely because of these fea-tures of the UK's labour market and society that the British Keynesians tended to attribute wage and price increases to 'cost–push' factors such as trade union greed. Quite logically, they downplayed the monetary causes of inflation, refused to see inflation as a purely economic problem and advocated incomes policies as the appropriate, largely political response. Monetarists in the UK had inevitably to devote more critical attention to incomes policies than their counterparts in the USA. To a far greater degree than in the USA an important undercurrent in British monetarism was that the government should reduce the political power of the trade union movement. Controlling the money supply had less direct relevance to wage and price setting in the nationalized industries than in the private sector. When Mrs Margaret (later Lady) Thatcher scrapped the machinery of incomes policy in 1979 and prepared for showdowns with the large public sector trade unions, she knew that money supply control was not a complete prescription for economic policy.[9] (In *Monetarism: An Essay in Definition* – published by the Centre for Policy Studies in 1978 – I said, 'The strength of the correlation between monetarist sympathies and a liberal or conservative approach to political problems is not an accident'. Essay 6, 'The political economy of monetarism', on pp. 127–45, is based on a chapter in the CPS pamphlet.)

Even apparently technical beliefs about the determination of national income had a more political tinge in the UK than in the USA. All monetarist economists agree that the equilibrium level of nominal national income is related to the quantity of money, and that the rates of increase in nominal national income and prices are affected by the rate of increase in the quantity of money.[10] It follows that – if a government is pursuing a money supply target in order to influence the rate of inflation – a key policy question is the interaction between fiscal and monetary policy. Suppose that a government is simultaneously receiving advice from Keynesian economists (who think that national income is a multiple of investment and government spending, and believe in the primacy of fiscal policy) and monetarist economists (who think that national income is determined by the quantity of money and believe in the primacy of monetary policy). Suppose that – as a muddled response to the advice received – the government increases the budget deficit in order to stimulate demand and raise employment, and at the same time reduces the rate of money supply growth in order to combat inflation. Will the expansionary budget deficit or the restrictive money supply target dominate the future path of national income? Which will win, fiscal policy or monetary policy?

In the 1970s this issue was of considerably greater importance in the UK than in the USA. Under the Labour government from 1974 to 1979, the budget deficit (as measured by the public sector borrowing requirement [PSBR]) averaged almost 7 per cent of gross domestic product (GDP), the highest figure for such an extended period since the Second World War. Although the USA had its budget deficit problems, these were not on the same scale. (In evidence to a House of Commons committee in 1980 Friedman repudiated the notion of a relationship between the PSBR/GDP ratio and the rate of money supply growth. Later, in 1984 Friedman even expressed complacency about the USA's own budget deficits, when they had moved out to almost 4 per cent of gross national product.)[11] British Keynesians thought that reductions in the budget deficit would lower demand and raise unemployment, but a money supply target had been introduced for anti-inflationary reasons in July 1976. The monetarist view was that the growth rate of the money supply would dominate the effect of fiscal policy on demand and inflation, and that expansionary fiscal policy was futile once the money supply target was in place. Extra government spending would not add to demand, but merely crowd out private spending. (I wrote an article in *The Times* on 23 October 1975, which is reprinted as Essay 8 on pp. 177–80, setting out this argument. The article set me on a train of thought that led to the advocacy of medium-term fiscal rules. I realized when writing it how shocking it must have seemed to most university-based economists, since it implicitly endorsed the anti-Keynesian 'Treasury view' of the inter-war period. It was described as 'not convincing' by Kathleen Burk and Sir Alec Cairncross in their study '*Goodbye, Great Britain': The 1976 IMF Crisis* more than 15 years later.)[12]

If the monetarists were right, fiscal policy should not be used to manage demand. Rather, because large budget deficits might be financed to some extent from the banking system and so create new money balances, the existence of a money supply target argued that the budget deficit should be kept under control. A case could be made for gradual reductions in the ratio of the budget deficit to GDP, in order to facilitate declines in the growth rate of the money supply.[13] The Medium-Term Financial Strategy (or MTFS) announced in the 1980 Budget set out a path for reductions in both the money supply growth rate and the PSBR/GDP ratio over the next four years, in accordance with this thinking. In consequence, fiscal policy was demoted from its long-standing position as the most revered (and allegedly most powerful) weapon in the official macroeconomic armoury. Instead it was to have a subordinate status as an adjunct of monetary policy. The need to integrate medium-term budgetary planning with monetary control was basic to British monetarism, but scarcely figured in the American academic literature.

The UK debate was now to move out of the scholarly journals and seminar rooms, and briefly to hold a central role in the political stage. Large numbers of Keynesian economists in British universities were upset by the announcement of the MTFS, as it signalled the end of fiscal fine-tuning. The 1981 Budget caused disquiet to turn into outrage. Despite sliding demand and rising unemployment in 1980, the Thatcher government, with Sir Geoffrey (now Lord) Howe as Chancellor of the Exchequer, decided to *reduce* the deficit by an increase in taxes amounting to 2 per cent of GDP. To the Keynesians, who believed that the budget deficit should be *increased* in a recession to bolster demand, the tax increases were folly. In their view, the tax increases would intensify the downturn and raise unemployment, and the 1981 Budget was an exercise in macroeconomic illiteracy.

Three hundred and sixty-four economists in British universities signed a letter of protest to *The Times*. The initiative in drafting the letter had been taken by two leading Cambridge economists, Professors Frank Hahn and Robert Neild. In a covering letter requesting that signatures be confined to 'present and past teaching officers and equivalent staff' Hahn and Neild said: 'We believe that a large number of economists in British universities, whatever their politics, think the Government's present economic policies to be wrong and that, for the sake of the country – and of the profession – it is time we all spoke up.' The letter itself warned that 'present policies will deepen the depression, erode the industrial base of our economy, and threaten its social and political stability'.[14] This was the Keynesians' most public attack on the monetarist direction of government policy at that time. In effect, 'the 364 threw down the gauntlet and invited the monetarists (who were far fewer in numbers) to a duel of ideas'. (The last sentence appears in Essay 12, 'Criticizing the critics of monetarism', where the context of the 1981 Budget is discussed on p. 250. Essay 9 presents a theoretical critique of the income-expenditure model which was the conceptual basis of the letter from the 364 economists.)

Since the government refused to change its policies in response to the letter, the duel of ideas would implicitly be decided by a subsequent passage of events. Did the depression deepen, was the industrial base eroded, and were Britain's social and political stability at risk? While any debate about the real world is coloured by the participants' biases and cannot avoid some selectivity in its appeal to fact, the consensus view is that the 364 were wrong. Despite the tax increases, demand and output started to grow again shortly after the 1981 Budget, and from early 1983 growth was at an above-trend rate for six years. Productivity growth in manufacturing was particularly rapid in the 1980s, while such indicators of instability as inflation and strike activity behaved better in the 10 and 20 years after the 1981 Budget than in the previous 10 and 20 years. (The controversy about the sequel to the 1981 Budget is covered in Essay 10, pp. 206–29, which includes an exchange between the author and Professor Stephen Nickell, the Warden of Nuffield College, Oxford.)

By the mid-1980s the revival of the economy seemed to validate the claims that 'money matters' and 'monetary policy matters more than fiscal policy'. Fiscal fine-tuning had been dropped in 1980 and 1981, and it has not returned. The 1980 Budget has been followed by over 25 years of medium-term financial rules, even though their original rationale – that excessive budget deficits would risk high money supply growth and inflation – has faded from view. (Essay 5, pp. 112–22, asks 'Is anything left of the "Keynesian revolution"?' and notes that since the late 1980s the conduct of fiscal policy has largely ceased to seek a rationale in theoretical macroeconomics.) In this respect a fair conclusion is that monetarism defeated the Keynesians in the battle of ideas and its recommendations replaced theirs in actual policy-making. Similarly, no government since 1979 – including the Labour government in power since 1997 – has seen fit to reintroduce incomes policy or to restore the political influence of the trade union movement. Indeed, it is not going too far to say that public discussion of incomes policy as a means of inflation control has stopped altogether.[15] The monetarists have won that argument too. (As noted in Essay 11, 'Assessing the Conservatives' record' on pp. 235–44, inflation was lower in the final five years of Conservative rule from 1992 to 1997 than in the last five years of the preceding Labour government from 1974 to 1979, although no incomes policy was in force from 1979 whereas it had been applied for most of the 1960s and 1970s.)

But other debates were not settled by the economy's behaviour in the 1980s. Having apparently defeated the Keynesians on fiscal fine-tuning and incomes policy, and having established among the chattering classes the principle that 'money matters', the monetarists became embroiled in a civil war among themselves about the exact ways in which money affects the economy. One dispute was about how the quantity of money is determined. Several economists thought that the quantity of money is best interpreted as a multiple of the monetary base and proposed that the Bank of England should vary the monetary base in order to control the quantity of money.[16] Another quarrel was about the relative significance of different monetary aggregates in macroeconomic analysis. The main view in the late 1970s had been that a broadly defined measure, including virtually all bank deposits, was the most useful and important, but in the early 1980s a counter-argument developed that narrow money – or even the monetary base by itself – was the key aggregate.[17] Leading officials and economists at the Treasury were persuaded by the narrow-money school, which was associated with Sir Alan Walters and Professor Patrick Minford, two of Thatcher's favourite economists. Mr Nigel (now Lord) Lawson, the Chancellor of the Exchequer, became an enthusiast for a particularly narrow measure of money, M0, and dropped broad money targets in October 1985.

The annual growth rate of broad money quickly accelerated to almost 20 per cent, not far from what it had been in the crazy boom of 1972 and 1973. The economy's reaction was similar, with surges in asset prices followed by buoyant spending by both households and companies. By mid-1988 the balance of payment's deficit had widened alarmingly. With signs of rising inflation increasingly apparent, interest rates were raised abruptly. By late

1989 clearing bank base rates were up to 15 per cent. One interpretation of these events is that they confirmed, yet again, the validity of the monetary approach to macroeconomic fluctuations and the monetary theory of inflation. The Conservatives had been vocal in the late 1970s and early 1980s about the need to restrict money supply growth in order to limit inflation, and from 1979 the Prime Minister herself had emphasized that there would be no 'turning back' on this central part of their strategy. Given these commitments, the Lawson boom between 1986 and 1989 has to be described as an episode of 'shocking incompetence'. (I used this phrase in commentary on the 2004 Wincott Lecture given by Sir Alan Budd, in which Budd defended macroeconomic policy in the late 1980s and early 1990s. I was amazed by the turn of events from 1985 and criticized government policy in a sequence of articles and papers, many of them in *The Times*. Some of the articles were brought together and republished in my 1992 collection, *Reflections on Monetarism*.)[18]

But that was not how the overwhelming majority of British economists saw it. Their Keynesian sympathies and their antipathy to the use of monetary policy to control inflation were unchanged. Hardly anyone viewed the connection between high money growth and inflation in those years as justification for the restoration of money supply targets expressed in terms of broad money.[19] Instead key opinion-formers – notably Mr Samuel (now Sir Samuel) Brittan of the *Financial Times* – were attracted by the low inflation and apparent macroeconomic stability being achieved by members of the European Monetary System (EMS). The EMS imposed a fixed exchange rate on the nations who belonged to it, while monetary policy was orchestrated by West Germany's Bundesbank. The Bundesbank – which had persevered with broad money targets since the mid-1970s – had the best anti-inflation credentials of any major European central bank. A fierce debate developed between supporters and opponents of EMS membership, which required a two-year period of qualification in the so-called 'exchange rate mechanism' (ERM) before full entry.

Since most economists in British universities were self-proclaimed Keynesians and since the majority of them in the late 1980s supported EMS membership via the ERM route, it might seem that a commitment to a fixed-exchange rate is one aspect of 'British Keynesianism'. In fact, a wide diversity of views is held by different Keynesians on this topic. For most of his life Keynes preferred a floating exchange rate and 'a managed currency' to a fixed exchange rate and the acceptance to an external monetary discipline.[20] But here, as in other areas of economics, the Keynesians had by the 1980s moved quite a long distance from Keynes himself. For the many academic Keynesians who favoured EMS membership in the late 1980s it had the important virtue that interest rates could be set by reference to the exchange rate and not the behaviour of the money supply. Membership of the EMS was an alternative to monetarism and its 'mumbo-jumbo'.[21] (The contrast between Keynes's views on the exchange rate regime and those of most British Keynesians is discussed in Essay 3 on 'Keynes, the Keynesians and the exchange rate', pp. 55–76.)

As inflation increased towards a double-digit annual rate in the autumn of 1990, leading opinion-formers decided that the UK suffered from a chronic inability to run its own economy properly. All the main newspapers – backed up by most academic advice – welcomed the decision to join the EMS announced on 5 October 1990. The outcome was a disaster. Because of reunification between West and East Germany, and subsequent heavy government expenditure, the Bundesbank was forced to raise interest rates and pursue a tight monetary policy in 1991 and 1992. The higher interest rates affected all other members of the EMS, including the new applicant, the UK, which had started out with a clearing bank base rate of 14 per cent. The UK's housing and commercial property markets were crippled by dear money, and its economy suffered a severe downturn in demand and output. On Wednesday, 16 September 1992, a speculative attack on the pound in the foreign exchanges led to the UK's exit from the ERM. The boom–bust cycle of the years between 1986 and 1992, under a government which had initially espoused 'monetarism', had proved just as bad as the boom–bust cycle between 1971 and 1975, which had gone far to discredit Keynesianism.

The sequel to the fiascos of the ERM and Black Wednesday (as 16 September 1992 became known) was highly pragmatic. Ideology, rhetoric and 'isms' were out. The Chancellor of the Exchequer, Mr Norman (now Lord) Lamont, dispensed with intermediate targets altogether and introduced a target for the ultimate policy goal, inflation. The annual increase in the RPIX index (that is, the retail price index excluding mortgage interest payments) was to lie towards the lower end of a 1 to 4 per cent band 'by the end of the current parliament' (which was expected to be in 1996 or 1997). The minutes of the monthly meetings between the Chancellor of the Exchequer and the Governor of the Bank of England were to be published, making the Bank of England more openly involved in interest rate decisions. Ministers were to receive the advice of a Treasury Panel of Independent Forecasters (or so-called 'wise men') as well as that of Treasury officials.[22] The Treasury announced that it would monitor a wide range of variables, including both the exchange rate and broad money, in its macroeconomic assessments.

No one could have forecast in late 1992 the virtual miracle that was about to happen.[23] After the 20-year sequence of blunders and mishaps in policy-making, and of booms and busts in the economy itself, the new system of inflation targets has proved a total success. At the time of writing (mid-2006) inflation targets have been in force for almost 15 years. The target – slightly changed with a move to the consumer price index in December 2003 – has been met in every year, while the economy has not just avoided boom–bust cycles, but achieved an unprecedented degree of stability in output and employment. The Conservative government was not targeting high employment in 1992 when the system started and no formal pledge about 'full employment' has been made under the Labour government since 1997. Nevertheless, employment levels – measured as the proportion of men and women of working age actually in jobs – have been higher over the last decade than in the so-called 'era of full employment' in the 1950s.

III

A debate about the intellectual ownership of this extraordinary period has not yet really started, but sooner or later it seems inevitable. (Perhaps this book will help to start the ball rolling.) It is clear that Old Keynesianism – the Keynesianism of fiscal expansionism and incomes policies – cannot take any credit. As explained here, the Thatcher government abandoned incomes policy in 1979 and dropped fiscal activism in the 1980 Budget, and neither has come back. But money-supply-target monetarism – the monetarism of the early years of the Thatcher government – also receives no prizes. Sure enough, in 1992 Lamont included broad money in his long list of variables that were worth monitoring and the Bank of England's *Inflation Report* contains analyses of money supply developments. However, interest rate decisions are rarely related to the money supply and, if they are, it is because the money supply is thought to affect more directly important macroeconomic variables (such as asset prices).

The heart of the current system is that the Bank of England varies short-term interest rates in order to influence the rate of growth of demand and to keep the level of output roughly at trend.[24] The rationale for keeping output at its trend level can be described in more formal terms. The difference between the actual and trend levels of output can be defined as 'the output gap', and expressed as a percentage of the trend level. The empirical evidence is that the change in inflation is a function of the output gap, being positive when output is above trend (that is, the output gap is positive) and negative when output is beneath trend. It follows that – if the inflation target is being met at present and if output is at trend (that is, the output gap is zero) – the inflation target will continue to be met while the output gap remains at zero. This system is subject to various kinds of shock (such as big movements in commodity prices, because of international developments beyond UK control), but – once the inflation target has been met over an extended period – expected inflation ought to be very close to target inflation. All being well, the presumed inertia of expectations should stabilize the rate of nominal wage growth and so prevent external shocks upsetting the system.[25]

Inflation targets have now been introduced in a large number of countries.[26] In influential academic circles the associated system of macroeconomic control has come to be labelled 'New Keynesianism'. The explanation for this terminology is to be sought in journal articles and academic seminars remote from the original debates over Keynesianism and monetarism in the UK. While British policy-makers were grappling with such down-to-earth matters as monetary base control, distortions to sterling M3 and the cyclical behaviour of the PSBR, a number of (almost exclusively) American economists extended the monetarist critique of the effectiveness of fiscal policy. The argument was developed into a wider claim that – if rational agents expected a macroeconomic policy change – they would be able to anticipate its impact and so render it ineffective. One of their favourite accompanying arguments was that the two sides of a balance sheet cancel out, so that the behaviour of organizations (such as banks) with balance sheets could not affect anything important in the economy.[27] Paradoxically, the effect of this argument was to demolish traditional monetary economics, since most money nowadays takes the form of bank deposits and is predominantly a liability of the banking system.[28] (Essays 14 and 15, on pp. 281–315 and pp. 316–29 respectively, present a practitioner's view of relationships between money and the economy, in which bank deposits are extremely important to agents' expenditure decisions.)

The exponents of this rather nihilist type of thinking became known as the New Classical School. For many people New Classical Economics went much too far. A counter-argument developed, among again (almost exclusively) American economists, that the wide range of price and wage rigidities found in the real world preserved the macroeconomic potency of monetary policy. The phrase 'monetary policy' was understood here as the variation of the money market rate (which is one, but only one, measure of 'the rate of interest') by the central bank to influence the growth of aggregate demand. This theoretical viewpoint was married with the idea of basing interest rates on the output gap to engender 'New Keynesian macroeconomic policy'.[29]

Once a label has been attached to a body of ideas – particularly a quite influential body of ideas – that label tends to stick. However, it has to be said that 'New Keynesianism' has almost nothing to do with Old Keynesianism of the British sort (that is, the Keynesianism of the 364, with fiscal fine-tuning, incomes policies and enthusiasm for state investment). As noted earlier, the Keynesians of the 1960s and 1970s insisted on the unimportance of monetary policy, basing their view on the supposed interest-inelasticity of investment spending and, indeed, of aggregate demand as a whole. The Old British Keynesians were particularly dismissive of the Bank of England and 'the Bank rate tradition'. But New Keynesianism regards central-bank decisions on interest rates as the virtual factotum of macroeconomic policy. Obviously, this makes sense only if aggregate demand is responsive to interest rates. Meanwhile New Keynesianism is almost completely silent on fiscal policy and its devotees have little to say on the merits of public ownership.[30]

Further, New Keynesianism has only the slightest of connections with the Keynes of *The General Theory*. In *The General Theory* the key 'rate of interest' was the yield on long-dated bonds, which Keynes saw as being determined by the interaction of the demand to hold a broad measure of money (dominated by bank deposits) with the quantity of money created by the banking system (that is, mostly by the commercial banks). By contrast, in New Keynesianism the vital interest rate is the money market rate set by the central bank. But the money market rate and the long-bond yield are distinct phenomena, with their movements often being of very different amounts and sometimes in opposite directions. There are dozens of statements in *The General Theory* and other works by Keynes in which he criticized an exclusive focus on the short-term rate in the money market and urged the much greater importance of the long-term rates set in the bond market.

Why, then, do members of the New Keynesian school call themselves 'Keynesian'? Part of the answer is to be sought in an attitude shared with the New Classical School. This is an aversion to any kind of macroeconomic theorizing in which the commercial banks, and the broadly defined money aggregates, play a significant role. The New Keynesians are agreed that the interest rate under central bank control should not be geared to the meeting of money supply targets. In line with their theoretical commitments, they instead advocate that the central bank rate should be set by 'looking at everything', although with a particular focus on the output gap. They criticized the Bundesbank for following broad money targets in 1990s and now they criticize the European Central Bank (ECB) for following the same approach.[31] The denigration of money supply targets helps with the marketing of their ideas, as it lets other people know that they are not 'monetarist'. And does it not follow, if monetarism and Keynesianism are taken to define the entire stage of macroeconomics, that economists who are not the monetarist must be Keynesian? Indeed, if the economists concerned are very trendy and know all about quadratic loss functions, should not they be allowed to call themselves 'New Keynesian'?[32]

Ironically, the New Keynesians have adopted – as a central tenet in their creed – an idea which is undoubtedly monetarist in origin. They believe that monetary policy should be organized to deliver price stability (or, at any rate, the low inflation rate specified in an inflation target). A compelling argument for a wholehearted commitment to price stability was made by Friedman in his 1967 presidential address to the American Economic Association, when he proposed that there is no long-run trade-off between unemployment and inflation. Friedman's related proposition – that a so-called 'natural rate of unemployment' is associated with a stable rate of price change – lies at the core of New Keynesianism. An implication of Friedman's thinking is that an artificially defined 'full-employment rate of unemployment' lower than the natural rate is accompanied by an ever-accelerating rate of inflation and, hence, that the pursuit of full employment by macroeconomic means is a mistake. As this accelerationist hypothesis was the knockdown argument against old-fashioned Keynesianism, its adoption by the New Keynesians is remarkable. Whereas in Old Keynesianism full employment was the main policy goal and fiscal policy was the principal means to achieve it, New Keynesians concentrate on inflation and regard monetary policy as virtually omni-competent in their favoured inflation-targeting regime.

IV

For participants in the debates between Keynesianism and monetarism in the 1960s and 1970s, and indeed for people who are interested in those debates for their wider message about politics and society, the rotation of labels may be bewildering.[33] Part of the trouble here is the iconic status of Keynes in economics. Whatever its weaknesses, his *General Theory* did provoke a rethinking of the causes of business fluctuations and determined the contents of macroeconomics courses in universities for at least the next 70 years. Keynes was also the principal intellectual influence on the financing pattern of Britain's war effort between 1939 and 1945, making him – by association – the Churchill of economics. It is hardly surprising that any school of thought should try to capture his name as part of the branding exercise. But – to repeat – New Keynesianism has little to do with the Old Keynesianism, largely UK originated and UK based, which is the type of Keynesianism mostly under review in this collection of essays.

Indeed, a case can be made that the best way to characterize the policy-making framework now dominant across the industrial world is 'output-gap monetarism'. As explained in the last few paragraphs, two notions – of *a trend level of output* (that is, of a zero 'output gap') associated with unemployment at its natural rate (and, magically, with a rate of price change which neither accelerates nor decelerates), and of *a trend rate of output growth* which keeps the output gap at zero – are basic to New Keynesianism.

But these notions are derived from Friedman's accelerationist hypothesis, even if Friedman himself never spelt it out.[34] In the 1970s and 1980s they would have been regarded as a specifically monetarist. To the extent that (virtually) all economists now accept both the absence of a long-run trade-off between unemployment and inflation and the primacy of monetary policy over fiscal policy, they are 'monetarists' in the sense that would have been understood in Britain in the late 1970s and early 1980s. They have become monetarists, whether they like it or not. (The phrase 'output-gap monetarism' is used in Essay 13, 'Has macroeconomic stability since 1992 been due to Keynesianism, monetarism or what?'; see pp. 262–76).

Readers may wonder about my own position in the various debates. I have been an advocate of the ideas called 'British monetarism' in this book since the mid-1970s and remain so. It will be clear from the following collection that I believe these ideas have been largely responsible for the dramatic improvement in macroeconomic policy-making in the period. I expect that most British economists – particularly the self-styled 'Keynesians' in British universities – will disagree. So be it. But I would be grateful if – when they disagree – they rely on logic and fact, and not rhetoric and authority, to pursue the debate. The Hahn–Neild campaign to organize the 1981 letter to *The Times* rested on two assumptions, that 'the profession' could be defined as the group of economists teaching in universities and that the latter had authority because it expressed 'the profession's' view. But 'the truth' of a statement depends on its logical integrity and empirical verifiability (or falsifiability, if one prefers Popper's way of putting it), not on the job held by the person making it. The notion that only people who teach in universities can propound 'the truth' was wrong then and it is wrong now.

I should make clear, finally, that I regard Keynes as the greatest ever economist, even though I am far from agreeing with everything he said and wrote. If my views on the British Keynesians of the immediate post-war generation are much more negative, I do not wish to deny the continuing relevance of Keynes's work to contemporary economic problems. (I wish more people would read what Keynes actually said! That is one message of Essays 1 and 2, pp. 33–45 and pp. 46–54 respectively.) Part of Keynes's greatness was that his theoretical work was motivated by practical problems and intended to have a real-world application; its real-world relevance was therefore of greater importance than its technical rigour. As noted by John Kay in a recent obituary notice on Kenneth Galbraith: 'Economists are learning again, as Keynes knew and Galbraith never forgot, that economics derives value from its contribution to public affairs and to everyday life.'[35] For all their faults, I hope these essays derive some value from having made a contribution of that kind.

NOTES

1. Attitudes towards macroeconomic policy have changed radically in the last 20 years. Some readers may be bemused that the views summarized under 'Keynesianism' in this paragraph were ever held by a large and influential group of economists. However, the problem with substantiating the thumbnail sketch of Keynesianism (which is of course 'Old British Keynesianism' of the kind which flourished in the 1960s and 1970s) given here is not the lack of references, but the profusion. On, first, the efficiency of fiscal policy in managing demand, see as an example the remarks on p. 45 of R.J. Ball, *Money and Employment* (London: Macmillan, 1982). A vast number of references could be given on, secondly, the commitment to full employment and the validity of fiscal policy as a means of achieving it, but – for a flavour of the literature – see chapters 13 and 14 of D. Winch, *Economics and Policy: a Historical Study* (London: Hodder and Stoughton, 1969). Finally, for a relatively early advocacy of incomes policy, see chapter 10, 'The way forward', of A. Shonfield, *British Economic Policy Since the War* (Harmondsworth: Penguin, 1958), which included the remark 'the success or failure of the trade unions in controlling their members will determine the level of prices – and nothing else' (p. 278).

2. As with note 1, a vast number of references are potentially available, but see – for a recent illustration – the opening remarks at the start of the paper on 'The case against the case against discretionary fiscal policy' by A. Blinder, pp. 24–61, in R.W. Kopcke, E.M.B. Tootell and R.K. Triest (eds), *The Macroeconomics of Fiscal Policy* (Cambridge, MA: MIT Press, 2006. 'Times change. When I was introduced to macroeconomics as a Princeton University freshman in 1963, fiscal policy – and by that I mean I *discretionary* fiscal *stabilization* policy – was all the rage . . . In those days, discussions of monetary policy often fell into the "Oh, by the way" category, with a number of serious economists and others apparently believing that monetary policy was not a particularly useful tool for stabilization policy' (ibid.)

3. By 'the rate of interest' Keynes meant 'the yield on long-dated bonds'. He did not mean 'the rate set by the central bank by open market operations in the short-term money market'. However, the discussions on the subject in *The General Theory* are muddled and inconsistent. This has subsequently been the source of great confusion in monetary economics and the theory of macroeconomic policy-making.

4. A. Leijonhufvud's *On Keynesian Economics and the Economics of Keynes* is particularly good on the place of investment interest-inelasticity in Old British Keynesianism. See Leijonhufvud, *On Keynesian Economics and the Economics of Keynes* (New York: Oxford University Press, 1968), p. 405. The subject is picked up below on pp. 64–5, in Essay 3 on 'Keynes, the Keynesians and the exchange rate'.

5. See E.D.N. Worswick and P.H. Ady (eds), *The British Economy in the Nineteen-Fifties* (Oxford: Clarendon Press, 1962), p. 419. A book on *The Labour Government's Economic Record: 1964–70*, edited by an Oxford economist, W. Beckerman, and published in 1972 (London: Duckworth), contained chapters on 'Fiscal policy for stabilization', 'Policy towards nationalised industries', 'Labour market policies' and 'Economic planning and growth', and not a single index reference to interest rates, the money supply or the quantity of money. Beckerman himself, and the authors of the chapters on fiscal policy and labour market policies, were among the 364 economists who signed the letter to *The Times* in 1981 condemning 'monetarist policies'.

6. The economics and television journalist, Peter Jay, noticed the deterioration in the macroeconomic outcomes from the late 1950s, proposing in his 1975 Wincott Lecture 'the dilemma hypothesis' that – unless the commitment to full employment were abandoned – inflation would accelerate from one cyclical peak to the next. 'The problem is only beginning to be noticed very late in the day because it operates transcyclically rather than intracyclically'. See P. Jay, *The Crisis for Western Political Economy* (London: Andre Deutsch, 1984), p. 42.

7. Friedman did publish at length on the UK in *Monetary Trends in the United States and the United Kingdom* (Chicago and London: University of Chicago Press, 1982), but that

was after 'British monetarism' (as it is understood in this volume) was already up and running. Friedman's influence in the UK in the 1970s owed much to the work of the London think tank, the Institute of Economic Affairs, and the writings of Peter Jay on *The Times* and Samuel Brittan on the *Financial Times*.

8. The USA did have an incomes policy during the Nixon administration of the early 1970s, but this was exceptional.

9. See, for an example of the Conservative government's attitude towards the public sector unions, M. Thatcher, *The Downing Street Years* (London: HarperCollins, 1993), p. 143. The relationship between belief in the importance of money to the economy and support for market mechanisms is clear from surveys of economists' attitudes and is almost an empirical regularity in itself. See J. Aschheim and G.S. Tavlas, 'On monetarism and ideology', *Banca Nazionale del Lavoro Quarterly Review*, June 1979, pp. 167–86.

10. Note that this proposition is considerably more troublesome than it seems, because some monetarist economists believe that a narrow money measure (or even the monetary base itself) is the key one for monetary analysis, whereas others favour broadly defined money measures. A much cited theoretical critique of the significance of broad money measures (dominated by bank deposits and so influenced in size by the behaviour of the banking system) was given by Fama in his 1980 paper on 'Banking in a theory of finance'. (E. Fama, 'Banking in a theory of finance', *Journal of Monetary Economics*, vol. 6, 1980, pp. 39–57.) I have argued consistently that broad money is of far greater importance than narrow money in the determination of asset prices and national income. See, for example, 'Credit, broad money and economic activity', pp. 171–90, in T. Congdon, *Reflections on Monetarism* (Aldershot, UK and Brookfield, USA: Edward Elgar, 1992), as well as T. Congdon, *Money and Asset Prices in Boom and Bust* (London: Institute of Economic Affairs, 2005) and T. Congdon, 'Broad money vs. narrow money: a discussion following the Federal Reserve's decision to discontinue publication of M3 data', *London School of Economics Financial Markets Group Special Paper Series*, no. 166, May 2006.

11. Friedman's precise words were 'There is no necessary relation between the size of the PSBR and monetary growth' in *Memoranda on Monetary Policy* (London: Her Majesty's Stationery Office, 1980), p. 56. In my opinion Friedman was largely wrong about this. The relationship between big budget deficits and rapid monetary growth is very clear in hyperinflations, and is also evident (although perhaps less obvious) in milder situations. It is easy to show that, when steady states are being compared, the rate of money supply growth is a positive function of the ratio of the budget deficit to national income if two ratios – the ratio of public debt in non-bank hands to national income and the ratio of the banking system's claims on the private sector to its total assets – are given. (See my paper 'The analytical foundations of the medium-term financial strategy' in the May 1984 issue of the Institute for Fiscal Studies' journal, *Fiscal Studies*, reprinted in pp. 65–77 of Congdon, *Reflections on Monetarism*.) A key item on the agenda of the Thatcher government in 1979 was the liberalization of the financial system, which implied – almost inevitably – a *rise* in the ratio of the banks' claims on the private sector to their total assets. The prospect of rapidly growing bank credit to the private sector reinforced the case for budgetary restraint. As far as I am concerned, strong public finances are an essential element in any framework of macroeconomic stability.

12. K. Burk and A. Cairncross, *'Goodbye, Great Britain': The 1976 IMF Crisis* (New Haven, CT and London: Yale University Press, 1992), pp. 146–7. As noted, my argument had the effect of reinstating 'the Treasury view' of the 1920s and 1930s. The Treasury view was associated with Keynes's contemporary and sometime antagonist Sir Ralph Hawtrey, who has been described as 'the Treasury's in-house economist in the inter-war period'. (G.C. Peden, *Keynes and His Critics: Treasury Responses to the Keynesian Revolution 1925–46* [Oxford: Oxford University Press for the British Academy, 2004], p. 16.) Hawtrey's analysis was used by the Treasury in the 1920s to resist demands for extra public works expenditure. (The definitive paper was R. Hawtrey, 'Public expenditure and the demand for labour', *Economica*, vol. 5, 1925, pp. 38–48.) According to Hawtrey, extra public works spending 'can only increase employment if accompanied by

the appropriate monetary or credit expansion, and this latter would in any case increase employment whether accompanied by increased public spending or not'. (Peden, *Keynes and His Critics*, p. 62.)

13. I made this case in the late 1970s in a number of newspaper articles and stockbroker research papers, and in evidence to the House of Commons Expenditure Committee. Some of the material is reprinted in T. Congdon, *Reflections on Monetarism* (Aldershot, UK and Brookfield, USA: Edward Elgar for the Institute of Economic Affairs, 1992), part 1, section 3, 'The rationale of the medium-term financial strategy', pp. 36–77.

14. The organization of the campaign to collect signatures for the letter is described in an appendix to P. Booth (ed.), *Were 364 Economists All Wrong?* (London: Institute of Economic Affairs, 2006). For the full wording of the letter, see p. 176.

15. But see pp. 484–90 of R. Layard, S. Nickell and R. Jackman, *Unemployment: Macroeconomic Performance and the Labour Market* (Oxford: Oxford University Press, 2nd edition, 2005) for continued advocacy of incomes policies.

16. Variants of 'monetary base control' were proposed in the early 1980s by, for example, Brian Griffiths of the City University Business School (who became head of the Policy Unit at No. 10 Downing Street in1985) and Gordon Pepper of the stockbroking firm, W. Greenwell & Co. The Bank of England quietly, but effectively, resisted the proposal. (See C.A.E. Goodhart, M.D.K.W. Foot and A.C. Hotson, 'Monetary base control', *Bank of England Quarterly Bulletin*, June 1979, pp. 149–59, for a review of the arguments.) I opposed monetary base control in a number of pieces, such as 'First principles of central banking', *The Banker*, April 1981, pp. 57–62. My 1982 book on *Monetary Control in Britain* argued that there was a trade-off between the precision of a system of money supply targets on the one hand and the freedom and efficiency of the banking system on the other. (T. Congdon, *Monetary Control in Britain* [London: Macmillan, 1982].) In the 15 years from 1992 it has been possible – without monetary base control – to reconcile a liberalized and largely deregulated banking system with an almost constant annual inflation rate of 2 to 2.5 per cent. The monetary base debate is dead.

17. See note 10 for an introduction to this debate. Useful comments on the debate are to be found, for example, in G. Pepper, *Restoring Credibility: Monetary Policy Now* (London: Institute of Economic Affairs, 1992), pp. 10–17, and P. Temperton, *UK Monetary Policy: The Challenge for the 1990s* (London: Macmillan, 1991), pp. 23–98.

18. For the commentary on Budd's lecture, see pp. 43–55 of A. Budd, *Black Wednesday* (London: Institute of Economic Affairs, 2005). (The phrase 'shocking incompetence' appeared on p. 55.) For my pieces in *The Times*, see *Reflections on Monetarism*, pp. 115–94.

19. I dissented from the majority position. In *Monetarism Lost: And Why It Must Be Regained* (London: Centre for Policy Studies, 1989) I argued that a system of broad money targets – like that which had been in existence from 1976 to 1985 – should be reintroduced. Is it fair to ask – so many years later – 'could the continuation of the 1976–85 arrangements have had a worse outcome than the disastrous boom–bust cycle that was actually experienced in the 1986–92 period?'?

20. By a 'managed currency' Keynes meant – essentially – the variation of interest rates to keep the growth of bank credit and deposits at a low, stable, non-inflationary rate, without regard to the effect of interest rates on the exchange rate. See J.M. Keynes, *A Tract on Monetary Reform* (1923), reprinted in *The Collected Writings of John Maynard Keynes*, vol. 4, D. Moggridge and E. Johnson (eds) (London: Macmillan for the Royal Economic Society, 1971), pp. 141–54. Lord Skidelsky has pointed out to me that, by promoting the Bretton Woods system of fixed exchange rates in his negotiations with the USA at the end of the Second World War, Keynes may have changed his mind. For the larger good of a liberal world economy, he was prepared to accept that UK monetary policy ought to be subordinated to external influences. For Keynes's defence of his own position in a celebrated speech to the House of Lords on 18 December 1945, see R. Skidelsky, *John Maynard Keynes 1883–1946: Economist, Philosopher, Statesman* (London: Macmillan, 2003), pp. 819–20.

21. In the early 1990s the phrase 'monetarist mumbo-jumbo' was often used by Samuel Brittan in his columns in the *Financial Times*.
22. I was appointed to the Treasury Panel in December 1992 and remained a member until the general election in May 1997. Mr Gordon Brown, the Chancellor of the Exchequer in the new Labour government, brought the Panel to an end. By giving operational independence for interest rate decisions to the Bank of England, Brown ended both the central position of the Treasury in the conduct of macroeconomic policy and Treasury ministers' need for a high volume of macroeconomic advice.
23. I forecast favourable medium-term combinations of inflation and output growth in 'Better economic prospects in the mid-1990s: why the growth/inflation trade-off will improve in coming years', pp. 1–17, *The State of the Economy* (London: Institute of Economic Affairs, 1993). However, I thought that the improvement would be cyclical and further episodes of incompetent macroeconomic management would happen in due course. Happily, that surmise has been wrong so far (summer 2006). The depoliticization of interest rate decisions – combined with the neutralization of fiscal policy by medium-term rules – has been vital here, as noted by Budd in his 2002 Julian Hodge lecture. (See note 24.)
24. The Bank of England sometimes says that its decisions are based on 'a suite of models'. On other occasions it highlights its quarterly macro-econometric model. ('The new Bank of England quarterly model', *Bank of England Quarterly Bulletin*, vol. 44, no. 2, summer 2004, pp. 188–95.) For the prominence of the output gap in the thinking of members of the Monetary Policy Committee and in interest-rate setting, see Sir Alan Budd, 'The quest for stability', Julian Hodge Institute of Applied Macroeconomics annual lecture, Cardiff, given on 25 April 2002, republished in autumn 2002 issue of *World Economics* (Oxford: NTC Economic and Financial Publishing), vol. 3, no. 3.
25. Notice, in the way that the argument is presented, that expectations – not money supply growth – seem to determine inflation. Mervyn King, as Governor of the Bank of England, has written: 'Because inflation expectations matter to the behaviour of households and firms, the critical aspect of monetary policy is how the decisions of the central bank influence expectations . . . The precise "rule" which central banks follow is less important than their ability to condition expectations.' (See M. King, 'Monetary policy: practice ahead of theory', pp. 9–24, in K. Matthews and P. Booth [eds], *Issues in Monetary Policy* [Chichester: John Wiley and Sons, 2006].) The quotation is from pp. 13–14. But would an expected inflation rate of 2 per cent a year remain realized and 'expected' if the central bank consistently presided over a double-digit annual rate of money supply growth? The expectations-determine-outcomes doctrine – which is a by-product of New Classical Economics and has become quite fashionable in some academic circles – seems to me another of the many misunderstandings under which monetary economics has laboured over the decades. How many times does it have to be reiterated that inflation is caused by faster growth of the quantity of money than the quantity of output? In qualification, on 10 May 2006 King did say, 'in the long run, if you have rapid growth of broad money, you are going to get inflation'. (Quoted in *The Economist*, 13 May 2006, p. 35.)
26. Inflation targets were first introduced in New Zealand, when Donald Brash was governor of the Reserve Bank (that is, the central bank).
27. The elimination of the banking system from monetary economics can be rationalized by the application of the Modigliani–Miller theorem to banks, as in Eugene Fama's article 'Banking in a theory of finance', *Journal of Monetary Economics*, vol. 6, no. 1, pp. 39–57.
28. 'Fama's attack on the problem of integrating monetary theory and value theory is radical: he simply abolishes monetary theory.' K.D. Hoover, *The New Classical Macroeconomics: A Sceptical Inquiry* (Oxford and Cambridge, MA: Basil Blackwell, 1988), p. 95.
29. The key reference is R. Clarida, J. Galí and M. Gertler, 'The science of monetary policy: a New Keynesian perspective', *Journal of Economic Literature*, vol. 37, no. 2, 1999, pp. 1661–707. For a sympathetic appraisal of New Keynesian macroeconomics, see G. Zimmermann, 'Optimal monetary policy: a New Keynesian view', *The Quarterly Journal of Austrian Economics*, vol. 6, no. 4, winter 2003, pp. 61–72.

30. The 'Bank rate tradition' was the practice of varying Bank rate in order to influence the exchange rate and the economy. Bank rate was first used as a means of protecting the Bank of England's gold reserve in the 1830s and fluctuated widely over the next 100 years. It stayed at 2 per cent – apart from a few weeks in 1939 – from 1932 to 1951. These were the years – including the Second World War and the post-1945 nationalizations, and accompanied by extensive quotas, rationing and controls – when the Keynesian doctrine of the interest-inelasticity of demand became established. Hawtrey defended the Bank rate tradition in his *A Century of Bank Rate* (London: Frank Cass, 1962, first published in 1938). On p. 263 he referred to 'the deplorably prevalent tendency to disparage, distrust or ignore the Bank rate tradition' and on p. 264 he denounced proposals to manage demand by fiscal action. But Hawtrey's confidence in a high interest-rate elasticity of demand had become unusual by the late 1930s.

31. In the early years of the new single European currency the ECB defended its adherence to broad money targets in a number of articles, with the research led by its first chief economist, Otmar Issing. See, for example, a short article on 'Inflation forecasts derived from monetary indicators', pp. 22–4, in the June 2006 issue of the ECB's *Monthly Bulletin*.

32. The idea of using a quadratic loss function to derive 'optimal monetary policy' (which would enable the fluctuations of the output gap to be minimized) was proposed by Svensson in papers for academic conferences in 1998 and 1999. See L. Svensson, 'Inflation targeting as a monetary policy rule', *Journal of Monetary Economics*, vol. 43, 1999, pp. 607–54. Clarida, Galí and Gertler said, on p. 1662 of their 1999 *Journal of Economic Literature* article: 'we adopt the Keynesian approach of stressing nominal price rigidities, but at the same time base our analysis on frameworks that incorporate the recent methodological advances in econometric modelling (hence the term "New").' As should be clear from the text, I regard the notion of attaching the New Keynesian label to the sort of macroeconomics propounded in the Clarida, Gali and Gertler paper as rather silly. I am not alone in protesting against the extraordinary flexibility of the contents of 'New Keynesianism'. See, for example, the entry on 'Bastard Keynesianism' by J. Lodewijks, pp. 24–9, in J.E. King (ed.), *The Elgar Companion to Post Keynesian Economics* (Cheltenham, UK and Northampton, MA, USA: Edward Elgar, 2003). It also seems to me that the technical complexity of the concepts put into play by Svensson and others is disproportionate to their empirical verifiability and practical usefulness.

33. Another school of thought is Post-Keynesianism. The main themes of Post-Keynesianism are the importance of money and financial markets to macroeconomic outcomes, but with an insistence that – in accordance with Keynes's own work – money and financial markets are not neutral in their effects on the economy. Post-Keynesians also hold that money is created 'endogenously' (that is, within the economy by the banking system rather than outside the economy by central banks). Because banks and the financial system affect demand and output in Post-Keynesian theory, Post-Keynesianism is quite distinct from New Keynesianism of the Clarida, Gali and Gertler variety, as well as from the New Classical Economics. It has its own journals, a large literature and a conference subculture. The *Elgar Companion* by King, mentioned in note 32, gives a good sample of the Post-Keynesians' interests.

34. See the Appendix to this Introduction for further discussion.

35. J. Kay, 'Goodbye Galbraith', *Prospect*, June 2006, p. 12.

APPENDIX: THE ORIGINS OF THE CONCEPT OF 'THE OUTPUT GAP'

The origins of the phrase, 'the output gap', when used in a Friedmanite, natural-rate-of-unemployment setting, are obscure. I seem to have been one of the first economists to use it in presentations to investment clients in the mid and late 1980s. However, researchers at the International Monetary Fund (IMF) and the Organisation for Economic Co-operation and Development (OECD) – now almost completely unsung heroes – probably 'got there first'.

A quotation from a paper I wrote for the March 1991 issue (which reviewed the forecast made in an earlier exercise on the same lines in September 1989) of my firm's *Monthly Economic Review* is very clear:

> A number of concepts will define the analytical approach . . . [T]he first is the idea of 'potential output'. This is the level of output at which the pressure of demand is in line with the economy's capacity to supply, at which – in consequence – inflation is stable. Associated with potential output are certain levels of unemployment and capacity utilization. [Secondly,] the level of unemployment at which pay settlements (and so inflation) are stable is known among economists as the 'natural rate of unemployment'. When actual output is equal to potential output, the actual rate of unemployment is likely to be equal or close to the natural rate of unemployment. There is no specific name for the degree of capacity utilization which keeps the inflation rate stable, but this concept also hovers in the background of the discussion. The third idea is the rate at which potential output grows over time, which may be called the underlying or 'trend' growth rate. If the economy were continuously to grow in line with its trend rate, and if actual output were continuously in line with potential output, inflation would be stable. It should be emphasized – since people are sometimes sloppy in their use of words – that this does not mean that the price level would be stable. To reduce inflation it is necessary to have actual output beneath potential output. This introduces our fourth concept, the 'output gap'. When actual output is above potential output, there is a 'positive output gap'; when it is beneath potential output, the output gap is 'negative'. A positive output gap is accompanied by rising inflation, a negative output gap by falling inflation. A positive output gap is usually the result of a boom, after an extended period of growth above its trend rate; a negative output gap, by contrast, is the sequel to recession.

However, I had been using the idea of the output gap in client presentations for several years before this. The key proposition was that the change in inflation depended on the level of the gap. It followed – since every well-patterned business cycle has four phases (phase one, of above-trend growth while the level of output is beneath trend; phase two, of above-trend growth while the level of output is above trend; phase three, of beneath-trend growth [or falling output] while the level of output is still above trend; and phase four, of beneath-trend growth [or falling output] while the level of output is beneath trend) – that two phases have counter-intuitive, 'unexpected' outcomes. These phases are the first, when growth is above trend and yet (because the output gap is negative) inflation is falling or at least not rising, and the third, when growth is poor (or output is even going down) and is accompanied (because the output gap is positive) by rising inflation and/or a failure of inflation to decline. To generalize rather boldly, the first phase sees high positive returns for stock market investors, whereas the third phase is bad news. Investors should be geared up in phase one, but be liquid in phase three. (I am aware that academic exponents of 'rational expectations' view recurrent patterns in stock market cycles as impossible. That is their problem.)

As noted above, the structure of the analysis in the March 1991 paper replicated that in a *Monthly Economic Review* of September 1989. But I had been using the framework well before 1989. In a note to clients of 2 August 1988 I wrote:

> The point is that inflation increases because the economy is operating with an inadequate margin of spare resources. Unemployment is beneath the rate (the so-called 'natural rate') consistent with stable wage settlements, while capacity utilisation is excessive. *To dampen inflation it is necessary to restore an appropriately high margin of spare resources. A slowdown from strongly above-trend growth to trend growth is not enough to do the trick. Instead at least two or three quarters of beneath-trend growth are needed* . . . We doubt that beneath-trend growth will be recorded before early 1989 or that inflation will moderate before early 1990.

(The italics were in the original. In the event, beneath-trend growth started in the third quarter 1989, while the peak in the 12-month rate of retail price inflation came in the third quarter of 1990.)

When the 'output gap' is mentioned in academic literature, the usual reference is to a paper by Taylor in 1993. His 1993 paper proposed that central bank behaviour could be described by rules ('Taylor rules') in which the money market rate is based on the inflation rate and the output gap. But it neither contained the phrase 'the output gap' nor made large statements about the relationship between the output gap and inflation. I have found an OECD Working Paper of May 1989, by Raymond Torres and John Martin, with a clear statement of the principles of later output gap estimation.

> The particular concept of potential output which is currently being used by the OECD Secretariat refers to the level of output that is consistent over the medium-term with stable inflation. As such, this concept is clearly different from the maximum attainable level of output in an engineering sense that could be produced with given factors of production.

Torres and Martin refer to a 1987 IMF research paper (by C. Adams, P.R. Fenton and F. Larsen) and express thanks to the authors 'for supplying us with the IMF data on output gaps'.[1] (The Adams, Fenton and Larsen paper may include the phrase 'output gap', but I do not know, as I have so far been unable to track it down on the IMF website. If it did include the phrase and related passages with its rationale, the three authors deserve a Nobel Prize, because this is where the now dominant and very successful style of macroeconomic policy-making began.)

When I first used the phrase the 'output gap' in a natural-rate setting, I did not know of the OECD's work. (My 1991 paper did make any footnote reference to a 1990 IMF paper, which also appears in the notes to Essay 4 in this collection. I acknowledged a debt to Friedman for the idea of the natural rate of unemployment and, hence, of an output level associated with the natural rate.) I just found the concept of the gap useful for answering questions in which my clients were interested. It is indeed ideal for handling such questions as 'how long will growth have to run at a beneath-trend rate?' and 'what will inflation be two years from now?', the answers to which have a major bearing on share prices and bond yields. In the late 1980s I was not aware of the existence of earlier papers, academic or otherwise, in which the output gap had been mentioned. I was aware of the 'Okun gap' idea, which originated in a 1962 paper on 'Potential GDP: its measurement and significance', published by the American Statistical Association in its *Proceedings* (which is mentioned by Torres and Martin in their 1989 paper). But in neither this 1962 paper nor others did Okun use the phrase 'the output gap'.[2]

More fundamentally, Okun's gap is quite different from the 'output gap' notion conceived in the late 1980s. Okun took full employment as the policy goal, and his gap was the difference between actual output and potential output where potential output was output *at full employment*. In my 1991 paper I was – self-consciously – following Friedman. I took low, stable inflation as the policy goal. My output gap – like that of Torres and Martin – was therefore the difference between actual output and potential output where potential output was the output level associated *with the natural rate of unemployment*. This may sound like a quibble, but it is not.

Okun's gap between actual and potential gross national product (GNP) is zero at full employment. Otherwise – in Okun's own writings – the gap always takes a positive value, which increases with unemployment. So the higher is unemployment, the higher is the value of Okun's gap. Whether inflation is stable or not at full employment was not Okun's principal concern, but – as a self-proclaimed and articulate Keynesian – he certainly did not like the possibility that full employment might imply accelerating, or even high, inflation. Other writers – such as Samuelson's textbook on

Economics in its treatment of the subject – noted the possibility of over-full employment, which would be associated in the Okun way of thinking with a negative output gap. As a result, the output gap in the Okun sense becomes more negative, the *lower* is the unemployment rate and the stronger are the *upward* pressures on inflation.

By contrast, the gap in my 1991 paper is zero at the natural rate of unemployment. The gap takes a positive value when unemployment is beneath the natural rate and a negative value when it is above the natural rate. The output gap in my sense becomes more negative, the *higher* is the unemployment rate and the stronger are the *downward* pressures on inflation. The Okun notion of the gap is a product of Keynesian macroeconomics, in which the policy priority was high employment. My notion of the gap was derived from Friedman and – since it helps to formulate policy rules in an environment where low inflation is the key target for policy-makers – it is plainly part of the monetarist toolkit. (The Torres and Martin paper made no reference to Friedman, although – in my opinion – it should have done. It proposed a 'non-accelerating wages rate of unemployment', or NAWRU, which is virtually the same thing as the natural rate of unemployment apart from being clumsier in expression. They might be differentiated on the grounds that NAWRU is associated with stability of the rate of *nominal* wage change, whereas the natural rate is associated with stability of the rate of *real* wage change, but in practice movements in real and nominal wages are closely correlated.)

At any rate, the monetarist concept of the gap had virtually replaced Okun's by the mid-1990s and is now standard. How did this happen? My guess is that the output gap framework started in investment circulars and the international agencies, particularly the OECD and the IMF, and spread to the academic profession via the quality financial press and the centres of policy-making praxis (that is, finance ministries, central banks and again the international agencies). The output gap notion was certainly understood in the IMF and the OECD well *before* the Taylor 1993 paper. (For a comparison of the monetarist and Keynesian concepts of the output gap, see Table I.1 on pp. 25–6.)

When I joined the Treasury Panel in early 1993 one of my first inputs was a piece of work in which I showed that the *change* in inflation was better explained by the *level* of the output gap than by *the rate of change* of the output gap. It was on the basis of this relationship that I produced a medium-term forecast that was markedly more optimistic for the UK economy than that of other Panel members. (The economy was in phase one of the four-phase cycle. I had been similarly optimistic about the medium-term outlook in 1983 in the same circumstances, for the same reasons *and using the same analytical framework*, although not at that

Table I.1   Two concepts of the output gap

	Keynesian concept of gap	Monetarist concept of gap
Concept of output relative to which the gap is measured	Full employment level of output	Level of output associated with natural rate of unemployment, or 'natural rate of output'
Scale of numbers by which gap is measured	Only positive values, taking value of zero at full employment and rising with unemployment	Positive and negative values, taking value of zero at natural rate of output and positive with output above natural rate
Seminal paper(s)	Okun in 1962 American Statistical Association *Proceedings*/Paish in the 1950s, in association with Phillips, although both Paish and Phillips may have been sceptical about 'full employment' as goal	Friedman 1967 AEA presidential address, published in 1968, and Phelps 1967,* if from an otherwise Keynesian perspective/Paish in the 1950s in association with Phillips
View on the inflation process	Level of inflation a function of level of gap, and change in inflation a function of change in gap	Change in inflation a function of the level of the gap**
Name of associated hypothesis on wage formation	Phillips curve	Accelerationist hypothesis
View on output as a policy objective	To be maximized (implicitly at lowest previously attained unemployment rate), as any shortfall is very expensive because of Okun's Law	Output to be kept at natural rate, even if this is less than the maximum 'in an engineering sense'
View on inflation as a policy objective	Old 'Keynesian', that is, to be controlled by incomes policy, and control of inflation is secondary to achieving full employment, although with many variations	Meeting inflation target is paramount objective of policy and takes precedence over full employment
View on money and inflation	Monetary policy (for example, behaviour of bank deposits) not relevant	Output gap most reliable guide to direction of inflation in short run, but

Table I.1   (continued)

	Keynesian concept of gap	Monetarist concept of gap
	to inflation; labour market critical instead	relationship between money and prices holds in the long run, and short-run fluctuations in real money affect asset prices, demand and employment
Terminology	Initially 'GNP gap', following Okun; now 'output gap' in so-called 'New Keynesian' policy framework, with Taylor rules and so on, but 1993 Taylor paper did not use output gap phrase or refer to link with inflation	First use of 'output gap' phrase in monetarist sense uncertain, but probably in IMF/OECD and/or City circles (that is, practitioners) in the mid-1980s; Congdon gave very clear statement in 1991 and phrase appears in UK official documents at about same time
Implied position of macro decision-taking in the wider polity	Political, government to decide on right mix of inflation and unemployment	Technical, decision on interest rates can be delegated to committee of experts

Notes:
* E.S. Phelps 'Phillips curves, expectations of inflation and optimal unemployment over time', *Economica*, vol. 34, August 1967.
** In Friedman's 1967 presidential address the rate of change of real wages is a function of the divergence of unemployment from its natural rate, but in practice changes in real and nominal wages are closely correlated.

stage the output gap terminology.)[3] Paul Turnbull – who had worked with me at the stockbrokers L. Messel & Co. in the early 1980s and become chief London economist at Merrill Lynch in the late 1980s – and Gavyn Davies, chief international economist of Goldman Sachs, had already adopted the output gap idea. Mr Davies was also appointed to the Treasury Panel, and was interested in the work I submitted on the relationship between the gap and inflation. His team started to carry out analyses of the relationship between the output gap (in a natural-rate, monetarist setting) and inflation rates in the UK and indeed other countries. The Goldman Sachs research was (and is) very widely circulated, and is sometimes cited in John Taylor's papers.

Whatever the precise channels and mechanisms at work in the transmission of ideas, I am confident that the essentials of the output gap framework were common knowledge in the economics community in the City of London, and among research teams at the OECD and IMF, at least five years before it was absorbed into the so-called 'New Keynesianism' of technical academic articles. Indeed, within two or three years from the announcement of the UK's inflation target in late 1992 the notion of basing interest rate decisions on the monetarist, natural-rate concept of the output gap had taken hold. I am not claiming any originality for the underlying ideas which – in my opinion and as I have always said – come from Friedman. But I am protesting against the labelling of the now dominant policy-making framework as 'New Keynesian'. To use this label seems to me a radical departure from the traditional meaning of Keynesianism, a misrepresentation of how policy-making praxis developed in the late 1980s and 1990s, and a travesty of how thought on policy-making should have been characterized as it responded to that praxis. (The phrase 'output-gap monetarism' – mentioned above – again comes to mind and seems more accurate. Some economists have suggested that the framework should be called 'the New Normative Economics' or the 'the New Consensus Monetary Policy'. This is less eye-catching, but far less objectionable.)

Addendum: Since writing this Appendix, I have read further around the subject and need to add some points. The 1987 Adams, Fenton and Larsen paper did indeed include the phrase 'the output gap', where the gap was measured relative to the natural rate of output and was therefore the monetarist concept, as I have defined it. Adams, Fenton and Larsen said in a footnote that their gap concept originated in a paper by Jeffrey Perloff and Michael Wachter at the April 1978 Carnegie-Rochester conference on public policy. (The conference volume, edited by Karl Brunner and Allan Meltzer, was published by North Holland in 1983 as *Three Aspects of Policy and Policy-making*.) Perloff and Wachter said that their paper was in the Okun tradition, claiming that Okun had been worried in his 1962 paper that demand management policy should be consistent with non-accelerating inflation. In his comment Robert Gordon praised Perloff and Wachter's work in 'an innovative paper', but denied that the accelerationist hypothesis had been formulated in the early 1960s. By implication, Gordon disputed Perloff and Wachter's attempt to place themselves in the Okun/Keynesian tradition. Gordon nevertheless emphasized that what Perloff and Wachter had done – by generalizing the analysis of the labour market in Friedman's 1967 presidential address to the whole economy – was important. (He proposed the phrase 'the natural rate of output', probably for the first time. Friedman had not used it in 1967.) But in their contributions to *Three*

Aspects of Policy and Policy-making neither Perloff and Wachter nor Gordon referred explicitly to the Friedman 1967 address or used the phrase 'the output gap'. The phrase was used by Charles Plosser and G. Schwert in their comment. Further, in one brief but perceptive paragraph Plosser and Schwert noted that the gap notion was ambiguous, because it could be calculated relative to a full-employment level of output or the natural rate of output.

Since the early 1990s macroeconomic outcomes have improved to a remarkable extent across the industrial world. Do some of the economists mentioned in this addendum – the economists who pioneered the output gap framework – deserve the Nobel prize? Well, someone does.

Notes

1. See J.B. Taylor, 'Discretion vs. policy rules in practice' *Carnegie-Rochester Conference Series on Public Policy*, vol. 39, 1993, pp. 195–214, and R. Torres and J.P. Martin, 'Potential output in the seven major OECD countries', *OECD Department of Economics and Statistics Working Papers*, no. 66 (Paris: OECD, May 1989).

2. See J.A. Pechman (ed.), *Economics for Policy-making: Selected Essays of Arthur M. Okun* (Cambridge, MA : MIT Press, 1983). In qualification, Okun used the words 'the GNP gap' several times. Other writers may then have used the phrase 'the output gap' in the 1970s and 1980s when they meant Okun's 'GNP gap', although – I confess – my reading at the time was not wide enough to notice this. See p. 19 of John A. Tatom, 'Economic growth and unemployment: a reappraisal of the conventional view', *Federal Reserve Bank of St. Louis Review*, October 1978, pp. 16–22, for an isolated use of the phrase 'output gap' in the late 1970s. (Tatom's gap was the same as Okun's, but he differed from Okun in believing that employment was less responsive to output.) In the 1950s the British economist, Frank Paish, used notions of 'productive potential' and 'the margin of unused potential' in an account of the business cycle, *including the effect of 'the margin of unused potential' on inflation and the balance of payments*. See, particularly, the sixth and seventh chapters of F.W. Paish, *How the Economy Works* (London: Macmillan, 1970). But Paish – worried particularly by the UK's external payments deficits – did not make the crucial step of stating that one, and only one, level of output would be associated with a stable wage and price inflation.

3. For my optimism in 1983, see 'A confident forecast of prosperity in the mid-1980s', pp. 107–11, in Tim Congdon, *Reflections on Monetarism* (Aldershot, UK and Bookfield, USA: Edward Elgar, 1992), based on an article in *The Spectator* of 28 May 1983. The point was that – if inflation accelerated without limit while unemployment was beneath the natural rate – it ought, symmetrically, to decelerate without limit (and eventually be replaced by falling prices) while unemployment was above the natural rate. So an economy with unemployment well above the natural rate could enjoy both above-trend trend and falling inflation for a period. 'The [UK] economy can look forward to the happy combination of lower unemployment and lower inflation' (p. 109). The generalization of these ideas – resulting in the propositions that potential output would be associated with no change in inflation, a situation with output beneath potential (that is, a negative output gap) with falling inflation and a situation with output above potential (that is, a positive output gap) with rising inflation, and finally that the change in inflation depended on the level of the gap – was obvious. For my optimism in 1993, see 'Submission by Professor Tim Congdon', pp. 25–31, in *Report by the Panel of Independent Forecasters* (London: H.M. Treasury, February 1993), and note 23 to the Introduction in this volume.

PART ONE

Keynes and the Keynesians

Most British economists in the 40 years from 1945 regarded themselves as 'Keynesians', but this did not mean that they read Keynes. It was easier to absorb Keynesianism by studying macroeconomics textbooks (which from the late 1940s presented the multiplier theory of national income determination developed in books III and IV of The General Theory*) and by listening to the leading Keynesians of the day (Kahn, Harrod, Mrs Joan Robinson, Kaldor). But the leading Keynesians had their own agenda. Most of them had studied in the Cambridge of the 1930s and 1940s, where some form of socialist society was seen as an ideal to be admired and supported. Their political tendencies had an important effect on the kind of economics they liked to do. Marx himself had said that a communist society would have no use for money and banks, while even in a mixed economy (such as Britain had become by the 1950s) the 'planning' of state-owned industries could replace the resource allocation role performed by the financial system in a free market economy. The Keynesians therefore downgraded the teaching of monetary economics and denied that the quantity of money had a significant role in the economy.*

Ironically, Keynes himself was fascinated by money and finance. The result was that over time the Keynesians lost touch with what Keynes had actually written. In the first essay here, 'Were "the Keynesians" loyal followers of Keynes?', based on a piece which appeared in Encounter *in 1975, I contrast the views on inflation expressed in Keynes's writings with those articulated by the leading Keynesians in the 1970s. Keynes was an intellectual chameleon, but undoubtedly he thought that inflation had monetary causes, and he had little time for centralized control over prices and incomes. The Keynesians' advocacy of incomes policy therefore had no justification in Keynes's work. (In a rather similar piece, entitled 'Keynes on Inflation' in the 1981* Federal Reserve Bank of Richmond Economic Review, *Thomas Humphrey even suggested that there were 'enough monetarist elements' in Keynes's analysis 'to qualify him as at least a partial monetarist as far as inflation theory is concerned'.)*

The misrepresentation of Keynes was made easier by the complexity of The General Theory. *The second essay, 'What was Keynes's best book?', endorses and elaborates a brief comment in Skidelsky's biography of Keynes, by arguing that* The Treatise on Money *(published in 1930) is superior to* The General Theory *(1936). The essay is an expansion of a review of the second volume of Skidelsky's biography, which appeared in* The Spectator *in November 1992, just a few weeks after the pound was expelled from the European exchange rate mechanism on Black Wednesday. Who can say what*

Keynes would have thought of the debates about the ERM which were such a prominent feature of British politics in the late 1980s and early 1990s? But for virtually all his career he was opposed to basing interest rate decisions on the exchange rate, particularly if the exchange rate were fixed as part of an international gold standard. The case against gold was spelt out in, for example, his 1923 Tract on Monetary Reform, *a book praised by the arch-monetarist Milton Friedman. So it was curious that most Keynesian academic economists were vocal protagonists of the ERM in the late 1980s. The most likely explanation was that they saw a fixed exchange rate as an alternative to money supply targets, which the majority of them abominated. As I noted in an inaugural lecture to an honorary professorship at Cardiff Business School in November 1990, Keynes had in fact proposed a policy regime rather like money supply targeting in the* Tract. *The intellectual origins of the Keynesians' friendliness towards the ERM were to be sought not in Keynes, but in the UK policy-making elite's (and particularly the Bank of England's) long commitment to the gold standard.*

1. Were the Keynesians loyal followers of Keynes?

Tribal warfare is not the most attractive feature of contemporary economics, even if it is much the most exciting. But the vigour of debate occasionally makes it less careful and precise. Distinguished economists become misled by their own slogans and tend to assert glibly what they know should be argued cautiously. One particular vice is the habit of attaching a brand name to a school of thought, not with the intention of designating a common theme, but with that of heightening rhetorical impact. It is right to be suspicious of this tendency because it conveys a possibly spurious impression of unanimity, of a confederation of intellects, which can persuade non-participants in the debate by sheer force of numbers. But there can be a still more serious reason for distrust. When the confederation becomes known by a special name there is a danger that the name can give a distorted idea of the quality of its intellectual weaponry. The danger is greatest when the name used is that of a much revered warrior, now dead, who achieved a number of famous victories in his lifetime.

In economics, the revered warrior in all confrontations is still John Maynard Keynes. A quote from Keynes, no matter how slight and trivial, appears to silence opposition. It has the same force as an appendix of mathematical reasoning or a half-dozen learned articles. It can be a powerful blow in debate and, indeed, it can sometimes serve as a substitute for thought. It is important, therefore, to examine carefully the credentials of any group which calls itself 'Keynesian'. In the 1960s and 1970s the Keynesian label was attached to a body of economists in England, principally from Cambridge University, who held distinctive views on the problem of inflation control. In choosing this label they had – or believed they had – a great advantage. It was then – and remains today – a commonplace that Keynes was worried above all by the depression of the 1930s and the attendant unemployment, and that his work on inflation was insubstantial and can be neglected. The Keynesians therefore had freedom to propound their own views as those of Keynes. This freedom amounted to a licence to counterfeit his intellectual coinage.[1]

In fact, it is not true that Keynes was uninterested in inflation. He lived through the most rapid inflation of the twentieth century: that between

1914 and 1920, which ravaged the British financial system and devastated the currencies of most European countries. His writings on inflation are extensive. The post-war British Keynesians' views on inflation can be compared with, and checked against, Keynes's own position. It emerges that several leading strands in Keynesian thought cannot be said to have their origins in Keynes's work. The claim of a close correspondence between the two was based on a myth – a myth which was carefully nurtured by a number of economists who collaborated with Keynes in the 1930s, but who outlived him and propagated an influential, but spurious, oral tradition. Tribes, even tribes of economists, need myths. They serve as both emotional support and a sort of shared intellectual cuisine. This particular myth must be exploded. A summary of the Keynesian position is of course needed to define the debate. The account here tries to do justice to Keynesian thought, despite the obvious and unavoidable danger that, by highlighting its central elements, its variety and subtlety may not be sufficiently acknowledged.

I

The British Keynesians of the 1960s and 1970s saw the inflationary process as almost exclusively a question of 'cost–push'. A number of forces were identified as responsible for rising costs of production throughout the economy and prices were raised in response to higher costs, in order to preserve profit mark-ups. This cost–push process was contrasted with 'excess demand' explanations of inflation, in which the causes were said to be too much demand for labour (which, then, raised wages and costs) and goods (which enabled firms to raise prices without fearing loss of business). Of the forces driving up costs, trade union bargaining pressure (or 'pushfulness') was usually given priority, although rising import costs might also be mentioned. The Keynesians were ambivalent in their attitude to the union movement, because it was regarded as both the cause of a self-defeating jostling between different groups for a higher share of the national cake (which they deplored) and the agent of income redistribution in favour of the lower classes (which they applauded). Nevertheless, they made numerous criticisms of the trade unions and some of them were scathing. At one extreme Lord Balogh – who served as an economic adviser to Harold Wilson, the Prime Minister from 1964 to 1970 – was outspoken and unhesitating in his condemnation. Others were more circumspect. In his contribution to a book on *Keynes: Aspects of the Man and his Work* (based on the first Keynes seminar which was held at the University of Kent in 1972), Dr Roger Opie – a don at New College, Oxford – attributed their behaviour to the economic context in which they operated. It was, he said, the experience of past high employment which had given unions the taste of power, while the combination of organized labour and oligopolized industry had given them the opportunity to exercise it without limit.[2] Professor Joan Robinson recognized the conflict between the public aims of the labour movement as a whole and the private, self-interested objectives of the individual union. In her view, although the vicious inflationary spiral caused by wage-bargaining did 'no good to the workers', nevertheless it remained 'the duty of each trade union individually to look after the interests of its own members individually'.[3]

Accompanying this hostility, open or disguised, to the trade unions, was a set of beliefs about the operation of the labour market. Wages were deemed to be set not by demand and supply, but by bargaining. According to the Keynesians, workers did not move quickly and easily from industry to industry and from firm to firm in response to the incentives of better pay and prospects. The labour market was instead characterized by rigidities and imperfections, and wage determination took place in an environment of 'countervailing power', without respect for fairness or for social justice. ('Countervailing power', was a phrase invented by the American Keynesian, Professor Kenneth Galbraith.) Moreover, the imperfections in the labour market were matched by imperfections in the production and supply of goods. Opie's reference to 'oligopolized industry' was typical. Occasionally even the retailers took their share of the blame. As Sir Roy Harrod put it, the distributors were 'sometimes up to a little mischief'.

In short, the core of cost–push inflation was the conflict between managers, trade unionists and the non-unionized as they struggled endlessly to increase, or at least preserve, their share of the national product. The timing and size of the demands placed on the economy were not thought to have a primarily economic explanation. The principal influences were instead social and psychological, and they operated continuously. The outcome of the distributional struggle was not determined by productivity, but by power, with the strike threat being a crucial determinant.

What, then, was the Keynesians' answer to cost–push inflation? It was direct intervention by the government in the form of prices and incomes policies. The Keynesians were united in this, and in the 1970s they probably convinced a majority of the academic economics profession in the UK.[4] Few clearer statements of support can be found than that from Sir Roy Harrod in *Keynes: Aspects of the Man and his Work*, where he wrote, 'I am myself a definite advocate of what we call an "incomes policy". I believe there must be direct interference'. To the Keynesians a prices and incomes policy served many functions. It was, first and foremost, a weapon to fight inflation. But it was more than that. By enabling a central authority to

monitor price movements, it superseded – or, at least, overrode – the
monopoly bargaining power of large firms and the trade unions. It could
thereby contribute to attempts to distribute economic rewards more fairly.
Indeed, it could become a means of attaining social justice.[5]

What of the uses of monetary correctives? These were scorned. To quote
Harrod again: 'I do not think it is any good saying that banks can stop
inflation – saying, let them reduce the money supply. How can the
poor banks reduce the money supply? What actually happens is that
wage-earners get a demand granted which must raise costs.'[6] If monetary
methods had been adopted they would have caused unemployment, and
this was thought to be unacceptable. It would have been the negation
of Keynesianism if unemployment were the best method of fighting rising
prices.

The Keynesian position had the merit of internal consistency. If an economist believed that 'greed' and 'envy' were the causes of inflation, he or
she was logical to doubt the efficacy of such indirect methods of control as
changes in taxation and interest rates. It was much easier to legislate against
greed and envy directly, by laying down statutory limitations on their
effects. Keynesianism was also consistent with a particular perception of
reality and an associated approach to policy-making. If monopoly power
were pervasive, and if markets were stunted by imperfections and rigidities,
there was an evident futility in applying remedies which worked on the
assumptions of ubiquitous competition and the responsiveness of supply
to incentives. But – as we shall see – the Keynesians' position was not consistent with that of Keynes. Their policy prescriptions had no foundation
in his written work and were incompatible with fundamental aspects of his
economic philosophy.

But surely, it might be said, the Keynesians must have been basing their
case on some element of Keynes's thinking. Was there any kinship between
their arguments and his? In fact, there was an assumption common both to
their way of thinking and the most important part of Keynes's work. It was
a technical assumption, slipped into the interstices of the theoretical structure and, for that reason, one whose significance was easily overlooked. It
was the assumption in books III and IV of *The General Theory of
Employment, Interest and Money* (1936) that the analysis was to be conducted in terms of 'wage-units'.

Keynes was not concerned in his investigation of unemployment with the
relationship between capital inputs and output. The vital relationships were
those between employment, output and demand. The function of the wage-
unit assumption was that it enabled his analysis to focus on these relationships 'provided we assume that a given volume of effective demand has a
particular distribution of this demand between different products uniquely

associated with it'. The wage-unit was defined as the sum of money paid to each 'labour-unit' or, in effect, each worker.[7] This was a very useful assumption. Keynes could proceed to the determination of output and employment without needing a prior theory of the determination of the money wage and without troubling himself too much over microeconomic details. It might seem to follow that Keynes considered money wages to be given exogenously, perhaps as a result of bargaining.

The subtle effect of the wage-unit assumption on later thinking was noticed in Sir John Hicks's *The Crisis in Keynesian Economics*. The validity of analysis conducted in wage-units turned on what Sir John calls 'the wage theorem', that 'when there is a general (proportional) rise in money wages, the normal effect is that all prices rise in the same proportion'.[8] Given the wage theorem, it was immaterial what the particular money wage might be. The relationships between liquidity preference, the investment function, and the rest – the hub of Keynes's economics – were unaffected. Consequently, it became a convenient and innocuous simplification to assume a fixed money wage. Further, the relationship between aggregate demand and the money wage could be neglected.

This chain of thought – or, rather, this compound of faulty thought-habits and pseudo-empirical hunches – was the source of all the trouble. Keynes made the wage-unit assumption because it facilitated his theoretical task. He could grapple more quickly with the issues of demand and employment, once the awkward (but, to him, supererogatory) problem of money wage determination was put to one side. But this did not mean that he thought money wages were determined exogenously in the real world. Unfortunately, the Keynesians came to think just that. It is almost comical to picture Sir Roy Harrod indulging in an elaborate exegetical hunt – just before an academic conference in the 1970s – to find some justification for his conjecture:

> I have searched through his writings very carefully, not long ago – for the purpose of discovering anything he had to say about what we call 'cost–push inflation'. I could find only one short passage in Keynes, just a couple of sentences, where he said . . . Of course the wage-earners might demand more than corresponding to their rise in productivity, might demand more and get more . . . You can find those words if you search; I ought to give you chapter and verse, but I have not put down the page reference; they are there all right.[9]

The fact is that Keynes wrote almost nothing about 'what we call "cost–push inflation"'. The 'one short passage' may or may not be a figment of Sir Roy's imagination. The many thousands of words written by Keynes on inflation as an excess demand phenomenon are palpable and, to anyone who 'searches through his writings very carefully', rather obtrusive.

There are, however, many echoes between the Keynesians' and Keynes's views on social fairness. His writings at times resemble a roll-call of the class structure of a late industrial society, with references to profiteers, rentiers and unions scattered throughout the pages. The passages on income distribution in *How to Pay for the War* describe the upward swirl of the wage–price spiral particularly well. Here, indeed, it might be said, is the endless social struggle for a higher proportion of the national income.[10] But it is difficult to infer Keynes's attitude to the labour movement from his writings. He was certainly alerted to its potential impact on the organization of the markets in factor services. In one of his public speeches he described trade unionists as, 'once the oppressed, now the tyrants, whose selfish and sectional pretensions need to be bravely opposed'.[11] But the harshness of the observation was unusual. Perhaps it was an isolated piece of bravura intended more for public relations purposes than as an expression in inner conviction. In *The General Theory* (and elsewhere) the unions are a fact of life; they are not the subject of a favourable or adverse judgement.

II

But, if there are some reasons for attributing Keynesian views to Keynes's intellectual legacy, there are many more reasons for denying a strong connection between the two. Before moving on to an examination of Keynes's theory of inflation, it is essential to challenge a widespread misapprehension: that Keynes knew nothing about, and was uninterested in, the price mechanism or, more generally, in what we would now call microeconomics. This is simply untrue.[12] His awareness of the virtues (within limits) of the price mechanism saved him from the common assumption among the Keynesians that official interference to restrain rises in the absolute price level – or, more explicitly, prices and incomes policies – has no damaging repercussions on the configuration of relative prices. He doubted the effectiveness of price controls, with his scepticism based on first-hand knowledge of conditions in the inflation-ridden European economies after the First World War. (He visited both Germany and Russia in the early 1920s.) In *The Economic Consequences of the Peace* (1919), he wrote, 'The preservation of a spurious value of the currency, by the force of law expressed in the regulation of prices, contains in itself, however, the seeds of final economic decay, and soon dries up the sources of ultimate supply.' A page later he added, 'The effect on foreign trade of price-regulation and profiteer-hunting as cures for inflation is even worse'.[13] He derided the 'bread subsidies' which were common at the time.

Similarly, he regarded centralized control of the wage level as problematic in a democracy. There are recurrent passages in Keynes – particularly when Britain returned to the gold standard (in 1925) – where the need to bring down the level of wages is stressed (if the exchange rate had to be unnecessarily raised). But it was precisely the impracticality of efforts to depress the general wage level which made adjustments of the exchange rate expedient. In 1931, just before Britain left the gold standard, he wrote that the reduction of all money wages in the economy 'if it were to be adequate would involve so drastic a reduction of wages and such appallingly difficult, probably insoluble, problems, both of social justice and practical method, that it would be crazy not to try [the alternative of import restrictions]'.[14]

Of course, the Keynesians could argue in the 1970s – and like-minded people might argue today – that people have become habituated to regulation and control. The improvement in communications has made it that much easier to administer and police a prices and incomes policy. It might be contended that in these altered circumstances Keynes would revise his views, acknowledging some merits in legally imposed limitations on wage and price rises. It is impossible to argue with this. The conjecture might be true, but surely no one can give a definite answer one way or the other. What is clear is that there is nothing in Keynes's writings which explicitly envisages and endorses a prices and incomes policy, and there is much in their mood and tenor which is contemptuous of its makeshift predecessors in the 1920s.

What, then of Keynes's views of the inflationary process? The first point is that Keynes regarded inflation as an excess demand phenomenon. There is very little, if anything, in his writings to suggest that he regarded it as something else. Perhaps the most lucid and consecutive discussion to be found in his work is in chapter 21 of *The General Theory* on 'The theory of prices' (and, more especially, between pages 295 and 303). Paradoxically, however, it is rather hard to use this section for our purposes. The difficulty is that Keynes thought the proposition that inflation was due to excess demand so self-evident that he did not bother to argue it. The discussion consists of permutations of assumptions, all of which derive from a theoretical position of extreme orthodoxy. No alternative to excess-demand inflation is contemplated, let alone explored.

The form of the discussion is to put forward, as a pivot for further argument, the principle that, 'So long as there is unemployment, employment will change in the same proportion as the quantity of money; and when there is full employment, prices will change in the same proportion as the quantity of money'.[15] The validity of this principle is shown to depend on five conditions. Only one of the five conditions is concerned with the institutional context of wage-bargaining. It is the tendency for the wage-unit – or, in effect, money wages – to rise before full employment has been reached. Let me quote the relevant passage in full: 'In actual experience the wage-unit does not change continuously in terms of money in response to every small change in effective demand; but discontinuously. These points of discontinuity are determined by the psychology of the workers and by the policies of employers and trade unions'.[16] In other words, the significance of the union movement is recognized. But the exercise of bargaining power depends on prior changes in 'effective demand'.

This was plainly thought to be the normal run of events. These 'discontinuities' represented 'semi-inflations' which 'have, moreover, a good deal of historical importance'. It is not surprising that Keynes saw unions as susceptible to the same economic pressures as firms or individuals. In his lifetime, the membership of the union movement was substantially reduced on two distinct occasions – between 1921 and 1924, and between 1929 and 1932. In both instances the cause was the downturn in demand. To summarize, Keynes believed there to be an interplay between institutions and economic forces. He did not believe, as the Keynesians of the 1970s sometimes appeared to do, that institutions dictate to or overwhelm these forces, and that politics always trumps economics.[17]

Whereas Keynes hardly ever attributed trade unions a causal role in inflation, there are in *The General Theory* and other places an abundance of passages in which inflation is 'a monetary phenomenon'. (The claim that inflation is 'a monetary phenomenon' is associated with the famous American economist, Professor Milton Friedman.) Indeed, on one occasion Keynes gave a definition of inflation which was stated in terms of the money supply. He did not dither between two competing modern definitions, of 'rising prices' and 'aggregate demand in excess of aggregate supply'. Instead, in his words, 'From 1914 to 1920 all countries experienced an expansion in the supply of money relative to the supply of things to purchase, that is to say Inflation.'[18]

Moreover, the emphasis on money in the inflations of the First World War is consonant with the dominant themes of Keynes's depression economics. The more simple-minded explanations of Keynes's theory often concentrate unduly on the need for public works to raise spending. But this neglects the cause of inadequate private investment, which was too much liquidity preference or, roughly speaking, the behaviour of the demand for money.[19] When savings take the form of liquid holdings (such as bank deposits) rather than illiquid holdings (like plant and machinery), the demand for goods declines and there is unemployment. The traditional answer was to lower the rate of return on liquid holdings, until savers shifted back into illiquid. But Keynes saw that, in certain extreme circumstances, there might be psychological and institutional barriers to a sufficient downward reduction in the rate of interest. It followed from this that monetary policy, intended to engineer changes in interest rates, could not by itself cause a recovery of demand. The potential impotence of monetary policy had to be remedied, in his words, by 'a somewhat comprehensive socialization of investment'. If investment were in state hands, it could be undertaken with larger ambitions than mere profit-maximization. In particular, it could be stepped up in order to promote higher employment.

However, if the risk that monetary policy might become impotent in a depression is one of the principal conclusions of Keynes's economics, there is no foundation for the widespread Keynesian attitude that 'money does not matter'. Keynes's writings are replete with references to the banking system and financial assets. It would be remarkable if he thought them irrelevant to problems of economic policy in normal circumstances. (Of course, the 1930s were not normal circumstances. But it should be remembered that three out of the eight historical illustrations in chapter 30 of *A Treatise on Money*, the book which preceded *The General Theory*, were analyses of inflations. Keynes did think about the longer time span.[20])

In Keynes, the monetary variable under discussion was usually the rate of interest (the price of money) rather than the money supply (its quantity). This has subsequently been a fertile and persistent source of disagreement between the Keynesians and others. The Keynesians say that no support is to be found in *The General Theory* or elsewhere for the mechanistic rules advocated by, for example, Milton Friedman of the Chicago School, in which the monetary variable emphasized is the quantity of money. It is true that nowhere in Keynes is there a forthright recommendation for stable growth of a monetary aggregate. But there are sections of *A Tract on Monetary Reform* which come remarkably close to this standard monetarist position.[21] (Keynes's proposal for 'a managed currency' is discussed in more detail in Essay 3, on pp. 61–3.)

Of course, Keynes was in no position to talk with confidence about fluctuations in money supply growth, because he lived in an age before full statistics were available. The rate of interest, on the other hand, was something known and observable. There are extensive passages in *A Treatise on Money* (1930) where Keynes was examining such measures of the money supply as he could find, and trying to identify relationships between them on the one hand and nominal asset prices and national income on the other. The two most interesting cases were in Britain in the decade after the First World War and in the USA between 1925 and 1930.[22] There were mismatches between changes in the money supply and nominal national income changes, which, interestingly, he attributed to 'lags' between 'profit' and 'income inflations'. The discussion in these pages is a fascinating attempt to understand the transmission mechanism of monetary policy.

Keynes's tendency to focus on the price of money, rather than its quantity, may also have reflected his involvement in insurance and fund management. He was active in City finance and speculation throughout the 1920s and 1930s, and to some extent looked at the monetary situation in the same way as bankers and brokers. Bankers, who have to arrange loans from day to day, think of the demand for credit as fickle and volatile, while economists, who look at a range of monetary aggregates as measured by long-run time series, regard it as continuous and stable. Bankers see interest rates, which give signals of credit availability, as the determining variable, while monetary economists have a greater tendency to watch the money supply. Keynes mostly thought in interest rate terms. But this does not mean that, in the general run of events, he distrusted the effectiveness of monetary policy as a method of changing demand, output and employment. A clear statement of his position is again to be found in *A Treatise on Money*. The authorities have, he said, no control over individual prices (like those of cars or meat) in the economic system. Nor do they have *direct* control over the money supply because the central bank must act as lender of last resort. But they do determine one price, 'the rate of discount', or the rate of interest. It is this which gives them leverage over the system as a whole.[23]

III

One final point, which is perhaps decisive in refuting the Keynesians, needs to be made: it is that when Britain was confronted with nasty outbreaks of inflation during his lifetime, Keynes supported policies of a traditional, demand-restrictive nature. It has been too readily assumed that the years from 1914 to 1945 were of prolonged and unremitting depression, characterized by falling or stable prices, and that Keynes was therefore never called upon to offer advice on the control of inflation. This is quite wrong. In early 1920, Britain was in the midst of an inflationary boom of proportions which have never been paralleled before or since. (Conditions in 1973 and 1974 were, in some respects, rather similar.) In both 1918 and 1919 money wages soared by nearly 30 per cent a year, and even by February 1920 there seemed no sign of an early release from the grip of the price explosion which had inevitably followed.

The Chancellor of the Exchequer, Austen Chamberlain, asked for an interview with Keynes to obtain his opinion on the right course of action. Chamberlain later summarized his impression of the interview as, 'K.

would go for a financial crisis (doesn't believe it would lead to unemployment). Would go to whatever rate is necessary – perhaps 10 per cent – and would keep it at that for three years'.[24] Shortly afterwards Keynes prepared a 15-point memorandum in which he amplified his advice. Perhaps its most startling feature is the similarity between the economic issues of early 1920 and those of late 1974, and only a little less startling is Keynes's set of recommendations to deal with the problems. He wanted stiff and harsh deflation.

Is this document an aberration? Would Keynes have retracted it with the benefit of hindsight and of the breakthroughs in economic thought he pioneered in the 1930s? In 1942 he was shown his 1920 memorandum. He was not in the least repentant. Far from thinking his position too iconoclastic, he acknowledged that other economists at the time had thought exactly the same and that they had been equally right. To quote:

> As usual the economists were found to be unanimous and the common charge to the contrary without foundation! I feel myself that I should give today exactly the same advice that I gave then, namely a swift and sharp dose of dear money, sufficient to break the market, and quick enough to prevent at least some of the disastrous consequences that would then ensue. In fact, the remedies of the economists were taken, but too timidly.[25]

There is no need to go any further. The argument could be reinforced by an analysis of Keynes's views of war finance, but there is already enough evidence to validate the main contentions of this essay. There was almost nothing in Keynes's writings, philosophy or work which coincided with the views on inflation policy held by the British Keynesians of the 1960s and 1970s. They favoured direct government interference to keep prices down; he scorned price regulation as ineffective and harmful. They considered inflation to be a cost–push phenomenon; he never envisaged it as anything but a phenomenon of excess demand. They dismissed monetary policy; he thought the one sure answer to inflationary excess was 'a swift and severe dose of dear money'.

Were the Keynesians really loyal followers of Keynes?

NOTES

1. The best-known Keynesians in this country in the 1960s and 1970s were Sir Roy Harrod, Lord Kahn, Lord Kaldor and Joan Robinson. Kahn, Kaldor and Mrs Robinson stayed at Cambridge, but Sir Roy Harrod taught at Oxford for most of his academic career. Although Cambridge was the home of Keynesianism, many economists in universities throughout England professed Keynesian affiliations, and it is, perhaps, misleading to locate it too precisely in geographical terms. Throughout the essay, Keynesianism

means the body of beliefs of this group of economists, and the Keynesians were these economists. A distinction is therefore being drawn between Keynesian economics and Keynes's economics. A similar distinction was made in A. Leijonhufvud's *On Keynesian Economics and the Economics of Keynes* (New York: Oxford University Press, 1968), although Leijonhufvud was concerned with the whole body of Keynes's economics whereas I am only interested in his work on inflation.

2.   Roger Opie, 'The political consequences of Lord Keynes', in D.E. Moggridge (ed.), *Keynes: Aspects of the Man and his Work* (London: Macmillan, 1974), p. 87.

3.   Joan Robinson, *Economic Philosophy* (Harmondsworth: Penguin, 1962), p. 131.

4.   In 1990 the Institute of Economic Affairs published *British Economic Opinion: A Survey of a Thousand Economists* by M. Ricketts and E. Shoesmith. When asked for their views on the proposition 'Wage–price controls should be used to control inflation', 5.4 per cent of respondents 'agreed strongly' and 28.3 per cent agreed 'with reservations', while 14.4 per cent neither agreed nor disagreed. However, attitudes towards wage and price controls would undoubtedly have been more positive 15 or 20 years earlier.

5.   Sir Roy Harrod, 'Keynes's theory and its applications', in Moggridge (ed.), *Keynes: Aspects*, pp. 9–10; and Opie, in Moggridge (ed.), *Keynes: Aspects*, p. 86. The 1970s saw suggestions that there was such a thing as a 'just price' and that 'social considerations' should enter into price determination. See A. Jones, *The New Inflation* (London: Andre Deutsch, 1973), particularly chapters 5 and 6.

6.   Sir Roy Harrod in Moggridge (ed.), *Keynes: Aspects*, p. 9.

7.   J.M. Keynes, *The General Theory of Employment, Interest and Money* (London: Macmillan, Papermac edition, 1964, originally published 1936), pp. 41–3. See, particularly, the footnote on pp. 42–3.

8.   Sir John Hicks, *The Crisis in Keynesian Economics* (Oxford: Blackwell, 1974), pp. 59–60.

9.   Sir Roy Harrod in Moggridge (ed.), *Keynes: Aspects*, p. 9. Other examples: 'It would be most inappropriate for me to stand up here and tell you what Keynes would have thought. Goodness knows he would have thought of something much cleverer than I can think of' (pp. 8–9); and: 'I do not think we can tackle it without direct interference. They do seem to be doing this rather more effectively in America now than here having tribunals, boards, call them what you will, responsible for fixing maximum price increases. I am sure we have got to come to that, and, as our Chairman very kindly hinted, I had a letter in *The Times* on this very subject yesterday' (p. 10).

10.   J.M. Keynes, *How to Pay for the War* (1940), which originally appeared as articles in *The Times* on 14 and 15 November 1939, with pp. 61–70 reprinted in R.J. Ball and P. Doyle (eds), *Inflation* (Harmondsworth: Penguin, 1969), pp. 21–7.

11.   J.M. Keynes, 'Liberalism and labour' (1926), reprinted in *Essays in Persuasion* (London: Macmillan, 1931), p. 341.

12.   An amusing footnote on this theme appeared on pp. 70–71 of D.E. Moggridge (ed.), *Keynes: Aspects of the Man and his Work*. It was at Joan Robinson's expense. She had supported the notion that 'Maynard had never spent the 20 minutes necessary to understand the theory of value', sublimely unaware that as a matter of fact (as is clear from one of the notes to her publisher) he had acted as referee to her very book on the subject.

13.   E. Johnson and D.E. Moggridge (eds), *The Collected Writings of John Maynard Keynes*, vol. II, *The Economic Consequences of the Peace* (London: Macmillan for the Royal Economic Society, 1971, originally published in 1919), pp. 151–2.

14.   Keynes, *Essays in Persuasion*, p. 284. The alternative of import restrictions was the one preferred in the context of the passage quoted, but Keynes was in favour of a devaluation if it was politically possible.

15.   Keynes, *General Theory*, p. 296.

16.   Keynes, *General Theory*, p. 301.

17.   The frailty of institutions in the face of economic imperatives was one theme of G.A. Dorfman, *Wage Politics in Britain* (London: Charles Knight, 1974). See, particularly, chapter 2 on the inter-war period.

18.   Keynes, *Essays in Persuasion*, p. 60.

19. There is a fascinating discussion of the notion of liquidity preference, and its connection with investment flexibility, in the second part of Sir John Hicks, *The Crisis in Keynesian Economics*.

20. Johnson and Moggridge (eds), *The Collected Writings of John Maynard Keynes*, vol. VI, *A Treatise on Money: The Applied Theory of Money* (London: Macmillan for the Royal Economic Society, 1971, originally published in 1930), pp. 132–86.

21. Johnson and Moggridge (eds), *The Collected Writings of John Maynard Keynes*, vol. IV, *A Tract on Monetary Reform* (London: Macmillan for the Royal Economic Society, 1971, originally published in 1923), pp. 141–8.

22. Keynes, *Treatise*, pp. 155–61 and pp. 170–75.

23. Keynes himself put 'direct' in italics (p. 189) of the *Treatise*, presumably because he thought that a rise in the price of money would cause people to economize on its use and, therefore, the authorities could indirectly control the money supply. The belief that a central bank should not hold down the money supply directly, because it has the lender-of-last-resort function, is a very typical banker's attitude. Incidentally, it is one reason why Friedmanite economists and central bankers often do not see eye to eye.

24. S. Howson, ' "A dear money man"? Keynes on monetary policy, 1920', *The Economic Journal*, June 1973, p. 458.

25. Howson, ' "A dear money man" ', p. 461.

2.   What was Keynes's best book?

Large numbers of books and papers are still being written about Keynes in the opening years of the twenty-first century. As the Introduction to the current volume showed, the name 'Keynes' continues to have enormous brand value in economics and has been appropriated by diverse bodies of thought, some of which have only a loose connection with Keynes's own teaching. How should Keynes's work now be viewed? What was its purpose and does it remain relevant? From the perspective of the early twenty-first century, what was his most interesting and durable contribution? What was his best book?

I

Keynes can be seen as an analyst and defender of managed capitalism, the man who showed how harmful fluctuations in business activity could be smoothed out by well-judged government action and who therefore made the market economy work more efficiently. As such, he might be represented as a hero of the Right. Alternatively, he can be interpreted as the champion of the public sector, the foremost advocate of the large-scale nationalization of the British economy which occurred in the late 1940s. If so, he is one of the great thinkers of the Left. The diversity of appreciations of Keynes stems from the difficulty of locating his work in the political spectra of twentieth-century Britain.

Born in 1883, he grew up in the ordered and stable world of late-Victorian and Edwardian England. He was the son of a Cambridge don and was himself to become a Fellow of King's College. One aspect of the order and stability of British society in his youth and early adulthood was its currency, the pound sterling. It had been tied to gold since the late seventeenth century and had much the same value (in terms of the things it would buy) in 1910 as 200 years earlier. When Keynes first started to think about the theory of credit and money, most people believed that the value of money would be roughly the same when they died as when they were born.

Britain's currency stability was ruptured by the First World War. The government resorted to the printing presses to finance military spending. The result was a severe inflation, which led to a large gap between labour costs in Britain and competitor nations, the suspension of the gold standard and a devaluation of sterling against the dollar. The central question for economic policy in 1919 was, 'should Britain return to the gold standard and, if so, at what exchange rate?' The consensus of the great, the good and the orthodox was that Britain should return to gold as soon as possible, with the gold price (in terms of sterling) the same as it had been in 1914. There was much to be said in favour of the orthodox view, not least that it had been the traditional response in previous post-war contexts. Britain's rulers had refused to accept a permanent devaluation of the pound (against gold) after the wars of William III and the Napoleonic Wars.

Keynes's most important insight in the early 1920s was that the gold standard was obsolete. As is well known, he opposed the particular exchange rate against the dollar ($4.86 to the pound) implied by the restoration of the pre-war gold price. He thought, correctly, that the British and American price levels were out of line at the $4.86 exchange rate and that the attempt to bring the price levels into balance (that is, to reduce British prices) would be deflationary, and would lead to unnecessary declines in output and employment. When the Chancellor of the Exchequer, Winston Churchill, decided to return to gold, Keynes brought his criticisms together in a celebrated pamphlet on *The Economic Consequences of Mr. Churchill*. Keynes's analysis was fully vindicated by events. Britain suffered a general strike in 1926 and a few years of industrial semi-stagnation, whereas other nations enjoyed the prosperity of the Roaring Twenties. Keynes's reputation as an economic analyst, commentator and adviser was hugely enhanced.

But his attack on the gold standard was over a much wider front than the criticism of one particular gold price. Keynes saw that the growth of banking systems in the century of peace before 1914 had dramatically reduced the use of gold in transactions. By the beginning of the twentieth century virtually all significant payments, including international payments, were in paper money. In a formal sense gold remained the ultimate bedrock of the system and people appeared justified in believing that their paper was 'as good as gold'. But, in truth, changes in the quantity of paper money (that is, bank notes and deposits) had become both the principal regulator of the business cycle and the main determinant of the price level. In this new world fluctuations in the quantity of gold were accidental, their impact on monetary policy was capricious and their relevance to meaningful policy goals (the stability of output and prices) was highly debatable. What was the point of the gold link? Surely, gold's continuing prestige relied on superstition and tradition, and had no rational, scientific basis. As Keynes remarked in his 1923 *Tract on Monetary Reform*, gold had become 'a barbarous relic'.

Both *A Tract on Monetary Reform* and *The Economic Consequences of Mr. Churchill* were based on newspaper articles. Neither pretended to be serious academic tomes. Keynes's journalistic activity was frantic at this stage of his career and seems to have been motivated by the desire to have a big income. (He received £4000 for organizing some supplements to the *Manchester Guardian Commercial* in 1922, a sum equivalent to about £125 000 in the money of 2007.) However, the two short books identified the vital monetary question of the twentieth century. If governments could no longer rely on the gold standard, how should the task of monetary management be performed? Even if the British government had restored the gold link at a more sensible exchange rate than $4.86 to the pound, would it really have been advisable to make interest rates depend on the fluctuating moods of the foreign exchange markets and the accidents of gold-mining technology?

Keynes wanted to replace the gold standard by a managed currency, where the essence of the management task was to control the level of bank credit (and of bank deposits, which constituted most of the quantity of money) by a number of instruments which were just beginning to be understood. Bank rate – the rate of interest set by the Bank of England in its money market activities – was a traditional weapon of considerable power. But Keynes was also attracted to the practice of influencing banks' reserves by open market operations, which was being developed in the USA by the newly created Federal Reserve System under the leadership of Benjamin Strong. (The Federal Reserve had been founded in 1914 and was a much younger institution than the Bank of England.) Keynes had no doubt that currency stabilization was vital to the preservation of the market economy. As he remarked in the *Tract*: 'The individualistic capitalism of today presumes a stable measuring-pod of value, and cannot be efficient – perhaps cannot survive – without one.'[1]

Keynes took his analysis further in a two-volume work, the *Treatise on Money*, published in 1930. It was a remarkable production, combining abstract analysis with detailed descriptions of monetary institutions and particular historical episodes. It expressed Keynes's considerable interest in international currency matters and theorized on the role that banking arrangements might play in macroeconomic instability. It went much further than the *Tract* and his miscellaneous pamphlets in setting out an agenda for monetary reform in a world which had outgrown gold. But its publication coincided with the worst collapses in demand and output ever inflicted on the international economy, and the most humiliating setback for the capitalist system. American industrial production fell by 45 per cent between 1929 and 1932. Even worse, in some countries (although not Britain) the recovery from slump was gradual and reluctant. Political extremism took hold in leading industrial nations, notably Germany, Italy

and the Soviet Union, and many intellectuals thought that the serious political debate had been polarized between Communism and Fascism. Keynes
decided that yet more analysis and explanation were needed. In 1936 he
published his *General Theory of Employment, Interest and Money*, a book
which is usually regarded as the start of modern macroeconomics. Indeed,
it is often described as the greatest book on economics written in the
twentieth century.

Its emphasis was rather different from the *Tract* and the *Treatise*. Like its
predecessors, it contained ample discussion of interest rates and money,
and of their relationships with other variables and their impact on the
economy. But its main innovation was a new theory of the determination
of national income. National income could be seen, according to Keynes,
as a multiple of the level of investment. Unfortunately, investment undertaken by private agents was highly variable from year to year, because it was
susceptible to volatile influences from financial markets and erratic swings
in business sentiment. In an extreme case – later given the soubriquet the
'liquidity trap' by another Cambridge economist, Dennis Robertson –
investors might be so afraid of future capital losses that, even if the central
bank injected new money into the economy, they would not buy bonds at
a higher price and force down the rate of interest. In other words, the lack
of confidence might be so severe that monetary policy had become
ineffective in boosting demand. The answer, so Keynes told the world, was
for investment to be undertaken to a much greater extent by the public
sector. In his words, there should be a 'somewhat comprehensive socialisation of investment'. Moreover, fiscal policy should be used actively to stimulate spending in recessions and to restrain spending in booms.

The message of *The General Theory* was political dynamite. By implication governments were right to nationalize important industries, because
this would make it easier for them to prevent economic instability and
reduce unemployment. Further, they were wrong to rely exclusively on the
old technique of Bank rate (and even some of the new American techniques
of monetary policy), which had seemed adequate in the predominantly
private enterprise economy of the Victorian era (and the USA in the
Roaring Twenties). Indeed, a careless reader of *The General Theory* might
conclude that monetary policy was of little interest in understanding
macroeconomic fluctuations.

II

The author of *A Tract on Monetary Reform* in 1923 had seemed concerned
to preserve 'individualistic capitalism'. The author of *The General Theory*

in 1936 celebrated the imminent prospect of a 'somewhat comprehensive socialisation of investment'. Which was the authentic Keynes? What did he really say? Or were there several contradictory spirits in the same man, and did his work have many meanings? In the second volume of his magnificent biography of Keynes, Skidelsky made the controversial suggestion that 'the *Treatise* and not *The General Theory* was Keynes's classic achievement'.[2] For at least four reasons, that verdict looks far more persuasive from the standpoint of the early twenty-first century than it would have done in, say, 1952 or 1962.

First, *The General Theory* is distressingly hard to read. While its subject matter is inescapably complex, Keynes did not make it accessible to the general reader. The first sentence of the preface warned that the book was 'chiefly addressed to my fellow economists', but the second expressed a hope that it would be 'intelligible to others'. But the truth is that the book's contents were unintelligible even to economists until they were further clarified by Keynes in short subsequent papers, and translated into diagrams and equations by disciples and critics. Samuelson – who in due course became one of Keynes's vocal admirers – admitted *The General Theory* 'is a badly written book'. It was 'poorly organized' and abounded in 'mares' nests of confusions'. Indeed, 'I think I am giving away no secrets when I solemnly aver – upon the basis of vivid personal recollection – that no one else in Cambridge, Massachusetts, really knew what it was all about for twelve or eighteen months after publication'.[3] Part of the trouble was that Keynes, keen to emphasize the originality of his contribution, used familiar terms in unfamiliar ways and had to devote several pages to explaining what he was about.[4] This would have interrupted the flow of the argument in any circumstances, but the problem was compounded by both repetition and digression. (*The General Theory* contained an appendix on the accountancy of depreciation, and a chapter on mercantilism and various contemporary monetary cranks. Neither had much to do with the main argument.) The *Treatise on Money* was also a rather unwieldy book and it had its fair share of esoteric terms, but it was more direct in its message and easier to read.

Secondly, *The General Theory* has little to say about banks and credit creation, and almost nothing about international finance. But, as the author of the *Tract* and the *Treatise* was fully aware, any attempt to understand the real-world problems of monetary management is also necessarily an attempt to understand the behaviour of banking systems and internationally traded currencies. As Hicks noted, 'the *General Theory* is the theory of the closed economy. If we want to read what Keynes said on the theory of international money . . . we have to go to the *Treatise*'.[5]

True enough, *The General Theory* makes countless references to money and interest rates. But – unlike the *Treatise* – it does not distinguish clearly between the central bank and the commercial banks, and between legal-tender monetary base assets (always worth their nominal value, by law) and the deposits issued by commercial banks (which might not be repaid in full if banks went bust). When Keynes was writing, the collapse of hundreds of American banks, because of loan losses and their inability to meet deposit obligations, was a central fact about the American economic scene. Deposits were not as good as notes, and the notion of 'money' was heterogenous and difficult to define. But in *The General Theory* Keynes treated all money assets identically, as a single homogenous mass, in the apparent belief that the potential insolvency of private commercial banks was not an important element in financial and economic instability. To quote Hicks again, 'Money, in the *General Theory*, is stripped to its bare bones; we get no more of the monetary system than is necessary for a particular purpose. The *Treatise* is a Treatise on Money, in a way that the other is not.'[6]

Further, by identifying certain special and unusual conditions in which the interest rate could not be reduced by central bank policy (that is, in the conditions Robertson labelled 'the liquidity trap'), the *General Theory* misled two generations of British economic policy-makers into thinking that monetary policy-making was trivial in normal times. They thought that they could neglect banking, money and monetary policy, with disastrous results in two boom–bust episodes. (The Heath–Barber boom of the early 1970s and the Lawson boom of the late 1980s are analysed from a monetary perspective in Essay 14 later in this book.)

Thirdly, in a significant sense *The General Theory* was a less general book than the *Treatise*. The *Treatise* was an attempt to produce a comprehensive text covering everything of importance in the monetary field. In addition to describing a range of banking institutions, the *Treatise* was clear that the problem of maintaining balance in an investment portfolio involved money and a variety of other securities, including bonds *and equities*.[7] Implicitly, the level of the equity market (and indeed of other asset prices) was influenced by the quantity of money. But – apart from one or two exceptional passages – in *The General Theory* portfolio balance is reduced to the choice between money *and fixed-interest bonds alone*.[8] If fixed-interest bonds are taken as representative of capital assets as a whole, this truncation of the problem of portfolio balance might appear harmless. But Keynes's narrowly restricted approach to portfolio balance in *The General Theory* was essential to a critical part of its argument.

By taking 'bonds' as the alternative to money, Keynes could make statements about the relationship between the quantity of money and the yield on bonds, and by regarding the yield on bonds as synonymous with the 'rate of interest', he could make grand claims to be propounding a new theory of the monetary determination of interest rates. In this theory a change in the quantity of money would usually alter the equilibrium rate of interest, with the rate of interest adjusting until the demand to hold money balances was equal to the actual quantity of money in existence. Keynes was not shy about the virtues of this theory, which he opposed to an alternative 'classical' view in which changes in the rate of interest were responses to differences between savings and investment. By denying the validity of the classical view, he was able to cast aspersions on the efficiency of market mechanisms and the self-adjusting properties of a capitalist economy dominated by private property. But these aspersions were legitimate only if the monetary theory of interest rate determination were correct, while its correctness depended on the assumption that bonds were the only non-money assets in the economy.

An obvious question needs to be asked. If the range of non-money assets were widened to include equities, houses and commercial real estate, would Keynes's monetary theory of 'the rate of interest' still hold water? The answer must be 'not necessarily, because so much would depend on investors' expectations and the scope for substitution between bonds and other assets'. If – starting from equilibrium – the quantity of money were increased in an economy with equities and real estate, logically the equilibrium values of both equities and real estate would advance, at least in the short run. The dividend yield on equities and the rental yield on real estate would fall, on just the same lines as – according to Keynes – the price of bonds ought to rise and the 'rate of interest' on bonds to decline.

However, in the medium and long runs the result of the money injection, and the drop in asset yields and surge in asset prices, might well be a boom in the economy and inflation. If so, holders of fixed-interest bonds would see the real value of their investment fall. It follows that the initial reaction of alert, forward-looking investors to an increase in the quantity of money might be to sell bonds in the search for a yield high enough to compensate for future inflation. An increase in the quantity of money would lead to a *rise*, not a *fall*, in the equilibrium 'rate of interest'. In short, if the analysis of *The General Theory* were made more general (and closer in fact to that of the *Treatise*) by adding extra assets, the monetary theory of 'the rate of interest' would crumble into incoherence.[9] One of Keynes's difficulties was that he wanted his 'rate of interest' (that is, his bond yields) to be susceptible to central bank action in normal conditions, but – as he well knew – central banks did not typically deal in long-dated bonds. Sometimes he wrote as if the central bank's task was the setting of the 'rate of interest' at the short end, which would affect the much more important long-dated bond yields almost by sympathetic magic. But in the real world long-dated bond yields do not move mechanically with the money market rate. As Keynes admitted, he had 'slurred over' problems of definition.[10] The *Treatise* – which did not make extravagant boasts about a new theory of interest rate determination – was less ambitious, but also more satisfactory.

Finally, the practical results of Keynes's recommendations in and after *The General Theory* have become tarnished. In Britain the 'somewhat comprehensive socialisation of investment' of the late 1940s led to mismanagement and inefficiency in nationalized industries on a scale which only became fully recognized following privatization under the Conservatives in the 1980s.[11] It speaks volumes that the Labour government elected in 1997 left the transport and energy utilities in private hands, with the problematic exception of the railways. Fiscal activism failed to stabilize output and employment in the late twentieth century, and in most countries has been replaced by fiscal rules, typically with a medium-term orientation. In the 1980s and early 1990s the large budget deficits endorsed by some Keynesians threatened financial ruin for Italy and other significant countries. By contrast, the issues raised by the *Tract* and the *Treatise* are very much alive, and the conclusions drawn by the early Keynes are still surprisingly viable. The *Tract*'s argument became particularly pertinent when the USA ended the convertibility of the dollar into gold in 1971 and thereby broke the last remnant of a gold-based currency system. The method of currency management proposed by Keynes in 1923 – to stabilize the growth of bank credit and the money stock – has clear affinities with the actual behaviour of one of the great modern central banks, the European Central Bank. It has also been adopted – if more reluctantly – by other central banks, such as the American Federal Reserve and the Bank of England, at various times in the last 30 years.

Keynes's contribution is far more substantial than his overrated *General Theory*. The *General Theory* represents only a fraction of all the words he wrote on economics, while the range of his work includes a major book on probability theory, essays in biography, and dozens of topical articles on politics and culture. As a sponsor of the Bloomsbury Group, he helped to change the moral climate of inter-war Britain. It must be conceded that – despite its faults – the *General Theory* did stimulate a revolution in macroeconomic thinking. But the *General Theory* can be more easily understood if it is seen as a sequel to the *Treatise on Money*, which is in many ways a superior piece of work. For all his ambiguities, complexities and wrong turnings, Keynes was the central intellectual influence on British economic policy – and indeed on British public life – in the twentieth century.

NOTES

1. D. Moggridge and E. Johnson (eds), *Collected Writings of John Maynard Keynes*, vol. IV, *A Tract on Monetary Reform* (London: Macmillan, 1971, originally published 1923), p. 36.
2. R. Skidelsky, *John Maynard Keynes*, vol. 2, *The Economist as Saviour 1920–37* (London: Macmillan, 1992), p. 337.
3. Samuelson's remarks appeared in his contribution to S. Harris (ed.), *The New Economics* (New York: Alfred A. Knopf, 1948). They were quoted by Murray Rothbard in his contribution to M. Skousen (ed.), *Dissent on Keynes* (New York: Praeger, 1992). See p. 184 of Skousen.
4. According to H. Johnson, the *General Theory* gave 'old concepts new and confusing names' and emphasized 'as crucial analytical steps that' had 'previously been taken as platitudinous'. E.S. Johnson and H.G. Johnson (eds), *The Shadow of Keynes* (Oxford: Basil Blackwell, 1978), p. 188.
5. Sir John Hicks, *Critical Essays in Monetary Theory* (Oxford: Clarendon Press, 1967), p. 189.
6. Hicks, *Critical Essays*, p. 189.
7. As Patinkin noted, the money-holders' choice in the *Treatise on Money* was between bank deposits and 'securities', whereas in the *General Theory* it was between money and bonds. Don Patinkin, *Keynes' Monetary Thought* (Durham, NC: Duke University Press, 1976), pp. 38–9.
8. The restriction of wealth to money and bonds continues to affect textbook writers to the present day. A standard text – *Macroeconomics* by Dornbusch and Fischer – says, in a discussion of the demand for money: 'The wealth budget constraint in the assets market states that the demand for real [money] balances . . . plus the demand for real bond holdings . . . must add up to the real financial wealth of the individual.' So, 'the decision to hold real money balances is also a decision to hold less real wealth in the form of bonds'. R. Dornbusch and S. Fischer, *Macroeconomics* (New York: McGraw-Hill, 6th edition, 1994), p. 103. Surprisingly, the adoption of the limited definition of wealth follows shortly after an excellent account of real-world assets, which refers at length to equities and houses. Keynes's awareness that he spoke of 'the rate of interest' in a dangerous way is evident in a footnote on p. 151 of the *General Theory*, in which he said that high stock market valuations had the same stimulatory effect on investment as a low rate of interest.
9. The argument that an increase in 'the quantity of money' reduces 'the rate of interest' begs many questions, not least the meaning of the phrases 'the quantity of money' and 'the rate of interest'. Keynes's analysis related to 'the short period' (that is, with the capital stock fixed) and assumed an economy in which the only non-money assets were bonds. But, as soon as one thinks of an economy with several assets, including equities, houses and other forms of real estate, and in which agents look ahead over many periods, it is possible – as explained in the text – for an increase in the quantity of money to lead to higher inflation expectations, a *fall* in bond prices and a *rise* in the rate of interest. Keynes's theory of the monetary determination of the rate of interest would then disintegrate. The point will be elaborated in my *Money in a Modern Economy* (forthcoming), to be published by Edward Elgar.
10. A. Leijonhufvud, *On Keynesian Economics and the Economics of Keynes* (New York and London: Oxford University Press, 1968), p. 152.
11. The political implications of the *General Theory* were highly topical in the late 1930s and enhanced its influence on the public debate. In 1954 Joseph Schumpeter remarked: 'There cannot be any doubt that it [*The General Theory*] owed its victorious career primarily to the fact that its argument implemented some of the strongest political preferences of a large number of modern economists.' This quotation appeared in Don Bellante's contribution to Skousen (ed.), *Dissent on Keynes*, p. 119.

3. Keynes, the Keynesians and the exchange rate

One of the most quoted remarks in economics comes in the final chapter of Keynes's *General Theory of Employment, Interest and Money*, where he says:

> the ideas of economists, both when they are right and when they are wrong, are more powerful than is commonly understood. Indeed the world is ruled by little else. Practical men, who believe themselves to be quite exempt from any intellectual influences, are usually the slaves of some defunct economist. Madmen in authority, who hear voices in the air, are distilling their frenzy from some academic scribbler of a few years back.[1]

Keynes believed that his book would be a particularly powerful 'intellectual influence' on such 'practical men'. He hoped that, by adopting his recommendations of increased state ownership and the counter-cyclical variation of public investment, the government would in future be able to prevent large swings in unemployment. He wanted to harness the fiscal powers of the state to make the trade cycle obsolete.

For about 25 years after the Second World War British economists thought that Keynes's ambition had been largely fulfilled. Of course, there were fluctuations in economic activity in the 1950s and 1960s. But these fluctuations, known as 'stop–go cycles', were mild by comparison with those in the inter-war period or the nineteenth century. Although unemployment varied in the course of the stop–go cycle, it never – even at the most immobile point of the 'stop' – amounted to more than a fraction of what it had been in the 1930s. This improvement, the so-called 'Keynesian revolution', was taken to be the triumph of modern economic theory over a number of ancient financial prejudices, notably the doctrine that the government should balance its budget. In the late 1960s no British economist expected the next 25 years to see large cyclical fluctuations in economic activity. The trade cycle may not yet have been obsolete, but it was thought to have depreciated to the point of insignificance.

Unhappily, these expectations were to prove wrong. The next 25 years were to see three major cyclical episodes. The first was the Barber boom of 1972 and 1973, followed by the severe downturn of 1974 and 1975; the second, from early 1978 to mid-1979, could be called the Healey boomlet, and gave way to the recession of 1980 and early 1981; and the third was the Lawson boom of mid-1986 to mid-1988, which preceded the recession of 1990 to 1992. These episodes were not as extreme as the slump of the early 1930s, but they were comparable – in the amplitude of the fluctuations and other characteristics – to the trade cycles of the nineteenth century. They were certainly more noticeable than the stop–go cycles of the immediate post-war decades. The questions arise, 'why did these large cyclical fluctuations come back?', 'what mistakes were governments making?' and 'were their mistakes tactical and accidental in nature, or the result of a strategic misunderstanding of how the economy works?' More pointedly, why did the madmen in authority behave as they did? And to which defunct economists were they listening?

In attempting to answer these questions the approach here will be largely historical. As we shall see, the reference to 'defunct economists' will not be purely rhetorical. The aim will be to consider why British economists, and hence the British government, were so unprepared for the problems of the 1970s and 1980s. The underlying assumption is that events cannot be understood without an explanation – or at least an interpretation – of why people thought in the way they did. This essay will therefore be mostly an exercise in the history of ideas, particularly ideas about macroeconomic policy.

I

The notion of 'macroeconomic policy' is very modern. In the eighteenth century no one believed that the government had either the ability or the responsibility to manage the economy. Cyclical fluctuations in economic activity were sometimes pronounced, but these were regarded as acts of God like the weather or earthquakes. In particular, theorizing about the role of money in the trade cycle was rudimentary. In previous centuries the money stock had consisted entirely of metals, particularly gold and silver, and the quantity of money had therefore been determined by the past production of gold and silver mines. There had been little scope to substitute paper for these metals, because of the lack of trust in paper alternatives. However, as the eighteenth century wore on, Britain's political stability and the development of a satisfactory legal framework encouraged people to carry out an increasing proportion of their transactions in bank notes and bills of exchange. These paper instruments – whose validity depended on credit – came increasingly to perform the monetary functions of the precious metals.

But the growth of paper credit introduced a new risk. This was that the individuals and organizations issuing the paper alternatives to the precious metals might not be able to redeem them at their face value. A goldsmith banker might issue a note recognizing an obligation to repay the bearer on demand a particular weight of gold or silver, and the note might circulate widely and with perfect creditworthiness for many months or even years. But, if one of its holders presented it to the goldsmith banker and he was unable – for any reason – to pay over the stated quantity of precious metal, his entire note issue would fall into disrepute and this part of the money stock would no longer be able to circulate. Sudden collapses in the credit-worthiness of paper lay behind some of the most severe cyclical fluctuations of the eighteenth century, even though precious metals continued to be the most important monetary asset. London bankers tried to anticipate the dangers by opening accounts and establishing a good relationship with the Bank of England, on the understanding that the Bank would act as a source of precious metals in an emergency. Country bankers in turn opened accounts and established good relationships with the London bankers.

The legislative response to these developments was twofold. First, restrictions were placed on the ability of private banks to issue notes, although these restrictions were surprisingly late in coming and were more a feature of the nineteenth than the eighteenth century. Secondly, the Bank of England – which was seen as the core institution from an early stage – was required in successive Bank Charter Acts to redeem its note liabilities at a fixed price in terms of the precious metals. The price of gold was fixed at £3 17s 10½d an ounce by Sir Isaac Newton in 1717, while the first denominationalized notes were printed in 1725.[2] In other words, the Bank of England was mandated to protect a fixed exchange rate between its paper liabilities and the precious metals. After the Napoleonic Wars Parliament deprived silver of much of its former monetary role and established gold monometallism as the basis of Britain's money in 1821. Thereafter the essential features of Britain's monetary arrangements, and indeed the defining characteristics of the classical gold standard in this country, were the fixed gold price of £3 17s 10½d an ounce and the ready convertibility of notes into gold and vice versa.

The logic of this system is easy to analyse and defend. Let us take it for granted that the public at large wants a money which is fairly reliable in terms of its ability to purchase non-monetary things. In this context precious metals have one key advantage as a monetary asset. Because they are highly durable, virtually all of the last period's stock of metals survives into the current and next periods. Further, as long as mining technology changes only slowly and there are no new discoveries, the production of new gold and silver in any one period should be only a small fraction of the stock of these metals accumulated over past centuries. As a result the stock of precious metals is very stable over time. Since it is therefore unlikely to increase more rapidly than world output, the price of commodities in general should be roughly stable in terms of the precious metals.

From this point of view, the introduction of paper alternatives to be precious metals is potentially dangerous. The production of paper money requires almost no resources. The quantity of paper money – unlike the quantity of precious metals – can be easily multiplied tenfold or a hundredfold. If this multiplication of the quantity of money occurs in a short period with no matching increase in output, the value of money is certain to collapse. Public policy could anticipate this problem by insisting that paper be convertible into gold at a fixed price. If the fixed exchange rate between paper and gold is maintained, and if the value of gold remains reasonably stable in terms of commodities, then the value of paper should also remain reasonably stable in terms of commodities. Here was the rationale for the gold standard in the nineteenth century. With paper anchored to gold at a fixed exchange rate the growth of paper money could not have systematic inflationary consequences

The gold standard was a success. Although the economy was subject to occasional cyclical disturbances and the price level varied both within these cycles and over longer periods, nineteenth-century Britain was a model of financial stability. Such was the admiration for Britain's achievement that by the 1880s most other major industrial countries had also adopted gold as the basis for their monetary systems, creating the international gold standard of the late nineteenth century. The 'rules of the game' were well known. The central bank of every participating country had to preserve the convertibility of its note liabilities into gold at the agreed fixed exchange rate. The paper/gold exchange rate within each country implied certain exchange rates between the paper currencies of the participant countries. If an exchange rate came under pressure, the consequent external drain on the central bank's gold reserve had to be countered by raising interest rates. On the other hand, when a central bank's gold reserve was ample, it could cut interest rates. In the case of the Bank of England, its interest rate decisions were determined fairly mechanically by watching the proportion between its gold holdings and its deposit liabilities.[3] By the late nineteenth century its gold holdings varied mainly because of international pressures, rather than domestic changes in financial confidence. The practice of relating interest rate decisions to gold holdings and the exchange rate became deeply entrenched. The dependence of interest rates on international financial developments increased, even as the UK's weight in the world economy – and hence its share of the total world gold stock – diminished.

But another and quite different approach to monetary policy would have been possible, and had indeed been intimated by some economists many years before. It would have relied on two revolutionary ideas which emerged in the debates on British financial policy during the Napoleonic Wars, debates which in their complexity and sophistication can fairly be described as the matrix of modern monetary theory. The urgency of those controversies arose because, under the strains of war, the Bank of England had been forced to suspend the convertibility of its notes into gold in 1797. There was widespread public concern that the value of the notes, which continued to circulate as currency, would decline steadily. The vital question was how to stabilize the real value of the notes in the absence of the fixed anchor with gold.

The first of the two revolutionary ideas was that of the 'general price level'. Nowadays the concepts of an overall price level, of a price index which quantifies it and of an inflation rate measured by changes in the index are so commonplace that we rarely stop to think about them. That was not so in the 1790s. People were aware of the need to have a reliable monetary unit and standard of value, but they were not sure how best to formalize this need in precise numerical terms. Thus, when David Ricardo wrote about the depreciation of the currency in a famous pamphlet of 1810 he gave it the title, *The High Price of Bullion, a Proof of the Depreciation of Bank Notes*. He thought of currency depreciation in terms of the price of gold, not in terms of a general price level. However, there had already been innovators who had seen the potential for applying index numbers to the problem. According to Schumpeter:

> A great step toward full realization of the importance of the method was made in 1798, when Sir George Shuckburgh Evelyn presented a paper to the Royal Society in which, with apologies for treating a subject so much below the dignity of that august body, he used an index number – of a primitive kind no doubt – for measuring the 'depreciation of money'.[4]

The approach became progressively more refined in the course of the nineteenth century and in 1922 the American economist, Irving Fisher, published a monumental work on *The Making of Index Numbers*. One of the motives of this work – and, indeed, one of Fisher's strongest professional interests – was to define a price index whose stability would be the prime objective of monetary policy.

The second revolutionary idea, and perhaps an even more fundamental one, was to recognize that the nature of the inflationary process was radically changed by the introduction of paper money. With the functions of money increasingly being performed by paper instruments, the quantity of such instruments could affect the prices of goods and services. The link between the quantity of gold and its price had been the central interest of earlier monetary commentators. But, as more notes and bills of exchange entered the circulation, economists began to surmise that the connection might be between the quantity of all forms of money, both gold and paper, and the price level. The starting point for their analyses was the crude but serviceable principle that the greater the quantity of paper credit, the higher the price level. By extension, the higher the rate of increase in paper credit, the faster the rate of inflation.

The most impressive early work on these ideas was *An Inquiry into the Nature and Effects of the Paper Credit of Great Britain* by Henry Thornton, published in 1802. The timing of this great book, five years after the Bank of England's suspension of gold convertibility, was not an accident. Thornton was convinced that the widespread acceptability of paper in payments was an advantage to a country and, in particular, that it helped Britain to face wartime pressures on its economy.

> Paper credit has . . . been highly important to us. Our former familiarity with it prepared us for the more extended use of it. And our experience of its power of supplying the want of gold in times of difficulty and peril, is a circumstance which . . . may justly add to the future confidence of the nation.[5]

Nevertheless, Thornton was aware of the dangers inherent in a system of paper credit. He emphasized that an excessive issue of bank notes would lead to rises in the price level, while warning, on the other hand, that sharp contractions of the note issue could cause downturns in economic activity. His advice to the Bank of England was therefore to 'limit the amount of paper issued, and to resort for this purpose, whenever the temptation to borrow is strong, to some effectual principle of restriction; in no case, however, materially to diminish the sum in circulation, but to let it vibrate only within certain limits' and 'to afford a slow and cautious extension of it, as the general trade of the kingdom enlarges itself'.[6]

Here is the kernel of a new approach, the beginnings of the idea of 'monetary policy' or even 'macroeconomic policy'. Decisions on monetary management are no longer motivated by the gold price or an exchange rate between paper and a metal. Instead the central bank is understood to have fairly deliberate goals, to stabilize the price level and, as far as possible, to avoid large fluctuations in economic activity. Moreover, it is to achieve these goals by trying to control 'the sum in circulation' or, as we would now say, by regulating the money supply. This way of conducting monetary policy – where the quantity of paper money is the target of central bank action – is clearly quite different from the earlier approach, with its focus on a particular gold price or exchange rate.[7]

II

Thornton's hint of a new style of monetary regulation was not taken up in his lifetime. On the contrary, the gold standard became established, gained increasing credibility and flourished until the First World War. But after 1918 another phase of intense monetary controversy began. The problem – just as it had been after the Napoleonic Wars – was whether Britain should restore the gold standard at the pre-war parity.

The majority of bankers, politicians and so-called 'practical men' associated the gold standard with the stability and prosperity of the Victorian period. Perhaps without thinking very hard about the issues, they wanted to return to the gold standard. This point of view was expressed officially in the reports of the Cunliffe Committee, in 1918 and 1919, which said that restoration should occur as soon as possible. However, a small group of economists were sceptical, believing that the success of the gold standard in the nineteenth century had been largely a fluke and preferring a more deliberate and (as they described it) scientific approach to monetary policy. Their inspiration came from the great tradition of ad hoc and more or less amateur theorizing on the trade cycle in the nineteenth century, which had begun with Thornton and was developed in later decades by such authors as Tooke, Overstone, John Stuart Mill, Alfred Marshall, Bagehot and Hartley Withers. The theories were rather miscellaneous, but a common theme was that fluctuations in demand, output and the price level were driven by variations in the growth rates of credit and money.

The foremost sceptic about the gold standard was John Maynard Keynes. In his *Tract on Monetary Reform*, published in 1923, he identified the risk that gold could be kept in line with output only through chance discoveries of the metal. In any case, since Britain held only a small part of the world's gold stock, a return to the pre-war standard would leave it vulnerable to changes in other countries' demand for gold. There was no alternative to managing the currency:

> If providence watched over gold, or if Nature had provided us with a stable standard ready-made, I would not, in an attempt after some slight improvement, hand over the management to the possible weakness or ignorance of boards and governments. But this is not the situation. We have no ready-made standard. Experience has shown that in emergencies ministers of finance cannot be strapped down. And – most important of all – in the modern world of paper currency and bank credit there is no escape from a 'managed' currency, whether we wish it or not; convertibility into gold will not alter the fact that the value of gold itself depends on the policy of the central banks.[8]

The answer, then, was not to go back to a fixed gold price, but to have a 'managed currency'. But how, in more specific terms, should a managed currency work? What objectives should policy-makers have and how should these objectives be achieved?

Keynes was clear about what he wanted. He was against not only the gold standard, but also a fixed exchange rate between the pound and the dollar, since this would leave Britain too much at the mercy of the American Federal Reserve. Although he recognized that 'an internal standard, so regulated as to maintain stability in an index number of prices, is a difficult scientific innovation never yet put into practice', that was nevertheless the ideal he favoured: 'I regard the stability of prices, credit and employment as of paramount importance.'[9] He referred with enthusiasm to Irving Fisher, as the pioneer of price stability as against exchange stability.

The *Tract* also devoted much space to the principles and practice of monetary management. In Keynes's view, 'The internal price level is mainly determined by the amount of credit created by the banks, chiefly the Big Five' and 'The amount of credit . . . is in its turn roughly measured by the volume of the banks' deposits'.[10] There is a certain lack of clarity in these remarks, since it is not obvious whether it is the assets or liabilities side of banks' balance sheets that Keynes wanted to emphasize. But, if we agree that new lending creates deposits, this would be no great problem. The discussion of the mechanics of monetary control was also rather confusing. Keynes seemed to oscillate between two views, one that the size of banks' balance sheets is a multiple of their cash reserves, which can be determined by open-market operations, and another that 'adequate control' over an important part of banks' assets (that is, their advances and bills) 'can be obtained by varying the price charged, that is to say the bank rate'.[11]

But the technical complications should not be allowed to hide the essence of the 'managed currency' as Keynes envisaged it. The ultimate target should be the stability of the domestic price level, not the gold price or the exchange rate; and that target should be attained by managing the growth rate of banks' balance sheets, through interest rate variations if appropriate. It would be a matter of comparative indifference in practical terms whether the intermediate target here were taken as bank credit, bank deposits or a broad measure of the money supply, although the relevant pages in the *Tract* are a little muddled and ambiguous on the subject. It might also not add much to say that Keynes's managed currency had a certain amount in common with latter-day 'monetarism', since that begs the question of how monetarism should be defined.[12] But there cannot be much doubt that – for most of his career – Keynes disliked having a fixed exchange rate as a policy target and paid close attention to credit and monetary variables when assessing economic prospects. That, on a careful reading of the texts, should be uncontroversial.

At first Keynes's proposals for a managed currency got nowhere. Britain returned to the gold standard in 1925, with unhappy consequences for economic activity and employment, just as Keynes had expected. But after the departure from the gold standard in 1931, and the subsequent disintegration of international monetary order, Britain willy-nilly had the managed currency that Keynes advocated. Domestic objectives, not the gold price or the exchange rate, dominated policy-making in the 1930s. Until late in his career Keynes insisted that domestic objectives, not external, should have priority. In a speech on the proposed International Monetary Fund in the House of Lords in May 1943, he said:

> We are determined that, in future, the external value of sterling shall conform to its internal value, as set by our own domestic policies, and not the other way round. Secondly, we intend to keep control of our domestic rate of interest. Thirdly, whilst we intend to prevent inflation at home, we will not accept deflation at the dictates of influences from outside. In other words, we abjure the instruments of bank rate and credit contraction operating through an increase in unemployment as a means of forcing our domestic economy into line with external factors. I hope your Lordships will trust me not to have turned my back on all I have fought for. To establish these three principles which I have just stated has been my main task for the last 20 years.[13]

It would be natural to assume that the post-war 'Keynesian revolution' would reflect the implementation of a macroeconomic policy directed to domestic priorities. That, indeed, is how some of the hagiographers have seen it. They have claimed that official policy in the first 25 years after 1945 was dominated by the aim of maintaining the domestic goal of full employment. Since a much closer approximation to full employment was achieved in these years than in the inter-war period, that may seem a reasonable assertion. However, monetary policy was certainly not organized in the way that Keynes had recommended in the *Tract on Monetary Reform* or in his May 1943 speech to the House of Lords.

On the contrary, the lodestar for interest rate decisions was the pound's exchange rate against the dollar. For 22 years, from 1945 to 1967, the pound was constrained by the Bretton Woods regime of fixed exchange rates and kept close to its central parity. (Admittedly, a big devaluation occurred in 1949, but the $2.80 rate was then maintained until 1967.) It was true that sterling's explicit link with gold had been broken and that the Bank of England did not redeem its note liabilities with any precious metal, as it had done before 1914. But the pound was tied to the dollar and the dollar was fixed to gold at the official price of $35 an ounce. Britain may no longer have been on a formal gold standard, but sterling maintained a constant, if indirect and perhaps rather clandestine, relationship to gold for many years after Keynes's death.

In these years of fixed exchange rates, academic and official interest in monetary policy dwindled steadily. Indeed, it could be argued that Keynes's *General Theory* was both the climax and the terminus of the nineteenth-century tradition of trade-cycle theorizing, in which credit and money had been so important. Afterwards the overwhelming majority of British economists downplayed the significance of credit and money in macroeconomic fluctuations and inflation. There were at least three reasons for the new neglect of monetary analysis.

The first was that Keynes himself had been moving in this direction late in his career. At the time of the *Tract* he believed, with few qualifications, in the ability of interest rate changes to manage the currency and so to achieve desired macroeconomic outcomes. But in the 1930s very low interest rates were unable to prevent the persistence of high unemployment. One task of *The General Theory* was therefore to identify those circumstances in which low interest rates would be ineffective in stimulating investment and encouraging employment. He suggested that there could be a situation, a so-called 'liquidity trap', where people were so shell-shocked by the deflationary environment around them that they could not be induced to move out of cash into other assets. The deflation could not be countered by central bank action to cut interest rates. Keynes went on to advocate that the government take direct responsibility for investment in order to offset the possible impotence of interest rates. In his words, 'it seems unlikely that the influence of banking policy on the rate of interest will be sufficient by itself to determine an optimum rate of investment. I conceive, therefore, that a somewhat comprehensive socialization of investment will prove the only means of securing an approximation to full employment'.[14]

This argument – linking the alleged ineffectiveness of monetary policy to wholesale nationalization – was one of the most influential and important in Britain's post-war political economy. In the 1950s and 1960s it gave economists a rationale both for a modishly left-wing sympathy towards state ownership, and for suppressing the teaching of monetary economics. It is very unlikely that this is what Keynes wanted. As the *Tract* made clear, a managed currency would have required a strong and detailed understanding of monetary institutions. Even *The General Theory* says far more about interest rates and monetary policy than it does about nationalization. But that Keynes contributed to the belittling of monetary economics, even of his own great work in the area, cannot be denied.

The second reason for the growing indifference towards monetary policy was that for almost 20 years, from 1932 to 1951, interest rates were virtually constant. Bank rate was held at 2 per cent throughout the period, apart from a brief (and insignificant) interruption at the beginning of the Second World War. Since hardly any interest rate changes occurred, there seemed little practical benefit in analysing the results of such changes. As interest rates had clearly not been much of an influence on business conditions for such a long period, economists thought they could ignore the possibility that interest rates might become important in the future. Even in the 1950s and 1960s interest rate variations were small for most of the time. In British universities theorizing about the effect of interest rates on the economy – and so about monetary policy in the large – became moribund.

Thirdly, during the Second World War, and for many years afterwards, the British economy was subject to a wide variety of administrative controls of one sort or another. Rationing, conscription and the requisitioning of resources for the armed forces had a clear military function and could not be accepted for long in peacetime. But other restrictions – such as exchange controls, tight planning controls on building materials, controls on new issues and so on – survived long after the war had ended. Many civil servants and politicians thought that the economy could be run better by relaxing or tightening these controls than by relaxing or tightening monetary policy. Their ideal was not Keynes's 'managed currency', which would have been fully compatible with market capitalism, but a semi-socialist mixed economy with extensive economic planning. In the late 1940s and 1950s a large number of British economists undoubtedly welcomed the retention of controls and a commitment to planning.

If this seems a strong statement, it needs to be emphasized that 1963 saw the publication of an official document on *Conditions for Faster Growth*, which enjoined a more active government role in industry, with the full blessing of the then Conservative government. In 1964 the Department of Economic Affairs, with even more interventionist objectives, was established by the newly elected Labour government of Mr Harold Wilson. Mr Wilson had previously been an economics don at Oxford University and his government introduced large numbers of academic economists into Whitehall. It is a fair comment that none of these economists was much bothered by monetary policy, but all of them were fascinated – in one way or another – by the potential of 'economic planning'. One kind of control was particularly important in the monetary field, direct quantitative restrictions on bank lending. With credit kept under control by such means, the role of interest rates in macroeconomic policy was rarely discussed.

By the late 1960s hardly any British economist thought that interest rates could or should be varied to influence domestic economic variables. The immensely influential National Institute of Economic and Social Research never mentioned the money supply, on any of its definitions, in its *Reviews*. It only occasionally referred to credit variables and even then the focus was on hire purchase rather than mortgage lending. Whole volumes were written on macroeconomic policy with hardly any comment on money. For example, in a book on *The Labour Government's Economic Record: 1964–70*, edited by Wilfred Beckerman and published in 1972, there was only one index reference to 'the money supply', whereas there were 17 to the National Economic Development Council, 21 to the National Board for Prices and Incomes, and no less than 41 to the National Plan and 'Planning'.[15] In the early 1970s the Cambridge Economic Policy Group was established with the support of such well-known figures as Lord Kaldor and Professor Robert Neild. The much publicized recommendations in its *Economic Policy Reviews* almost never contained remarks on monetary policy, unless they were dismissive. According to one article in its March 1977 issue, 'In our view there is no justification at all for incorporating a target for domestic credit expansion in official economic policy'.[16] (As mentioned in the Introduction, and noted again below on p. 69 and in Essay 9, Neild was one of the organizers of the letter to *The Times* from the 364 which protested against the 1981 Budget.)

An extraordinary somersault had been accomplished. Whereas in 1923 the managed currency favoured by Keynes had seen the restraint over credit growth as central to monetary regulation, in the 1970s Cambridge economists and, indeed, most economists in British universities saw no merit in targets for credit and monetary growth. Many of them saw no point in analysing credit or monetary trends at all. Inflation was better understood, in their view, by watching the behaviour of wages and the exchange rate. The readiness of staff at the National Institute and the Department of Applied Economics to adopt the label of 'Keynesian' was the more remarkable in that it overlooked huge chunks of Keynes's own writing. These economists did not seem to appreciate that their ways of thinking were a betrayal of Keynes's ideas. Instead their loyalty was to second-rate textbooks which regurgitated, for decades after they had lost any practical relevance, the dangers of the liquidity trap and interest-inelastic investment.

The questions arise, 'how then was the Keynesian revolution accomplished?' and 'what were the techniques of economic policy which gave the British economy its stability in the first 25 years after the war?' If Keynes's managed currency was forgotten by most British economists, who or what should be awarded the medals for the relative financial tranquillity of the immediate post-war decades? It is here that we come to a yet greater paradox. There can be hardly any doubt that the key economic constraint on British governments in those years was the avoidance of sterling devaluation. Whenever policy-makers embarked on unduly stimulatory policies, the pound would come under downward pressure on the foreign exchanges and the resulting 'sterling crisis' would oblige the government to think again. It was the succession of sterling crises, and the need to check them by credit restrictions and/or higher interest rates, which kept inflation under control.

Since the pound/dollar rate was the lynchpin of the system, American monetary policy determined British monetary policy. Fortunately, American monetary policy in the first 25 years after the war was a model of anti-inflationary prudence and counter-cyclical stability. As Keynes had noted in his May 1943 speech to the House of Lords, 'the instruments of bank rate and credit contraction' would be dictated from outside Britain in a fixed-exchange-rate system. But it was precisely these instruments which not only kept the UK price level in line with the world price level (of traded goods, expressed in terms of a common currency), but also delivered the full employment, low inflation and cyclical moderation of the post-war period. The exchange rate played a positive and benign role in British macroeconomic management. Keynes's suspicion of international financial influences on monetary policy-making proved misplaced.

Before we discuss what happened after the pound/dollar link was broken, another irony needs to be mentioned. American monetary policy in the first two decades after the Second World War was unquestionably a success compared with other periods, both before and after. But why? Many of the good decisions can be attributed, of course, to the professionalism of the staff of the Federal Reserve System and the budgetary restraint of Presidents Truman and Eisenhower. But there was another factor at work. One of the reasons for the Federal Reserve's tightening of monetary policy in the late 1950s was to protect the dollar on the foreign exchanges and, in particular, to preserve the $35-an-ounce gold price. Gold was still the bedrock of the Bretton Woods system. Does it follow from this argument that the Keynesian revolution was not the result of the discretionary demand management and fiscal fine-tuning so much praised in the textbooks? Can the happy stability of the 1950s and 1960s instead be seen to rest on two fixed exchange rates, the $2.80 rate between the pound and the dollar, and the $35-an-ounce official price of gold? Was the prosperity of that period due not to the final abandonment of the 'barbarous relic', but rather to the UK's membership of the Bretton Woods system and the world's last inarticulate clinging to a gold anchor?

III

The two exchange rates were scrapped in the early 1970s. In August 1971 the American government suspended the dollar's convertibility into gold, because of the rapid decline in its gold reserve, while in June 1972 the pound left the embryonic European 'currency snake', after belonging for less than two months. Sterling's exit from the snake was to inaugurate a period of deliberate floating. We have already seen that one of the key preconditions for wise domestic monetary management – namely, a deep and extensive understanding of monetary economics among professional economists – no longer existed in Britain. Very few academic economists were interested in the pre-Keynesian tradition of trade-cycle analysis, the acknowledged classics of monetary theory or contemporary monetary institutions. As a result there was no longer any heavyweight intellectual obstacle to rapid domestic credit and monetary expansion. The external barrier to inflationary policies, which had been imposed by a fixed exchange rate for over 20 years, was now also removed.

The scene had been set for the Barber boom of the early 1970s. There is little point in describing that boom in detail once more. Suffice it to say that credit and monetary growth were extraordinarily fast by any previous standards. But most British economists were unconcerned about the potential inflationary repercussions and instead celebrated the very rapid output growth from mid-1972 to mid-1973. (The level of GDP, at factor cost, expenditure based, was 8.6 per cent higher in real terms in the middle two quarters of 1973 than in the middle two quarters of 1972. Domestic demand grew even faster.) On 7 May 1973 Mr Peter Jay, the Economics Editor of *The Times*, wrote an isolated article entitled, 'The boom that must go bust'. The *National Institute Economic Review* judged in the same month that, 'there is no reason why the present boom should either bust or have to be busted'. The *Review* was undoubtedly representative of professional economic opinion.

Later it became uncontroversial that something had gone horribly wrong. The current account deficit on the balance of payments was a post-war record in 1974 and in mid-1975 the inflation rate hit 25 per cent. In 1976 Mr Healey, the Chancellor of the Exchequer, introduced money supply targets in order to establish a monetary framework for reducing inflation. These targets opened up the possibility that interest rate changes might be determined by the behaviour of monetary growth rather than by the exchange rate. The targets were expressed in terms of broad money, which is dominated by bank deposits. Broad money targets were to survive for almost a decade, until they were dropped in late 1985. Although the need for some kind of money target, or a so-called 'nominal framework', was widely accepted, it would be wrong to think that academic economists were much involved in its introduction. On the contrary, the case for money targets was urged most vigorously by City economists and in the financial press, notably in *The Times*.[17]

The heyday of broad money targets was in early 1980, only a few months after the Thatcher government had come to power. At about the same time as the announcement of the medium-term financial strategy in the Budget of that year, the government published a Green Paper on *Monetary*

Control. It set out the rationale and the method of operation of broad money targets. In its words, 'The Government's policy is . . . to sustain downward pressure on prices by a progressive reduction of the rate of growth of the money supply over a period of years'.[18] (This statement clearly implied that monetary growth caused inflation.) The reduction in monetary growth was to be accomplished partly by curbing public sector borrowing from the banks (which depended on the total amount of public sector borrowing minus sales of public sector debt to non-banks) and partly by discouraging bank lending to the private sector. Although sceptical that the private sector's demand for bank finance was responsive to interest rates in the short run, the Green Paper's aversion to quantitative credit restrictions left interest rates as the only instrument available to regulate credit expansion. It followed that interest rates were to be raised if monetary growth was ahead of target, but lowered if it was behind target.

In effect, the Green Paper on *Monetary Control* set out an approach to monetary policy which – in its emphasis on the credit counterparts to deposit growth and its focus on domestic rather than external objectives – had clear similarities to Keynes's scheme for a 'managed currency' in the *Tract on Monetary Reform*. Moreover, in a number of speeches Sir Geoffrey Howe, the then Chancellor of the Exchequer, argued that the exchange rate had to be allowed to float if the government was to have the freedom over interest rates required to achieve its money supply targets. Interest rates were to be governed by domestic criteria, with a view to attaining price stability, rather than by the exchange rate.

The question of what happened to broad money targets, and the system of financial control associated with them, is not much debated now. There is hardly space here to provide a detailed history of British economic policy in the early 1980s.[19] However, certain salient points are essential to the argument. In late 1980 monetary growth ran far ahead of target, obliging the government to keep interest rates high despite a deepening industrial recession. The exchange rate rose to remarkable levels and by early 1981 was clearly overvalued. Most economists, appalled by this turn of events, urged the government to ease the deflationary pressures. They wanted it to pay more attention to the exchange rate and less (or none at all) to domestic monetary trends.

But in the Budget of March 1981 the government raised taxes in order to keep public sector borrowing within the targets stated in the Medium-Term Financial Strategy. Two professors of economics at Cambridge – Frank Hahn and Robert Neild – organized a letter to *The Times* from 364 economists at British universities, which claimed that the government's policies 'will deepen the depression, erode the industrial base of the economy and threaten its social and political stability'. The 364 economists were wrong. The British economy began to recover only a few months after it had been written and above-trend growth was maintained from late 1983 to 1989. (See the discussion about the 1981 Budget and its sequel in Essays 9 and 10, on pp. 181–229.)

But to assume therefore that the letter from the 364 had no influence would be a very serious mistake. It accurately reflected the overwhelming consensus of British academic opinion. Whenever officials from the Treasury or the Bank of England took part in academic conferences, both in these years and later, they were subjected to a barrage of scorn for obeying their political masters and implementing money supply targets. The constant sniping took its toll. Perhaps even more important, there was only limited academic interest in the technical operation of the system of monetary management actually at work in the early 1980s. A substantial literature developed on the merits of an alternative system of monetary base control, but this was not strictly relevant to the day-to-day problems facing the Treasury and the Bank of England. For example, whereas City newsletters and circulars discussed the problem of 'overfunding' in some detail in 1984 and 1985, it received hardly any comment in academic journals. The reason was simple. There were very few university economists who respected what the government was trying to do, namely, to combat inflation by reducing the rate of broad money growth. ('Overfunding' was the practice of selling more public sector debt to the non-bank private sector than the budget deficit, in order that the excess proceeds could be used to reduce the banks' claims on the public sector, and hence reduce both banks' assets and their deposit liabilities.)

So when broad money targets were scrapped in late 1985 there was general relief in university economics departments that, at long last, the government had returned to sanity. 'Sanity' was to be understood, in their view, as the former style of macroeconomic management with interest rate changes determined largely by the pound's fortunes on the foreign exchanges. The government nevertheless retained monetary targets, at least in form. Few people outside the Treasury took these targets, which came to be expressed in terms of narrow money rather than broad money, all that seriously. City commentators noted that the quantity of notes and coin, which is the main constituent of the officially favoured narrow money measure, M0, is determined by the current economic situation, rather than being a determinant of the future behaviour of demand and output. It followed from this that narrow money could not have any casual role in the inflationary process.

Keynes had, in fact, made precisely the same point in the *Tract* over 60 years earlier. He remarked that, in the circumstances of the early 1920s, 'Cash, in the form of bank and currency notes, is supplied *ad libitum*, that is in such quantities as are called for by the amount of credit created and the internal price level established'. It followed that: 'the tendency of today – rightly I think – is to watch and control the creation of credit and to let the creation of currency follow suit, rather than, as formerly, to watch and control the creation of currency and to let the creation of credit follow suit'.[20] Keynes's preference for watching bank credit and deposits rather than currency (in the form of coin and notes) was partly a by-product of his aversion to gold. Under the Bank Charter Act of 1844 the Bank of England had been required to restrict the fiduciary note issue (specifically, that part of the note issue not backed by gold holdings in its Issue Department) and gold had remained, in principle, the ultimate reg-ulator of the quantity of notes. But Keynes wanted 'the volume of paper money' (that is, notes) to be 'consequential . . . on the state of trade and employment, bank rate policy and Treasury bill policy', so that the 'gov-ernors of the system would be bank rate and Treasury bill policy'. He therefore made 'the proposal – which may seem, but should not be, shock-ing – of separating entirely the gold reserve from the note issue'. If this were done, monetary policy would be free to serve the government's proper objectives, which in his view were, of course, the 'stability of trade, prices and employment'.[21]

The Treasury's adherence to M0 in the mid and late 1980s was half-hearted. Nevertheless, as Keynes would have expected, it had unfortunate consequences. Because it is an indicator rather than a cause of inflation, it failed abjectly to give advance warning of future inflationary trouble. The role of two self-styled 'monetarist' advisers to the government, Sir Alan Walters and Professor Patrick Minford, in this failure needs to be men-tioned. In the early 1980s they were both critical of the importance attached to credit and broad money, and advocated that narrow money be given a more prominent role. Conservative politicians did not trust the great mass of left-leaning British academic economists, but they did consult the ideologically sound Walters and Minford. The advice of these two economists was therefore instrumental in undermining the framework of monetary management which was in existence *before* Mrs Thatcher and her Treasury ministers started listening to them.

In his book *Britain's Economic Renaissance* Sir Alan Walters observed that it is money in the 'transactions sense that plays the central role in the theoretical structure and the proposition of monetarism'. He gave paying a bus fare as an example of the kind of transaction he had in mind, and dis-tinguished this sharply from 'credit'. (To quote, 'You pay your bus fare with money; you do not offer the fare collector a promissory note.'[22]) But, what-ever the role of money in this 'transactions sense' in either Walters's or the British government's understanding of monetary economics during the

1980s, it had actually been superseded several decades earlier by the leaders of economic thought.

The whole point of Keynes's critique of classical monetary theory was that it overlooked the position of money in a portfolio of assets. If the demand to hold money rose for reasons of increased liquidity preference, the demand to buy goods and services would fall. In Keynes's extreme case of the liquidity trap, the ability of money's non-transactions role to expand indefinitely could become the jinx of the capitalist system. Hicks also saw the need to locate money in a framework of portfolio choice, proposing that the principle of marginal maximization should be borrowed from micro-economics.[23] Friedman's attempt to restate the quantity theory related the demand for money to wealth, as well as income and other variables.[24] Walters's neglect of these basic ideas, and their many implications, is further testimony to British economists' lack of insight into the role of credit and money in macroeconomic fluctuations. Walters and Minford agreed with the majority of Keynesian economists in British universities that Nigel Lawson, as Chancellor of the Exchequer, was correct to abandon broad money targets in late 1985. They were part of the extensive coalition of academic economists which regarded the monitoring of trends in credit and broad money as unnecessary.

IV

The sequence of events after the scrapping of broad money targets in 1985 had clear similarities to that after the abandonment of a fixed exchange rate in 1971 and 1972, except that the boom evolved somewhat more slowly. The focus of monetary policy again became the exchange rate. In late 1985 and early 1986, with the dollar falling rapidly on the foreign exchanges, the exchange rate did not signal a need for higher interest rates. The pound itself fell heavily in late 1986, particularly against the Deutschmark, but this was interpreted as a necessary and welcome result of lower oil prices. (In 1984 exports of oil had amounted to almost £15 billion, equivalent to almost 20 per cent of total exports of goods. The pound was widely seen as a 'petro-currency'.)

From March 1987 to March 1988 sterling was deliberately kept in a band of 2.95 to 3 against the Deutschmark. However, with German interest rates so much beneath those in Britain, this external factor argued for an easing, rather than a tightening, of domestic monetary policy. In effect, from late 1985 to early 1988 there was no meaningful external constraint on domes-tic monetary policy. The external environment allowed rapid growth of domestic credit and fast monetary expansion, just as it had after the ending of the dollar's convertibility into gold in August 1971 and the pound's exit from the European snake in June 1972. Interest rates fell, credit growth accelerated and the growth rate of broad money – no longer dampened by overfunding – also increased. By late 1986 the economy was undoubtedly growing at an above-trend rate. By mid-1987 it was in a full-scale boom. The mood of businessmen, particularly get-rich-quick property specula-tors, was an almost exact replica of that in the Barber boom 15 years earlier. Indeed, the bank lending and broad money numbers themselves were remarkably similar. (See Essay 14, on pp. 281–315, for further discussion.)

But did British economists, of either the Keynesian or narrow money schools, object? Did they warn that the boom would inevitably end in a worse payments deficit, a rising inflation rate and a need for a sharp cycli-cal downturn to offset the excesses of the boom? Sadly, it is hardly neces-sary to answer these questions. The clear majority of them – in the universities, the official policy-making machine and the City – raised no objections and issued no warnings. On the contrary, the consensus macro-economic forecast in 1986, 1987 and early 1988 was that the economy was about to slow down to a trend rate of output growth without any rise in interest rates. (This tendency to predict a slowdown two to three quarters from the current quarter was so widespread and persistent that it became known as 'forecasters' droop'.) All of the so-called leading forecasting bodies – the London Business School, the National Institute, the Treasury and their many imitators – believed that the inflation rate in the late 1980s would be similar to, or lower than, that in the mid-1980s.[25]

Without an appropriately valued fixed exchange rate to guide interest rate decisions, academic economists were slaphappy about the medium-term implications of grossly unsustainable domestic monetary trends. The indifference of academic opinion gave economic advisers in the civil service and the Bank of England a pretext for not alerting their political masters to the foolishness of policy.[26] The Lawson boom of the late 1980s – like the Barber boom of the early 1970s – was the result of British economists' lack of recognition of how credit and money affect demand, output, employ-ment and inflation. It was due, above all, to a great vacuum in intellectual understanding. The Lawson boom was followed, like the Barber boom, by a sharp rise in inflation and a recession. It therefore wrecked the greatest asset the Thatcher government had in the general elections of 1983 and 1987, a high reputation for managerial competence in running the economy and controlling inflation. These consequences can be fairly described as the revenge of the 364.

However, there was no excuse for the vacuum in intellectual understand-ing. Keynes had set out over 60 years earlier in his *Tract on Monetary Reform* how a system of monetary policy focused on domestic objectives should work. The key intermediate indicators in the *Tract* were the growth rates of credit and bank deposits (or, as we would now say, broad money), just as they were in the original medium-term financial strategy declared in 1980. Keynes's agenda in the *Tract* should be seen as the logical culmination of many decades of analysis and theorizing about the trade cycle. This tradition of British monetary economics began with Thornton and Ricardo, and proceeded through (among others) John Stuart Mill, Bagehot and Alfred Marshall, to Keynes's contemporaries, Dennis Robertson and Ralph Hawtrey. But it withered and died in the 1940s and 1950s. It suffered, most of all, from the deliberate and ideologically motivated neglect of an economics profession far more interested in planning how a semi-socialist economy might work in the future than in understanding how a free-market economy had operated in the past (and does now operate and will indeed continue to operate in the future).

The closing phase of the Lawson boom saw a vigorous debate between those economists who favoured membership of the European monetary system and others who wanted to maintain policy independence. As noted in the Introduction, the dominant position in the UK economics establishment – with its strong Keynesian leanings – was to support EMS membership. This was a bizarre twist, in two ways. The fixing of the exchange rate was not the currency regime endorsed in the great mass of Keynes's writings on the topic, while the effect of linking the pound with the Deutschmark was to subordinate UK interest rates to decisions taken by the avowedly monetarist Bundesbank.[27] Indeed, if the UK had turned out to be a long-term participant in European monetary unification, it would have lost control of both monetary and fiscal policy. It is fair to ask, 'was this how "the Keynesian revolution" was supposed to end?' And, if one wants to find the 'defunct economists' to blame for the muddles and disasters of the 1970s and 1980s, is it not justified to suggest that the academic Keynesians – most of whom never paid much attention to Keynes's early work in the *Tract* – should be identified as the culprits?

In the event the pound joined the Exchange Rate Mechanism, a necessary period of apprenticeship in the full EMS, in October 1990. But it stayed inside the ERM for less than two years, enduring a recession far worse than the EMS advocates had envisaged. Comparisons were drawn between the decision to accept the exchange rate discipline of the ERM in 1990 and the decision to accept the exchange rate discipline of the gold standard in 1925, to which Keynes had so eloquently objected. The pound was expelled from the ERM on 16 September 1992 in circumstances of extreme international humiliation. The UK has subsequently both eschewed a fixed exchange rate link with any other currency and declined to participate in European monetary union. It has also – somehow – been able to run its own currency and economy with an impressive degree of stability, arguably on the lines of the 'managed currency' adumbrated by Keynes in his 1923 *Tract on Monetary Reform*. (The story of how this achievement should be interpreted is taken up in Essay 13.)

NOTES

1. D. Moggridge and E. Johnson (eds), *Collected Writings of John Maynard Keynes*, vol. VII, *The General Theory of Employment, Interest and Money* (London: Macmillan, 1973, originally published 1936), p. 383.
2. V.H. Hewitt and J.M. Keyworth, *As Good as Gold: 300 Years of British Bank Note Design* (London: British Museum Publications in association with the Bank of England, 1987), p. 27.
3. C.A.E. Goodhart, *The Business of Banking, 1891–1914* (London: Weidenfeld and Nicolson, 1972), pp. 195–208.
4. J.A. Schumpeter, *History of Economic Analysis* (London: George Allen and Unwin, 1954), p. 256.
5. H. Thornton, *An Enquiry into the Nature and Effects of the Paper Credit of Great Britain* (Fairfield, NJ: August M. Kelly, 1978, reprint of version edited by F.A. von Hayek and published by George Allen and Unwin in 1939; originally published 1802), p. 276.
6. Thornton, *Paper Credit*, p. 259.
7. I am not suggesting that Thornton was opposed to the gold standard. In fact, his 1811 contributions to two House of Commons debates show that he was strongly in favour of it. See *Paper Credit*, p. 346. I am claiming only that his writings hinted at the possibility of a different approach.
8. Moggridge and Johnson (eds), *Collected Writings of Keynes*, vol. IV, *A Tract on Monetary Reform* (London: Macmillan, 1971, originally published 1923), p. 136.
9. Moggridge and Johnson (eds), *Keynes*, vol. IV, *Tract*, pp. 126–7 and p. 140.
10. Moggridge and Johnson (eds), *Keynes*, vol. IV, *Tract*, pp. 141–2.
11. Moggridge and Johnson (eds), *Keynes*, vol. IV, *Tract*, pp. 142–5.
12. I discussed some of the definitional problems in my contribution 'British and American monetarism compared', pp. 38–72, in R. Hill (ed.), *Keynes, Money and Monetarism* (London: Macmillan, 1989). (This paper is reprinted in this volume as Essay 7 on pp. 146–72.)
13. Lord Kahn, *On Re-reading Keynes* (London: Oxford University Press for the British Academy, 1975), pp. 22–3.
14. Moggridge and Johnson (eds), *Keynes: General Theory*, p. 378.
15. W. Beckerman (ed.), *The Labour Government's Economic Record: 1964–70* (London: Duckworth, 1972), pp. 340–41.
16. F. Cripps and M. Fetherston, 'The role of monetary policy in economic management', *Economic Policy Review*, March 1977, p. 54.
17. Tim Congdon, *Monetarism: An Essay in Definition* (London: Centre for Policy Studies, 1978), pp. 11–13. See also chapter 6, 'How Friedman came to Britain', pp. 172–202, of W. Parsons, *The Power of the Financial Press* (Aldershot, UK and Brookfield, US: Edward Elgar, 1989).
18. Bank of England and HM Treasury, Cmnd. 7858 *Monetary Control* (London: HMSO, 1980).
19. See my pamphlet, *Monetarism Lost* (London: Centre for Policy Studies, 1989), for a more detailed description of the evolution of monetary policy in the 1980s.
20. Moggridge and Johnson (eds), *Keynes: Tract*, pp. 145–6.
21. Moggridge and Johnson (eds), *Keynes: Tract*, pp. 153–4.

22. Alan Walters, *Britain's Economic Renaissance* (New York: Oxford University Press, 1986), pp. 116–17.
23. This is a reference to Sir John Hicks's famous paper on 'A suggestion for simplifying the theory of money', written before Keynes's *General Theory*.
24. Milton Friedman's 'The quantity theory of money: a restatement', a paper originally published in 1956, said that 'the demand for money is a special topic in the theory of capital'. It was the theoretical launching-pad of the so-called 'monetarist counter-revolution'.
25. Professor Patrick Minford of Liverpool University argued late into the boom that slow growth of M0 presaged an early return to 3 per cent inflation. This was not the first time that Minford had been disastrously wrong by using M0 for forecasting purposes. He warned in late 1985 that, because of slow M0 growth, 'we now have the tightest monetary policy we have ever had' and maintained that 'a stalling in the growth rate, unless immediate action is taken to reduce interest rates, is now increasingly likely'. See p. 45 of J. Bruce-Gardyne and others, *Whither Monetarism?* (London: Centre for Policy Studies, 1985). These remarks were made on the eve of the strongest boom for 15 years.
26. According to one former civil servant, even Mr Denis Healey – who as Chancellor of the Exchequer had made the announcement that introduced broad money targets – did not really believe in them. 'To ascribe paternity for the MTFS to Denis Healey seems to me to be going too far. He was described at the time as an unbelieving monetarist, meaning that he adopted monetary targets only with a view to inspiring confidence in the financial world, which did believe in them.' Leo Pliatzky, *The Treasury under Mrs Thatcher* (Oxford: Basil Blackwell, 1989), p. 122.
27. In any case, other European countries did not suffer the illusion that full membership of the EMS specified a complete anti-inflationary policy. They also followed domestic financial targets stated in terms of credit and/or broad money. In their regard for narrow money, it was British economic policy-makers and their advisers who had become idiosyncratic. The Bank of England stopped publishing data on M0 in early 2006.

PART TWO

The So-called 'Keynesian Revolution'

The two essays in this section are exercises in debunking. The notion of 'the Keynesian revolution' is so well established that it might seem frivolous to challenge it. But – if the phrase means the adoption of discretionary fiscal policy to manage demand and thereby to secure full employment – a strong case can be made that the UK did not have a 'Keynesian revolution' at all. In his final years Keynes was a dominant figure in British public life, but he seems to have irritated a significant number of Treasury and Bank of England officials. In one notorious exchange a senior Treasury official, Sir Herbert Brittain, was told to his face that he was 'intellectually contemptible'. That may not have mattered if Keynes had remained in control of events, but he died in 1946 whereas Brittain was closely involved in Home Finance (including the preparation of the annual Budget) until his retirement in 1957. Brittain used his immediate post-retirement leisure to write a book on The British Budgetary System. *It made no mention of Keynes and defended principles of public sector accountancy (such as the distinction between above-the-line and below-the-line expenditure items), which had originated in Gladstone's day. Only in the 1960s and 1970s did Keynesian thinking come to dominate the Treasury, but by then British governments were not free to vary the budget deficit because of constant worries about the balance of payments and the weakness of sterling.*

The first essay in this section, 'Did Britain have a "Keynesian revolution"?' (based on a paper given to a conference at Gresham College in February 1996), discusses the rather confused conduct of fiscal policy in practice. It denies that Keynesianism determined fiscal policy in the post-war decades, except perhaps for a couple of years in the early 1970s. A statistical test in the appendix shows that that the budget deficit was not varied inversely with the output gap between 1948 and 1974 (which it ought to have been if policy had been Keynesian). After the mid-1970s Keynesianism – in the sense of fiscal fine-tuning – was dropped. For a few years in the late 1970s and early 1980s lip-service was paid to the idea that the budgetary position should be consistent with a targeted rate of growth of the money supply. While practice was again rather different from theory, this was a form of monetarism. Whatever one's views on the two systems of thought, both Keynesianism and monetarism did at least try to apply economic theory to a practical problem. But in the late 1980s unsophisticated notions of 'balance' and 'prudence' took over, and economic theory was put to one side. The New Labour government of 1997 enunciated two fiscal rules which, despite being routinely described as 'modern' in official documents, could be most readily justified in neo-Gladstonian terms. The second essay, 'Is anything left of the "Keynesian revolution"?', remarks on the similarity of the reasoning behind these supposedly new rules and the conventions of public sector accounting advocated by Brittain almost 40 years earlier.

4. Did Britain have a 'Keynesian revolution'?

The common understanding of the phrase, 'the Keynesian revolution', is a reappraisal of the theory of fiscal policy after the publication of Keynes's *The General Theory of Employment, Interest and Money* in 1936, followed by the practical adoption of the new ideas by the major industrial countries in the 1940s and 1950s. Specifically, whereas before the Keynesian revolution governments' priority in fiscal policy was to maintain a balanced budget, afterwards the budgetary balance was varied contra-cyclically in order to reduce fluctuations in economic activity. Britain is often regarded as the home of the Keynesian revolution. For example, the opening sentence of chapter VII of Christopher Dow's *The Management of the British Economy 1945–60* asserts, 'There is probably no country in the world that has made a fuller use than the UK of budgetary policy as a means of stabilizing the economy.'[1] The characterization of British macroeconomic policy as 'Keynesian' in the immediate post-war decades has become routine and unchallenged in standard textbooks.

A detailed narrative account of the evolution of fiscal policy in the Keynesian direction has been provided in the USA by Herbert Stein's *The Fiscal Revolution in America*. Stein describes the immense initial enthusiasm of young American economists, such as Samuelson and Boulding, for *The General Theory* in the late 1930s. As a result,

> By 1940 Keynes had largely swept the field of the younger economists, those who were soon to be 'back-room boys' in Washington and who, when they reached the age of forty-five or so, would be ready to come into the front room when John F. Kennedy became President in 1961.[2]

No similarly organized story has been told about the UK, perhaps because the policy revolution is deemed to be so self-evident that an analysis of personalities and events is unnecessary. (As discussed in the three essays in the first part of this book, Keynes himself had rather different attitudes and emphases from the Keynesians.[3])

The purpose of this essay is to suggest that, between the 1940s and 1970s, both the thinking behind British macroeconomic policy-making and the actual conduct of policy were far from the Keynesian model. As there is little question that after the mid-1970s fiscal policy ceased to be Keynesian in either form or substance, the essay raises doubts about whether Britain ever had a Keynesian revolution. To throw more light on the issue, statistical tests are conducted of the relationship between changes in the budget position and the level of economic activity. The results of these tests are reported in the appendix. They show that the level of economic activity was not a significant influence on the change in the cyclically adjusted budget position in the supposedly Keynesian period between 1948 and 1974. (Less surprisingly, it was also not a significant influence between 1975 and 1994.) On this basis, the answer to the question, 'Did Britain have a Keynesian revolution?' is 'No'.

Of course, the demonstration that statistically there never was a Keynesian revolution does not rule out the possibility that, from time to time, key decision-takers did respond to their advisers and alter fiscal policy in a Keynesian manner. It may even be consistent with their desire to conduct fiscal policy on Keynesian lines all the time. Plans to vary the budget balance contra-cyclically may have been frustrated by sterling crises, of which there were many between 1945 and the mid-1970s, and other external shocks, such as the Korean War in 1950 and 1951. The absence of a Keynesian revolution in fact does not exclude the possibility that there was a Keynesian revolution in intention. The essay's first task has to be a review of the structure of macroeconomic policy-making, and the ideas held by policy-makers, from the 1930s onwards.

I

Keynes was appointed to the Economic Advisory Council, a high-level body set up to advise the government on economic matters, at its formation in 1930. It was the successor to a similar committee, created in 1925, to advise the Cabinet. The importance of this appointment should not be exaggerated, because – in the words of Lord Bridges – both the 1925 committee and the Economic Advisory Council were throughout the 1930s 'rather remote from the active centre of things'.[4] In particular, Keynes failed in 1931 and 1932 to halt the public expenditure cuts advocated by the May Committee, despite his ferocious and well-known attack on them in the *New Statesman*.[5] These cuts were a classic example of government expenditure being dominated by budget-balancing principles, instead of by the requirements of the business cycle. They were also an important part of the provocation for the new theories expressed in *The General Theory*.

Despite Keynes's apparent ineffectiveness in the policy debate of the early 1930s, the Economic Advisory Council set the precedent for professional economists to supplement civil service advice on key issues in economic policy. Because of the imperative to reach the best possible decisions in wartime, the Economic Advisory Council was followed in 1939 by a Central Economic Information Service in the Cabinet Office. It had a full-time staff of economists and statisticians, and they were given the job of assembling in one place information about production which had previously been available only from a wide variety of sources. This had obvious significance for the organization of military output, but it also made possible the first estimates of national income and expenditure. Early in 1941 the Central Economic Information Service was split into two, with the economists becoming the Economic Section of the Cabinet Office and the statisticians the Central Statistical Office. The service's work made possible the publication of the first National Income White Paper, which informed the tax decisions taken in the Budget on 7 April 1941 by Sir Kingsley Wood, the Chancellor of the Exchequer.

According to Sabine, '1941 . . . was the watershed year when the Budget could at last be seen to be performing its correct dual function of raising the taxation required and restricting purchasing power.'[6] The connection between tax decisions and consumer spending power – and so, by extension, between the government's financial position and aggregate demand – had been emphasized by Keynes in articles in *The Times* on 'How to Pay for the War', where he developed the idea of an 'inflationary gap'. The gap, the excess of the nation's *ex ante* propensity to spend over its *ex ante* ability to supply, made sense conceptually only in the context of his theory of national income determination. 'It is impossible to divorce the practice of the Kingsley Wood regime from the theories of Keynes, particularly 'in the recasting of Budget mathematics to highlight the gap'.[7] Dow agrees that 1941 was the turning point. 'Since 1941 almost all adjustments to the total level of taxation have been made with the object of reducing excess demand or of repairing a deficiency.'[8]

Keynes is also attributed with a role in the authorship of the 1944 White Paper on *Employment Policy*. The *Employment Policy* White Paper is widely regarded as the charter for demand-management policies in the post-war period, largely because of its reference to 'a high and stable level of employment' as an objective of official policy. However, the actual wording of the White Paper is far from enthusiastic in its endorsement of a Keynesian purpose for fiscal policy. One passage reads, 'To the extent that the policies proposed in this Paper affect the balancing of the Budget in a particular year, they certainly do not contemplate any departure from the principle that the Budget must be balanced over a longer period'. Further, 'An undue growth in national indebtedness will have a quick result on confidence. But no less serious would be a budgetary deficit arising from a fall in revenues due to depressed industrial and commercial conditions'.[9] It is plainly implied that depressed conditions might not justify discretionary action to expand the budget deficit.

At any rate, by the late 1940s ministers and many civil servants recognized that the annual Budget ought to be framed with a view to influencing the level of economic activity. In 1948 Sir Stafford Cripps combined the functions of Chancellor of the Exchequer with that of Minister for Co-ordination of Economic Affairs. In his Budget speech of 1950 he said, 'Excessive demand produces inflation and inadequate demand results in deflation. The fiscal policy of the Government is the most important single instrument for maintaining that balance.'[10] This is clear and straightforward, and undoubtedly represents an official stamp of approval for Keynesianism.

There is also no question that – when it was given – the statement was uncontroversial and commanded support from all parts of the political spectrum. The Conservative Party came to power in 1951 and made more deliberate use of monetary policy than its predecessor. Most notably, it allowed Bank rate to rise from 2 per cent (where it had been stuck, apart from a brief period at the start of the Second World War, since 1932) to 2½ per cent in November 1951 and 4 per cent in March 1952. Thereafter Bank rate was varied mostly in response to the vicissitudes of the exchange rate. But monetary policy was not thought to have a major part to play in influencing demand. Because it was assigned to the task of stabilizing foreign exchange sentiment towards the pound, fiscal policy could instead be used for the vital aim of managing the domestic economy and trying to secure, on average, a high level of employment. The 1941 and other wartime Budgets has set a precedent for the use of fiscal policy in peacetime. Fiscal policy was taken as being more or less equivalent to discretionary changes in tax, since public expenditure was judged too inflexible for short-run demand management.[11] Further, tax changes mattered mostly because of their impact on consumption, not on investment. Investment had the drawback that it was volatile and difficult to forecast, and so it seemed less amenable to fiscal policy treatment. In Ian Little's words, commenting on fiscal policy in the 1950s, 'in almost all respects, taxation (and, more generally, fiscal policy) is superior to monetary policy'.[12]

By the start of the 1960s economists began to feel more confident about quantifying the effect of tax changes on demand. As they could estimate the link between tax changes and consumption, and since consumption was the largest component of aggregate demand, they believed they had leverage over the economy as a whole. '[T]he procedure of official forecasting is designed to fit in with the procedure of budget-making.'[13] To quote Little again, writing in 1961,

Mr. Heathcoat-Amory was the first Chancellor to predict demand in percentages in his 1960 Budget speech. More recently, Mr. Selwyn Lloyd has said, 'I believe it will be within our power to expand at the rate of 3 per cent per annum over the next five years, but to do this our exports will have to rise at approximately double this rate'.

Little welcomed the shift to forecasts of demand constituents in percentage terms, concluding his references to Heathcoat-Amory and Selwyn Lloyd with the remark 'Let us hope these are straws in the wind of change.'[14]

II

Superficially, informed views on fiscal policy theory and the actual conduct of fiscal policy had made a comprehensive shift from primitive pre-Keynesian budget balancing in the early 1930s to sophisticated Keynesian demand management in the early 1960s. This shift seems to have been comparable to that in the USA, as described by Stein in his *The Fiscal Revolution in America*. The standard textbook characterization of the period as 'the age of Keynes' appears to be justified.

However, even at the level of ideas, the Keynesian triumph was far from complete. Influential writers in the Keynesian camp themselves concede that official thinking was more muddled and ambivalent in this period than commonly thought. In particular, the conventions for measuring the various categories of public expenditure, taxation and the differences between them harked back to the budget-balancing orthodoxies of the pre-Keynesian era. For example, in his book on *The Management of the British Economy* Dow protested against the survival of accounting practices which originated in the Exchequer and Audit Departments Act of 1866 or even earlier. To those well versed in the precepts of modern macroeconomics, 'The traditional Exchequer accounts have constantly to be explained away as misleading.' Indeed, in a footnote Dow admitted that the references to fiscal policy in the 1944 White Paper on *Employment Policy* were 'highly confused', because of tensions between economists working in Whitehall and 'the guardians of the older Treasury tradition'.[15]

Moreover, these guardians of the older tradition did write, quite extensively, about how they thought the public finances should be organized. In 1959 Sir Herbert Brittain, a recently retired senior Treasury official, published a book on *The British Budgetary System*, to serve as 'a new and comprehensive account of our budgetary system and of the parliamentary and administrative arrangements that are part of it'. He saw his book as following in the wake of *The System of National Finance* by Lord Kennet and Mr Norman Young, which had previously 'filled that role'. The book

contained not a single reference to Keynes. Indeed, it is not going too far
to say that, in certain respects, Brittain's description of budgetary arrangements appeared to be deliberately anti-Keynesian. Chapter III, on 'The
general design of the Budget', placed a section on 'Prudent finance' before
sections on 'Social and political questions' and 'Broad economic and
financial policy'.

The comments on budget deficits under the 'Broad economic and
financial policy' heading were highly traditional. Not only must the deficit
be as low as possible in the interests of control, but also 'regard must be
had to the fact that any deficit inevitably means an increase in the national
debt'. Brittain noted the doctrine that 'an indefinite increase in the national
debt does not matter so long as the rate of increase is less than the rate of
increase in national income', but rejected it on the grounds that the tax
burden depended on the size of all transfer payments and not on the debt
interest charge alone. '[I]t may be dangerous to mortgage in advance any
given part of the increase in revenue for the debt charge, irrespective of
other possible claims.'[16] The section's verdict was that 'dangerous results'
might proceed from a lack of confidence in the public finances. Finally, a
footnote was attached, claiming that most of the 1944 *Employment Policy*
White Paper, and in particular the passage in paragraphs 74 to 79 'dealing
with Central Finance', had stood up 'to the test of post-war expenditure'.[17]
Paragraphs 74 to 79 were exactly those which had reiterated the virtues of
balancing the budget over the business cycle.

How should this balancing of the budget be defined? The central principle of the Treasury's fiscal conservatism was that the budget should be balanced 'above the line'. The distinction between items above and below the
line was related, but not identical, to the distinction between income and
capital. The crucial difference was that recurrent items of capital expenditure were regarded as above the line, 'as there is no case for spreading it
over a period, and to borrow every year would only increase the cost over
the years by unnecessary payments of interest'.[18] So borrowing was legitimate to cover the cost of exceptional, non-recurrent capital expenditure,
but that was all. The intended aim of this type of fiscal conservatism was
to prevent the national debt rising faster than the stock of capital assets
owned by the government. The cyclical state of the economy was a secondary consideration. Further, in prosperous conditions extending over
several cycles the result of applying such rules would be to keep the national
debt growing more slowly than national income.

Which set of ideas – the Keynesian contra-cyclical activism described by
Dow and Little or the fiscal conservatism defended by the Treasury knights –
was in fact the predominant influence in the late 1940s, the 1950s and early
1960s? On some interpretations the data give a clear-cut answer. As noted by

Robin Matthews, writing in 1968, 'throughout the post-war period the Government, so far from injecting demand into the system, has persistently had a large current account surplus . . . [G]overnment saving has averaged about 3 per cent of the national income'.[19] A surplus of this kind would be the likely outcome of applying the above-the-line/below-the-line methodology favoured by Brittain and traditional Treasury knights, since it would correspond to the recurrent capital costs covered by revenue. The ratio of the UK's national debt to its gross domestic product fell sharply from 1945 to the mid-1970s, despite the charter for permissive deficit financing which Keynes was supposed to have given policy-makers in his *General Theory*.

Matthews continued, provocatively, to assert that fiscal policy appears 'to have been deflationary in the post-war period'. However, there is an important theoretical objection to this conclusion. The characterization of fiscal policy is beset with ambiguities. Quite apart from all the uncertainties about specifying the appropriate concept of the budget balance, fiscal policy can be measured and described in terms of either the *level* or the *change* in the budget balance. Matthew's conclusion depends on the premiss that fiscal policy is best described in terms of the level of the budget balance. A counterargument could be made that the change in the balance, appropriately defined, is the government's discretionary response to the economic situation and is therefore a better way of thinking about 'policy'.

Fortunately, several studies have been made of the relationship between the economy and changes in the budget balance in the first 25 years after 1945. Hansen, conducting a statistical review of *Fiscal Policy in Seven Countries 1955–65* for the OECD, judged that fiscal policy in the UK, measured in terms of changes in the cyclically adjusted deficit, had been destabilizing over the period.[20] (In other words, action had been taken to increase the deficit when the economy was operating at an above-normal level and to reduce it when economy was below normal.) In his narrative account *The Treasury under the Tories 1951–64*, Samuel Brittan was also highly critical. In 1971 he published *Steering the Economy*, a revised and updated version of *The Treasury under the Tories*. In it he suggested that 'Chancellors behaved like simple Pavlovian dogs responding to two main stimuli: one was "a run on the reserves" and the other was "500,000 unemployed" – a figure which was later increased to above 600,000.'[21] Even Dow – who made such strong claims for the historical reality of the Keynesian revolution in the early chapters of *The Management of the British Economy 1945–60* – acknowledged in later chapters that practice and out-turn had been very different from theory and plan. In the event many 'adjustments of policy were occasioned by the balance of payments', not the level of unemployment relative to a desired figure. The external interference had the result that,

[a]s far as internal conditions are concerned . . . budgetary and monetary policy failed to be stabilizing and must on the contrary be regarded as having been positively destabilizing. Had tax changes been more gradual, and credit regulations less variable, demand and output would probably have grown much more steadily.[22]

The conclusion must be that, over at least the first two-thirds of the period from 1945 to the mid-1970s, fiscal policy was not Keynesian in the normally understood sense. The trend level of the budget deficit was determined by 'the older Treasury tradition', with its emphasis on the sustainability of government debt relative both to national income and the size of the public sector's stock of capital assets. Policy-determined variations in the deficit around this trend level were largely motivated by the balance of payments and the state of the pound, not by the counter-cyclical requirements of the domestic economy and unemployment. Moreover, many economists active at the time must have been fully aware that there was a sharp divergence between the actual conduct of fiscal policy and their Keynesian views of what fiscal policy ought to have been.

The election of the Labour government in October 1964, with Harold Wilson as Prime Minister, was accompanied by a large influx of professional economists into Whitehall. Many of them thought fiscal policy could and should be used to manage the economy. But economic policy in the years from 1964 to 1970 was again dominated by the balance of payments. The government sought financial help from the International Monetary Fund after the pound's devaluation in November 1967. The Budget of 1968 contained the largest tax increases since 1945, with fiscal policy specifically designed to curb the current account deficit. Unhappily, the current account's initial response to devaluation was slow. In June 1969 the government and the IMF reached agreement on further measures, with the Letter of Intent referring to a target for domestic credit expansion of £400 million in the 1969/70 year. Domestic credit expansion (DCE) was a new policy indicator, essentially equal to all new bank credit extended to the public and private sectors. DCE to the public sector was equal to the public sector borrowing requirement (PSBR) minus net sales of public sector debt to non-banks. A target for DCE implied some sort of limit on the budget deficit and so precluded contra-cyclical action to lower unemployment.

One result of the IMF's involvement in British macroeconomic policy was to make the PSBR – a cash measure of borrowing, which integrated readily with monetary analysis – the most prominent measure of the budgetary position. This led to a substantial modernization of the lexicon of fiscal policy, but policy itself was certainly not Keynesian. Most Keynesians were scornful of the IMF medicine, on the grounds that it was merely a refurbishment of old sound finance doctrines. But the current account of the balance of payments was converted, after adoption of the IMF's prescription, from deficit in 1968 to large surplus in 1970. Indeed, a common refrain in 1970 and 1971 was that the fiscal contraction of 1968 had not turned the balance of payments round, whereas the monetary squeeze of 1969 had worked. The effectiveness of fiscal policy was compared unfavourably with that of monetary policy.

Another theme in policy-making circles in the early 1970s was that the UK's poor long-term record on economic growth could be largely blamed on undue anxiety about the balance of payments and the exchange rate. For example, Brittan argued that a balance-of-payments deficit was a non-problem, since the drain on the UK's foreign exchange reserves could be halted simply by allowing the exchange rate to float.[23] The editor of an important collection of essays on *The Labour Government's Economic Record 1964–70* judged in 1972 that, because of the reluctance to devalue the pound earlier, 'the Government never achieved any room for manoeuvre . . . It is little wonder that they were eventually blown off course'.[24]

The intellectual groundwork had been laid for the aggressive expansionism of macroeconomic policy in the two years to mid-1973. Policy-makers were determined that the exchange rate would not be allowed to hold back economic growth. Credit restrictions were relaxed in late 1971 and a highly stimulative Budget was introduced by the Chancellor of the Exchequer, Mr Anthony (later Lord) Barber, in March 1972. In response to the inevitable resulting weakness of the pound, the exchange rate was floated in June 1972. In 1973 gross domestic product rose by over 7 per cent. But the trend growth rate of the UK economy remained much as before and the 'Barber boom' led to severe overheating. Inflation (as measured by the 12-month increase in the retail price index) rose to double-digit rates in 1974 and peaked at 26.9 per cent in August 1975, while the current account of the balance of payments incurred the heaviest deficits (relative to GDP) in the post-war period.

In the subsequent policy debates, the policy thinking behind the expansionism of the early 1970s was often labelled 'Keynesianism'. This may be rather unfair, since Keynesianism encompasses a wide variety of positions about the relative importance of the different branches of policy and is merely 'an apparatus of thought' (in Keynes's own words), not a well-defined set of rules about policy. Two years in the early 1970s (from mid-1971 to mid-1973) may nevertheless be the only phase in the entire post-war period when policy was properly Keynesian, uncluttered by the constraints of the fixed exchange rate (as before 1971) or by an entirely different framework of thought (as after the mid-1970s). At the time, the Barber boom was regarded as Keynesian in intention by those who decided policy and as

Keynesian in form by the majority of commentators. It was also an unmit-
igated disaster. The euphoria of 1973 was followed over the next two years
by the worst recession, the highest inflation and the widest payments gap in
the post-war period.

III

After some point in the mid-1970s it no longer makes any sense to describe
British macroeconomic policy as 'Keynesian'. Textual and narrative analysis has to admit that there is scope for debate about whether fiscal policy
was Keynesian between 1945 and 1974, but there is no doubt about the
period from 1979. Policy-makers, official advisers to Treasury ministers and
commentators are all agreed that – after the election of the Conservative
government under Mrs (later Lady) Thatcher – fiscal policy was determined by non-Keynesian considerations.

But that leaves undetermined the precise moment between 1974 and 1979
when fiscal policy-makers consciously and deliberately abandoned
Keynesian thinking. Of course, the notion of a 'precise moment' is misleading. The attitudes of the key politicians, advisers and academics were
in constant flux. They changed at different times to different degrees and in
different ways from one person to another. Mr Denis (later Lord) Healey,
who was Chancellor of the Exchequer from 1974 to 1979 and took a closer
interest in the niceties of economic theory than most chancellors, made a
fascinating appraisal in his autobiography, *The Time of My Life*. He found
the PSBR so vulnerable to the economic cycle that it was 'impossible to get
[it] right', which – in his opinion – undermined the heavy emphasis on the
PSBR in 'the so-called "budget judgement"', which in turn determined the
extent to which taxes or spending should be raised or lowered'.[25] But he was
also suspicious of dependence on the money supply, as 'the monetary statistics are as unreliable as all the others'. His response was to become 'an
eclectic pragmatist'.[26] This may sound like a fudge, but it had an important
consequence. After noting that when he arrived at the Treasury in 1974 it
was still Keynes's intellectual 'slave', Healey ventured the comment 'I abandoned Keynesianism in 1975'.[27]

But the private and retrospective reflections of a Chancellor of the
Exchequer are not the same as the public and transparent passage of events.
For most observers 1976 was the crucial turning point. Heavy selling pressure on the foreign exchanges hit the pound in the spring, obliging the government to introduce a package of expenditure cuts and other policy
changes. On 22 July Healey announced a target for the growth of the money
supply, on the M3 measure (including bank deposits), of 12 per cent during

the 1976/77 financial year. It was the first time that a target for monetary growth had been included in an official statement on macroeconomic policy. As the pound remained under pressure in the next few months, the government again sought help from the IMF in late September. The IMF made a loan, but attached the condition that DCE should not exceed £9 billion in 1976/77, £7.7 billion in 1977/78 and £6 billion in 1978/79. As in the late 1960s, this implied a constraint on the amount of bank credit extended to the public sector and so on the size of the budget deficit. Fiscal policy could not be focused on the management of domestic demand and the maintenance of high employment, because it had to give priority to an externally imposed target.

In the event the government easily met the IMF's targets and the pound staged a spectacular recovery in 1977. However, the inflationary trauma and exchange rate crises of the mid-1970s stimulated drastic rethinking about both the theory and practice of macroeconomic policy-making. This rethinking has been given the generic brand name of 'monetarism'. Arguably 'monetarism' was – and remains – an even more disparate body of thought than Keynesianism, but the label cannot now be shaken off. In the mid-1970s two central tenets of monetarism were that high inflation was caused by high monetary growth and that targets to restrict monetary growth were therefore the key to controlling inflation. A large budget deficit undermines the task of monetary restraint, because there is a risk that the government will have to finance its deficit from the banking system. In that case the banks add claims on the government to their assets and incur deposit liabilities to the private sector on the other side of the balance sheet. These deposits are money. A target for monetary growth therefore implies some limit on the budget deficit. It needs to be emphasized that the limit is determined by the logic of monetary targeting. It applies whether or not the government is borrowing from the IMF, and irrespective of the exchange rate regime it has adopted (that is, irrespective of whether the exchange rate is fixed or floating).

The potential monetary consequences of excessive budget deficits demonstrate the interdependence of fiscal and monetary policy. If a decline in monetary growth is necessary in order to lower inflation, cuts in the PSBR are also an essential element in the programme. It follows that policy should be expressed in terms of both monetary growth and the fiscal position, and that these should be seen as two sides of the same coin of 'financial policy'. (In effect, financial policy absorbs both monetary and fiscal policy.) Moreover, the UK's inflationary plight in the mid-1970s was such that a rapid deceleration in monetary growth would cause a severe recession and soaring unemployment. So – for those persuaded by the broad thrust of the monetarist case – it was generally accepted that the reductions in monetary growth and the PSBR should be phased over a number of years. Official policy should look not just to the next budget and the next year ('the short run'), but should be framed within a three- to five-year context of financial rehabilitation. Here lay the justification for medium-term macroeconomic planning, with the budget deficit geared to restoring medium- and long-run financial stability. Policy should not try to manipulate demand and employment from year to year in a Keynesian manner.[28]

Ideas of this kind were developed particularly among London-based policy-making and policy-advising circles in the crises of the mid-1970s. These circles included the Treasury, the Bank of England, some stock-broking firms in the City and what might be termed 'higher economic jour-nalism'.[29] The intellectual input from economists in universities outside London was minimal. In fact, most academic economists remained wedded to Keynesianism, a preference which led to sharp debates between the university-based profession and policy makers in the 1980s. The London Business School played a vital role in promoting the new ideas. In 1977 Mr Terry (later Lord) Burns and Mr Alan (later Sir Alan) Budd proposed a medium-term financial plan in the London Business School's *Economic Outlook*. In 1979 the same two authors wrote an article in the same publi-cation on 'The role of the PSBR in controlling the money supply'. In 1981 a book of *Essays in Fiscal and Monetary Policy* contained a paper by them on 'The relationship between fiscal and monetary policy in the London Business School model'. It made strong claims that 'The relationship between fiscal and monetary policy is a very close one, and under a floating exchange rate the prime determinant of monetary variations is changes in fiscal policy' and – even more ambitiously – 'Changes in the monetary aggregates are an "efficient" estimate of overall policy stance'.[30] The paper had originally been given at seminars organized by the Institute for Fiscal Studies in 1977 and 1978.

This emphasis on monetary variables as the best indicators of policy, combined with the linking of the fiscal and monetary policy in a medium-term context, set the scene for the introduction of the Medium-Term Financial Strategy (MTFS). The Thatcher government made clear soon after its election in June 1979 that it saw control of the money supply as necessary and sufficient to curb inflation. It was forthright in its rejection of Keynesian prescriptions. On 5 October 1979 a meeting to discuss medium-term financial planning was held at the Treasury between Sir Geoffrey (later Lord) Howe, his officials and a number of outside econo-mists known to be monetarist in their doctrinal affiliations. Sir Frederick Atkinson, of Keynesian leanings, retired in late 1979 and was replaced as Head of the Government Economic Service by Burns on 1 January 1980.

In the Budget of 26 March 1980 the first version of the MTFS was announced. It set out targets to reduce the ratio of the PSBR to GDP from 3¾ per cent in the 1980/81 financial year to 3 per cent in 1981/82, 2¼ per cent in 1982/83 and 1½ per cent in 1983/84, and in parallel gradually to lower the rate of increase in the sterling M3 measure of money.

Two points need to be made about the original MTFS. First, it did not envisage a return to a balanced budget at any date and its supporters did not appeal to old-fashioned balanced-budget rhetoric to defend their position.[31] Second, the rationale for targeting the PSBR was to support monetary control, which had increasingly been seen in the late 1970s as more fundamental to the macroeconomic outlook than fiscal policy.

The existence of the fiscal targets in the MTFS is crucial to understanding the 1981 Budget, which was the final nail in the coffin of Keynesianism at the policy-making level. The year 1980 saw the deepest recession in the post-war period, with GDP dropping by almost 2½ per cent. In early 1981 output was undoubtedly well beneath its trend level. Meanwhile the pound had been a strong currency for over 18 months and there was no external constraint on fiscal relaxation. But the government decided to increase taxes by over £4 billion, equivalent to almost 2 per cent of GDP. In the event, the economy began to recover in the middle of 1981, which gave encouragement to the beleaguered policy-makers in Whitehall that they were on the right lines. Despite setbacks in other branches of macroeconomic policy, the government persevered with the fiscal component of the MTFS. By the mid-1980s the PSBR/GDP ratio was down to the levels envisaged in the original MTFS. However, the official rationale for PSBR targeting changed markedly. In 1980 sterling M3 grew well above the top of its target range, greatly embarrassing the government, which had at first placed heavy emphasis on this measure of money as the keystone of macroeconomic policy. In response, the target was 'quickly abandoned (although not formally) as the government came to recognize [sterling M3's] apparent misleading behaviour'.[32] (Given the drastic nature of the volte-face on sterling M3, it may be worth mentioning that the DCE target contained in the IMF's Letter of Intent in 1976 was broadly defined. It was equal to the increase in sterling M3 and the banking system's external liabilities; it therefore related to commercial bank credit and not merely to credit extended by the central bank. Whatever the government's view by 1981, the IMF had certainly thought that the behaviour of sterling M3 was important five years earlier.)

With the money supply dethroned, there was no longer any sense in justifying PSBR targets by their contribution to monetary control. Instead the emphasis shifted to such considerations as the need to prevent debt rising too fast relative to GDP and, more specifically, to avoid an excessive burden of debt interest. The downfall of the monetary argument for fiscal restraint was also attributable in part to evidence from Professor Milton Friedman to the Treasury and Civil Service Committee of the House of Commons. Friedman, universally acknowledged as one of the intellectual founders of monetarism, told the Committee that the concern with the PSBR was 'unwise', partly 'because there is no necessary relation between the size of the PSBR and monetary growth'.[33]

The defence of PSBR targeting instead relied increasingly on the need to secure long-run fiscal solvency. An illustration of the new approach was the publication of a Green Paper on *The Next Ten Years: Public Expenditure and Taxation into the 1990s*, in conjunction with the 1984 Budget. This was the first Budget presented by Mr Nigel (later Lord) Lawson, who was to remain Chancellor until 1989. Paragraph 56 of the Green Paper projected the PSBR/GDP ratio into future years and noted that, 'net of debt interest little or no change in the PSBR is assumed'. It continued, 'on this basis the tax burden for the non-North Sea sector can be reduced to the extent that public expenditure falls more than North Sea tax revenues as a share of GDP'.[34]

This sounds complicated, but the essential message was that any success in controlling non-interest public expenditure would in future be translated into tax cuts. The PSBR/GDP ratio might decline, but only as a consequence of lowering the ratio of debt interest to GDP. There was no mention in the Green Paper of adjusting the PSBR to combat the business cycle (on Keynesian lines) or of lowering it in order to dampen monetary growth (as favoured by the monetarists). The Green Paper is interesting in three ways: first, as early evidence of Lawson's preference for tax cuts over budgetary discipline; second, for its dichotomy between the policy implications of interest and non-interest expenditure; and, third, because of its medium- and long-term planning perspective. The PSBR/GDP ratio was intended to drop to 1 per cent by 1993/94, helped by the projection of a sufficiently large decline in the ratio of debt interest to GDP. Separately, Lawson described a PSBR/GDP ratio of 1 per cent as 'the modern equivalent of a balanced Budget'.[35] A PSBR/GDP ratio of 1 per cent had earlier been judged compatible with long-run price stability in a paper published in the London Business School's *Economic Outlook* in 1983.[36]

The 1984 Green Paper was a theoretical document. The out-turns in practice were very different. In the late 1980s the economy experienced a strong and unforeseen boom in activity, which gave the usual cyclical boost to the public finances. The PSBR declined to less than 2 per cent of GDP in the 1986/87 fiscal year and turned into a small surplus in 1987/88. In 1988/89 the surplus widened to £14.7 billion or 3 per cent of GDP. The attainment of a surplus in 1987/88 and the extent of the surplus in 1988/89 were not predicted by the Treasury. In the 1988 Budget Lawson took the unusually benign fiscal performance as an opportunity to reinstate the doctrine of a balanced budget. His budget speech condemned the deficits recorded by previous Labour administrations, noting that 'profligacy' had bought 'economic disaster' and 'national humiliation', as well as adding 'massively to the burden of debt interest'. Lawson saw the doctrine of a balanced budget as 'a valuable discipline for the medium term'. Further, 'henceforth a zero PSBR will be the norm. This provides a clear and simple rule, with a good historical pedigree.'[37]

The aim of balancing the budget (in the sense of keeping the PSBR at zero) over the cycle remained the cornerstone of fiscal policy from the 1988 Budget until the 1997 general election. It was reiterated during the early 1990s, when in a deep recession the government once again incurred heavy deficits. As in the similar circumstances of 1981, the two budgets of 1993 raised taxes sharply in order to restore a satisfactory fiscal position over the medium term. But the official argument for a balanced budget was less strident and ideological, and far more pragmatic, than the case for medium-term PSBR reductions in the early 1980s. As in the Lawson period, it continued to rely on broad notions of stability and solvency. It eschewed Keynesian demand-management considerations and was rather casual about the interdependence of fiscal and monetary restraint. In Burns's words in 1995, now as Permanent Secretary to the Treasury delivering the South Bank Business School annual lecture,

> Essentially we have two objectives, low inflation and stable public finances. We have two instruments, interest rates and fiscal policy. Both instruments can have an impact on inflation but only fiscal policy can ensure stable public finances on a sustained basis. Intuitively, therefore, it seems clear that monetary policy will bear the main burden of delivering low inflation with fiscal policy taking the burden of delivering sound public finances.

This formulation was rather vague and later in the lecture Burns conceded that there were 'no hard and fast rules' for fiscal policy. But he made one exception, the need to contain 'debt service costs and the level of total debt outstanding in a way that avoids being caught in a debt trap where it is only possible to finance debt interest charges by higher levels of borrowing'.[38]

One interpretation of these remarks is that they represented a return to long-run solvency concerns of a kind emphasized by the Treasury knights in the 1930s and 1940s. The reference to runaway debt-interest costs in Burns's 1995 lecture had more than a passing resemblance to the section in the 1944 *Employment Policy* White Paper which warned about 'the charge on the Exchequer' from excessive public debt. Burns's views might therefore be regarded as the rejection of Keynesianism and the restoration of old-fashioned sound finance doctrines. However, it is important to note major differences in definition and emphasis from earlier positions. No official statement on fiscal policy in the 1980s and 1990s was expressed in terms of the old distinction between above-the-line and below-the-line items. In this respect the principles of sound finance, as they were understood in the closing years of the 1979–97 Conservative government, departed significantly from their counterparts in the inter-war period and, indeed, from more distant Gladstonian precursors.

Instead of the aim to achieve balance or surplus above the line, the PSBR was the main benchmark of fiscal policy. The PSBR had initially been formulated inside the Treasury in the early 1960s, to help in the presentation of financial statistics. Its first major policy applications were in support of the IMF's balance-of-payments objectives in the late 1960s, and again in 1976 and 1977. In the early phase of the Thatcher government the announcement of a PSBR limit had been intended to buttress monetary restraint. To focus on the PSBR as a means of preventing excessive growth of debt was therefore a significant shift in its pattern of deployment. In fact, its position in discussions of long-run fiscal solvency is not particularly comfortable. It does not differentiate, as did the above-the-line/below-the-line distinction, between non-recurrent capital items and other types of expenditures. As a result, it does not have any clear message for the government's or the public sector's overall net assets (that is, its gross stock of financial and tangible assets, minus its debt). Moreover, as the government can both sell financial assets and borrow in order to on-lend to the private sector, there is no simple relationship between the PSBR and net debt.

These points did not – and do not now – invalidate the PSBR's legitimacy as a target or control variable. The alternatives also have their weaknesses. However, it is interesting to note that – if the old above-the-line/below-the-line distinction had survived – the public finances would have appeared to be in some disarray by the mid-1990s. The PSBR was held down during the Thatcher and Major Conservative administrations not by curbing current spending relative to revenues, but by restricting capital expenditure and taking in money from privatization. While the Treasury and its Conservative political masters acknowledged a long-run solvency constraint on fiscal policy, they defined it in a quite different manner from their predecessors before the supposed 'Keynesian revolution'.

At any rate, there is little doubt that, certainly since 1979, and perhaps since 1975 or 1976, fiscal policy was not regarded as 'Keynesian' by policymakers or their key advisers. There was a brief phase in 1979 and 1980 when fiscal policy could be characterized as 'monetarist' more than anything else. Later it became subordinate to 'sound finance', dressed up in modern terminology but with a rather incoherent rationale. Arguably the

Conservatives' zero-PSBR-over-the-cycle maxim was less restrictive of debt than the Treasury's old orthodoxies of the 1930s and 1940s. There were some similarities between the formulations of the 1990s and those earlier orthodoxies, but they were fortuitous, not consciously intended. Policy-makers sometimes admitted that they remembered what they were taught at university, namely that changes in the budget deficit could have significant effects on the level of demand in the economy.[39] But such considerations were secondary, or even tertiary, in actual policy decisions.

IV

The record of official statements, positions and speeches is therefore very far from unanimous that fiscal policy was conducted on Keynesian lines even in the period from 1945 to the early 1970s, while it is clear-cut that a marked shift away from Keynesianism occurred in the mid-1970s. But the analysis so far has been literary and textual. Like all such analysis, it has required selection from a wider mass of statements, and it has involved judgements about different actors' tone of voice and their balance of priorities. Necessarily, the selection has been to a degree arbitrary, and the judgements could be criticized as imprecise and subjective. An alternative approach is to review policy actions in statistical terms, which should put the analysis and conclusions on a more objective plane.

The broad meaning of the phrase 'Keynesian fiscal policy' is well known. If fiscal policy is on Keynesian lines, the budget deficit is increased when unemployment is 'high' and reduced when it is 'low'. The statistical test should therefore be designed to answer the question, 'Did policy-makers vary the deficit inversely with the level of unemployment?' But several statistical series could be deployed to handle this question. What are the right concepts of 'the budget deficit' and 'the level of unemployment'?

Several competing notions of the budget deficit are candidates. As already demonstrated, for much of the 1950s and 1960s the Treasury continued to frame budgetary decisions in accordance with the principle that the budget should be balanced 'above the line'. The above-the-line central government position is, however, too narrow to serve as a valid indicator of the underlying thrust of fiscal policy. It excludes many capital items and the effect of public corporations' transactions, yet some Keynesians insist that capital spending, particularly capital spending by the nationalized industries, ought to be a prime instrument of countercyclical fiscal policy.[40] On the other hand, the public sector borrowing requirement, which came to dominate public discussion of fiscal policy from the mid-1970s onwards, is too broad. It is affected by 'financial transactions', such as nationalization, privatization and government lending to industry and for house purchase. Such transactions do not constitute net injections into or withdrawal from aggregate demand.

According to most authorities, the best compromise between narrow and broad measures of the budgetary position is 'the public sector's financial deficit'.[41] This covers the entire public sector, but excludes the effect of purely financial transactions. It approximates to the difference between the flow of the public sector's receipts and expenditures, and this difference is usually taken to mean the addition to or subtraction from the circular flow of income which lies at the heart of the Keynesian theory of income determination. A complication is that the public sector's financial deficit is both an influence on and is influenced by the cyclical course of the economy. (Social security spending rises and falls with unemployment, while tax receipts vary inversely with it.) So discretionary policy action is best understood as and measured by its effect on the cyclically adjusted estimate of the deficit, not on the unadjusted deficit. In the statistical work in the appendix fiscal policy decisions are therefore measured by the change in the cyclically adjusted public sector financial deficit. (Various methods of cyclical adjustment are possible. See the appendix for the method adopted in this essay. Two sets of assumptions are used to obtain two separate estimates of the cyclically adjusted fiscal policy. The estimation of two such series helps in checking whether the conclusions are special and depend on the assumptions, or are more general and robust.)

The identification of the appropriate unemployment variable is also difficult. In the 1950s 'full employment' was widely thought to mean an unemployment rate, measured by the count of benefit claimants as a ratio of the workforce, of under 2 per cent.[42] But in the 1970s and 1980s economists stopped thinking about full employment as a single number, while various institutional changes to the structure of the labour market caused an increase in the level of unemployment consistent with a stable rate of price change (the so-called 'natural rate of unemployment'). In the late 1980s and 1990s the Conservative government's measures to increase labour-market flexibility may have reduced the natural rate. These ambiguities suggest that no long-run series for unemployment is altogether reliable as a guide to the state of the labour market.

A more general measure of activity in the economy is provided by 'the output gap', defined as the upwards or downwards deviation of output from its trend and usually expressed as a percentage of that trend.[43] Like assessments of the 'fullness' of full employment, calculations of the output gap depend partly on the analyst's methods. But the temptation and opportunity to manipulate the numbers is less with politically neutral GDP figures than with politically charged unemployment statistics. Further, cross-checks can be made between several different techniques for calculating output gaps, which limits the scope for the analyst to impose his own hunches and prejudices. Comparison is also possible with calculations made by, for example, the Organisation for Economic Co-operation and Development. (The method of calculating the output gap in this essay is explained in the appendix.)

The discussion has pinned down the statistical test more exactly as an attempt to answer the question, 'Did the cyclically adjusted public sector financial deficit (PSFD) vary inversely with the output gap?' If fiscal policy was Keynesian, the deficit ought to have increased when the level of output was beneath trend and declined when it was above trend. Table 4.1 in the appendix shows the output gap, the unadjusted PSFD/GDP ratio, and both the level and change in the cyclically adjusted PSFD/GDP ratio, estimated on one set of assumptions about the cyclical adjustment, and Table 4.2 the same numbers, but estimated on an alternative set of assumptions about the cyclical adjustment. Table 4.3 compares the numbers used here with separate estimates of the cyclically adjusted PSFD/GDP ratio given by the Treasury. This essay's estimates of the adjusted PSFD/GDP ratio are close to each other and the Treasury's figures. Very similar conclusions emerge on both sets of assumptions, with the encouraging implication that they are genuine and not an artefact of the chosen method of cyclical adjustment. Using the first set of numbers (that is, those in Table 4.1), three years (1963, 1976 and 1986) saw hardly any change in fiscal stance, while the output gap itself was close to zero. They can therefore be eliminated from the sample as having no clear message for the matter in contention. Of the remaining 43 years between 1949 and 1994 there were 22 years when the fiscal stance changed in a Keynesian manner (that is, inversely to the output gap), but 21 years when it did not. Keynesian fiscal policy was more common in the period to 1974 than afterwards, which is consistent with the view that the conduct of fiscal policy changed in the mid-1970s. Fiscal policy was contra-cyclical in 14 of the relevant 25 years to 1974 (that is, over 55 per cent of the years), but in only eight of the relevant 20 years from 1975 to 1994 (that is, in 40 per cent of the years).

More rigorous econometric tests have also been performed, with the change in the cyclically adjusted PSFD regressed on the level of the output gap. It turns out that in virtually all of the equations – no matter which cyclical-adjustment assumptions or period are chosen – the coefficient on the output gap is not significantly different from zero. In other words, fiscal policy was not 'Keynesian', in the usually received sense, in the period from 1949 to 1994 as a whole or in the two sub-periods, 1949 to 1974 and 1975 to 1994. On the face of it, there was no such thing as 'the Keynesian revolution'. (See the appendix for a fuller statement of these results.)

V

The great majority of British economists undoubtedly believe that something called 'the Keynesian revolution' did happen. There is room for discussion about its precise meaning, for example, on the question of whether 'fiscal policy' is best defined as the change or the level of the budget deficit. But the essence of the supposed 'revolution' – that in and after the 1940s British fiscal policy (however defined) was used contra-cyclically in order to dampen fluctuations in output and employment, and maintain a high average level of employment – is well known.

This chapter has cast doubt on the historical accuracy of this widely held view. First, it has denied that Britain ever had a Keynesian revolution in the usually understood sense. In the 30 years from 1941 fiscal policy was not in fact conducted in a Keynesian manner, whatever leading politicians and economists claimed at the time. Much policy thinking in this era certainly was Keynesian, but theory and practice were a long way apart. Second, the chapter has tried to describe the shift in policy thinking away from Keynesianism in the mid-1970s. There is little controversy that a shift of some sort occurred, although again its exact nature can be discussed. As has been shown, the government's rationale for action to restrict the PSBR varied over the years. Sometimes the official argument relied on a presumed relationship between the budget deficit and monetary growth; at others it reflected more traditional concerns about the accumulation of excessive debt which would be expensive to service. But official references to fiscal policy as an instrument for cyclical stabilization were perfunctory or frankly dismissive.

The majority of British academic economists were unsympathetic to the shift in thinking about fiscal policy, with their discontents registered most famously in the letter of 364 economists to *The Times* after the 1981 Budget. The frankness of policy-makers' rejection of Keynesian precepts by the early 1980s ought perhaps to have encouraged these economists to examine the substance of 'the Keynesian revolution' with care and scepticism. Whether the official ending of the Keynesian period (if it deserves the title) is dated as happening in 1975, 1976 or 1979, the statistical evidence is that the unresponsiveness of fiscal policy to the state of demand was much the same before as afterwards.

At any one period a great variety of personalities are involved in economic policy-making. As they often come with different perspectives, it would be naïve to expect them to propound a single monolithic view of policy-making. Moreover, when the period of analysis is extended to a few decades, the cast of personalities changes, and no one canonical statement of theory and practice can bind them all. Keynes was a great man and a benign influence on British economic policy, and it is understandable that British economists should want to pay homage to his *General Theory*. But the substance of policy-makers' actions may have little connection with their advisers' descriptions of strategic intent. More bluntly, what people do may be quite different from what they believe they are doing. The UK is the homeland of Keynesian thought, but in the actual conduct of British fiscal policy 'the Keynesian revolution' is and always has been an illusion.

NOTES

1. J.C.R. Dow, *The Management of the British Economy 1945–60* (Cambridge: Cambridge University Press, 1964), p. 178.
2. H. Stein, *The Fiscal Revolution in America* (Chicago, IL and London: Chicago University Press, 1969), p. 165.
3. Part of the explanation for the differences between Keynes and the Keynesians is to be sought in the complexity and obscurity of *The General Theory*. For example, while there can be little doubt that Keynes wished to promote fiscal policy relative to monetary policy, *The General Theory* says almost nothing about how exactly fiscal policy should be conducted. The American economist, Abba Lerner, tried to formalize the fiscal prescriptions implicit in *The General Theory* in his idea of 'functional finance' (that is, to run a deficit in a downturn and a surplus in a boom). But Keynes was critical of Lerner's proposals, asserting that functional finance 'runs directly contrary to men's natural instincts . . . about what is sensible'. R. Skidelsky, *John Maynard Keynes*, vol. 3, *Fighting for Britain 1937–46* (London: Macmillan, 2000), p. 276.
4. E.E.B. (Lord) Bridges, *The Treasury* (London: George Allen and Unwin, and New York: Oxford University Press, 1964), p. 90.
5. 'The Economy Report' and 'The Economy Bill', in D. Moggridge and Mrs E. Johnson (eds), *The Collected Writings of John Maynard Keynes*, vol. IX, *Essays in Persuasion* (London: Macmillan, 1972, originally published in 1931), pp. 101–5 and 145–9, originally based on articles published in *New Statesman and Nation* on 15 August and 19 September 1931.
6. B.E.V. Sabine, *British Budgets in Peace and War* (London: George Allen and Unwin, 1970), p. 300.
7. Ibid.
8. Dow, *Management of British Economy*, p. 198.
9. White Paper on *Employment Policy* (London: HMSO, 1944), pp. 25–6, paragraphs 77–9.
10. Bridges, *The Treasury*, pp. 93–4. The quotation is from p. 93.
11. Dow, *Management of British Economy*, p. 198.
12. I.M.D. Little, 'Fiscal policy', in G.D.N. Worswick and P.D. Ady (eds), *The British Economy in the Nineteen-Fifties* (Oxford: Oxford University Press, 1962), ch. 8, pp. 231–91. The quotation is from p. 251.
13. Dow, *Management of British Economy*, p. 161.
14. Little in Worswick and Ady (eds), *British Economy in Nineteen-Fifties*, p. 275.
15. Dow, *Management of the British Economy*, pp. 183–8. The quotations are from p. 183 and p. 187 respectively.
16. H. Brittain, *The British Budgetary System* (London: George Allen and Unwin, 1959), pp. 53–4. Brittain and Keynes clashed at meetings held in the Treasury in 1945 to prepare papers for the National Debt Enquiry. According to Peden (citing James Meade's papers, collected by Mrs Elizabeth Johnson and Donald Moggridge), Keynes told Brittain to his face that he was 'intellectually contemptible'. As Peden notes, the Sinking Fund for national debt – of which Brittain was apparently a defender – was not phased out until

1954, while the above-the-line/below-the-line distinction survived until the publication of an official paper on *Reform of the Exchequer Accounts* (Cmnd. 21014) in 1962. (See G.C. Peden, *Keynes and his Critics: Treasury Responses to the Keynesian Revolution 1925–46* [Oxford and New York: Oxford University Press for the British Academy, 2004], p. 12, p. 331 and pp. 349–50.) Peden also emphasizes in his book on the Treasury the durability of a doctrine introduced by Asquith in 1906 and 1907, that the only investments which should be financed by borrowing were those expected to produce a money return, and which would not rely on future taxation for the servicing of the borrowing involved. (Peden, *The Treasury and British Public Policy 1906–59* [Oxford: Oxford University Press, 2000], p. 39.) Tomlinson has said that in the 1950s 'day-to-day discussion of economic issues in government departments' was 'notable for extraordinary crudity'. (J. Tomlinson, *Public Policy and the Economy* [Oxford: Clarendon Press, 1990], p. 256.)

17. Brittain, *British Budgetary System*, p. 56.
18. Brittain, *British Budgetary System*, p. 43.
19. R.C.O. Matthews, 'Why has Britain had full employment since the war?', *Economic Journal*, vol. 78, September 1968, pp. 555–69. The quotation is from p. 556.
20. B. Hansen, *Fiscal Policy in Seven Countries 1955–65* (Paris: Organisation for Economic Co-operation and Development, 1969).
21. S. Brittain, *Steering the Economy* (Harmondsworth: Penguin, 1971), p. 455.
22. Dow, *Management of the British Economy*, p. 384.
23. S. Brittain, *The Price of Economic Freedom* (London: Macmillan, 1970).
24. W. Beckerman (ed.), *The Labour Government's Economic Record 1964–70* (London: Duckworth, 1972), p. 25.
25. D. Healey (later Lord Healey), *The Time of My Life* (London: Michael Joseph, 1989), p. 380.
26. Ibid., p. 382.
27. Ibid., p. 383.
28. See the papers, 'Monetarism and the budget deficit' and 'The analytical foundations of the Medium-Term Financial Strategy', in Tim Congdon, *Reflections on Monetarism* (Aldershot, UK and Brookfield, US: Edward Elgar for the Institute of Economic Affairs, 1992), pp. 38–48 and 65–77. A growing interest in a medium-term perspective can also be noticed in A. Budd, 'Economic policy and the medium term', in G.D.N. Worswick and F.T. Blackaby (eds), *The Medium Term: Models of the British Economy* (London: Heinemann, 1974), pp. 133–42.
29. See 'How Friedman came to Britain', in W. Parsons, *The Power of the Financial Press* (Aldershot, UK and Brookfield, US: Edward Elgar, 1989), ch. 6, pp. 172–202.
30. See the paper, 'The relationship between fiscal and monetary policy in the London Business School model', by A.P. Budd and T. Burns, in M.J. Artis and M.H. Miller (eds), *Essays in Fiscal and Monetary Policy* (Oxford: Oxford University Press, 1981), pp. 136–63. The quotations are from p. 136.
31. See 'Implementation and results of the strategy', in G. Maynard, *The Economy under Mrs. Thatcher* (Oxford: Basil Blackwell, 1988), ch. 4, pp. 58–92. But the claim on p. 65 that the MTFS had as its 'stated objective' a 'progressive . . . return to budget balance', is not correct. The balanced-budget goal surfaced in official statements much later, in 1988.
32. Maynard, *Economy under Mrs. Thatcher*, p. 66.
33. The quotation is from p. 56 of M. Friedman, 'Response to questionnaire on monetary policy', in House of Commons Treasury and Civil Service Committee (Session 1979/80), *Memoranda on Monetary Policy* (London: HMSO, 1980), pp. 55–62. As explained in note 11 to the Introduction, the author disagrees with Friedman's views on public finance.
34. HM Treasury, *The Next Ten Years: Public Expenditure and Taxation into the 1990s*, Cmnd 9189 (London: HMSO, 1984).
35. Nigel (later Lord) Lawson, *The View from No. 11* (London: Bantam Press, 1992), p. 812.
36. A. Budd and G. Dicks, 'A strategy for stable prices' *Economic Outlook* (Aldershot: Gower Publishing for the London Business School), July 1983, pp. 18–23.
37. Lawson, *View from No. 11*, p. 811.

38.   Sir Terence Burns, *Managing the Nation's Economy – the conduct of monetary and fiscal policy*, given as South Bank Business School annual lecture (London: HM Treasury, 1996), p. 5. Burns's 1995 lecture – in which interest rates and fiscal policy were taken to be independent instruments – was a long way from his London Business School papers of the late 1970s in which the interdependence of fiscal and monetary policies had been emphasized.

39.   '[T]here are very few practitioners who would argue that fiscal policy has no role to play at all in influencing demand . . .'. Burns, *Managing the Economy*, p. 5.

40.   See, for example, S. Howson (ed.), *The Collected Papers of James Meade, vol. 1: Employment and Inflation* (London: Unwin Hyman, 1988), pp. 6–25, 'Public works in their international aspect', originally published in 1933.

41.   A. Britton, *Macroeconomic Policy in Britain* (Cambridge: Cambridge University Press for the National Institute of Economic and Social Research, 1991), p. 215, but note Britton's warning on p. 217 that the cyclically adjusted public sector financial deficits 'do not identify policy acts, that is deliberate choices by government as distinct from the passive response of the system to events'.

42.   F.W. Paish, *Studies in an Inflationary Economy* (London: Macmillan, 1962), p. 327.

43.   For the introduction of the concept of the output gap, see the appendix to the Introduction. In the late 1980s and early 1990s the Organisation for Economic Co-operation and Development in Paris devoted some effort to preparing historical estimates of these gaps in its member nations. See C. Giorno et al., 'Potential output, output gaps and structural budget balances', *Economic Studies*, no. 24 (Paris: OECD, 1995).

STATISTICAL APPENDIX

The author would like to acknowledge the help received from Professor Kent Matthews of Cardiff Business School and Mr Stewart Robertson, senior economist at Aviva, in the preparation of this statistical appendix which is, in effect, a joint product of three authors. (Mr Robertson was working with the author at Lombard Street Research when the estimates were prepared.)

1. Collection and Estimation of the Data

Estimates of the 'output gap', the difference between the actual and trend level of national output expressed as a percentage of trend output, were the first requirement. The actual level of national output was measured by the office for National Statistics' series for gross domestic product at factor cost in 1990 prices, starting in 1948. Trend output was estimated by assuming that it was determined by the quantity and productivity of inputs of labour and capital. (This is sometimes known as the 'production function method', as production is represented as a function of inputs. The relative importance of the two inputs is calculated by assuming that their return is determined by their marginal products and their share in national output is equal to their quantity multiplied by the return. The income share in national output is assumed also to be their contribution to output. See C. Adams and T. Coe, 'A systems approach to estimating the natural rate of unemployment and potential output for the USA', published in the June 1990 *IMF Staff Papers*, for further discussion.)

Data for the labour force and the capital stock were supplied by the Organisation for Economic Co-operation and Development from 1963 onwards. A trend rate of growth of 'total factor productivity' (that is, the increase in the productivity of the two inputs) was obtained by smoothing the original figures by use of the Hodrick–Prescott filter. The use of the filter generates a potential output series with the characteristic that deviations of actual output from it sum to zero over the period as a whole. (Trend and actual output were equal in 1963. For years before 1963, when the OECD data for the capital stock and labour force were not available, trend output was estimated by taking a moving average.)

The Office for National Statistics publishes a series for the public sector's financial deficit back to 1948. In the chapter this deficit series was divided by gross domestic product at current market prices and multiplied by 100 to obtain the PSFD as a percentage of GDP. To calculate the change in the deficit/GDP ratio after cyclical adjustment, it was of course necessary to estimate a cyclically adjusted series for the level of the deficit/GDP ratio. As explained in the text, two distinct sets of assumptions were used to estimate this series. In both cases it was assumed that the difference between the actual and cyclically adjusted deficit depended on the output gap, for which a calculated series had already been prepared. (See the previous paragraph for this calculation. If output is beneath trend, tax revenues are also beneath trend, whereas various items of public expenditure, notably social security expenditure, are above trend.)

The first assumption was that the PSFD was affected by the output gap only in the same year. For the years 1948 to 1979 the cyclically adjusted PSFD/GDP ratio, expressed as a percentage, was lower (higher) than the actual PSFD/GDP ratio by 0.4 per cent of GDP for each 1 per cent of GDP less than (above) trend; for the years from 1980 to 1994 the coefficient was increased from 0.4 to 0.5, to reflect the increased size of the state sector. The second assumption was that the PSFD was affected by the output gap in the current and previous year, because, for example, of delays in tax payments. The coefficients 0.25 and 0.45 were assumed to hold for the first- and second-year effects from 1948 to 1979, while in the period from 1980 to 1994 the coefficients became 0.33 for the first year and 0.7 for the second year. The formula for the calculation was

$$\left(\frac{DEF}{Y}\right)_t = \left(\frac{DEF}{Y}\right)_t^* - aGAP_t - (b-a)GAP_{t-1} \qquad (4.1)$$

where *DEF* is the deficit, *Y* is gross domestic product, *GAP* is the output gap, *a* and *b* are the coefficients for the first- and second-year effects, and the asterisk denotes the cyclically adjusted value of the deficit/GDP ratio.

The estimates of the cyclically adjusted deficit/GDP ratio using the first set of assumptions are set out in Table 4.1; the estimates using the second set of assumptions are set out in Table 4.2. The justification for the sets of assumption used in the cyclical adjustment were provided in two studies. First, Bredenkamp (1988) suggested that the first- and second-year effects of a change in GDP relative to trend on the PSFD (as a percentage of GDP) were 0.25 per cent of GDP and 0.45 per cent of GDP. (See H. Bredenkamp, *The Cyclically-Adjusted Deficit as a Measure of Fiscal Policy*, Government Economic Working Paper, no. 102, April 1988.) Second, the Treasury updated Bredenkamp's paper in the winter 1990/91 issue of the *Treasury Bulletin* in an article on 'Fiscal developments and the role of the cycle', where it increased its estimates of the cyclical sensitivity of public finances and suggested the higher values of the coefficients, 0.33 and 0.7. (A further paper, *Public Finances and the Cycle*, was published as the *Treasury Occasional Paper No. 4* in September 1995.)

Table 4.1 *PSFD as a percentage of GDP, both unadjusted and after
cyclical adjustment according to first set of assumptions
described in text*

Year	Output gap as % of trend GDP	PSFD as % of GDP	Cyclically adjusted PSFD/GDP ratio, %	Change in adjusted PSFD/ GDP ratio, %
1948	−2.6	−2.3	−3.3	
1949	−3.3	−2.5	−3.8	0.5
1950	−1.6	−2.7	−3.3	−0.5
1951	−1.3	1.6	1.1	−4.4
1952	−3.0	3.5	2.3	−1.2
1953	−1.2	4.2	3.7	−1.4
1954	0.6	2.4	2.6	1.1
1955	1.9	2.0	2.8	−0.2
1956	0.5	2.6	2.8	0.0
1957	−0.3	2.4	2.3	0.5
1958	−2.7	2.0	0.9	1.4
1959	−1.0	2.3	1.9	−1.0
1960	1.5	2.7	3.3	−1.4
1961	1.0	2.7	3.1	0.2
1962	−0.8	2.8	2.4	0.7
1963	0.0	2.7	2.7	−0.3
1964	2.1	2.8	3.6	−0.9
1965	1.5	2.2	2.8	0.8
1966	0.3	2.2	2.3	0.5
1967	−0.7	3.6	3.3	−1.0
1968	0.8	2.1	2.4	0.9
1969	0.6	−1.0	−0.8	3.2
1970	0.1	−1.3	−1.3	0.5
1971	−0.6	0.6	0.3	−1.6
1972	0.0	2.4	2.4	−2.1
1973	5.2	3.7	5.8	−3.4
1974	1.8	5.6	6.4	−0.6
1975	−0.7	7.2	6.9	−0.5
1976	0.2	6.7	6.8	0.1
1977	1.1	4.2	4.6	2.2
1978	2.3	5.0	5.9	−1.3
1979	2.1	4.4	5.2	0.7
1980	−1.7	4.5	3.8	1.4
1981	−4.8	3.1	0.7	3.1
1982	−5.2	2.7	0.2	0.5
1983	−3.7	3.4	1.6	−1.4
1984	−3.9	4.0	2.0	−0.4

Table 4.1   (continued)

Year	Output gap as % of trend GDP	PSFD as % of GDP	Cyclically adjusted PSFD/GDP ratio, %	Change in adjusted PSFD/ GDP ratio, %
1985	−2.0	2.9	1.8	0.2
1986	−0.1	2.1	2.0	−0.2
1987	2.2	1.1	2.2	−0.2
1988	5.0	−1.4	1.1	1.1
1989	5.3	−1.0	1.7	−0.6
1990	3.8	0.3	2.2	−0.5
1991	−0.3	2.5	2.3	−0.1
1992	−3.3	6.3	4.6	−2.3
1993	−3.9	7.6	5.7	−1.1
1994	−3.0	6.6	5.1	0.6

Source: Office for National Statistics and see text.

Table 4.2   *PSFD as a percentage of GDP, both unadjusted and after cyclical adjustment according to second set of assumptions described in text*

Year	Output gap as % of trend GDP	PSFD as % of GDP	Cyclically adjusted PSFD/GDP ratio, %	Change in adjusted PSFD/ GDP ratio, %
1948	−2.6	−2.3	−2.9	
1949	−3.3	−2.5	−3.8	0.9
1950	−1.6	−2.7	−3.7	−0.1
1951	−1.3	1.6	1.0	−4.7
1952	−3.0	3.5	2.5	−1.5
1953	−1.2	4.2	3.3	−0.8
1954	0.6	2.4	2.3	1.0
1955	1.9	2.0	2.6	−0.3
1956	0.5	2.6	3.1	−0.5
1957	−0.3	2.4	2.5	0.6
1958	−2.7	2.0	1.2	1.3
1959	−1.0	2.3	1.5	−0.3
1960	1.5	2.7	2.9	−1.4
1961	1.0	2.7	3.3	−0.4
1962	−0.8	2.8	2.8	0.5
1963	0.0	2.7	2.7	0.1
1964	2.1	2.8	3.3	−0.6
1965	1.5	2.2	3.0	0.3

Table 4.2   (continued)

Year	Output gap as % of trend GDP	PSFD as % of GDP	Cyclically adjusted PSFD/GDP ratio, %	Change in adjusted PSFD/GDP ratio, %
1966	0.3	2.2	2.6	0.4
1967	−0.7	3.6	3.4	−0.8
1968	0.8	2.1	2.2	1.2
1969	0.6	−1.0	−0.7	2.9
1970	0.1	−1.3	−1.2	0.5
1971	−0.6	0.6	0.4	−1.6
1972	0.0	2.4	2.3	−1.9
1973	5.2	3.7	5.0	−2.7
1974	1.8	5.6	7.1	−2.1
1975	−0.7	7.2	7.4	−0.3
1976	0.2	6.7	6.7	0.7
1977	1.1	4.2	4.5	2.2
1978	2.3	5.0	5.8	−1.3
1979	2.1	4.4	5.4	0.4
1980	−1.7	4.5	4.7	0.7
1981	−4.8	3.1	0.9	3.8
1982	−5.2	2.7	−0.7	1.6
1983	−3.7	3.4	0.3	−1.0
1984	−3.9	4.0	1.3	−1.0
1985	−2.0	2.9	0.7	0.6
1986	−0.1	2.1	1.3	−0.6
1987	2.2	1.1	1.8	−0.5
1988	5.0	−1.4	1.1	0.7
1989	5.3	−1.0	2.6	−1.5
1990	3.8	0.3	3.6	−1.0
1991	−0.3	2.5	3.8	−0.2
1992	−3.3	6.3	5.1	−1.3
1993	−3.9	7.6	5.1	0.0
1994	−3.0	6.6	4.2	0.9

Source: Office for National Statistics and see text.

The figures for the cyclically adjusted deficit/GDP ratio in the regression work (described below) related to calendar years and, as already noted, extended back to 1948. The Treasury has published its own estimates of the cyclically adjusted PSFD/GDP ratio on a fiscal year basis from 1963/64 to 1986/87. These estimates are compared with those of the authors in Table 4.3. The differences in the estimates are due to revisions to the data, different assumptions about the cyclical adjustment factor and different assumptions about the output gap.

Table 4.3   *Public sector financial deficit estimates used in essay compared*
               with the Treasury's own estimates

Year	Treasury unadjusted	Treasury cyclically adjusted	CSO unadjusted	Adjusted by first set of assumptions	Adjusted by second set of assumptions
1963/64	3.3	3.0	2.7	2.9	2.9
1964/65	2.3	2.8	2.7	3.4	3.2
1965/66	1.7	2.1	2.2	2.7	2.9
1966/67	2.6	2.6	2.6	2.6	2.8
1967/68	4.2	4.6	3.2	3.1	3.1
1968/69	0.8	0.9	1.3	1.6	1.5
1969/70	−1.7	−1.5	−1.2	−0.9	−0.8
1970/71	−0.4	−0.4	−0.8	−0.8	−0.8
1971/72	1.1	1.1	1.1	0.8	0.9
1972/73	3.0	2.8	2.8	3.3	3.0
1973/74	4.6	5.5	4.2	6.0	5.5
1974/75	6.7	7.4	6.0	6.5	7.2
1975/76	7.3	6.8	7.1	6.9	7.2
1976/77	5.7	5.1	6.1	6.3	6.2
1977/78	4.4	4.2	4.4	4.9	4.8
1978/79	4.8	5.1	4.9	5.7	5.7
1979/80	3.9	4.9	4.4	4.9	5.2
1980/81	5.0	5.2	4.2	3.0	3.8
1981/82	2.0	1.2	3.0	0.6	0.5
1982/83	2.9	2.3	3.0	0.6	−0.5
1983/84	3.7	3.5	3.6	1.7	0.6
1984/85	4.0	3.8	3.7	2.0	1.2
1985/86	2.3	2.1	2.7	1.9	0.9
1986/87	2.5	2.4	1.9	2.1	1.4

Note: All figures are percentage of GDP.

2.   Statistical Relationships between the Change in the Cyclically Adjusted PSFD/GDP Ratio and the Level of the Output Gap

As argued in the text, fiscal policy would have been Keynesian if the cyclically adjusted PSFD/GDP ratio had increased when output was beneath trend (that is, there was a negative 'output gap') and decreased when output was above trend. The test is therefore to regress the change in the cyclically adjusted PSFD/GDP ratio on the level of the output gap for both estimates of the PSFD/GDP ratio and for all three time periods, that is, 1948–94, 1948–74 and 1975–94.

(a) **Regression results using the first estimate of the cyclically adjusted PSFD/GDP ratio (that is, the PSFD is affected by the output gap in the current year only)**

1948–94

$$DUND_t = 0.03 * OGAP_t + 0.293 * DUND_{t-1} \qquad (4.2)$$

R-squared $= 0.074$; only the coefficient on the lagged dependent variable is significant.

Note that here and in the other equations $DUND_t$ is the change in the underlying (that is, cyclically adjusted) public sector financial balance (expressed as a percentage of GDP at market prices) and $OGAP_t$ is the output gap as a percentage of potential output. (If the public sector financial deficit falls from 2.3 per cent to 1.6 per cent of GDP, then $DUND_t$ takes a value of 0.7).

1948–74

$$DUND_t = 0.048 * OGAP_t + 0.358 * DUND_{t-1} \qquad (4.3)$$

R-squared $= 0.095$; only the coefficient on the lagged dependent variable is significant.

1975–94

$$DUND_t = 0.022 * OGAP_t + 0.149 * DUND_{t-1} \qquad (4.4)$$

R-squared $= 0.031$; only the coefficient on the lagged dependent variable is significant.

In none of the three equations for the different periods was the coefficient on the output gap term significant.

(b) **Regression results using the second estimate of the cyclically adjusted PSFD/GDP ratio (i.e. the PSFD is affected by the output gap in the current and previous year)**

1948–94

$$DUND_t = 0.112 * OGAP_t + 0.319 * DUND_{t-1} \qquad (4.5)$$

R-squared $= 0.141$; only the coefficient on the lagged dependent variable is significant.

1948–74

$$DUND_t = 0.09 * OGAP_t + 0.448 * DUND_{t-1} \qquad (4.6)$$

R-squared = 0.163; only the coefficient on the lagged dependent variable is significant.

1975–94

$$DUND_t = 0.148 * OGAP_t + 0.055 * DUND_{t-1} \qquad (4.7)$$

R-squared = 0.17; neither coefficient is significant.

Again, in none of the three equations for the different periods was the coefficient on the output gap term significant. (It is curious that the six coefficients on the output gap terms are in fact all positive, whereas they ought to have been negative if policy had been on Keynesian lines. But, as the coefficients are all small and none of them is statistically significant, not too much should be made of this.)

5. Is anything left of the 'Keynesian revolution'?

The conduct of British fiscal policy has changed during the post-war period, reflecting both the pressure of events and the evolution of thinking about macroeconomic policy. This essay reviews the changes in policy approach and relates them to the ultimate objectives of macroeconomic policy. Two objectives are usually emphasized, high (or full) employment and price stability, although equilibrium in external payments and economic growth are sometimes also mentioned.

The argument will be that between the 1940s and the 1980s attempts were made to replace atheoretical Treasury orthodoxies with policy approaches clearly grounded in macroeconomic analysis. Unhappily, the two main approaches – Keynesianism with its focus on fiscal policy and monetarism, to be understood as a reliance on monetary policy which sought its rationale in the quantity theory of money – were to conflict. The differences between them were radical in principle, and led to bitter disputes in practice. Despite these tensions, all economists involved in the debates on fiscal policy between the 1940s and the 1980s appealed to macroeconomic theory and analysis to support their positions. However, in the 1980s – and more particularly in the 1990s – the debates fizzled out, while the fiscal ground rules became disconnected from the understood objectives of macroeconomic policy. Despite their authors' insistence on their modernity, the new ground rules had many echoes of those espoused in the Treasury before the 1940s.

I

The key precept in fiscal policy until the post-war period was that the government should balance its budget. The concept of budget balance depended on a distinction between 'above-the-line' and 'below-the-line' items, with the aim being to maintain the balance (or even achieve a small surplus) above-the-line. The distinction was related, but not identical, to that between current and capital expenditure. In essence, recurrent items of capital expenditure were deemed to be 'above-the-line' and their cost had to be covered from current revenue, which would be predominantly taxation. Borrowing was legitimate to cover the cost of exceptional, non-recurrent items of capital expenditure, but that was all. Continuous borrowing to meet the cost of recurrent capital expenditure was rejected, as it 'would only increase the costs over the years by unnecessary payments of interest'.[1] Implicitly, high levels of debt interest were regarded as misguided, even dangerous. Although they were an internal transfer between different citizens of the same nation (from taxpayers to bondholders), they raised the tax burden with adverse consequences for incentives and economic efficiency. These definitions and conventions originated in the era of Gladstonian sound finance in the late nineteenth century. They were affiliated to distinctions between the Consolidated Fund and the National Loans Fund set out in the Exchequer and Audit Departments Act of 1866. To macroeconomists who had absorbed Keynes's ideas in his *General Theory* of 1936 they were old-fashioned hocus-pocus. The Keynesians believed that the budget balance should instead be varied to influence the level of demand in the economy and, at a further remove, the number of people in work. While Keynes's own prescriptions for fiscal policy were never stated with much precision, most Keynesians thought that the right concept of the budget balance was that which measured the net 'injection' or 'withdrawal' of demand to or from the economy. In their writings, this can be most readily interpreted as the change in the public sector's financial deficit (or surplus), where the financial deficit is the net incurral of financial liabilities to other agents. The PSFD has no clear or necessary connection with the budget balance above-the-line.

So the debate about fiscal policy in the 1940s and 1950s can be viewed as being between the guardians of old Treasury traditions and the apostles of Keynesian theories of demand management. The debate ran partly in terms of definitions, but it was also, more substantively, about the purposes of policy. The Keynesian theorists portrayed themselves as more rigorous, scientific and modern, partly because they were focused on a standard aim of macroeconomic policy, namely to sustain high employment. A familiar textbook account of the period is that enlightened Keynesianism vanquished benighted Treasury orthodoxies, with contra-cyclical adjustment of the budget deficit being vital to the attainment of full employment. According to Winch in his 1969 study of *Economics and Policy*, 'Post-war stabilisation policy in Britain has mainly been conducted in terms of tax changes designed, for example, to stimulate private investment and, more important from a quantitative point of view, to influence consumer spending by altering the level of disposable income'. Further, economic management on these lines enjoyed 'comparative success' in the immediate post-war decades.[2]

The debate between the Treasury mandarins and the Keynesian evangelists was in reality far more even-handed than the textbook story suggests. An important study by Matthews, published in 1968, emphasized that 'throughout the post-war period the Government, so far from injecting demand into the system, has persistently had a large current account surplus . . . [G]overnment saving has averaged about 3 per cent of the national income'.[3] The persistence of a 'large current account surplus' may have been due to the application of the old Treasury rules, because it would be the logical by-product of financing a significant proportion of capital spending (the recurrent element) from taxation. Indeed, public sector accounts continued to refer to the distinction between above-the-line and below-the-line items until the early 1960s. These notions survived, despite repeated criticism – and even outright mockery – from academic Keynesians.

A White Paper, Cmnd. 2014, on *Reform of the Exchequer Accounts*, was published in 1962 and seems to mark the watershed between Gladstonian and Keynesian fiscal accountancy, although it is rarely mentioned in books about the period. Also significant were developments, in far from glorious circumstances, during the Labour government of 1964–70 led by Mr Harold (later Lord) Wilson. Wilson had himself been an economist before entering politics and in its early years his administration saw the recruitment of large numbers of academic economists to Whitehall. Most of these economists had strongly Keynesian sympathies. Unfortunately, from the outset the Wilson government was plagued by a weak balance-of-payments position and it was obliged to devalue the pound in November 1967. As the balance of payments did not improve quickly, the British government borrowed from the International Monetary Fund (IMF) in 1968. In addition to imposing certain conditions for its loan, the IMF introduced new measures of both monetary and fiscal policy. Its target for the British authorities was stated in terms of 'domestic credit expansion (DCE)', which can be regarded as the sum of new bank credit extended to all UK domestic agents (that is, to the public and private sectors combined).

The thinking was that the balance-of-payments deficit would be roughly equivalent to DCE minus the growth of the money supply. (Bank credit would create new money balances, unless the expenditure it financed went to foreign suppliers.) So – for any given rate of money supply growth – control over DCE would strengthen the balance-of-payments position. As bank credit to the public sector was part of DCE, the IMF guidelines implied some limit on the total of public sector borrowing which might, potentially, be financed from the banks. This total was known as 'the public sector borrowing requirement' or PSBR for short. (The PSBR was essentially a cash measure of the deficit, since it was a cash concept that was most readily integrated with monetary policy.)

The acceptance of IMF restrictions on Britain's public finances implied that satisfactory balance-of-payments outcomes had a higher policy priority than the achievement of full employment. This was undoubtedly a setback for the Keynesians. However, the IMF's involvement in policy-making in the late 1960s had another and rather different long-term significance. The vocabulary and form of macroeconomic policy shifted, giving more scope for monetary variables such as money supply growth, domestic credit expansion, bank credit to the private sector, non-bank financing of the budget deficit and, crucially for the future, the PSBR. It was this shift – not the Keynesians' ridicule in the 1940s and 1950s – that finally expunged the Victorian notions of sinking funds, above-the-line deficits and such like from the copybook maxims of British public finance. (The concepts of the Consolidated Fund and the National Loans Fund survive to this day.)

The move to floating exchange rates in the early 1970s gave policy-makers a new freedom from the external balance-of-payments constraint on fiscal and monetary expansion. They abused their freedom totally. DCE and money supply growth ran at fantastic rates in 1972 and 1973, far higher than anything previously recorded in the post-war period. The PSBR, which had been in small surplus in the 1968/69 fiscal year, recorded a deficit equal to 9 per cent of GDP at market prices in the 1974/75 fiscal year. The annual rate of retail price inflation exceeded 25 per cent in early and mid-1975, in conjunction with a vast current account deficit on the UK's balance of payments. In the autumn of 1976, the government again sought assistance from the IMF, which – as in 1968 – spelt out its targets in terms of DCE and the PSBR.

In this environment of macroeconomic anarchy, a number of British economists rejected the Keynesian principles held by the majority of their profession, and advocated monetary control as the right answer to inflation. A new body of thought, conventionally known as 'monetarism', began to influence policy thinking. The government had already introduced a target for money supply growth in July 1976, a few months before seeking IMF help, and refined it in conjunction with IMF officials in the closing months of the year.

Monetarism was – and remains – a heterogenous set of ideas, and its diversity is analysed in other essays in this book. But, according to one very influential strand of British monetarist analysis in the late 1970s, control over money supply growth was essential to the control over inflation, while quantified targets for the PSBR facilitated control over money supply growth.[4] This strand of analysis received an obvious impetus from the two episodes of IMF borrowing, but the UK met its money supply and DCE targets easily in 1977, and its dependence on IMF support was short-lived. Much valuable analysis on the relationships between the budget deficit and money supply growth was home-grown, with the London Business School and City stockbroking firms (notably by Gordon Pepper at W. Greenwell & Co.) making important contributions.

When the Thatcher government came to power in 1979, the central themes of macroeconomic policy were avowedly monetarist. In the Budget of 1980 the medium-term financial strategy (MTFS) was announced, with multi-year targets for both the PSBR and money supply growth. However, if this was British monetarism's sunny high noon, the sky soon became overcast. The validity of the approach to macroeconomic policy implied by the MTFS was challenged by totally unexpected developments. In the summer and autumn of 1980 the money supply target was exceeded by a wide margin, and yet economic activity deteriorated and inflation started to fall sharply. Monetarist theory, with its emphasis on the link between money growth and inflation, looked silly. Meanwhile opponents of monetarist thinking assembled an array of expert opinions about macroeconomic theory and policy for the Treasury and Civil Service Committee of the House of Commons. The committee's report was damning in its repudiation of the relationship between the PSBR and money supply growth, which was the analytical kernel of the MTFS. According to officials active at the time, the role of money supply targets in policy decisions was downgraded as early as the autumn of 1980. Nevertheless, broad money targets continued until 1985 and – to that extent – the proposition that a large budget deficit undermined monetary control still had official blessing. The retention of the PSBR – which, to repeat, is a cash concept that can be related to the government's bank borrowing and, hence, to money growth – had a logical basis in economic theory.

II

The development of post-war British fiscal policy until the mid-1980s can now be summarized. There had been two main battles of ideas. The first had been between Treasury orthodoxies and Keynesianism. Whereas Treasury orthodoxies could be fairly characterized as having no clear meaning for any of the ultimate policy objectives, Keynesianism's ultimate objective was – very explicitly – the achievement of full employment. According to the textbooks, this battle was resolved in favour of the Keynesians at some point between 1940 and 1970, with most authorities taking the view that the 1941 Budget was the critical turning point. Further, the textbooks judge that – whatever the ambiguities about the exact date of its adoption by officialdom – Keynesianism was a success. Crucially, the application of its ideas is reputed to have been the dominant reason for the impressively low unemployment recorded in the 1950s and 1960s.[5]

The second battle was between the Keynesians and monetarists in the 1970s, as policy-makers and economists close to them grappled with double-digit inflation. The monetarists urged that macroeconomic policy as a whole concentrate on lowering inflation and that, by means of PSBR targets, fiscal policy be made subsidiary to money supply targets. Plainly, Keynesians and monetarists had divergent views about the best way of formulating fiscal policy, about the manner of fiscal policy's interaction with the rest of policy-making and about the effects of fiscal policy on the economy at large. These divergences were deeply felt and publicly disputed. But, equally plainly, both the Keynesians and monetarists validated their views on fiscal policy by reference to understood objectives and received theory. They were a long way apart, as the Keynesians stressed the goal of full employment, whereas the monetarists were concerned almost exclusively with inflation. Nevertheless, their discourse made a recognizable appeal to 'macroeconomics', in the sense of an intellectual discipline that was much more than glib formulae that could easily be converted into newspaper headlines.

Strong arguments can be presented that neither 'the Keynesian revolution' nor 'the monetarist counter-revolution' amounted to all that much. The Keynesian revolution was far less substantial in actual fiscal practice than it was as a set of nostrums and aspirations shared by a large number of university dons; the monetarist counter-revolution was retrospectively dismissed by the media as a temporary political fad, since it had never had a serious hold on the long-term policy-making establishment in the Treasury and the Bank of England. Subsequent narrative accounts of the period by the key players suggest that the media's characterization of the official attitude towards monetarism was accurate.[6] However, this leaves much unexplained. If neither Keynesian nor monetarist approaches to fiscal policy held sway by the late 1980s, then what set of ideas did influence policy?

The question may not have seemed particularly pressing during the boom in the final years of Nigel (later Lord) Lawson's period as Chancellor of the Exchequer. The public finances recorded large surpluses, as tax revenue was boosted by excessive domestic expenditure. At any rate, in the 1988 Budget Lawson took the opportunity to spell out a new rule for fiscal policy, that 'henceforth a zero PSBR would be the norm'. The rationale for this apparent restoration of the principle of a balanced budget was that it provided 'a clear and simple rule, with a good historical pedigree'. Further, the balanced budget rule would – according to Lawson in his book of memoirs, *The View from No. 11* – give the Treasury 'a useful weapon in the unending battle to control public spending'. Among other arguments for a balanced budget, he referred to 'the burden of debt service and therefore the tax level in years to come'.[7] (A large deficit would add to the debt and debt-servicing costs, and hence increase future taxes.)

Lawson's discussion of the zero PSBR rule – in both the Budget speech of 1988 and his memoirs – referred only tangentially to the debate between the Keynesians and monetarists which had raged in the 1970s and early 1980s. Indeed, the comment on debt interest and the virtues of expenditure restraint echoed many statements from senior Treasury officials in the 1930s and 1940s, almost as if the Keynesian/monetarist debate had never been. But one of Lawson's claims – that the zero PSBR rule had 'a good historical pedigree' – was misinformed. Even in 1988 the PSBR was hardly an historical concept. It had been introduced to the UK as recently as the early 1960s, while at no point in the following 25 years had a zero PSBR been the main guideline for fiscal policy. The PSBR is an altogether different measure of the fiscal position from the balance above-the-line, which had in fact been the focus of Treasury attention in the early and middle decades of the twentieth century.

The tendency of the Lawson years was therefore to downplay the macro-economic objectives over which the Keynesians and monetarists had fought so furiously. The government did not have a target for unemployment, as in the heyday of full employment policies, but it did not have a specific target for inflation either. Instead fiscal policy seemed to be motivated by rather old notions, such as the need to deliver long-run fiscal solvency and tight expenditure control. One item of expenditure in particular, the debt interest burden, was mentioned often in official speeches, in line with the comments in Lawson's memoirs. The Conservatives remained in office for almost eight years after Lawson's resignation in October 1989, and kept his zero PSBR rule. The aim of maintaining a balance was not particularly controversial. Economists with a monetarist background were happy with a zero PSBR, since that did not pose a threat to monetary control, while many Keynesian economists had come to accept that the goal of full employment could no longer be pursued merely by means of demand management.

However, the concept of the PSBR came under increasingly sceptical scrutiny. Embattled Treasury politicians and civil servants routinely relied on the PSBR target as their principle obstacle to more public spending. The concept of the PSBR was therefore reviewed and questioned. The critics seemed to think that the definition of the term, rather than the sequence of political choices being made by ministers, was to blame for the lack of particular kinds of public spending. For example, the PSBR was attacked by supporters of more public housing. They thought it was anomalous that extra capital spending by public corporations increased the PSBR, as the public sector had another asset (that is, public housing) to match increased debt. A report in 1995 from the Chartered Institute of Housing and Coopers & Lybrand considered 'whether there are alternatives to the current emphasis on the PSBR which would avoid undue constraints being imposed on investment by public corporations.'[8]

The election of a Labour government in 1997 aroused high expectations of a change in the fiscal rules, including the demotion of the PSBR from its pivotal role. In a sequence of statements in late 1997 and 1998 Gordon Brown, the new Chancellor of the Exchequer, did indeed greatly alter the *form* of the fiscal policy framework. (Whether he also altered the *substance* is more debatable.) Building on proposals in the Labour Party's election manifesto, in June 1998 the government published a paper on *Stability and Investment for the Long Term*. The PSBR had already been renamed 'the public sector net cash requirement (PSNCR)'. As widely hoped by lobbyists for more public expenditure, it was now downgraded in the list of fiscal concepts and ceased to be the subject of any policy rule. Instead, the government set two new rules for fiscal policy. The first – the so-called 'golden rule' – said that, over the business cycle, the government would borrow only to invest and not to fund current spending; the second – termed 'the sustainable investment rule' – intended that 'net public debt as a proportion of GDP will be held over the economic cycle at a stable and prudent level'.[9]

One consequence was that the critical variable for control purposes became the balance on the current budget or 'public sector current budget'. The golden rule implied that this should be nil or even in surplus. Of course, if the PSCB were balanced, and yet capital spending financed by borrowing were to increase sharply, the PSNCR (or PSBR, to use its old title) could explode. The purpose of the second rule was therefore to limit public sector debt. However, the words first chosen to defend the rule – 'stable' and 'prudent' – were mealy-mouthed. Neither of the government's two rules had an obvious link with macroeconomic theory, as conventionally understood. Indeed, *Stability and Investment for the Long Term* contained almost nothing about the relationship between fiscal policy and employment, on Keynesian lines, and no mention whatsoever of any measure of the money supply. The silence on the money supply contrasted sharply with Treasury statements in the same subject area 15 year earlier under the Conservatives or 20 years earlier under the then Callaghan–Healey Labour government. Plainly, the Treasury no longer had much interest in the relationship between fiscal policy and money supply growth. An observer might ask whether its political masters – and presumably its officials – remembered anything about the theoretical rationale for the initial programmes of PSBR/PSNCR reduction in the late 1970s.

So what were the arguments for the Labour government's new rules? According to *Stability and Investment for the Long Term*, the new spending control regime was to be 'based on the distinction between current and capital spending' (p. 20). Spending on capital items 'creates assets which support services and benefits taxpayers in future years as well as now' (p. 20). The golden rule was therefore 'fair', because 'those generations that benefit from public spending should also meet the cost' and it would ensure inter-generational equity by matching 'the costs and benefits of public spending across generations' (p. 21). What about the second rule, that total debt should be kept under control, even if borrowing were to finance investment? In the crucial paragraph, a reference to sustainability was tacked on to the emphasis on stability and prudence. Fiscal policy settings were described as 'sustainable' if 'on the basis of reasonable assumptions, the government can continue to meet its current spending and taxation policies indefinitely while continuing to meet its debt interest obligations' (p. 22).

In short, the golden rule was concerned with intergenerational equity, while the 'sustainable investment rule' would clearly be breached if debt interest were rising much more rapidly than national income. New Labour politicians apparently believed that they were entering unexplored territory. The White Paper on the Comprehensive Spending Review – published in July 1998 – was replete with references to modernity. In his foreword, the Prime Minister, Tony Blair, relentlessly emphasized how up to date he and his government were. The idea of 'money for modernisation' was – he said – a 'new principle'. The first chapter said that the overall spending plans would result in 'a modern and flexible role for the Government', while the Treasury would 'oversee a capital modernisation fund to provide for additional innovative projects'. Even the National Health Service would have its own 'modernisation fund'.

But how modern were the new fiscal rules? It is interesting to compare the New Labour views in *Stability and Investment for the Long Term* with the thoughts of Sir Herbert Brittain, an old-style Treasury knight, in his book on *The British Budgetary System* published in 1959. New Labour claimed that, under the golden rule, borrowing – and the associated increase in the national debt – could be justified if it were for investment purposes; Brittain observed that '[a] good deal of borrowing below-the-line may be offset by productive assets and to that extent . . . the increase in the national debt on this account need not cause undue alarm'.[10] New Labour and Brittain were clearly thinking in much the same way. The government's 'sustainable investment rule' was partly addressed to the danger of an ever-rising debt interest bill; Brittain noted that borrowing to finance current spending might stimulate the economy, but 'in future years . . . the general taxpayer will have to find the interest which has to be paid to the holders of the newly-created debt'.[11] Again, the reasoning of self-consciously avant-garde Labour politicians was similar to that of a fuddy-duddy Treasury knight of the 1950s.

Brittain was also eloquent about inter-generational equity, particularly in the context of debt-financed war expenditure. He doubted that borrowing did in fact shift the burden between generations. As he noted,

> [w]ar borrowing – like any other borrowing – means that various members of the public lend to the State . . . the unspent portions of their incomes in return for some form of claim on the State in the future; and that claim is satisfied out of the taxation or borrowing of future years. But all this amounts to is that, in those future years, value is being transferred within the country from one set of people to another from one generation.[12]

Stability and Investment for the Long Term referred to the then current academic fashion for calculating 'generational accounts', which estimated 'each generation's net tax and benefit position over their respective remaining lifetimes', and said that the Treasury was working with outside economists to produce such accounts for the UK.[13] This sounded new and forward-looking. In fact – as is evident from the Brittain quote – Treasury officials had been thinking about the subject, in much the same terms, over 40 years earlier.

III

In conclusion, the new fiscal rules introduced by the Labour government in 1997 and 1998 resemble a number of old fiscal rules which prevailed before the so-called 'Keynesian era'. They cannot be easily related to the recognized objectives of macroeconomic policy or justified by an appeal to macroeconomic theory. More specifically, they have no direct relevance to either the maintenance of high employment or the control of inflation. Their rationale instead runs in terms ('stability', 'prudence', limiting the debt interest burden, matching new debt with productive assets) which Treasury officials of the 1930s and 1940s would recognize, understand and approve, if they could somehow be reincarnated. The new rules are quite unlike the Keynesian principle that policy-makers should relate the budget deficit to aggregate demand and employment; they are also indifferent to the monetarist claim that an excessive budget deficit may need to be financed by monetary means and so lead to inflation. While monetarism (in the British sense, explained in Essay 7) and New Labour's brand of sound finance both endorse small budget deficits or balanced budgets, the authors of the two key rules – such as Ed Balls, the Chief Economic Adviser to the Treasury between 1999 and 2004 – have usually been rude towards monetarism when they have paid it any attention at all. Macroeconomic theory and analysis had some influence on fiscal policy between the 1950s and late 1980s, although the precise nature of that influence can be disputed. But macroeconomics has little or no relevance to the fiscal rules now in force.

This conclusion may sound critical and negative. It is not intended to be. The squabbles of macroeconomists in the 20 years to the mid-1980s were not particularly edifying and did not reach satisfactory, widely accepted answers. Further, a case can be made that – in terms of results – fiscal policy was better before the 1960s and after the mid-1980s than it was in intervening period when macroeconomics-based advice was in the ascendancy. But New Labour's technocrats must not pretend that their fiscal framework is innovative and modern. Such claims ignore the long-standing emphasis on sound finance in Britain's historical record. The golden rule and the sustainable investment rule are best interpreted not as new departures, but as the latest footnotes to that record.

NOTES

1. H. Brittain, *The British Budgetary System* (London: George Allen and Unwin, 1959), pp. 53–4.
2. D. Winch, *Economics and Policy* (London: Hodder and Stoughton, 1969), p. 313 and p. 315.
3. R.C.O. Matthews, 'Why has Britain had full employment since the war', *Economic Journal*, 78 (1968), pp. 555–69. The quotation is from p. 556.
4. T.G. Congdon, *Monetary Control in Britain* (London and Basingstoke: Macmillan Press, 1982), pp. 35–45.
5. For a sceptical assessment of the historical reality of the Keynesian revolution, see T.G. Congdon, 'Did Britain have a Keynesian revolution? Fiscal policy since 1941', in J. Maloney (ed.), *Debt and Deficits: An Historical Perspective* (Cheltenham: Edward Elgar, UK and Lyme, USA 1998), pp. 84–115, of which a revised version is reprinted here as Essay 4 on pp. 81–111.
6. N. Lawson, *The View from No. 11* (London and New York: Bantam Press, 1992), pp. 447–60.
7. Lawson, *The View from No. 11*, pp. 811–12.
8. J. Hawksworth and S. Wilcox, *Challenging the Conventions: Public Borrowing Rules and Housing Investment* (Coventry: The Chartered Institute of Housing, 1995), p. 3.
9. HM Treasury, *Stability and Investment for the Long Term* (London: HMSO, 1998), p. 20.
10. Brittain, *Budgetary System*, p. 53.
11. Brittain, *Budgetary System*, p. 53.
12. Brittain, *Budgetary System*, p. 175.
13. HM Treasury, *Stability and Investment*, p. 22.

PART THREE

Defining British Monetarism

Inescapably monetarism in the British context is connected with the premier-
ship of Margaret Thatcher between 1979 and 1990 and so with 'Thatcherism'.
But the origins of 'Thatcherite monetarism' lay somewhat further back, in the
disastrous Heath–Barber boom of the early 1970s and the shambles of macro-
economic policy-making in the mid-1970s. As she explains in the first volume
of her autobiography The Path to Power, *Thatcher was attracted to mon-*
etarism because 'the technical arguments and insights were so completely in
harmony with my fundamental instincts and early experience' (M. Thatcher,
The Path to Power *[London: HarperCollins, 1995], p. 568). No one should*
be surprised that a grocer's daughter believes in free markets, sound money and
balanced budgets. The first essay here – which is a heavily rewritten version of
a chapter in the author's Monetarism: An Essay in Definition *– sets mon-*
etarism in the wider political context. It tries to explain why supporters of
monetary control tend also to advocate the liberty of the individual, to support
the free play of market forces and to favour private ownership over state own-
ership. (The pamphlet Monetarism: An Essay in Definition *was published in*
1978 by the Centre for Policy Studies, the think tank founded by Thatcher and
Sir Keith [later Lord] Joseph in 1974. Mr Alfred [later Sir Alfred] Sherman
asked me to write it after seeing my essay on Keynes and the Keynesians in
Encounter *in 1975. The* Encounter *essay is the first in this collection.)*

The bungles in British economic policy in the 1970s were specifically British
and the attempts to restore some sort of order were also specifically British.
Two core themes were the reduction in the budget deficit and the need to inte-
grate fiscal policy with money supply targets. The themes came together with
the adoption of the Medium-Term Financial Strategy in the 1980 Budget,
with Thatcher herself strongly sympathetic to the objective of a more bal-
anced budgetary position. In the resulting style of policy-making, monetary
control depended on curbing the amount that the government borrowed from
the banks combined with restraint over bank lending to the private sector. This
was different from the approach espoused by American monetarists (such as
Milton Friedman), in which the key to targeting the rate of money supply
growth was management of the monetary base. So a 'British monetarism' had
to be differentiated from an 'American monetarism', as in the second essay
here 'British and American monetarism compared', based on a paper origin-
ally given at a one-day conference on Keynes and monetarism at the
University of Kent in 1987. Interestingly, it was easy to illustrate the Anglo-
American differences in the 1980s with references to Keynes's work dating
from the 1920s and 1930s.

Mayer's The Structure of Monetarism *is probably the most well-regarded book on the definition of monetarism. (T. Mayer,* The Structure of Monetarism *[New York and London: W.W. Norton], 1978.) Mayer has written to me that – in his opinion – 'British monetarism' is not really monetarism. Fair enough, but the definition of intellectual movements is difficult. No one doubts that a set of ideas called 'monetarism' did influence British public policy in the late 1970s and the 1980s, and that in some respects the resulting changes to policy were lasting. (By implication, there must also have been a group of people in the UK who were 'monetarists', more or less, whatever they subsequently say about the matter.)*

6. The political economy of monetarism

It is always a double-edged compliment to characterize an idea as fashionable. The description tends to suggest impermanence and fragility, as if the idea in question could be shrugged off as a topical irrelevance. In the case of monetarism in the 1970s and 1980s, this danger was particularly acute. Many of its detractors found that the sharpest critical approach was to admit that it had gained widespread support, but to imply that such support fluctuated with the ebb and flow of opinion, and made no real difference to economic knowledge.[1] This sort of attack was unfair. Certain propositions branded as 'monetarist' were not, in fact, distinctive of any school of thought, but formed part of the core of received economic theory. Moreover, many distinctively monetarist themes, far from being an evanescent response to the inflationary excess of the 1970s, had been recognized in one form or another for decades or even centuries.

The Keynesians in Britain were hostile – or at least apathetic – towards the teaching of monetary economics in British universities and the application of monetary theory in policy-making. But the allegation that monetarism was a fashion and nothing else was strange, since the monetary tradition in British economics was at one time full of vitality. Indeed, in the first half of the twentieth century Cambridge was the acknowledged centre of monetary theory, not just in Britain but in the world, with original contributions from Marshall, Pigou, Robertson and, above all, Keynes. In the 1950s and 1960s this legacy was neglected. The leading economists at Cambridge, who called themselves 'Keynesians' and enjoyed the esteem conferred by Keynes's name, scoffed at small and diminishing bands of diehards in provincial universities who obstinately insisted on the importance of money.[2] They also isolated Dennis Robertson, who had worked closely with Keynes in the 1920s (although quarrelling with him in the mid-1930s) and had become Cambridge's foremost monetary theorist. (According to the author of Robertson's intellectual biography, Keynes' influence at Cambridge 'lived on through his disciples, and the battles Robertson fought with them in the Faculty over teaching arrangements and new appointments continued to shadow his declining years'.[3]) Arguably, the strength of opposition to monetarism, and the lack of intellectual preparedness in the policy-making establishment when it was confronted by the double-digit inflation which followed the Barber boom of 1972/73 and the Lawson boom of the late 1980s, was due to the Cambridge Keynesians' pooh-poohing of the quantity theory of money in the 1950s and 1960s. Would it then be right to blame Keynes himself for Britain's economic difficulties in the 1970s?

I

The reply to this question reveals much about the development of economic thought in Britain. One point must be made straight away. The titles of Keynes's four main books on economics – *Indian Currency and Finance* (published in 1913), *A Tract on Monetary Reform* (1923), *A Treatise on Money* (1930) and *The General Theory of Employment, Interest and Money* (1936) – suggest that Keynes was obsessed by money and finance.[4] Further, there is no doubt that he always considered the influence of money on fluctuations in output and employment to be fundamental. He thought that the weakness of economics in his day was its inability to reconcile the determination of individual prices by supply and demand with the determination of the aggregate price level by the quantity of money. His aim in *The General Theory* was

> to escape from this double life and to bring the theory of prices as a whole back to close contact with the theory of value. The division of economics between the theory of value and distribution on the one hand and the theory of money on the other hand is, I think, a false division. The right dichotomy is, I suggest, between the theory of the individual industry or firm and the distribution between different uses of a *given* quantity of resources on the one hand, and the theory of output and employment *as a whole* on the other hand. So long as we limit ourselves to the study of the individual industry or firm on the assumption that the aggregate quantity of employed resources is constant . . . it is true that we are not concerned with the significant characteristics of money. But as soon as we pass to the problem of what determines output and employment as a whole, we require the complete theory of a monetary economy.[5]

Keynes devoted over 30 years of study to analysing the interaction of the real and financial sides of a capitalist economy. It is true that at the outset he considered money to be a benign or at worst harmless contrivance for facilitating transactions, whereas at the end he had convinced himself that it could be the jinx of the free enterprise system. But, whether the existence of money was beneficial or pernicious, he had no doubt that money mattered. That an influential set of academics was able so easily and successfully to promote a 'Keynesianism' in which decisions to spend were severed from the quantity of money and interest rates was an extraordinary intellectual fabrication. How did money-less 'Keynesianism' emerge? What were its main elements and can they be related, even distantly, to *The General Theory*?

It has to be conceded that the Keynesian approach of the 1970s – as adopted, for example, by the Treasury and the National Institute – was not altogether divorced from Keynes's thinking. The principal Keynesian theoretical construct is the income-expenditure model of aggregate demand determination. Reduced to its essentials this model says that demand depends on how much economic agents decide to spend and that certain categories of spending (such as exports and government expenditure) are 'exogenous'. That is, they do not depend on the current level of national income, but instead regulate its future value by the multiplier process. The Treasury econometric model, which by the mid-1970s already had scores of equations, was nothing more than an elaboration of this simple insight.

The income-expenditure model is advanced in *The General Theory*, constituting the subject matter of books II to IV. These take up 160 of the 385 pages and are the work's analytical heart. The model is expressed in wage-units which may be equated with the wage payment to the average worker. This device could be represented as purely technical. It has the great convenience that, if demand is measured in so many wage-units, an increase in demand leads to an identical increase in the number of wage-units and, as long as wages are constant, to an identical increase in the number of men in work. The wage-unit assumption therefore facilitates the determination of demand, output and employment. (In the 1930s it enabled Keynes to proceed quickly from the level of aggregate demand to the level of employment, an undoubted merit when mass unemployment was the major economic problem.) But expository convenience is obtained at significant cost in theoretical completeness, because the result is that – within books II to IV – *The General Theory* has no method of determining the wage-unit.

For this reason book V of *The General Theory* is concerned with 'Money-Wages and Prices'. Now a key issue becomes the determination of the wage unit itself. Not surprisingly, the hypothesized effects of changes in the quantity of money are very different in this book from what they are in books II to IV. In books II to IV an increase in the money supply lowers the rate of interest, stimulates activity and does not change the price level; in book V, by contrast, a rise in the money supply boosts effective demand and 'the increase in effective demand will, generally speaking, spend itself partly in increasing the quantity of employment and partly in raising the level of prices'.[6] In the extreme case of full employment monetary expansion leads only to inflation. Clearly, the income-expenditure model is outlined in books II to IV *before* the discussion of wages and prices because it is valid only if the wage-unit is constant. Keynes was fully aware of the ramifications, and the peculiarities, of the wage-unit assumption when he organized the argument of *The General Theory*.

But the Keynesians of the immediate post-war decades overlooked these qualifications. Their income-expenditure models – both in the textbooks and in large-scale forecasting models – were (and still are, in the early twenty-first century) constructed in real terms, as if a change in wages could not occur while income and expenditure were being determined. Within the model context the absence of a clear economic mechanism for determining price and wage level changes was defensible. It is a common property of Keynesian forecasting models that an *x* per cent rise in wages is sooner or later accompanied by an *x* per cent rise in prices, implying that the real purchasing power of earnings and, hence, consumption and national income are unaffected. But the habit of forecasting the macroeconomic aggregates in real terms had very serious consequences. It persuaded the economists concerned to believe that real variables and the level of inflation were determined by two separate processes, and it allowed them to banish money from their models. As Keynes recognized, his theory was not able to disentangle the effects of a money supply increase on real output and the price level (except, of course, in long-run equilibrium when quantity-theory conclusions hold). The Keynesians came to believe not only that national income depended on decisions to spend, but also that decisions to spend had no systematic connection with the main items in the economy's balance sheet (the level of the nominal and real money supply, the market value of stocks and shares, house prices and other real estate values). If money and asset prices had major effects on expenditure, the empirical validity of the income-expenditure model would be undermined and the whole conceptual edifice of Keynesianism – as the term was understood in Britain's policy-formation establishment – would dissolve.[7]

As this account demonstrates, the story of the degeneration of Keynes's pure theory to the Keynesian 'orthodoxy' of the 1970s was quite complicated. But it could be argued that one theme of this story was the reinstatement of an invalid dichotomy. The dichotomy was invalid because it separated two aspects of the economy which, in the real world, are intertwined. One aspect was the determination of national income in real terms by the level of demand; and the other was the determination of the rate of inflation by supposing that collective bargaining drives up wage costs (that is, Keynes's wage-unit) and, in the same proportion, the price level. Here lay the intellectual origin of the Keynesian assertion that effective demand had no bearing on the increase in prices and the theoretical background to the advocacy of incomes policies. If spending changes output and not prices, demand management is a useless instrument for controlling inflation. Reliance ought instead to be placed on direct political and administrative action. That such action might distort the structure of relative prices was a minor drawback to the typical Keynesian economist because his income-expenditure model was aggregative and did not bother itself with the supply-and-demand problems of individual business people.

The dichotomy under discussion here was an associate of 'a technique of thinking' in which the signalling function of relative price movements was regarded as unimportant. Of course the signalling function of relative price movements is basic to microeconomics. The 'apparatus of mind' of some British Keynesians in the 1970s was therefore a kind of anti-economics. The advocacy of 'planning', the suppression of microeconomics and the neglect of monetary economics were interrelated. It was consistent that the Department of Applied Economics in Cambridge – where this type of anti-economics was developed most fully – should in the late 1970s propose an 'alternative economic programme' including import controls. Perhaps more than any other single factor it was this anti-economics which was responsible for the succession of misguided policies, both microeconomic and macroeconomic, pursued by the British government in the 1960s and 1970s.[8] (Fortunately, import controls were never implemented, but they were the subject of extensive, unnecessary and largely misguided discussion about them during the various crises of the 1970s. Economists disagree about many things, but there is a strong professional consensus that import controls reduce welfare and are a mistake.)

Moreover, the dichotomy that was central to the Keynesian anti-economics resembled the classical dichotomy rebutted by Keynes. The classical dichotomy said that the output of the individual industry depended on supply-and-demand and the aggregate price level on the quantity of money. Keynes insisted that via the rate of interest, money affected relative prices, output and the aggregate price level, and that money, banking and asset markets had profound effects on demand and employment. The Keynesian dichotomy of the 1960s and 1970s was, in some respects, even more unrealistic than the classical because – in its extreme forms – it dispensed with money altogether. Keynes, who thought that 'as soon as we pass to the problem of what determines output and employment as a whole we require the complete theory of a monetary economy', would surely have repudiated it. The income-expenditure models of the Treasury and the National Institute were sometimes characterized as a 'vulgar', 'hydraulic' or 'bastardised' version of what 'Keynes really said'.[9] But that was too flattering. They simplified to the point of misrepresentation and would be better described as fakes.

The resistance to monetarism in Britain cannot be attributed to the fact that Keynes was an Englishman, rather than an American or European, and that he therefore had a disproportionate intellectual influence in Britain. It was not his fault that, from his death and particularly from the early 1960s, the prestige of monetary economics at Cambridge collapsed. Indeed, monetarism could be interpreted not as an assault on Keynes's work, but as an attempt to rescue it from his successors. Friedman compared Keynes's disillusionment with the stability of capitalist financial markets in the 1930s with similar views held by Henry Simons, a professor of economics at the University of Chicago. He also described Keynes's monetary theory as 'sophisticated and modern'.[10] By contrast, one would not have guessed from the sort of statements which emanated from the National Institute or the Department of Applied Economics at Cambridge in the 1970s that Keynes had a monetary theory or, indeed, that such an entity as monetary theory, whether derived from Marshall, Keynes or Friedman, was worth discussing at all. The lack of sturdy intellectual defences against monetary abuse on the scale of the 1972–74 period, when the annual rate of money supply growth exceeded 20 per cent, and the 1985–88 period, when it approached 20 per cent, is not to be explained by Keynes and the special position he holds in the pantheon of British economists.

II

Part of the explanation for the shrillness of the debates between Keynesians and monetarists was that much more than textbook economics was at stake. As its critics understood, monetarism was not – and is not – politically neutral. It was an ally of a certain disposition towards political problems. This disposition was basically liberal, but, since the need to respect existing institutions was also emphasized, it had conservative implications. It was not tendentious to associate it with such thinkers as Hayek and Oakeshott, although Hayek in his later years disowned technical monetarism. The purpose of this and the next section is to identify some of the links between monetarism, liberalism and conservatism.

Money is usually termed 'the medium of exchange', but this does not go far enough. The phrase, 'the instrument of choice', brings into stronger relief its significance for a liberal philosophy. Of course, choice exists in a barter economy, but the possibilities for transacting are more circumscribed. Because money is universally accepted, its introduction into an economy reduces the size of the stock of goods that merchants need to engage in trade. It thereby lowers marketing costs and extends the area in which consumers are able to select the combination of products most suited to their preferences. This extension of choice is an essential preliminary to widespread specialization. If it is expensive to trade, the market may be too small to allow an individual to concentrate on one form of production. But, with exchange facilitated by a universally accepted instrument of choice, the division of labour can begin. The ensuing gains from economies of scale and experience were first described by Adam Smith in *The Wealth of Nations*, and they have formed part of the folklore of the free market economy ever since. The division of labour can, of course, be taken a long way in a socialist, centrally planned economy, but traditionally it has been a process associated with market freedom and decentralized decision-taking. The advances in productivity associated with the division of labour are an effective illustration of how self-interested individuals, not working at the behest of a single co-ordinating unit under government control, can achieve a harmonious and socially optimal result. It is one component, and perhaps the most persuasive component, of the argument for permitting the 'invisible hand' to allocate resources without interference from the state.

Hayek reinforced this argument by pointing out the dependence of a complicated economy on the fragmentation of knowledge, on the fact that each member of society can have only a small fraction of the knowledge possessed by all and that each is therefore ignorant of most of the facts on which the working of society rests.[11] Here, too, the role of money is crucial. It is a common standard of value, a numeraire in which the value of all goods may be expressed. Its presence excuses traders from having to inform themselves of the price of a good in terms of other goods (such as the exchange ratio of wheat into coffee, of cars into furniture, and so on), since it is instead adequate to know the price of a good in terms only of the money numeraire (how many pounds have to be paid for a particular weight of wheat, of different makes of car, and so on). Since the amount of information required for successful marketing and trading is reduced by this device, energies are released for other tasks and economic efficiency is improved. The advantage conferred by money in this respect is weaker if its quantity and, consequently, its exchange relationship to goods in general (that is, the overall price level) change too much in a short space of time. The monetarist distrust of sharp fluctuations in the money supply finds here its most basic rationale.

The connection between money and freedom therefore pivots on Adam Smith's theory of the division of labour and Hayek's concept of the division of knowledge. One of the characteristics of economists who believe in these ideas is that they respect the relative price structure which arises from free production and exchange. They consider that – except in certain special circumstances which need to be carefully (and sceptically) specified – unfettered market forces set prices which achieve the right equilibrium between consumer wants and scarce resources. Not surprisingly, monetarists recommend a high degree of wage and price flexibility since restrictions on price movements impede the attainment of this equilibrium. Such restrictions sometimes stem from monopoly power, but governments and regulatory bodies are often to blame.

In the UK in the 1960s and 1970s pay and price controls designed to curb inflation were the most prominent form of government interference. Although they were commonly formulated as if they were to be impartial in effect (for example, the same percentage pay increase was allowed to the whole labour force), they always discriminated in practice. It is almost part of the definition of a dynamic economy that the relative price structure should come under pressure from different rates of productivity growth in different industries, varying income elasticities of demand and so on. To proclaim the same proportional pay increase for every worker or price increase for every good was to freeze the relative price structure and weaken its allocative power. That might have been an acceptable price to pay if prices and incomes policies did in the end deliver lower inflation, but experience showed that they did not.

The monetarists' condemnation of incomes policies stemmed partly from their philosophical attitude towards market freedom and partly from the failure of such policies when attempted in practice. Of course, if it could be shown that monetary mismanagement was the cause of inflation, that lent weight to the proposition that monetary responsibility was a sufficient policy response. Direct controls, with the infringement of freedom they entailed, were unnecessary. This conclusion could not be reached by the more extreme Keynesians since money formed no part of their system. Their world view was such that only changes in wages could account for changes in the aggregate price level and only political measures to check the collective greed of the unions could prevent prices from rising.[12]

The divide between monetary and non-monetary approaches to British inflation in the 1960s and 1970s was related to another fundamental split in economic theory, between those theories which say the distribution of income is determined by productivity and those which say it is determined by comparative bargaining power. The productivity theories belong to the neoclassical strand in economics and the power theories to the Marxian.[13] In the post-war decades the thought-habits associated with the wage-unit assumption placed the Keynesians on the Marxian side. (Schumpeter did indeed once refer to the more left-wing representatives of the cause as 'Marxo-Keynesians'.)[14] Nevertheless, much of the reasoning in *The General Theory* itself is conducted in terms of standard price theory and book V makes explicit references to a marginal-productivity basis for wages. Because the wage-unit assumption implied that wages were not governed by the workings of their income-expenditure model, but were given by forces outside the model, it was open to the Keynesians to attribute pay movements, and the balance between wages and profits, to political factors. The frequent references to union militancy in Keynesian writings were a logical consequence. In the more embroidered versions phrases such as 'class conflict' and 'revolutionary struggle' even made an appearance. On this reckoning, inflation was a manifestation of 'social crisis', a sign that the system was under threat from tension between selfish workers and profiteering capitalists.

Since the problem was seen as political, so was the supposed solution. Hence, there was a need for the government to involve itself in peace-making between the different groups, by laying down pay and profit limits to be binding on all of them. Keynes's wage-unit assumption therefore culminated in centralized pay negotiations between, on the one hand, the 'peak organizations' of labour and capital, and, on the other, the government and the leading politicians of the day. Moreover, in the opinion of some Keynesians, these negotiations ought not only to help in overcoming inflation, but ought also to contribute to the attainment of 'social justice'. According to Opie, writing in 1974, 'certainly all Keynesians in the early days and most Keynesians later on were radical in some sense or other, and few would have shrunk from the egalitarian implications' of increased government activism in the economy.[15] By permitting larger pay increases to the low-paid than the well-off an incomes policy could reduce inequality. The Keynesians considered this a desirable end, partly because equality was good in itself, but also partly because they felt that the prevailing distribution of income, being determined by power, had no worthwhile economic function.

Monetarist-inclined economists took the opposite view. Their sympathies were with the neoclassical school of pricing and distribution. Because they believed that the relative price structure reflected market forces, they saw wages – which were also prices, the prices of labour – as being determined by supply and demand. A worker is paid for what he produces; if he is paid less than his product, employers are induced to compete for his labour services until his wage rises and their surplus is removed; if he is paid more, he is either made redundant or obliged to suffer a wage cut. There is a definite, if rough-and-ready, justice in this equating of pay with marginal productivity because it matches reward to effort and skill. Centralized pay controls disturb this equivalence and, aside from the potentially harmful side effects in the misallocation of labour, they tend to lead to industrial unrest. The monetarist suspicion of income policies was validated, therefore, not merely by the tenet that inflation was caused by excessive monetary expansion, but also by acceptance of the structure of relative wages, salaries and other rewards determined by market forces. (The typical

monetarist view was that – if the market-determined pattern of income distribution offended against some distributive principle or other – it should
be remedied by the tax system, not by interference in relative prices and
wages. In qualification, this preference for tax-based redistribution is widespread among professional economists and should not be associated too
closely with monetarism.)

To summarize, the monetarists' criticism of income policies was part of
a broader defence of economic freedom. Economic freedom was seen as
beneficial because of the gains arising from the Smithian division of labour
and Hayek's division of knowledge. A trustworthy instrument of choice, in
the form of a monetary unit which maintained a constant value (or, at any
rate, a degree of stability) through time, was thought necessary for the
smooth operation of the free market economy which the monetarists
favoured.

III

By its intrinsic nature, money is private, not public, property. Since the state
is able to manufacture money at zero (or minimal) cost, it has no need to
hold large money balances. For most of the twentieth century central governments in the industrial world financed their expenditure partly by a continuous overdraft from the banking system. The government's money
holdings are negligible in most countries, but the banks lend it large sums
for ongoing commitments by taking up issues of Treasury bills and other
short-dated paper. (Again, local authorities and public corporations can
never face bankruptcy, because the government will bail them out, however
extreme their financial incompetence. One consequence of their immunity
from risk is that they do not need to have sizeable balances in the banks.)
British money supply statistics confirm these observations. At the end of
1976 – when the debates between Keynesianism and monetarism were
livening up – the M3 measure of money totalled £45.1 billion, while
deposits held by the public sector were about £0.9 billion. Public expenditure was over 45 per cent of national output, but money held by public
sector bodies was a mere fiftieth of money held by the private sector. (The
situation was much the same at the end of 2005. Sterling deposits held by
the public sector at UK 'monetary financial institutions' – that is, banks
and building societies – were £28.7 billion, whereas such deposits held by
the private sector amounted to £1324.7 billion)[16] Evidently, no private
sector agent can operate with the same financial freedom as the government. Every individual and company outside the public sector must own
some cash or bank deposits, or risk the possibility of going bankrupt

because of an inability to service debt. There are far-reaching – although often overlooked – implications for stabilization policy. Monetary control is not a complete macroeconomic agenda. Guidelines for fiscal policy, and government spending in particular, also need to be spelt out.[17]

The political message of Keynes's macroeconomic theory was that, because of the instability of the speculative demand for money, monetary policy was an unsound tool for regulating demand and that greater reliance should be placed on fiscal policy. So it might on occasions be necessary to combat recessions by raising public expenditure. Keynes had not noticed that money was relevant only as a determinant of private sector fluctuations. By contrast, as explained above, the public sector can borrow from the rest of the economy almost at will and cannot be constrained by a lack of liquidity. One of the major flaws latent in his advocacy of fiscal activism was therefore hidden from Keynes.

This flaw came gradually to be exposed in the 1960s and 1970s. The Keynesian predilection for using public expenditure as a demand regulator aided those politicians and bureaucrats who wanted, for ideological reasons, to see remorseless expansion of the public sector.[18] It would not have mattered if, after recessions were accompanied by spending increases, booms saw equivalent spending cuts. But that was not the way the cycles worked out. Instead, recessions induced public spending increases and booms prompted restrictive monetary policy. The private sector was disadvantaged in either situation. When demand was weak, the government's inclination to stimulate public expenditure was not associated with comparable pressures to raise private expenditure; and, when demand was strong, the resort to higher interest rates was detrimental to the private sector alone.

The tendency of this asymmetry to expand the size of the state, which was implicit in Keynesianism, was reinforced by the characteristics of government employment. Because such employment is only rarely justified by marketed output, the government cannot dismiss employees on the grounds that demand has dropped and sales revenue is insufficient. The state is quite unlike a private sector company subject to commercial disciplines which can offer a practically convincing (and morally reasonable) defence for declaring workers redundant if it does not have enough money to pay their wages. Private sector redundancies, the ultimate cause of which is often a cyclical downturn due to monetary restraint, can be attributed to the lack of demand for a particular product. They have a clear – if disagreeable – rationale, even to those who go without jobs. Since public sector output is financed by general taxation, the same argument cannot be made. It is more difficult to make redundancies in the public sector than in the private sector.[19]

There is a further, related point. Keynes's attack on the effectiveness of monetary policy did not stop with his call for the activation of fiscal policy. The point was that fiscal policy could have the necessary impact only if the public sector were sufficiently large. The logical corollary was, to use Keynes's own phrase, 'a somewhat comprehensive socialization of invest- ment'. An apparently technical and non-ideological judgement about the efficacy of monetary policy became the background to an openly socialist proposal. There was much to be said against Keynes's argument even on its own premises. For example, difficulties in predicting the consequences of monetary policy might be thought a reason for paying more attention to it, not less. Further, precisely because government employment was (and remains) more inflexible than private sector employment, variations in public expenditure were not (and still are not) an adaptable and easily deployed macroeconomic policy instrument.

But there was a more sweeping objection to the Keynesians' proposed harnessing of the state's fiscal powers for the short-term management of demand and output. The monetarists were critical of fiscal activism largely because they doubted that the relevant authorities – the government, the finance ministry and the central bank – had the wisdom, foresight and political detachment required for the role. According to one characteristic monetarist argument, the changeability of the lag between changes in the money supply and money national income did not validate the greater use of fiscal policy. Instead it justified abandoning the discretionary approach to economic policy altogether and the adoption of an automatic money supply rule. The crowding-out argument buttressed the monetarist posi- tion, because it implied that – once a money supply target was in place – an activist fiscal policy was futile and pointless. (See Essay 8, for a statement of the crowding-out argument made in an article in *The Times* in October 1975.) Aside from the crowding-out thesis, mainstream Keynesians had produced conflicting estimates of the size of the so-called 'multiplier' by which national income rises in response to an increase in government spending. Economists' uncertainties about the demand implications of public spending – about whether a £1 billion increase in public expenditure added £2 billion, £1 billion or nothing to effective demand in the economy – was symptomatic of wider difficulties with fiscal activism. These difficulties established a case for scepticism about Keynes's call for an overhaul of property relationships as radical as that implied by the phrase 'compre- hensive socialization of investment'. Donald Moggridge, the editor of Keynes's writings for the Royal Economic Society, once mentioned 'Keynes' tendency towards rather wild asides'.[20] Surely the recommenda- tion of a socialization of investment, on the spurious grounds that it was needed to make fiscal activism effective, was one such 'wild aside'.

The strength of the correlation between monetarist sympathies and a liberal or conservative approach to political problems in the debates of the 1970s and 1980s was not an accident. Money is one of the principal kinds of private property and variations in its quantity have most effect on the private sector. The 'Friedman money supply rule' was intended first and foremost as the answer to inflation, but – if adopted – it would also have gone some way to protect the private sector from the politicians. It is sometimes said that there is no intellectual connection between, on the one hand, monetarist macroeconomics and, on the other, an aversion towards excessive public expenditure and interventionist industrial policy. But support for sound money and free markets form part of a coherent and integrated political outlook. A socialist government could have a programme of constant money supply growth and a balanced budget, while maintaining a high ratio of public expenditure to national income and embarking on schemes for subsidizing or penalizing private industrial ventures. But a high ratio of public expenditure to national income reduces the scope for individually motivated choices and thus makes the management of the money supply less important. In addition, the more obvious is the state's determination 'to accelerate industrial change', and the more politicians and government officials arbitrate on the allocation of scarce inputs, the less important is the financial system's role of enforcing market-related priorities according to profitability. The monetarist advocacy of stable money sits easily with the defence of private property. Meanwhile, in Oakeshott's words, private property is the institution which 'allows the widest distribution and discourages most effectively great and dangerous concentrations of power' and, hence, is 'most friendly to freedom'.[21]

In an article in the November 1976 issue of *Encounter* Friedman tried to make more precise the warnings about how over-expansion of state spending might undermine political freedom. He advanced the notion of a 'tipping point', a particular ratio of public expenditure to national income at which political liberty is in peril and totalitarianism is imminent. For a fairly unsophisticated country, such as Chile, the tipping point might be 40 per cent; for a richer country, like Britain, it might be higher at 60 per cent.[22] These remarks received heavy criticism, notably from such leading economic commentators as Samuel Brittan on the *Financial Times*, as glib and unscientific. (At the time Brittan was usually sympathetic to monetarist ideas.) But Friedman's *Encounter* article, even if it could not substantiate the specific figure in contention, was based on some clear and indisputable features of political democracy. The vital contrast, in his view, was between political and economic markets. The political mechanism had 'the fundamental defect' that it is a system of highly weighted voting under which the special interests have great incentive to promote their own interests at the expense of the general public. The benefits are concentrated; the costs are diffused; and you have therefore a bias in the political market place which leads to ever greater expansion in the scope of government and ultimately to control over the individual.

The economic market was 'very different'.

> In the economic market – the market in which individuals buy and sell from one another – each person gets what he pays for. There is a dollar-for-dollar relationship. Therefore, you have an incentive proportionate to the cost to examine what you are getting. If you are paying out of your own pocket for something and not out of somebody else's pocket, then you have a very strong incentive to see whether you are getting your money's worth.[23]

Although in his *Encounter* article Friedman did not join this essentially political argument to his well-known economic prescriptions, it would not have been difficult to do so. Today, as in the 1970s, the machinery of the political market is oiled by votes. More generally, competing interest groups are able to extract resources from the state (which has a monopoly of coercion, and the powers to tax and to print money) if they can assemble voting coalitions. Whether the distribution of resources to particular groups then has any relation to economic merit or social justice is rather arbitrary. By contrast, in the economic market people receive income according to the value of what they produce, and can express their preferences for different products when they purchase goods and services. Production and consumption therefore respect individual choice and personal freedom; and the outcomes have an obvious logic, even if market forces are sometimes harsh and capricious. The lubricant of the economic market is money, and the advantages of the economic market are most obvious when the monetary system is in good working order. It is the hallmark of societies undergoing a hyperinflationary experience that pressures on the government to act as the guardian of particular sectional interests are particularly strong. In such circumstances some citizens may prefer the political market because the lack of a stable monetary unit reduces the efficiency of the economic market. Only when the value of money is steady and reliable over a period of years can the economic market develop to its full extent.[24]

IV

The last two sections showed that sound money furthers the widening of choice found in a free economy and lends support to the institution of private property. Both these themes connected monetarism with liberalism and conservatism in the 1970s and 1980s, and helped to account for the typical political attitudes of monetarist economists. This final section will suggest that an important theme in monetarist economics was scepticism about the rationalist and managerial style of politics which was dominant in the late twentieth century. Misgivings about this type of politics were expressed by Popper and Hayek and, more particularly, by Oakeshott in his *Rationalism in Politics*.

Keynesianism of the kind practised by Britain's policy-making establishment had several rationalist characteristics. It was highly ambitious in that it asked the state to pursue four goals – full employment, price stability, economic growth and balance-of-payments equilibrium – and to have a precise conception of what these goals were or should be. Once defined and (probably) quantified, these goals were to be sought by means of 'demand management'. Notice how the word 'management' had crept in, rather as if the state were a business and politicians were its board of directors. The concept of demand management presumed not only that policy-makers had a good grasp of the applicable economic theory, but also that the empirical relationships highlighted by theory were stable and reliable. Implicit throughout was the notion that the more scientific was the approach, the deeper would be policy-makers' understanding and the better would be their decisions. The electronic gadgetry of the Treasury model, with its pretence of giving exact answers to difficult questions, indicated the cast of mind involved. Also fundamental was the Keynesian assumption that all the requisite knowledge and wisdom could be concentrated in a few minds in Whitehall (or perhaps in Westminster and Whitehall, or in other versions in Westminster, Whitehall and a handful of colleges at Cambridge University). Ultimately the economy's fate – and that of dozens of industries and businesses across the land – was to be determined at a sort of central committee meeting where the crucial decisions were to be taken. (Hence, all the attention paid to meetings of the National Economic Development Council or 'confrontations' between the Chancellor of the Exchequer and the TUC [Trades Union Congress] or CBI [Confederation of British Industry].) The committee's decisions would have, if some Keynesian accounts were taken to their logical conclusion, a purely technical character, rather as though the problem of steering the economy were like that of steering a ship on an agreed course. Ideally, debate and uncertainty were to be banished, rather as if – in Keynes's own words – economics could be reduced to a kind of dentistry.

Monetarism was in conflict with the rationalist tendency in two main ways. First, it denied that enough was known for policies to be framed with the exactitude needed. Friedman's original case for the monetary rule was negative and sceptical. It was not based on an extravagant boast that he knew more about the economy than the Keynesians, but instead rested on the perhaps less vulnerable foundations of partial ignorance. Friedman argued that – precisely because so little was understood – it was sensible not to expect too much from monetary policy. A similar admission of incomplete knowledge came with his theory of the natural rate of unemployment. In the 1967 presidential address to the American Economic Association he said quite candidly that, although he thought the natural rate was an empirically valid concept, he could not measure it. This may be branded as obscurantist or applauded as prudent intellectual modesty, but either way it was not rationalist or managerial in its implications.

Secondly, monetarists distrusted the political authorities to whom Keynes felt the task of demand management should be granted. To Keynes, and arguably to most of the British upper and middle classes of his time, it was safe to believe that governments acted as servants of the community as a whole and that their members were basically honest and conscientious. This was plausible in the early twentieth century because Britain had been ruled by a political elite of unusually high quality for at least 150 years. The Benthamite and melioristic mood of Keynes and his establishment colleagues reflected this long tradition of honesty, fairness and decency in public life: it duped them into thinking that altruism among politicians was the rule rather than the exception. Henry Simons, and other social and economic observers in the inter-war USA, did not have the same respect for the political process. The American Constitution has many strengths, but the rough-and-tumble of democratic vote-catching in large American cities from the late nineteenth century was not edifying. Chicago School economists have tended to take a cynical view of politicians' motives, as Friedman's antithesis between the economic and political markets demonstrates. The monetarists of the 1970s were influenced by the new theory of public choice which was then emerging.[25] They were alert to the possibility that politicians, far from watching over the interests of the community as a whole, might put their own interest first. Taken to the logical extremes, public choice theorists argued that politics was to be analysed, not as the maximization of social utility, but as the maximization of politicians' utility. It followed that the government's powers in the economic sphere should be restricted. The monetary rule was seen as an effective barrier to political discretion. When consistently applied, it excluded 'management' of the exchange rate, 'management' of fiscal policy and 'management' of individual prices and incomes. The implied critique of Keynesianism was far-reaching. Monetarism and Keynesianism were motivated by quite different interpretations of democratic politics.

In the first three post-war decades Britain's experience of democracy became much more like the USA's, with the two main parties competing for votes by electoral promises in such areas as full employment and price stability. The boom of the early 1970s was a particularly blatant attempt to court political popularity by over-stimulating the economy. Precedents were to be found in the 1950s when the Conservatives held a general election in 1955 shortly after a Budget which cut income taxes and again in 1959 when Mr Macmillan's slogan of 'you never had it so good' was declared in the midst of an unusually vigorous cyclical upswing. Keynesianism – with its hope that governments would publicly commit themselves to full employment – encouraged a version of democracy in which political parties competed with each other to have the best management team. But managerialism refuted itself. By becoming embroiled in party politics, demand management lost its innocence and ceased to be a purely technical item on a committee's agenda. Moreover, as economic policy became increasingly contentious and political in nature in the 1960s and 1970s, macroeconomic outcomes got worse rather than better.

The progress of monetarism in public debate in the 1970s may be seen, therefore, as partly a reflection of the disillusionment with politicians which marked the decade. This disillusionment may in turn be attributed to a realization that rationalism in economic policy had not solved problems, but increased them, and had not made disagreement about policy less heated, but intensified it. But managerial economics and political democracy were, and are, confederates. Managerialism gives politicians plenty to say at elections and plenty to do in between them. An alternative set of ideas (such as monetarism) which envisages a smaller state and less adventurous economic policy may always be difficult to reconcile with the competitive, adversary style of contemporary democratic politics.

NOTES

1. One example will suffice. 'Monetarism, like Christianity, makes a comeback from time to time. When things get bad, even sceptics start paying lip service, just in case there is something in the doctrine which might conceivably save them from eternal damnation.' C. Johnson, in a review of G. Pepper's *Money, Credit and Inflation*, *The Business Economist*, vol. 22, no. 1, winter 1990, pp. 64–5.
2. Economists at provincial ('red-brick') universities and financial journalists were the main contributors to a pamphlet critical of the Radcliffe Report, *Not Unanimous*, which was published by the Institute of Economic Affairs in January 1960. Only one of the seven contributors (R.F. Henderson) was from Cambridge University. Henderson opened his chapter with a recognition of indebtedness to Dennis Robertson, but to no other Cambridge economists.
3. G. Fletcher, *Understanding Dennis Robertson* (Cheltenham, UK and Northampton, MA USA: Edward Elgar Publishing, 2000), p. 404.

4. The inclusion of *Indian Currency and Finance* in the list may seem surprising. But – arguably – this was the beginning of an interest in the place of gold in an international currency regime which continued until the Bretton Woods negotiations (and his House of Lords speeches on them) in the mid-1940s.
5. J.M. Keynes, *The General Theory of Employment, Interest and Money* (London: Macmillan, 1936), p. 293.
6. Keynes, *General Theory*, p. 296.
7. Money plays a crucial role in asset price determination, while sharp changes in asset prices affect expenditure. For more on these themes, see Essay 9 on pp. 181–205 and Essay 14 on pp. 281–315.
8. The phrases in quotation marks are taken from Keynes's famous introduction to the Cambridge Economic Handbooks, which he edited until 1936.
9. Mrs Joan Robinson – a left-wing economics don at Cambridge – used the phrase 'bastardised Keynesianism' to characterize the textbook income-expenditure model.
10. M. Friedman, *The Optimum Quantity of Money* (London: Macmillan, 1969), p. 84.
11. F. Hayek, *Law, Legislation and Liberty*, vol. 1 (London: Routledge and Kegan Paul, 1973), p. 14.
12. Shonfield's remark in his *British Economic Policy Since the War* (quoted in note 1 to the Introduction to this volume) – that 'the success or failure of the trade unions in controlling their members will determine the level of prices – and nothing else' – illustrated this sort of thinking.
13. Professor Maurice Dobb has made the distinction between the two types of theory particularly well in a number of books, notably in *Political Economy and Capitalism* (London: Routledge and Kegan Paul, 1970).
14. E.S. Johnson and H.G. Johnson, *The Shadow of Keynes* (Oxford: Basil Blackwell, 1978), p. 137. See also M. Skousen (ed.), *Dissent on Keynes* (New York: Praeger, 1992), p. 196.
15. See R. Opie, 'The political consequences of Lord Keynes', pp. 75–90, in D.E. Moggridge (ed.), *Keynes: Aspects of the Man and his Work* (London: Macmillan, 1974). The quotation is from p. 79.
16. *Financial Statistics* (London: Her Majesty's Stationery Office), September 1977, p. 51 and p. 74; *Financial Statistics* (London: The Stationery Office), July 2006, p. 58 and p. 78.
17. This was the point of the title of Keith Joseph's 1976 Stockton Lecture, 'Monetarism is not enough'. The title did *not* mean that monetarism was inadequate; it meant that control of the money supply had to be accompanied by restraint over public expenditure. To quote from the speech itself, 'Monetary contraction in a mixed economy strangles the private sector unless the state sector contracts with it and reduces its take in the national income'. M. Halcrow, *Keith Joseph: A Single Mind* (London: Macmillan, 1989), p. 113.
18. If this remark seems outlandish, see note 9 to Essay 12 in this collection, where George Orwell is quoted as saying – in 1945 – that communists keen 'to advance Russian interests at all costs . . . abound in England today'.
19. The case for money supply targets was advocated in the public debate at about the same time as the thesis that 'Britain had too few producers', because public sector employment (financed by taxes) seemed – almost continuously – to be rising faster than private sector employment (financed by sales revenue). The thesis was presented by R. Bacon and W. Eltis in an article in the *Sunday Times* in 1974, and in a book, *Britain's Economic Problem: Too Few Producers* (London: Macmillan, 1976). Between 1961 and 1979 public sector employment climbed at an annual compound rate of 1.3 per cent from 5.86 million to 7.45 million, while private sector employment contracted from 18.60 million to 17.94 million (The source for the data is *Economic Trends: Annual Supplement* [London: HMSO, 1988], p. 209.) During the 1979–97 Conservative government these trends were reversed, partly because of the privatization of nationalized industries.
20. See D. Moggridge, 'Keynes: the economist', pp. 53–74, in D.E. Moggridge (ed.), *Keynes: Aspects of the Man and his Work* (London: Macmillan, 1974). The reference to 'wild asides' is on p. 74.

21. M. Oakeshott, *Rationalism in Politics* (London: Methuen, 1962), p. 45. The remark appears in a review of Henry Simons's *Economic Policy for a Free Society*.
22. M. Friedman, 'The fragility of freedom', *Encounter*, November 1976, pp. 8–14.
23. It should be noted that the ideas put forward by Friedman in this article owed much to work on the theory of public choice done at the University of Western Virginia. See note 25 below.
24. The point may seem remote from the realities of Britain in the 1970s when inflation was running at 'only' 10 per cent a year. However, even this rate of price increases meant that the value of money over a five or ten year time span was highly uncertain and prohibitive of long-term contracts. The issue of long-term fixed-interest debentures and loan stocks on London financial markets practically ceased in these years. The general message is that – as inflation accelerates – the time horizon of the typical economic transector shortens until finally it is no more than a few hours or minutes. See an amusing footnote on p. 41 of J.M. Keynes, *A Tract on Monetary Reform*, in vol. IV of D.E. Moggridge and E. Johnson (eds), *The Collected Writings of John Maynard Keynes* (London: Macmillan, 1971).
25. The theory of public choice – which argues that public servants may put their own private interests ahead of the 'public interest' – was developed, mostly in the 1970s, by James Buchanan and Gordon Tullock. Its 'headquarters' are usually located as the Center for the Study of Public Choice at the Virginia Polytechnic Institute and State University. The public choice perspective was largely adopted by Chicago economists.

7.   British and American monetarism compared

The spread of monetarism in the 1970s did not occur by a simple process of intellectual conquest. In most countries monetarist ideas could not be incorporated in policy formation until they had adapted to local economic conditions and recognized existing traditions of monetary management. Although the framework of financial control assumed some monetarist characteristics in virtually all the industrial nations, each nation still retained distinctive institutional arrangements and policy approaches. The UK posed a particular problem. With its long history of monetary debate and practice, and with its unusually well-established institutional structures, it did not readily assimilate Chicago School doctrines. Nevertheless, in the late 1970s and early 1980s the media, leading politicians and the public at large believed that British macroeconomic policy was becoming progressively more monetarist. Perhaps the apex of monetarist influence on policy came in the Budget of 1980 with the announcement of the Medium-Term Financial Strategy, in which targets for both monetary growth and the budget deficit were stated for four years into the future. In a statement to regional city editors on 9 June 1980, Mr Nigel (later Lord) Lawson, Financial Secretary to the Treasury (later to be Chancellor of the Exchequer), said that the 'Medium-Term Financial Strategy is essentially a monetary – or, if you like, monetarist – strategy'.[1]

The purpose of this essay is to compare the 'monetarism' referred to by Nigel Lawson with the 'monetarism' which is conventionally associated with the Chicago School. The monetarism which once dominated policy formation in the UK is called British monetarism, and the monetarism of the Chicago School, American monetarism. Of course, these simple labels are to a degree misleading. So many ideas have been in play, and they have undergone such constant evolution, that there is an inevitable arbitrariness in talking of this monetarism, that monetarism or the other monetarism. Despite the difficulties, a short description of British monetarism is ventured in the next section. No precise definition is given of American monetarism, but Friedman's work and Mayer's book on the structure of monetarism are taken as broadly representative.[2] In the following four sections contrasts are drawn between British monetarism and American monetarism. The tensions between them were reflected in a number of per-plexities which are critical to understanding the decline and fall of mon-etarism in UK policy formation in the mid-1980s. The final section therefore discusses, among other things, the corrosive impact of certain dis-tinctively Chicagoan beliefs on the staying power of British monetarism in the policy debate.

It would be wrong to give the impression that there was a bitter transat-lantic intellectual duel. The divergence between British and American mon-etarism certainly did not reflect a controversy as intense or long-standing as that between monetarism and Keynesianism. However, there were points of contact between the two debates. Perhaps it is not surprising, in view of the range of his work, that Keynes himself touched on several of the topics which have subsequently been disputed between American and British monetarists. As we shall see, the relationship between his views and the Anglo-American monetary disagreements of the 1980s turns out to be complex and ambivalent.

I

The opening months of 1980, coinciding with the introduction of the Medium-Term Financial Strategy, have already been mentioned as a period of particular confidence in the virtues of monetary policy. Two official documents prepared at the time may be regarded as defining statements of British monetarism. The first is the March 1980 Green Paper on *Monetary Control*, which was the joint work of the Treasury and the Bank of England; the second is the *Memorandum on Monetary Policy* prepared by the Treasury for the Treasury and Civil Service Committee in June 1980.[3]

The focus of both documents was a target for the growth of broad money, measured by sterling M3. Sterling M3 consisted of notes and coin and nearly all deposit liabilities of the banking system. (Certificates of deposit [CDs] were included, but both deposits and CDs with an original term to maturity of over two years were excluded. Sterling M3 was renamed M3 in May 1987.) Sterling M3 was not monitored for its own sake, but as an intermediate target thought to have a definite – if rather elusive – rela-tionship with the ultimate target of inflation. The government's faith in this relationship was expressed strongly in the Treasury's *Memorandum on Monetary Policy*. While conceding that the mechanisms linking money and prices change over time and space, the *Memorandum* insisted that 'the proposition that prices must ultimately respond to monetary control holds whatever the adjustment process in the shorter term may be'.[4] An accom-panying note on 'The stability of the income velocity of circulation of money supply' stated that, although velocity had fluctuated in the previous 17 years, 'at times quite sharply', there appeared to be 'a clear tendency for the series to return to the underlying trend'.[5]

If the monetary targets were to be achieved, it was essential to understand what caused monetary expansion. The favoured account of the money supply process gave pride of place to bank credit. With the deposit liabilities of the banking system representing the greater part of broad money, it was logical to attempt to limit the growth of bank assets. Since the growth of bank assets depended on the extension of new credit to the public, private and overseas sectors, monetary control was guided by an analysis of the so-called 'credit counterparts'. More specifically, the authorities used a credit counterparts identity which set out the relationship between, on the one hand, the public sector borrowing requirement, sales of public sector debt to non-banks, bank lending to the private sector and a variety of external and other influences, and, on the other hand, the growth of broad money.[6]

The chosen approach to managing monetary growth was therefore to operate on the credit counterparts. Bank credit to the public sector could be influenced by varying the PSBR and the amount of public debt sold to non-banks; bank credit to the private sector was thought to be responsive to changes in interest rates; and bank credit to the overseas sector was related to intervention tactics on the foreign exchanges.[7] In this spirit, the Green Paper on *Monetary Control* began with the observation that: 'There are a number of policy instruments available to the authorities in influencing monetary conditions. Of these the main ones are fiscal policy, debt management, administered changes in short-term interest rates, direct controls on the financial system and operations in the foreign exchange markets'.[8]

Officials at the Treasury and the Bank of England had few illusions about the precision of monetary management by these means. Indeed, there was an uneasy slide from the use of the ambitious words 'control' in the title of the Green Paper to the more modest notion of 'influence' in the key opening paragraph. Nevertheless, the authorities were confident that, with their 'basic weapons', they could 'achieve the first requisite of control of the money supply – control, say, over a year or more'.[9]

Restraint over the budget deficit was seen as integral to monetary control over such annual periods. At Budget time a careful assessment was made of the consistency of the PSBR estimate with the broad money target, and the tendency of policy was to subordinate fiscal decision to the monetary targets. (As explained above on p. 119, the PSBR was renamed 'the public sector net cash requirement' [or PSNCR] in 1997.) In the early 1980s the humbling of fiscal policy was regarded as almost revolutionary, since it appeared to end the Keynesian demand-management role traditionally assigned to the government in post-war British political economy. The intention was not to vary the PSBR to counter cyclical ups and downs in the economy, but to ensure – in the words of the Treasury *Memorandum* – that 'the trend path' of the PSBR be 'downwards'.[10]

If the authorities were sceptical about their ability to target broad money over short-run periods of a few months, the government was reluctant to make exact predictions about how long it would take for inflation to respond to monetary restraint. The emphasis was very much on the medium-term nature of the commitment to monetary targets. It was readily conceded that a check to broad money this year would be followed by slower inflation not in the immediate future, but in two, three or perhaps even four years' time. This was, of course, consistent with the belief that the relationship between broad money and inflation was medium-term in character. One consideration thought particularly likely to confuse the money/inflation link in the UK was the influence of a powerful trade union movement on wages and prices. This influence was sometimes regarded as having autonomy from strictly economic variables, such as the state of demand and the level of unemployment. The size of the public sector, and its insensitivity to monetary conditions, was a special problem.[11]

To ask what Keynes would have thought about British monetarism, in its 1980 version, may seem an ahistorical impertinence. However, it is not far-fetched to see similarities between the system of monetary management envisaged by the Thatcher government in its early years and the idea of a managed currency advocated by Keynes throughout his life. Indeed, in one particularly interesting respect they coincided. The proposal for a managed currency was first made in *A Tract on Monetary Reform* (published in 1923), which was intended as a reasoned polemic against the gold standard. It contrasted the gold standard ('a barbarous relic') focusing on the stability of foreign exchange, and a managed currency ('a more scientific standard') with its goal of 'stability in an index number of prices'.[12] A preference for domestic price stability over a fixed exchange rate was also embodied in the Medium-Term Financial Strategy, as originally formulated. In the 1981 Mais lecture Sir Geoffrey Howe, the Chancellor of the Exchequer, remarked that, if monetary targets had been adopted, 'you cannot have it both ways and also hold the exchange rate at a particular level. If any inconsistency emerges, the monetary targets have to come first'.[13] In accordance with this prescription exchange intervention was minimal for several years in the early 1980s.

In summary, British monetarism could be said to have four distinctive features: (1) the selection of broad money as the appropriate intermediate target, and a consequent emphasis on the control of bank credit as the central task of monetary management; (2) as part of the overall control of credit, a belief that fiscal policy should be made consistent with monetary policy and lose the demand-management functions attributed to it in the 1960s and early 1970s; (3) an admission that the link between money and inflation was medium-term in nature and difficult to predict, partly because of the strength of British trade unionism; and (4) the avoidance of any specific exchange rate objective, for reasons which Keynes would probably have understood and approved.

II

The first area of disagreement between British and American monetarism lay in the relative emphasis placed on broad and narrow money, and in related questions about the implementation of monetary control. As we have explained, in Britain in the early 1980s broad money was the focus of policy-makers' attention. Although Friedman himself believed that all measures of money conveyed a valuable message (and had blessed broad money in the classic *A Monetary History of the United States* he wrote jointly with Anna Schwartz), there is no doubt that the majority of American monetarists favoured the monetary base or a narrow money aggregate as the best policy indicator. According to Mayer, the monetary base was chosen for two reasons. One was that the American monetarist's 'analysis of the money supply process' told him that this was 'the variable which best reflect[ed] monetary policy actions'; the other was that he believed 'the monetary base to be the best indicator of future changes in the money stock'.[14] Both aspects of Mayer's statement are important and need to be discussed, but to understand them a sketch of the American monetarists' view of the money supply process is required.

American monetarists, like their British counterparts, normally included bank deposits in their definition of the money supply.[15] Since banks (in the 1980s and now) have to be able to repay deposits with cash, they are obliged to hold a fraction of their assets in the form of cash or balances with the central bank. According to American monetarism, empirical investigation was said to demonstrate a reasonably stable ratio between cash and deposits over the long run, while the quantity of cash – a liability of the central bank – was fully under the monetary authorities' control. It was therefore claimed that changes in the quantity of cash, reflecting central bank operations, determined the level of bank deposits and, hence, of the money supply. Cash (that is, notes, coin and balances with the central bank) is also known as 'high-powered money', the 'monetary base' or the 'reserve base'. Economists who believed in this account of the money supply process tended also to favour deliberate variations in the quantity of cash as the main instrument of monetary policy. This system, known as monetary base control, was widely advocated by American monetarists. (A version of monetary base control was indeed implemented, briefly and rather reluctantly, by the Federal Reserve in a three-year experiment from 1979 to 1982.)

The first part of Mayer's statement is therefore readily explained. Changes in the monetary base were taken, by American monetarists, as the clearest guide to what the central bank had been doing, and so to the intended thrust of monetary policy. It is clear – from the previous section – that the approach of British monetarists was quite different. With bank deposits viewed as the counterpart to bank credit, British monetarists concentrated their attention on variables believed to be relevant to the behaviour of bank credit. By far the most important of these was the short-term rate of interest, set by Bank of England operations in the money market. The contrast with the American monetarist position, with its concern over the quantity of reserves rather than the price at which they were made available to the banking system, was radical. Moreover, whereas in British monetarism the level of bank lending to the private sector was seen as critical to the monetary outlook, American monetarists were largely indifferent to it.

Some doctrinal purists might protest at this stage that a preference for the interest rate over the monetary base cannot plausibly be attributed to monetarists of any kind, not even to 'British monetarists'. They might say that, if that is the implication of the definition of British monetarism given here, the definition is too idiosyncratic and peculiar to be taken seriously. The answer to this objection is to recall the pattern of public debate in the early 1980s. The official policy framework prevailing at that time, and the attitudes informing it, were labelled as 'monetarist' in the media, in Parliament and in many other contexts. Furthermore, its emphasis on broad money and the credit counterparts arithmetic did logically entail that close attention be paid to interest rates. Of course, to say that interest rates mattered was not to make them a target of policy. On the contrary, the intention was that interest rates (the instrument) were to be varied to influence credit and money (the intermediate targets) in order to exert leverage over the inflation rate (the ultimate target).

American reaction to monetary control procedures in Britain varied from technical puzzlement to frank outrage. A consequence of the British arrangements was that official sales of gilt-edged securities to non-banks often had to be stepped up in order to reduce the excessive quantity of deposits created by bank credit. In other words, long-term funding was a basic instrument of monetary policy. An official at the Federal Reserve Bank of New York remarked at a conference in May 1982 that this 'emphasis on selling intermediate and long-term securities to mop up money balances always sounds a bit strange to us'.[16] Friedman's comments to the Treasury and Civil Service Committee in 1980 were much sharper. He expressed incredulity at the opening paragraph of the Green Paper on *Monetary Control*. In his view: 'Only a Rip Van Winkle, who had not read any of the flood of literature during the past decade and more on the money supply process, could possibly have written' the key sentence with its list of instruments for influencing monetary conditions. He judged that: 'This remarkable sentence reflects the myopia engendered by long-established practices, the difficulty we all have of adjusting our outlook to changed circumstances.' He declared strong support for direct control of the monetary base instead of the British system.[17]

The dismay that many American monetarists felt – and still do feel – about the Bank of England's monetary control procedures did not go unnoticed in the UK. Several economists advocated that Britain adopt some form of monetary base control. The most notable were Professor Brian Griffiths of the City University (later to be head of the Prime Minister's Policy Unit at 10 Downing Street), Professor Patrick Minford of Liverpool University and Professor (later Sir) Alan Walters who was appointed the Prime Minister's Economic Adviser in 1981. As all three are British and have been called monetarists, it may seem odd that in this paper 'British monetarism' is associated with broad money, credit control and funding. It perhaps needs to be repeated that British monetarism is defined here as the system of macroeconomic management established in the late 1970s and early 1980s, not a set of beliefs held by self-professed monetarist economists. In the end the views of Minford and Walters became important as much because they challenged the existing policy framework as because they supported it.

What about the second part of Mayer's statement, that American monetarists followed the monetary base because it was 'the best indicator of future changes in the money stock'? It may or may not be true that the monetary base had this property in the USA. (Much depends on the economists and technical econometric papers one decides to trust.) But in the UK, where the institutional apparatus is different, the monetary base is not – and for several decades has not been – a reliable guide to future changes in the money stock on any definition. Under the British arrangements the Bank of England supplies cash in the required amounts to keep banks' balances at the daily clearing just adequate for them to fulfil their obligations.[18] In consequence, the quantity of cash held by the banks adjusts to the size of their balance sheets rather than the other way round. The monetary base is – and long has been – determined by what is happening in the economy today; it does not determine what banks, the money stock or the economy will do in future.[19] Indeed, one of the remarkable features of the British system is that – because of the flexibility of official money market operations – the banks can keep very low ratios of cash reserves to deposit liabilities. Since cash does not pay interest, this feature is attractive to profit-seeking overseas bankers. (In the 1980s this was one reason for the intensity of foreign competition in the British financial system. Since then other countries have also reduced banks' cash reserve requirements and the scale of the UK's relative advantage has diminished.)

American economists did not appear fully to understand either the method of operation or the purpose of the British practices. The same Federal Reserve official who was puzzled by the significance of funding in the UK was also 'struck by the minimal role that reserve requirements play in the monetary control process'. He wondered whether 'the amount of leverage available' was 'sufficiently large for the central bank to pursue monetary and other policy targets effectively in all seasons'.[20] But the point of the British system was that – in contrast to the situation in the USA – the quantity of cash reserves was not supposed to exert any leverage on the monetary targets. In his evidence to the Treasury and Civil Service Committee Friedman proposed some reforms which he thought would tighten the link between the base and the money supply. He noted that, in 1981, banks could hold a variety of assets to meet reserve requirements in the UK and suggested that:

> It would be highly desirable to replace this multiple reserve system by one in which only a single asset – liabilities of the Bank of England in the form of notes and coin (that is, base money) – satisfies reserve requirements. This is probably the most important single change in current institutional arrangements that is required to permit more effective control of the money supply.[21]

But Friedman was confused between a 12½ per cent reserve asset ratio which served an essentially prudential function and a 1½ per cent cash ratio which was the operational fulcrum of monetary policy. Since the confusion was shared to some degree by British economists and officials, it was perhaps excusable. But Friedman's imperceptiveness on the question reflected a wide gap between American and British approaches to monetary management and undoubtedly symptomized a certain amount of mutual incomprehension.

The differences between central bank techniques in the UK and USA are not new, but can be dated back to the early years of the Federal Reserve System. Unlike some recent participants in the debate, Keynes was well aware of their nature and origins, and devoted many pages of his *Treatise on Money* (published in 1930) to their analysis. He drew a contrast between 'the bank-rate policy' applied in Britain and the 'open-market policy' adopted in the USA. Essentially, the bank-rate policy involved a varying bank rate in order to control 'the aggregate of the central bank's assets', whereas open-market operations of the American kind produced 'a direct effect on the reserves of the member banks, and hence on the volume of deposits and of credit generally'.[22] Although Keynes saw some merits in a bank-rate policy, it is quite clear that he preferred an open-market policy. He expressed great admiration for Governor Strong of the Federal Reserve, whom he regarded as the pioneer of scientific open-market operations, remarking that:

> open-market operations can be so handled as to be quite extraordinarily effective in managing the currency. The successful management of the dollar by the Federal Reserve i.e. from 1923 to 1928 was a triumph – for the view that currency management is feasible, in conditions which are virtually independent of the movements of gold.[23]

The sympathy here for the American approach connects with some of his later themes, since he also considered that, 'whilst the bank rate may be the most suitable weapon for use when the object of the central bank is to preserve international equilibrium, open-market sales and purchase of securities may be more effective when the object is to influence the rate of investment'.[24] This fitted in neatly with Keynes's emphasis in *The General Theory* on the need to influence investment in order to mitigate fluctuations in output and employment.

However, it should be noted that in *The General Theory* Keynes says rather little about central bank techniques and almost nothing about the Federal Reserve. There is a short comment, in the 'Notes on the trade cycle' in chapter 22, about how 'the most enlightened monetary control might find itself in difficulties, faced with a boom of the 1929 type in America, and armed with no other weapons than those possessed at the time by the Federal Reserve System'.[25] But that is all. The implication seems to be that the severity of the American slump in the early 1930s, particularly by comparison with the mildness of the contemporaneous downturn in Britain, undermined the prestige of the Federal Reserve's procedures. Nevertheless, it is reasonable to conclude that – in this area of the technicalities of monetary control – Keynes inclined more towards American monetarism than British. In qualification, it also needs to be said that throughout this work Keynes referred repeatedly, and with evident belief in its importance, to 'credit', while in virtually all his discussions about monetary practice he was concerned about the behaviour of bank deposits and so of broad money. The focus on broad money was particularly obvious in his distinctions between income, business and savings deposits, and between industrial and financial 'circulations', in the first volume of the *Treatise on Money*.[26]

III

Basic to the Medium-Term Financial Strategy, and indeed to the monetarist enterprise in Britain more generally, was control over the fiscal position. Recognition of the importance of restricting public sector borrowing can be dated back to the mid-1970s, when extremely large budget deficits had been accompanied by difficulties in controlling the money supply and by fears that the substantial demands made by the public sector on the savings pool were crowding out private sector investment. Targets for the PSBR were included in the International Monetary Fund's Letter of Intent in December 1976, which set out conditions for its loan to the UK. In his speech to the Lord Mayor's dinner on 19 October 1978, Denis Healey – as Chancellor of the Exchequer in the then Labour government – said that the government was 'determined to control the growth of public expenditure so that its fiscal policy is consistent with its monetary stance'.[27] The stipulation of precise numbers for the PSBR in the Medium-Term Financial Strategy from 1980 onwards should not be seen as a surprise innovation, but as the logical culmination to events over several years.

The thinking behind this approach was implicit in the credit counterparts arithmetic. If bank lending to the private sector, external influences on money growth and public sector debt sales to non-banks were all given, there was – and, of course, still is – a direct accounting link between the PSBR/PSNCR and the growth of the money supply. For every £100 million of extra PSBR there was an extra £100 million of M3. If an excessive PSBR threatened the monetary target, high interest rates would be needed to discourage lending to the private sector or encourage more buying of public sector debt. According to Peter Middleton (later to become Sir Peter and also Permanent Secretary to the Treasury), in a seminar paper given in the 1977/78 academic year, 'as a general proposition, a big fiscal deficit will tend to lead to a rapid growth of money supply and/or to higher interest rates . . . It follows that it is essential to examine fiscal and monetary policy simultaneously and coordinate them as far as practicable.'[28]

This relationship between flows of public sector borrowing and the growth of the money supply can be easily reformulated in terms of the stocks of public sector debt, bank lending to the private sector and money.[29] The main conclusion is that, if the ratios of public debt and bank lending to gross domestic product are constant, a higher ratio of the PSBR to GDP is associated with a higher growth rate of broad money and so with more inflation. In practice, ratios of public sector debt and bank lending to GDP fluctuate substantially over time. But it is plausible that a government committed to extensive privatization of productive assets would favour, over the medium term, a rising ratio of private sector bank borrowing to

GDP, rather than a high ratio of public debt to GDP. In the early 1980s that implied a need for the PSBR/GDP ratio to be maintained at a low level for several years.

What about the American monetarists' attitude towards fiscal policy? In the late 1960s there was a fierce debate in the USA – known as the 'Battle of the Radio Stations' after the initials of the main researchers involved (AM, FM, for Ando–Modigliani, Friedman–Meiselman) – about the relative effectiveness of fiscal and monetary policy.[30] Arguably, it was the starting point of monetarism. Not only did it prompt Professor Karl Brunner to coin the term 'monetarist', but also it revolved around the idea – later to become a commonplace in the British policy debate – that discretionary changes in fiscal policy were misguided as a means of influencing the economy.

In view of this background, American monetarists might reasonably have been expected to welcome the demotion of fiscal policy in the Medium-Term Financial Strategy. Curiously, that was not the reaction. Friedman, in his evidence to the Treasury and Civil Service Committee, said that the attention paid to the PSBR targets was 'unwise', partly 'because there is no necessary relation between the size of the PSBR and monetary growth'.[31] Friedman's remarks were picked up by British critics of monetarism, notably by the Oxford economist, Christopher Allsopp, who was emboldened to claim that: 'The standard monetarist line is that it is only the money supply that matters for inflation control, and that fiscal policy has little direct effect on the economy, or on the ease or difficulty of controlling money.'[32] Although Friedman may have been particularly forthright in denigrating the place of PSBR control in British monetarism, there is no doubt that most American monetarists did not integrate fiscal policy into their thinking and policy advice. Thus a prescription for fiscal policy does not figure in Mayer's list of key monetarist propositions. The explanation might perhaps be sought in the separation of powers between the Federal Reserve (responsible for monetary policy) and the Treasury (which, along with other agencies, controls the Budget) in the American system. For these institutional reasons it made less sense to attempt to co-ordinate fiscal and monetary policy in the American macroeconomic context than in the British.

IV

There was never any pretence in British monetarism that x per cent growth of broad money over the next year would be followed by an exactly predictable y per cent growth of money GDP at an exactly known date in the future. It was readily admitted that the link between money and inflation was imprecise, while there were no illusions that the impact of monetary restraint on inflation would assert itself – or even be identifiable – over periods of time as short as three to six months. Instead, the connection between broad money and the price level was regarded as rather difficult to forecast and essentially medium-term in nature. When British monetarism was at its most influential, policy-makers probably thought in terms of an x per cent rate of broad money growth leading to an inflation rate of x plus or minus 2 or 3 per cent at some date two to four years away. That may sound too flimsy as a basis for decision-taking; but it is vital to remember the context in which British monetarism first made headway in the public debate. In the mid-1970s, when the inflation rate was frequently at about 20 per cent or more, politicians were less fussy about an annual error in forecasting inflation equivalent to 2 or 3 per cent of the index than they are in the early twenty-first century. Moreover, in the early 1980s there was little respect for computer-based macroeconomic forecasting methods which aspired to great exactitude. Such methods had totally failed to predict the scale of the inflationary retribution for the monetary policy mistakes of the Heath–Barber period.

American monetarists also refused to make bold claims about the precision of monetary impacts on the economy. Friedman coined an often repeated phrase when he said that the relationship between money and inflation was marked by 'long and variable lags'. In his evidence to the Treasury and Civil Service Committee, he cautioned that 'failure to allow for lags in reaction is a major source of misunderstanding'. After suggesting that 'for the US, the UK and Japan, the lag between a change in monetary growth and output is roughly six to nine months, between the change in monetary growth and inflation, roughly two years', he immediately inserted the qualification that, 'of course, the effects are spread out, not concentrated at the indicated point of time'.[33] Arguably, this reluctance to be specific reflected an aspect of monetarism highlighted by Mayer, a preference for small reduced-form models over large-scale structural models of the economy. According to Mayer, monetarists believed that the money supply affected the economy in so many ways that 'even a large structural model is not likely to pick them all up'.[34]

The differences between American and British monetarists in this area may not, therefore, seem to be all that wide. Keynes also recognized, although with reservations, the medium- and long-term validity of the money/inflation link. In chapter 21 of *The General Theory*, he said that the question of the relationship between money and prices outside the short period is 'for historical generalizations rather than for pure theory'. He continued by observing that, if liquidity preference (that is, the demand for money) tends to be uniform over the long run, 'there may well be some sort of rough relationship between the national income and the quantity of money required to satisfy liquidity preference, taken as a mean over periods of pessimism and optimism together'.[35] This is an interesting quotation because it shows that Keynes never dismissed the relevance of money to the long-run behaviour of prices, not even after the refinement of his theoretical ideas on the short-run determination of output in *The General Theory*. However, the section which contains the quotation also makes several references to wages and productivity as fundamental influences on prices. Keynes may have been reluctant to give a wholehearted endorsement to either a monetary or a wage-bargaining theory of the price level. Perhaps he thought that both had something to say.

Keynes's equivocation on the subject may have reflected the central position of the trade unions in British society. A strong and influential trade union movement continued for most of the first 50 or so years from the publication of *The General Theory* and obliged economists in the UK to pay trade unionism more attention than their counterparts in the USA. Not surprisingly, therefore, greater anxiety in the UK about the trade unions' impact on the labour market and the economy differentiated American and British monetarism, although the differences were more matters of emphasis than of substance. British monetarists were more prone to claim that trade unions, by disrupting the setting of market-clearing wages, aggravated the problem of unemployment. This argument was integrated into a specifically monetarist framework by saying that trade union activity increased the natural rate of unemployment. The point was that, in a situation such as the UK's where there had traditionally been strong political pressures to reduce unemployment below the natural rate, inflation expectations were contaminated by occasional phases of excess demand. As long periods of unemployment above the natural rate were then needed to remove the inflationary virus, and as these always involved restrictive and unpopular monetary policies, trade union activism indirectly stigmatized the deliberate use of monetary policy. British monetarists therefore accorded trade unions a more prominent and active role in the inflationary process than American monetarists.[36]

Friedman's position on the trade unions was that they could alter relative wages (that is, the ratio between union and non-union wages), but could not influence the absolute level of wages (that is, union and non-union wages combined) which was determined by, among other things, the money supply. Moreover, a given amount of trade union power could not explain continuing inflation. When asked at an Institute of Economic Affairs lecture in 1974 whether trade unions could increase the natural rate of unemployment, Friedman acknowledged that this was 'a very difficult question to answer', but reiterated that 'what produced . . . inflation is not trade unions, nor monopolistic employers, but what happens to the quantity of money'.[37]

The problem posed by trade unionism for British monetarism was exacerbated by the dominance of trade unionism in the public sector. While there are reasonably obvious transmission mechanisms between monetary policy and private sector inflation, it is far from evident how monetary policy affects the public sector. Wages and prices in government and nationalized industries are typically set by administrative fiat, and are sometimes remote from market forces. One exercise on the demand for money in the UK recognized this by regressing the money supply on private sector GDP, not GDP as a whole.[38] It did not occur to American monetarists – with the USA's small government sector and weaker trade unions – to be so fastidious.

V

The British economy also differed (and still differs) from the American in being smaller and more susceptible to international influences. Since this difference made British monetarists more concerned about external pressures on domestic monetary policy than their American counterparts, it stimulated a lively debate about the appropriateness of alternative exchange rate regimes. This debate has continued over many decades, with Keynes's argument for a managed currency in *A Tract on Monetary Reform* being one of the most seminal contributions. Indeed, it could be claimed that when Sir Geoffrey Howe expressed such a decided preference for monetary targets over a fixed exchange rate in 1981 he was echoing a famous passage in the *Tract* where Keynes set up an opposition between stability of prices and stability of exchange. In his words, 'If the external price level is unstable, we cannot keep both our own price level and our exchanges stable. And we are compelled to choose'.[39]

In the mid-1970s, however, Mr Healey failed to choose one or the other. Some interest rate changes were motivated by external factors, some by domestic considerations and some by both. The result was rather unhappy not just intellectually, but also practically, with 1976 seeing the most prolonged and embarrassing sterling crisis in the post-war period. The monetarist commitment to floating exchange rates in the early 1980s can be interpreted largely as a reaction to the muddles of the first three years of Mr Healey's Chancellorship. But a number of key theoretical inputs also moulded the climate of opinion and need to be mentioned. They can be dated back to the late 1960s, when leading economic journalists – egged on by Professor Harry Johnson of the University of Chicago and the London

School of Economics – thought that the abandonment of a fixed exchange rate would remove an artificial barrier to British economic growth. More immediately relevant in the late 1970s was work done by Laidler and Parkin at the Manchester Inflation Workshop.[40]

An episode in late 1977 is basic to understanding the clarity of the monetarist support for a floating exchange rate in 1980 and 1981. After the excessive depreciation of 1976 the pound revived in 1977, and for much of the year its rise was restrained by heavy official intervention on the foreign exchanges. (The Bank of England sold pounds and bought dollars, to prevent the value of the pound rising.) This intervention had the effect of boosting the money supply, which in consequence grew much faster than envisaged by the official target. The target was for an increase of 9 to 13 per cent in sterling M3 in the 1977/78 financial year, whereas the actual result was an increase of 15.1 per cent. Monetarist economists argued that the high monetary growth jeopardized the financial progress achieved under the International Monetary Fund programmes and that, after the usual lag, it would be punished by higher inflation. More conventional economists at the Treasury and elsewhere thought that a 'low' exchange rate was needed for reasons of export competitiveness. The debate was conducted at several levels and is reported to have been particularly intense within the official machine.

When the government stopped intervening and allowed the pound to float upwards in October 1977, the monetarists seemed to have won. But their victory was not final. Although they were vindicated by a sharp upturn in inflation in late 1979 and early 1980 (after a fairly standard Friedmanite two-year lag), there were constant complaints that the government's permissive attitude towards the exchange rate allowed undue exchange rate appreciation. Among the most active participants to the 1977 debate were economists at the London Business School. On the whole they favoured adhering to the money supply targets and allowing the exchange rate to float. A particularly notable contribution was made by Mr Terry (later Lord) Burns, who was to become the government's Chief Economic Adviser in January 1980.[41]

The views of British monetarists in the late 1970s and early 1980s on the choice of exchange rate regime were not radically different from those of their American counterparts. One of the classic statements on the merits of floating was given by Friedman in his 1950 paper on 'The case for flexible exchange rates'.[42] This paper was perfunctory in its treatment of the impact of foreign exchange intervention on money growth, which was basic to the UK debate in the late 1970s. But its mood, with its aspersions on the forecasting ability of central bank officials and its praise for market forces, was close to that of the Thatcher government in its early years. In his evidence to the Treasury and Civil Service Committee in 1980, Friedman said that 'of course' an attempt to manipulate the exchange rate would limit the authorities' ability to control the money supply. He also criticized the government's announced policy of preventing excessive fluctuations in the exchange rate. In his opinion, 'this exception is a mistake; better to leave the market entirely free . . . certainly for such a broad and efficient market as exists in British sterling'.[43]

As it happened, the government in 1980 and early 1981 did not make an exception, even for a patently excessive fluctuation in the exchange rate. The pound became seriously overvalued, reaching $2.42 in October 1980 compared to $1.63 in October 1976, and in February 1981 almost 5 to the Deutschmark compared with 4 one year earlier. These exchange rate oscillations were subsequently singled out as the principal policy disappointment of the monetarist experiment. Inevitably, there has been much soul-searching about the suitability of monetary targets in a small economy subject to all the volatilities of contemporary international finance. It is interesting that Keynes, when describing the alternatives of price stability and exchange stability in the *Tract*, conceded that the right choice must 'partly depend on the relative importance of foreign trade in the economic life of the country'.[44] Indeed, the book's final paragraph suggested that 'there are probably no countries, other than Great Britain and the United States, which would be justified in attempting to set up an independent standard'. Other countries could decide to peg their currencies to either sterling or the dollar until, 'with the progress of knowledge and understanding, so perfect a harmony had been established between the two that the choice was a matter of indifference'.[45]

VI

The period of strong monetarist influence over policy-making was short-lived, although its precise length is a matter for discussion and depends on whose version of events one selects. At one extreme it has been argued that broad money targets were discredited in July 1980 when the abolition of the 'corset' was followed by a jump of over 5 per cent in sterling M3 in only one month. (The corset was an artificial device for restricting credit, which imposed penalties on banks when their balance sheets increased faster than given percentage figures.) Officials quickly realized that the original sterling M3 target for the year to March 1981, which was for growth of between 7 and 11 per cent, was unattainable. They therefore sought forms of words to explain away – and, as far as possible, divert attention from – a serious monetary overshoot. In the end sterling M3 rose by 19.4 per cent in the

1980/81 target period. This wide divergence from target, combined with the apparent failure of high interest rates to bring M3 back under control, is said by some authors to have caused monetarism to be abandoned only a few months after it had been publicly proclaimed as official dogma.[46]

However, a more plausible account would treat the erosion of the system set up in early 1980 as a gradual process. There are various possibilities, but mid-1985 is probably best regarded as the terminal phase. It was then that broad money targets, and hence the defining features of British monetarism, were scrapped. Just as monetarism did not gain ground by a simple process of intellectual conquest, so it did not retreat through a straightforward failure to meet key practical tests. Instead there were a number of distinct and intermittent challenges to monetarist arrangements. Although none of them individually might have been decisive, their cumulative impact was difficult to resist.

The first major problem was the pound's clear overvaluation in late 1980 and early 1981. The reasons for sterling's appreciation have been much debated, but one thesis – that above-target broad money growth obliged the government to maintain high interest rates, and high interest rates drove up the sterling exchange rate – had obvious cogency and relevance. As we have seen, both Sir Geoffrey Howe and Keynes had argued, in their different ways, that 'you cannot have it both ways', and simultaneously control the domestic price level and the exchange rate. But the experience of 1980 and 1981 suggested that Britain should try to have it both ways. It was better to have an intellectually muddled monetary policy than a politically unacceptable industrial recession. In 1982 and 1983 official thinking was that the exchange rate should have some role in assessing monetary conditions, while the monetary targets should be retained. After severe exchange rate overvaluation had caused a drastic fall in industrial production between mid-1980 and mid-1981, the government was less concerned about the logical niceties of the matter than about avoiding further damage to the manufacturing base.

The second difficulty was that sterling M3 proved awkward to manage. The 1980 Green Paper on *Monetary Control* may not have been particularly optimistic about month-by-month control, but at least it thought that sterling M3 could be brought within target 'over a year or more'. The large overshoot in 1980/81 undermined the credibility of even that rather unambitious statement. When there was another overshoot in the 1981/82 financial year, with sterling M3 up by 13 per cent compared to a target range of 6 to 10 per cent, many economists agreed with the then chief Opposition spokesman on Treasury and economic affairs, Peter Shore, that sterling M3 had become 'a wayward mistress'. There was a widely held view that sterling M3 was no longer a reliable intermediate target and that policy should be stated more flexibly. For those who still favoured monetary targets in some form, the disappointments with M3 targeting implied that monetary base control deserved more sympathetic consideration. The disillusionment with broad money was accompanied by increased interest in narrow money, either in the monetary base itself (also known as 'M0') or in M1 (cash in circulation with the public, plus sight deposits).

These changes in official allegiances and informed opinion, away from money targets to the exchange rate and from broad money to narrow money, were largely determined by the pattern of events. But intellectual rationalization was not far behind. A key figure in the dethronement of sterling M3 was Sir Alan Walters. Although his credentials when appointed as the Prime Minister's Economic Adviser in 1981 were avowedly 'monetarist', his monetarism was different in character from the 'British monetarism' described here. He had been much influenced by the American enthusiasm for monetary base control and was doubtful about the merits of operating on the credit counterparts to achieve broad money targets. His preference was for a measure of money used in transactions, which he thought was best approximated in the UK's case by M1. Despite problems because of institutional change, he believed that, 'It is money in this transactions sense that plays the central role in the theoretical structure and the propositions of monetarism'. He judged that credit had 'but a minor role' and was correspondingly sceptical about 'such credit magnitudes as M3'. (However, the Alan Walters of the mid-1980s was different from the Alan Walters of the early 1970s. He had been critical of the explosion of *broad* money during the boom of the early 1970s, emphasizing a connection between it and rapid asset price inflation.)[47]

A consequence of the demotion of broad money was that less concern was felt about the rapid growth of credit in the private sector. Indeed, there was a school of thought – best represented by the Liverpool Research Group under Professor Patrick Minford – that bank lending to the private sector was always good for the economy, since it made possible more private sector spending and investment. High levels of lending were therefore welcomed, irrespective of the monetary repercussions. In some of its publications this group also suggested that large increases in broad money contained no inflationary threat. According to one issue of its *Quarterly Economic Bulletin*, credit – even credit in the form of bank lending – cannot be inflationary. Its argument was that, since borrowing by some individuals must be accompanied by lending by others, there is no net addition to or subtraction from wealth, and there should be no effect on behaviour. Thus, when both sides of a balance sheet increase: 'This is a straightforward portfolio adjustment and is not inflationary.'[48] Professor Minford, like Sir Alan Walters, had been much influenced by the American literature. As a reflection of this background, he regarded narrow money (particularly M0) as the most trustworthy money supply indicator and favoured monetary base control.

By 1983 and 1984 the views of Walters and Minford had been important in undermining the original monetarist arrangements. These arrangements suffered most from policy surprises and disappointments, and from criticisms from non-monetarist or frankly anti-monetarist economists. But the willingness of the two economists carrying the 'monetarist' label to repudiate certain aspects of the existing policy framework reinforced the suspicion and distrust with which British monetarism had always been viewed by the press, Whitehall and the majority of academic economists. Since Walters and Minford had undoubtedly been keen students of monetarist thought coming from the other side of the Atlantic, their susceptibility to its teachings meant that American monetarism contributed – if somewhat indirectly – to the decline of British monetarism.[49]

In another respect, however, Walters and Minford were loyal to the policy structure envisaged in 1979 and 1980. Although Walters promoted a 1981 report by Jurg Niehans, which identified sterling's sharp appreciation as a symptom of monetary tightness, he was adamantly opposed to attempts to manage the exchange rate by foreign exchange intervention. He wanted policy to be geared towards domestic monetary objectives and not towards the preservation of a fixed exchange rate or a target exchange-rate band. Indeed, he thought that these conditions still 'broadly' applied to the UK in 1985 when he wrote, in *Britain's Economic Renaissance*, that: 'The authorities announce that the level of short-term interest rates will depend primarily on the assessment of the movement in the monetary aggregates. The exchange rate is to be the object of benign neglect.'[50] Minford was equally hostile to systematic foreign-exchange intervention. In a paper first presented in 1980, he took it for granted that an 'independent monetary policy is possible' and noted that this 'presupposition is only valid under floating exchange rates'.[51]

Unlike the tendency to play down the significance of credit and broad money, the increasing official preoccupation with the exchange rate in the early and mid-1980s therefore cannot be ascribed to pressure from Walters and Minford, or to the influence of American monetarist ideas. In the end it was the completeness of the shift in official priorities from domestic monetary control to exchange rate stability which was primarily responsible for monetarism's downfall. Although several official statements had already hinted at the precedence of exchange rate stability as a policy goal, the Plaza Accord of September 1985 may have been the key turning-point. At the Plaza meeting the finance ministers of the five leading industrial nations decided that in future they should co-operate more actively to achieve an appropriate pattern of exchange rates. Thereafter the Chancellor of the Exchequer, Nigel Lawson, was constantly mindful of this international responsibility and gave less attention to domestic monetary issues.

Other considerations, more local and humdrum, pointed policy in the same direction. The standard British practice of long-term funding, which had so bewildered Federal Reserve officials in 1982, was beginning to cause technical problems in the UK's short-term money markets by mid-1985. The authorities decided that they could no longer 'overfund' the PSBR in order to keep broad money on target. Without this technique, which had proved immensely useful as a means of curbing the growth of the monetary aggregates, there were likely to be great difficulties meeting broad money targets.[52] In addition to all the other supposed weaknesses of broad money, sterling M3 was now condemned for complicating the management of the money markets. In his Mansion House speech on 17 October 1985 Lawson suspended the broad money target for the 1985/86 financial year.

This was effectively the end of British monetarism. Although ostensibly only 'suspended', broad money targets had in fact been abandoned. A broad money target was announced in the 1986 Budget, but the envisaged growth rate was so high that it was not a worthwhile constraint on inflation. Despite that, the target was soon exceeded and Lawson suspended it again. By late 1986 the UK was in the early stages of a vigorous boom driven by extraordinarily rapid growth in bank lending and broad money. Although the government refrained from fiscal reflation, the credit and money excesses of 1987 and early 1988 were curiously similar to those seen in the Barber boom of the early 1970s. This was richly ironic, since the inflation which followed the Barber boom had been largely responsible for policy-makers' initial receptiveness to American monetarist ideas in the late 1970s.

The government did announce and observe narrow money targets, expressed in terms of M0, throughout 1986 and 1987. But, as its champions ought to have known, M0 tracks recent movements in money transactions and does not influence the future behaviour of the economy. The behaviour of narrow money completely failed to warn the government about the widening payments gap and rising inflation trend which emerged in late 1988. If Lawson had a meaningful anti-inflation policy in these years, the key instrument was the exchange rate for the pound and the central idea was that exchange rate stability would ensure rough equivalence between inflation in the UK and other industrial countries. As the dollar was falling heavily from early 1985 because of the USA's enormous trade and current account deficits, it seemed sensible to watch the pound/Deutschmark exchange rate more closely than the pound/dollar rate or, indeed, the effective exchange rate against a weighted basket of other major currencies. Throughout 1987 sterling was held fairly stable in a band of 2.85 to 3 Deutschmark.

This shadowing of the Deutschmark meant that the UK was virtually an associate member of the exchange rate mechanism of the European Monetary System. Lawson had opted for an external financial discipline in preference to the domestic focus associated with money supply targets. Since this was obviously a major change in strategy from the early years of the Thatcher government, an active public debate developed about the advantages and disadvantages of full EMS membership. Most academic economists approved of Lawson's new approach and thought it a welcome change from the doctrinaire monetarism he had espoused as Financial Secretary to the Treasury in 1980. But old-style monetarists (as they now were being called) were mostly hostile to EMS membership, while Walters and Minford were particularly outspoken in their attacks on it. In *Britain's Economic Renaissance* Walters described the EMS as 'rather messy' and remarked that the periodic exchange rate realignments, far from being determined in an economically rational way, were 'grand political events which present many opportunities for horse-trading, threats, counter threats, bluff, etc.'.[53] In his view, it would be best if the UK had nothing to do with it. In adopting this position, Walters was following the mainstream monetarist tradition, in favour of freely floating exchange rates, associated with Friedman and Johnson.

After Walters had persuaded the Prime Minister, Mrs Margaret (later Lady) Thatcher, that the EMS was a bad idea, she was increasingly worried about how Lawson was organizing monetary policy. Their private disagreements became steadily more acrimonious and eventually could not be hidden from the press or their Cabinet colleagues. On 7 March 1988 Margaret Thatcher indicated to the Bank of England her wish that foreign exchange intervention be more limited in scale. The pound soon appreciated sharply against the Deutschmark. However, this did not foreshadow a return to money supply targets. In the Budget on 15 March Lawson did not reinstate a broad money target and even narrow money received a sharp snub. The M0 target was rendered ineffective, if only temporarily, by the admission, in the Treasury's *Financial Statement and Budget Report*, that no specific action would be taken to correct an overshoot which was expected to emerge early in the coming financial year.

By mid-1988 economic policy was in a fairly standard British muddle. The monetarist framework, as understood in 1979 and 1980, had been coherent and relatively simple in conception. It had been replaced by a confused and eclectic pragmatism reminiscent of the Healey Chancellorship in the mid-1970s. Government policy involved 'looking at everything' (the exchange rate, bank lending, house prices and the trade figures) and decisions were often the result of a lucky dip between options suggested by events in the financial markets. The UK had dropped broad money targets of a kind favoured by British monetarists; it had not adopted monetary base control as recommended by American monetarists; it had had an unsatisfactory experience with narrow money targets supported by American-influenced monetarists such as Walters and Minford; and it had equivocated before rejecting, at least provisionally, full membership of the EMS.

The many fluctuations in policy fashion in the 1980s should not be allowed to disguise a number of successes which were clearly attributable to the original monetarist programme. Most obviously, the inflation rate was reduced from an average of almost 15 per cent in the late 1970s to about 5 per cent in the five years from 1982. In view of the substantial monetary overshoots in 1980/81 and 1981/82, this achievement may have seemed more due to serendipity than scientific management. But in all of the next three financial years the broad money target was met, and in early 1985 the annual growth of sterling M3 was down to under 10 per cent. Meanwhile the government broadly adhered to the fiscal side of the Medium-Term Financial Strategy. The result was that in the years of moderate growth from 1982 to 1986 the ratio of public sector debt to national output was falling, while in the Lawson boom of 1987 and 1988 tax revenues were so buoyant that the government actually ran a large budget surplus. The UK was therefore saved from the worries about long-run fiscal solvency which troubled some other European nations.[54] The soundness of the UK's public finances was also, of course, in sharp contrast to the USA's problems with budget deficits throughout the 1980s. With the benefit of hindsight, fiscal issues seem to have been handled more prudently by British monetarists than their American counterparts.[55]

Indeed, there is something of a puzzle about the government's – or, at any rate, Nigel Lawson's – decision in 1985 to scrap the monetarist machinery with which it (and he) had been so closely associated five years earlier. As we have seen, there were many pressures tending to undermine the monetarist approach throughout the early 1980s, but one central point could not be overlooked. Monetarism had accomplished most of the original objectives held by its supporters as set out in the key policy documents of 1979 and 1980. Why, then, had the monetarist approach to macroeconomic policy disintegrated so quickly? Perhaps the main solvents were the hostility of the traditional policy-making establishment, particularly academic economists in the universities, and the incomprehension of many influential commentators in the media. The aversion of the policy-making establishment may have had political roots. It is a safe sociological generalization that the majority of university teachers in Britain did not like Mrs Thatcher and did not in the 1980s (and do not now) vote Conservative. They are more sympathetic to socialism or the mixed economy than to competitive capitalism. It would be consistent if they disliked monetarism as much for the free-market evangelism of its high priests as for its technical content. Also important in explaining their attitudes was that British economists had become habituated to basing macroeconomic policy on external criteria, notably the exchange rate, instead of analysing domestic monetary conditions. Officials at the Bank of England, which for most of its history had been charged with keeping the pound stable in value against gold or the dollar, undoubtedly found it more natural to adjust interest rates in response to exchange rate movements than to deviations of the money supply from its target level. (The historical roots for policy-makers' preference for external, exchange-rate-based signals are discussed above in Essay 3 on 'Keynes, the Keynesians and the exchange rate'.)

In this context the debates between British and American monetarists were important. In the circumstances of the early 1980s, when monetarism was very much on trial, the new system needed to be defended with simple and convincing arguments by a cohesive group of advocates. Instead the arguments were typically of extreme complexity, while often they were more heated between rival members of the monetarist camp than between monetarists and non-monetarists. The differences between the British and American methods provided material and personnel for these disputes, and therefore weakened the monetarist position in public debate. Samuel Brittan of the *Financial Times*, the UK's most influential economic commentator at the time, referred dismissively on several occasions to 'monetarist mumbo-jumbo', well aware that most of his readers were bored by technicalities. To him, and to many other people, membership of the EMS – with its uncomplicated exchange rate disciple – had great appeal.

There is a paradox here. Many critics of monetarism assumed the label of 'Keynesian' and clearly believed that their views were in a direct line of descent from Keynes himself. But, as we have seen, this is questionable. One theme throughout almost all of Keynes's career was that monetary policy should be directed to the attainment of domestic policy objectives (price stability and full employment), not to fixing the international value of the pound (either in terms of gold or another currency). In 1923 he mentioned in *A Tract on Monetary Reform*, with evident approval and sympathy, 'the pioneer of price stability as against exchange stability, Irving Fisher'.[56] It is intriguing that Irving Fisher is usually seen as an intellectual ancestor of Milton Friedman. But the determination of monetary policy by reference to domestic economic goals, and not to a numerically arbitrary exchange rate, was the central policy implication of Keynes's idea of a managed currency.

When Keynes wrote the *Tract* in 1923, Britain had extensive commercial influence throughout the world and its empire had an economic weight not much less than that of the USA. Its size relative to other countries justified it 'in attempting to set up an independent standard' as a complement to the dollar area. By contrast, in the late 1980s the UK was in a transitional and historically ambiguous position. It was no longer large enough to dominate a supra-national currency area, but it was not so small that membership of a European currency arrangement was self-evidently optimal. This dilemma, posed by the decline in British economic and financial power in the 65 years from the publication of the *Tract*, was basic to understanding policy-makers' resistance to a managed currency over the whole period. Perhaps the detailed blueprint for a managed currency would still have been unattractive if it had come not in the form of monetarism, but in a less ideologically unpalatable and far-reaching package. The trouble was that the Treasury and the Bank of England, knowing that the UK was in long-term financial retreat, lacked the self-confidence to make a managed currency work. American monetarists, coming from a large, self-contained economy, could more confidently recommend an ambitious and independent style of monetary policy than their British equivalents. It may always have been rather naïve to expect that ideas nurtured in the University of Chicago could be easily transplanted to Whitehall and Threadneedle Street.

At any rate, when the UK did eventually join the ERM (notionally as a stepping stone to the EMS) in October 1990, it was in the worst possible circumstances for the success of the enterprise. Intolerably high interest rates were needed to preserve the fixed rate with the Deutschmark. Home owners and small businesses were delighted by the drop in interest rates which followed the pound's expulsion from the ERM on 16 September 1992. The UK's association with the European fixed-exchange-rate system lasted less than two years, a shorter period than that of money-supply-target monetarism (from 1976 to 1985), and it was a fiasco. Since 1992 monetary policy has been guided neither by the exchange rate nor the money supply, but by a variety of indicators of which one – the output gap whose origins were discussed in the appendix to the Introduction – has probably been the most important. The UK has had a form of 'managed currency', although it is not the same as that proposed in the *Tract on Monetary Reform* and no one can know whether Keynes would have approved of how policy-making has evolved in the last 15 years. The Britain of the early twenty-first century is very different from that in which he lived.

NOTES

1. HM Treasury press release, 9 June 1980, Statement by Nigel Lawson, MP, Financial Secretary to the Treasury during his meeting with regional city editors.
2. T. Mayer, *The Structure of Monetarism* (New York and London: Norton, 1978). See, particularly, p. 2 for a list of 12 characteristic monetarist propositions.
3. *Monetary Control*, Cmnd 7858 (London: HMSO, 1980), and Memorandum by HM Treasury, pp. 86–95, in vol. II, *Minutes of Evidence of Third Report from the House of Commons Treasury and Civil Service Committee*, Session 1980–81 (London: HMSO, 1981).
4. Memorandum by HM Treasury, p. 90.
5. Note by HM Treasury on 'The stability of the income velocity of circulation of money supply', pp. 126–7, in *Third Report from the Treasury and Civil Service Committee*, Session 1980–81.
6. For an example of the approach see the chapter on 'Bank lending and monetary control' in C.A.E. Goodhart, *Monetary Theory and Practice* (London, Macmillan: 1984), pp. 122–45.
7. It should be added that interest rate changes acted not only on bank lending, but also on the ability of the authorities to sell gilt-edged securities as part of the funding programme.
8. *Monetary Control*, p. 1.
9. *Monetary Control*, p. 2.
10. Memorandum by HM Treasury, p. 89.
11. See, for example, J. Burton, 'Trade unions' role in the British disease: "An interest in inflation"', pp. 99–111, in A. Seldon (ed.), *Is Monetarism Enough?* (London: Institute of Economic Affairs, 1980), particularly pp. 105–6; and T.G. Congdon, 'Why has monetarism failed so far', *The Banker* (April 1982), pp. 43–9. The subject was also discussed in T.G. Congdon, *Monetarism: An Essay in Definition* (London: Centre for Policy Studies, 1978), particularly pp. 53–6.
12. J.M. Keynes, *A Tract on Monetary Reform* (1923), reprinted in *The Collected Writings of John Maynard Keynes*, vol. IV, eds D. Moggridge and E. Johnson (London: Macmillan for the Royal Economic Society, 1971), p. 126, p. 132 and p. 138. See Essay 3, pp. 61–3, for a more extended discussion of Keynes' proposal for a 'managed currency'.
13. HM Treasury press release, 12 May 1981. The Mais Lecture given by Sir Geoffrey Howe, QC, MP, Chancellor of the Exchequer, at the City University, p. 11. At about this time Howe's Treasury colleague and future Chancellor, Nigel Lawson, became convinced that an exchange-rate discipline in the form of the EMS was superior to 'targets for domestic monetary aggregates' in monetary policy-making. On 15 June 1981 he sent Howe a long note on the virtues of joining the EMS. (Nigel Lawson, *The View from No. 11* [London: Bantam Press, 1992], p. 111.)
14. Mayer, *Monetarism*, p. 27.
15. Few economists would regard the monetary base by itself as constituting a measure of the money supply. The Treasury was therefore rather iconoclastic in its attitude toward M0, which it apparently regarded as the full-scale aggregate when M0 was introduced in 1983. In both the USA and the UK the value of transactions in cash is less than 1 per cent of all transactions by non-bank agents.
16. The quotation comes from p. 71 of P. Meek, 'Comment on papers presented by Messrs. Forece and Coleby', in P. Meek (ed.), *Central Bank Views on Monetary Targeting* (New York: Federal Reserve Bank of New York, 1983), pp. 70–71.
17. The quotations are from p. 57 of M. Friedman, 'Response to questionnaire on monetary policy', in House of Commons Treasury and Civil Service Committee (Session 1979–80), *Memorandum on Monetary Policy* (London: HMSO, 1980), pp. 55–62. The self-confidence and assertiveness of Friedman's criticism of the UK authorities in 1980 looks misplaced, to say the least, in retrospect. At the time of writing (mid-2006) no central bank tries to target the quantity of money by controlling the monetary base. In Goodhart's words, writing in 1995, 'the debate over monetary base control appears

historical'. (The quotation is from C. Goodhart, *The Central Bank and the Financial System* [London: Macmillan, 1995], p. 261.) See also pp. 235–6 of Bindsell's *Monetary Policy Implementation: Theory, Past and Present* for critical comments on Friedman's position in the early 1980s. (Ulrich Bindsell, *Monetary Policy Implementation: Theory, Past and Present* [Oxford: Oxford University Press, 2004].)

18.   The arrangements are described in 'The role of the Bank of England in the money market', in *The Development and Operation of Monetary Policy 1960–83* (Oxford: Oxford University Press for the Bank of England, 1984), pp. 156–64.

19.   Econometric work may identify a contemporaneous link between the monetary base and one or other measure of the money supply, but that does not mean that the base 'explains' money rather than the other way round. If one wanted to predict the growth of M3 over the next six to 12 months, the level of monetary base today would not be much help, but forecasts of bank lending and the PSBR would be.

20.   Meek, 'Comment', p. 70.

21.   Friedman, 'Response', p. 58.

22.   J.M. Keynes, *A Treatise on Money: 2. The Applied Theory of Money* (1930), reprinted in *Collected Writings*, vol. VI (1971), pp. 224 and 225.

23.   Ibid., p. 231.

24.   Ibid., p. 225.

25.   J.M. Keynes, *The General Theory of Employment, Interest and Money* (1936), reprinted in *Collected Writings*, vol. III (1973), p. 327.

26.   Keynes, *Treatise 2*, in *Collected Writings*, vol. V (1971), pp. 30–32 and pp. 217–30. These distinctions anticipate the more celebrated analysis of the motives for holding money in *The General Theory*.

27.   HM Treasury press release, 19 October 1978. Speech by Rt Hon. Denis Healey, MP, Chancellor of the Exchequer, to the Lord Mayor's dinner.

28.   The quotation is from p. 97 of P.E. Middleton, 'The relationship between fiscal and monetary policy', in M.J. Artis and M.H. Miller (eds), *Essays in Fiscal and Monetary Policy* (Oxford: Oxford University Press, 1981), pp. 95–116.

29.   See pp. 21–3 of T.G. Congdon, 'The analytical foundations of the Medium-Term Financial Strategy', in M. Keen (ed.), *The Economy and the 1984 Budget* (Oxford: Basil Blackwell for the Institute of Fiscal Studies, 1984), pp. 17–29.

30.   Mentioned on p. 5 of J.L. Jordan, 'The Anderson Jordan approach after nearly 20 years', *Federal Reserve Bank of St Louis Review*, October 1986, pp. 5–8.

31.   Friedman, 'Response', p. 56.

32.   The quotation is from p. 2 of C.J. Allsopp, 'The assessment: monetary and fiscal policy in the 1980s', *Oxford Review of Economic Policy*, vol. 1, no. 1, Spring 1985, pp. 1–19.

33.   Friedman, 'Response', p. 59.

34.   Mayer, *Monetarism*, pp. 24–5.

35.   Keynes, *General Theory*, p. 306.

36.   Thus, for example, Laidler's awareness of trade union power may have been one reason for his advocacy of a 'gradualist' approach to the elimination of inflation. See D. Laidler on the case for gradualism, in Laidler, *Monetarist Perspectives* (Oxford: Philip Allan, 1982), ch. 5, pp. 176–7.

37.   M. Friedman, *Unemployment versus Inflation?* (London: Institute of Economic Affairs, 1975), pp. 30–35. The quotations are from pp. 32 and 33.

38.   A. Budd, S. Holly, A. Longbottom and D. Smith, 'Does monetarism fit the UK facts?', in B. Griffiths and G.E. Wood (eds), *Monetarism in the United Kingdom* (London: Macmillan, 1984), pp. 75–119.

39.   Keynes, *Tract*, p. 126.

40.   See, for example, M. Parkin and G. Zis (eds), *Inflation in Open Economies* (Manchester: Manchester University Press and Toronto: University of Toronto Press, 1976).

41.   See R.J. Ball and T. Burns, 'Long-run portfolio equilibrium and balance-of-payments adjustment in econometric models', in J. Sawyer (ed.), *Modelling the International Transmission Mechanism* (Amsterdam: North-Holland, 1979). It was Burns's position in the exchange rate controversy of 1977/78, and his papers on the interrelationship between

fiscal and monetary policy, which gave him a reputation as a monetary economist – or even as a monetarist – in the public debate and so led to his appointment as Chief Economic Adviser in January 1980. (See G. Howe, *Conflict of Loyalty* [London: Pan Books, 1994], p. 156.) In his paper on 'Exchange rate policy in the United Kingdom', in S. Holly (ed.), *Money, Inflation and Employment: Essays in Honour of James Ball* (Aldershot, UK and Brookfield, US: Edward Elgar, 1994), pp. 26–38, Budd highlights Ball's role in the 1977 debate. The final two sentences of Budd's paper read, 'The challenge was to incorporate the monetarist ideas into an empirical model of the UK economy. That is what Ball and his colleagues were able to do and that is why they played a major role in reshaping ideas and were able to contribute to a significant change in policy' (p. 37).

42. Reprinted in M. Friedman, *Essays in Positive Economics* (Chicago, IL: University of Chicago Press, 1953).

43. Friedman, 'Response', p. 53.

44. Keynes, *Tract*, p. 126.

45. Ibid., pp. 159–60.

46. G. Maynard, *The Economy under Mrs Thatcher* (Oxford: Basil Blackwell, 1988), p. 100.

47. A. Walters, *Britain's Economic Renaissance* (New York and Oxford: Oxford University Press, 1986), pp. 117 and 121. The description of M3 as a 'credit aggregate' was surprising. M3 consists of notes, coin and bank deposits. To say that its growth is driven by bank credit is *not* to say that bank deposits are the same thing as bank notes. (They evidently are not.) In any case, in the modern world where no money is backed by a commodity, the growth of M1 – or, indeed, even of M0 – is also driven by credit. (See T. Congdon, 'Credit, broad money and the economy', in D. Llewellyn [ed.], *Reflections on Money* [London: Macmillan, for the Economic Research Council, 1989], pp. 59–82.) Walters mentioned in a footnote on p. 118 of *Britain's Economic Renaissance* that he had used 'M3 statistics' to make an accurate prediction of 15 per cent inflation in 1974. See the footnote on p. 84 of T. Congdon, *Money and Asset Prices in Boom and Bust* (London: Institute of Economic Affairs, 2005) for more on Walter's shifting views on the money aggregates.

48. Liverpool Research Group in Macroeconomics, *Quarterly Economic Bulletin*, October 1987, p. 13. If this proposition were true, it would have drastic implications for economic theory and policy. But it overlooks the banks' liquidity-transformation role. Since cheques can be written against bank deposits and there is no loss of cheque-writing ability because of the existence of bank loans, the simultaneous expansion of deposits and loans increases the economy's liquidity and can change behaviour.

49. More direct damage to British monetarism came in other ways. For example, the *Observer* – which, under the lead of its Economics Editor, William Keegan, was strongly anti-monetarist – reprinted Friedman's 1980 evidence to the Treasury and Civil Service Committee. It correctly judged that this evidence would weaken the credibility of official policy. For the influence of the New Classical economist, Eugene Fama, on Minford's enthusiasm for M0, see note 37 to Essay 14 on p. 315.

50. Walters, *Renaissance*, p. 135.

51. P. Minford, 'The exchange rate and monetary policy', in W.A. Eltis and P.J.N. Sinclair (eds), *The Money Supply and the Exchange Rate* (Oxford: Clarendon Press, 1981), pp. 120–42. The quotation is from p. 121.

52. Again, see the chapter on bank lending and monetary control in Goodhart, *Monetary Theory*. On pp. 126 Goodhart noted that 'official reactions in the gilts market to developments in the monetary aggregates . . . have been relatively successful in offsetting unforeseen variations' in bank lending and other influences on broad money growth.

53. Walters, *Renaissance*, pp. 128 and 131.

54. These worries, which were particularly serious in Italy, Ireland and Belgium, are discussed in chapters 1–3 of T. Congdon, *The Debt Threat* (Oxford: Basil Blackwell, 1988).

55. Perhaps it should not come as a surprise, after his remarks to the Treasury and Civil Service Committee in 1980, that Friedman should say in a letter to *The Wall Street Journal* on 4 September 1984 that he did not regard the USA's budget deficit – then about 4 per cent of GDP – as a major issue or a cause for concern.

56. Keynes, *Tract*, p. 147.

PART FOUR

The Debate on the 1981 Budget

The Keynesianism of the first post-war generation gave a warm embrace to fiscal policy and cold-shouldered monetary policy. But hovering in the background was the awkward topic of the relationship between money and national income. Suppose that a decrease in the budget deficit occurred at the same time as an increase in the quantity of money. Which of the two policy forces would win? Would fiscal policy overwhelm monetary policy or not? Would Keynesianism refute the monetarists' quantity theory of money, or vice versa?

For any observer of British macroeconomic policy in the mid-1970s these questions were fundamental. As an economic journalist on The Times, *I was intrigued by the inconsistencies in official policy-making and the theoretical issues which they raised. The striking similarity of the rate of money supply growth in 1972 and the rate of inflation in 1975, as well as my reading around the subject, convinced me that the monetarists' theories were largely correct. But what did that mean for fiscal policy and the income-expenditure model? I argued in an article in* The Times *on 23 October 1975 (reprinted as the first essay in this part) that, once a money supply target had been announced, 'reflating by fiscal means is like pumping air into a tyre with a puncture – the puncture being massive sales of government bonds to the non-bank public'. The conjunction in the mid-1970s of fiscal expansionism and persistent demand weakness was 'the* reductio ad absurdum *of Keynesianism'. (The article was very slight, but I think it is worth inclusion here because of its relevance to the subsequent debates. It is a period piece and, although it was written over 30 years ago, I have left the contemporary references in the present tense.)*

The article in The Times *also conjectured that cuts in public spending and increases in taxes would not necessarily deflate demand. The rather cryptic explanation was that, 'Fewer bond sales would ensue, lowering interest rates, and promoting both investment and consumption'. I had no notion when I wrote the sentence that – only a few years later – it would be relevant to the justification of possibly the most controversial episode in British macroeconomic policy-making. The introduction of the Medium-Term Financial Strategy in the 1980 Budget, and the shoring-up of the fiscal targets in that strategy by large tax increases in the 1981 Budget, provoked fury from academic economists. As mentioned several times elsewhere in this book, 364 economists wrote a letter to* The Times *to protest against 'monetarist polices'. The second essay, on 'Did the 1981 Budget refute naïve Keynesianism?', criticizes the Keynesian income-expenditure model for its inability to incorporate monetary influences on assets prices and expenditure. It was written for a set of papers, edited by Philip Booth of the Institute of Economic Affairs (IEA), analysing the 1981 Budget on its twenty-fifth anniversary. Professor Stephen Nickell – who was then on the Monetary Policy Committee of the Bank of England and is now Warden of Nuffield College, Oxford – also contributed to the IEA volume, claiming that the 364 had 'turned out to be completely correct'. I disagreed with this verdict in a short comment and a further exchange followed. It is for others to decide who had the better of the argument.*

*(*Addendum*: The 1981 letter to* The Times *from the 364 is mentioned several times in these pages. The contents of the letter were as follows:*

> *The following statement on economic policy has been signed by 364 university economists in Britain, whose names are given on the attached list:*
>
> *We, who are all present or retired members of the economics staffs of British universities, are convinced that:*
>
> *(a) there is no basis in economic theory or supporting evidence for the Government's belief that by deflating demand they will bring inflation permanently under control and thereby induce an automatic recovery in output and employment;*
>
> *(b) present policies will deepen the depression, erode the industrial base of our economy and threaten its social and political stability;*
>
> *(c) there are alternative policies; and*
>
> *(d) the time has come to reject monetarist policies and consider urgently which alternative offers the best hope of sustained recovery.*

The letter was signed by 76 present or past professors, a majority of the Chief Economic Advisers to the government in the post-war period, and the President, nine of the Vice-Presidents and the Secretary-General of the Royal Economic Society.)

8. Do budget deficits 'crowd out' private investment?

The present worldwide recession is proving unusually stubborn. Large reflationary packages, involving cuts in taxation and higher public spending, have been announced in several leading Western economies, but the recovery so far has been fitful and uncertain. Accompanying the sluggishness of activity have been large public sector financial deficits, particularly in the United Kingdom, the United States and West Germany. These deficits were largely caused by the recession (as it has cut tax receipts), but at the same time they are seen as serving the benign function of combating the weakness of spending (because the deficits represent a demand injection into the economy).

It may be thought unorthodox to argue that the deficits – or, more correctly, the deficits in conjunction with the strategies adopted to finance them – have done nothing to abate the recession. But the argument is not difficult to make. The key point is that extra spending by public authorities has been offset by reduced spending by companies and individuals. The more that governments have kept up their expenditure, the harder it has been for the private sector to carry out its investment and consumption plans. The mechanisms involved are not particularly complex and should be easy to understand, but their implications for economic policy are drastic and sometimes overlooked.

First, large public sector deficits, when financed by debt sales to the general public, deter private investment. If the government sells bonds to non-bank private agents, it reduces their money balances and drives up interest rates. These higher interest rates lead industrialists to reconsider some of their projects and therefore crowd out investment that would otherwise have taken place. This 'crowding out' effect has been much discussed in the United States recently, but it is not a new idea.

Indeed, it closely resembles the pre-Keynesian 'Treasury view' which was fashionable in Britain in the 1930s. The Treasury in those days always resisted demands for deficit financing on the grounds that the money the government did not raise in tax revenue would have to be raised by borrowing, with the same net effect on demand. Higher public spending would merely pre-empt resources which would otherwise have been utilized by the

177

private sector. This apparently hard-faced attitude had been formed by experience of public works programmes in the 1920s. The Treasury found that, once these came to an end, there was a renewal of the initial problem, a lack of genuine jobs in private industry.

Old controversies can be tedious. In the 1930s the Treasury view was obviously misplaced because, with so many resources lying idle, the danger of less activity in one place because of more activity in another was minimal. The Treasury could have safely financed deficits by printing money. The result of the expansion in the money supply would have been to bring idle resources back into employment, not to push up prices. But Keynes never denied that in other circumstances 'crowding out' could be important.

More fundamentally, no one has ever doubted that, *with a given money supply growth rate*, a higher level of public debt sales must result in a lower level of bond issues by the private sector. Associated with the reduction in bond issues there is likely to be a reduction in capital spending and, in due course, less demand for labour. It would be rather brave to pass judgement here on the comparative merits of public spending and private investment, a question which is, after all, rather large. But the 'consensus' is that private investment is 'something we all need', 'a national priority' and 'essential for our survival'. Enthusiasm for public spending has, at any rate in the recent past, been less noisy.

Secondly, large sales of public sector debt induce higher savings by the personal sector and result in less consumption. The abnormally high level of personal savings found in the advanced economies this year can be largely explained in this way. It is interesting, for example, that the greatest departures from traditional savings behaviour have occurred in West Germany and the United Kingdom, which also have the largest public sector deficits (in relation to national income) of the major Western economies. In the first quarter of 1975 individuals in the United Kingdom saved 14.2 per cent of their disposable incomes and in the second quarter they saved 13.4 per cent. Throughout the 1960s the savings ratio averaged well under 10 per cent. Even in 1973, which at the time was thought to be an exceptional year, the savings ratio was 11.3 per cent. Much the same pattern is to be found in West Germany, although the level of savings has been consistently higher, with the savings ratio around 17.5 per cent this year. If people save more, they have less available to spend on consumption goods. The drop in demand for output is eventually reflected in the demand for labour and so counteracts the effect on employment of the public sector deficit.

Why should large public sector deficits prompt higher savings? The basic reason is the high interest rates which are inevitable if the government denies itself the easy option of financing its deficit by increasing the money supply. Most obviously, high interest rates give a good income to savers and affect the financial system profoundly. They make borrowing from banks and hire purchase companies more expensive, and encourage repayments of debt. (Note there is another, less noticed way in which they make saving worthwhile, as emphasized by Keynes in *The General Theory*. If interest rates are above their long-run level, the holder of fixed-interest public debt should make good capital gains when they come down.)

Although the level of interest rates is probably the best explanation of the recent financial behaviour of the personal sector, something of a controversy has developed over other possible influences. A thought-provoking suggestion was made in the Morgan Grenfell's latest *Economic Review*, edited by their economics director, Mr John Forsyth. The review argued that consumers try to keep their holdings of liquid assets in line with personal disposable income, because they need to have enough money or money-like assets to finance their transactions. If inflation is proceeding rapidly at say, 20 per cent per annum, they need to add 20 per cent to their existing holdings of liquid assets. Saving is sustained at a high enough level to ensure that this takes place.

The strands of the argument may now be brought together. If the government commits itself to a money supply target, public sector deficits and fiscal reflationary action have no further effect on economic activity. As part of a strategy to ignite recovery, they are more or less futile. They do virtually nothing to pull economies out of recession, and their only true effect is to alter the balance between the public and private sectors. Higher public expenditure, paid for by long-dated bond issuance, 'crowds out' private investment and causes higher personal savings. There is no positive effect on demand and no benefit to employment.

The refusal of Western economies to pick up despite massive doses of Keynesian reflationary 'action' can be largely explained by the greater awareness of monetary aggregates in the mid-1970s. In the 1960s central banks sometimes seemed to have no rationally formulated policy at all, apart from day-to-day marketry. But – to the extent that central banks had a policy – it was to maintain stable interest rates and allow the quantity of money to adjust to the economy. In that context extra government spending or lower taxation spilled over into the money supply and did stimulate economies. Now that the emphasis of monetary policy has changed, partly because of the lessons of the inflationary boom of 1971–73, fiscal policy is being neutralized by money supply responsibility. In these new circumstances reflating by fiscal means is like pumping air into a tyre with a puncture – the puncture being massive sales of government bonds to the non-bank public.

The argument can be taken a stage further. Governments reject calls for immediate massive cuts in public spending or sharp increases in tax rates on the grounds that they would deflate demand. The advice of a conventional 'Keynesian' economist would be that such steps would substantially aggravate unemployment and cause a needlessly severe cut in output. But no such consequences follow. Fewer bond sales would ensue, lowering interest rates and promoting both investment and consumption. If accompanied by the appropriate monetary measures, fiscal restraint need have no unfavourable effects on demand and employment.

Of course, there would be adjustment difficulties. If public sector employees are laid off as part of an economy campaign, they have to find jobs elsewhere. This takes time because of unavoidable labour market frictions, even if the demand is there. These difficulties give a warning against abrupt changes in fiscal policy. But they do not weaken the essential argument. In any case, difficulties of a different kind arise if public expenditure is uncontrolled and the money supply is held back: private sector employees are laid off and have to search for jobs in the public sector.

These qualifications need not be overdone. It is at last becoming clear that the coincidence and persistence of massive deficit financing with severe recession in most advanced economies signal the failure of fiscal policy. The present situation is the *reductio ad absurdum* of 'Keynesianism' – where Keynesianism is taken as the belief that an exclusive reliance can be placed on public spending and tax rates to control the economy. This belief, which never had any authority in Keynes's written work, is now being battered to death against a monetary brick wall.

9.   Did the 1981 Budget refute naïve Keynesianism?

The 1981 Budget was undoubtedly a turning point in British macroeconomic policy-making. It stimulated a sharp controversy about the role of fiscal policy in economic management, with 364 economists writing a letter to *The Times* in protest against the raising of £4 billion extra taxes (about 2 per cent of gross domestic product) in a recession. They warned that 'present policies will deepen the depression', and 'threaten . . . social and political stability'. It is fair to say, first, that the overwhelming majority of British academic economists disapproved of the 1981 Budget and, secondly, that they were quite wrong in their prognoses of its consequences. This essay discusses some of the issues in economic theory which it raised.

I

Until the 1930s the dominant doctrine in British public finance was that the budget should be balanced. Keynes challenged this doctrine, with many authorities citing his classic work – *The General Theory of Employment, Interest and Money* – as the rationale for discretionary fiscal policy (that is, the deliberate unbalancing of the budget, with deficits in recessions and surpluses in booms). In fact, the remarks on fiscal policy in *The General Theory* were perfunctory. The case for discretionary fiscal policy was made more explicitly in two articles on 'Paying for the war' in *The Times* on 14 and 15 November 1939.[1] These articles were a response to an unusual and very specific macroeconomic problem, the need to switch resources from peacetime uses to wartime production, but their influence was long-lasting. They assumed an approach to macroeconomic analysis, in which – given the present level of incomes – the sum of potential expenditures could be compared with the value of output at current prices. If potential expenditures exceeded the value of output, inflation was likely. In the 1939 articles Keynes noted that equilibrium could be restored by 'three genuine ways' and 'two pseudo-remedies'. After rejecting the pseudo-remedies (rationing and anti-profiteering), Keynes focused on the three 'genuine' answers – inflation, taxation and deferred savings. He opposed inflation, and recommended taxation and deferred savings to eliminate excess demand.

Over time Keynes's analysis had a powerful effect on official thinking. In a book published in 1982 Ball referred to 'the almost total acceptance of Keynesian prescriptions by economists, public servants and politicians of both left and right in the United Kingdom'.[2] The remarks in the two articles in *The Times* were elaborated in a theory of national income determination which took hold in the textbooks of the 1950s and 1960s. Quoting from Dow (from a book on *Major Recessions* published in 1998),

> Interpretation of events cannot depend on unstructured observation, but has to be based on assumptions . . . about the causal structure of the economy . . . Total demand is defined in terms of real final expenditure; its level (in the absence of shocks) is determined by previous income; its result is output, in the course of producing which income is generated; income in turn goes to determine demand in the subsequent period.[3]

In short, income determines expenditures which determine income and output which determines expenditures which determine income and output so on, as if in a never-ending circle. The circular flow of incomes and expenditure is conceived here as being between passive private sector agents with no way of adding to or subtracting from incomes from one period to the next, and without the inclination to vary the proportion of incomes that are spent. According to Dow's statement, the flow of private sector expenditures would proceed indefinitely at the same level, were it not for 'shocks'.

However, the textbooks did allow for additions to or subtractions from the circular flow by an active, well-intentioned and appropriately advised government. If the state itself spent above or beneath its tax revenue (if, in other words, it ran a budget deficit or surplus), it could add to or subtract from the circular flow.[4] The notion of a circular flow of income, and the related idea of the income-expenditure model of the economy (which was adopted in econometric forecasting in the late 1960s and 1970s), therefore made fiscal policy the favourite weapon in the macroeconomic armoury. If all went well, the fiscal additions to and subtractions from the circular flow could be designed to keep the economy at full employment with price stability (or, at any rate, acceptably low inflation). The official judgement on the size of these additions and subtractions, announced with accompanying political theatre every year in the Budget, was taken to be of great significance. For economists brought up to believe that the income-expenditure model was an accurate description of 'how the economy worked' (and that included probably over 90 per cent of the UK's university economists at the time), the 1981 Budget was shockingly inept. They saw it as withdrawing demand in any economy where expenditure was weak and unemployment rising, and so as being totally misguided.

The circular flow of income is a useful teaching aid and is understandably popular in university macroeconomics courses. However, it is a primitive and incomplete account of national income determination. If this is 'Keynesianism', it is 'naïve Keynesianism'. Substantial amendments are needed to bring the story closer to the truth – and indeed to the authentic Keynes of the major works.

At the level of the individual private sector agent, it is incorrect that income and expenditure are the same in every period for two reasons. The first is simple. As agents hold money balances, they can spend above income in any given period by running down these balances. (Of course, if they spend beneath income, they add to their money holdings.) The second is more troublesome. The motive of Keynesian analysis is to determine national expenditure and income, in order to fix the level of employment. So the relevant 'expenditures' are those which lead to output *in the current period* and so necessitate employment. It is evident that expenditure on existing assets – such as houses that were built decades ago, ships after they have been launched, antiques inherited from previous generations and so on – does not result in more employment. (They have been made *in past periods* and do not need to be made again.) But purchases and sales of assets, and of financial securities which establish claims to assets, are on an enormous scale. As with money, an individual agent can spend above income in any given period by selling an asset and spending the proceeds, or spend beneath income by purchasing an asset out of savings from current income. Goods can be bought with money arising from the sale of assets and assets can be bought with money arising from the sale of goods.

At the aggregate level, the situation becomes even more complicated. Suppose, to ease the exposition, that an economy has no assets. If the amount of money is given for the economy as a whole, decisions by individual agents to run down or build up their money balances cannot alter the aggregate amount of money. However, even in this asset-less economy the amount of spending can vary between periods if the velocity of circulation of money changes. Of course, if the amount of money increases or declines from one period to the next, that also allows the level of expenditures to change with the velocity of circulation constant.[5]

Now remove the assumption of an asset-less economy. Money is used in two types of transaction. The first type relates to current expenditure (that is, 'aggregate demand'), output and employment, and belongs to the circular flow; the second type relates to expenditure on existing assets. This second type leads to asset re-dispositions and, typically, to changes in asset ownership. Total transactions consist of both transactions in the circular flow *and transactions in assets*. It should be noted that this distinction is not new. In fact, it was made by Keynes in his *Treatise on Money*, which was published in 1930 before *The General Theory*. To adopt his terms, 'deposits' (money, in other words) were used partly in 'industry' and partly in 'finance'. The 'industrial circulation' was concerned with 'maintaining the normal process of current output, distribution and exchange, and paying the factors of production their incomes'; the 'financial circulation', on the other hand, was involved with 'holding and exchanging existing titles to wealth, including stock exchange and money market transactions' and even 'speculation'.[6] (Of course in the real world the same sum of money may be used in a transaction in goods one day and a transaction in assets the next. Money circulates endlessly. The distinction between the industrial and financial circulations – like any distinction relating to something as fluid as money – is to that degree artificial.)

How are these ideas to be put to analytical use? It is immediately clear that, with the quantity of money given, the value of aggregate demand can change for two reasons. First, money's velocity of circulation in total transactions may alter, with the relative size of Keynes' industrial and financial circulations constant. Secondly, the velocity of circulation of money in total transactions may stay the same, but the relative size of the industrial and financial circulations changes. It should be unnecessary to add that, if the quantity of money increases or decreases between periods, that introduces yet another potential source of disturbance.

In short, once the economy is allowed to have money and assets, the idea of a simple period-after-period equivalence of income and expenditure becomes implausible. The circular flow of income and expenditure would remain a valid description of the economy if the following were constant:

1. The quantity of money,
2. The velocity of money in total transactions, and
3. The proportion of transactions in the circular flow to total transactions (or, in Keynes's terminology in *The Treatise on Money*, the ratio between the industrial circulation and the industrial and financial circulations combined).

A brief glance at the real world shows that the quantity, the velocity and the uses of money are changing all the time. However, some economists brush these matters to one side and stick to a simple income-expenditure model when they interpret the real world. A common shortcut is to take expenditures as being determined in naïve Keynesian fashion and to claim that the quantity of money then adjusts to the level of expenditures. To quote from Dow again, 'Change in nominal GDP [that is, gross domestic product] determines change in broad money. Money is thus not the driving force in the economy, but rather the residuary determinant (*sic*)'.[7]

But Dow is simply wrong. Banks are forever expanding and contracting their balance sheets for reasons which have nothing whatever to do with the recent or current levels of nominal GDP. For example, when banks lend to customers to finance the purchase of old houses, land and long-established companies (that is, to finance the purchase of existing assets), they add to the quantity of money, but their activities do not in the first instance impinge on the industrial circulation. They have no immediate and direct effect on national income or expenditure. Nevertheless, agents have to reshuffle their money holdings and portfolios – in a second, third or more round of transactions – so that the extra money is again in balance with their wealth and current expenditure. The vital principle becomes that national income *and the value of assets* are in equilibrium, and so incomes and expenditure are likely to remain the same period after period, only when the demand to hold money balances is equal to the supply of such balances (that is, the quantity of money) at the end of each and every period, and when the quantity of money is constant. More briefly, national income is in equilibrium only when 'monetary equilibrium' also prevails. After all, it was Keynes himself who said, 'incomes and prices necessarily change until the aggregate of the amounts of money which individuals choose to hold at the new level of incomes and prices . . . has come to equality with the amount of money created by the banking system. That . . . is the fundamental proposition of monetary theory'.[8]

On this view changes in the quantity of money – particularly big changes in the quantity of money – shatter the cosy equivalence of income and expenditure which is the kernel of naïve Keynesianism. Indeed, a sudden sharp acceleration in the rate of money supply growth might create a severe 'monetary dis-equilibrium', and initiate adjustment processes in which first asset prices and later the prices of goods and services would have to change.[9] A 25 per cent jump in the quantity of money would – with some technical caveats – increase the equilibrium values of both national income *and national wealth* also by 25 per cent. One interesting possibility cannot be excluded. It might be that – in the period of transition from the old equilibrium to the new – some asset prices need to rise by more than 25 per cent, in order to stimulate excess demand in goods markets and motivate the required 25 per cent rise in national income. At any rate, any comprehensive account of the determination of national income economists must have a theory of money-holding behaviour and this theory has to recognize that money is only one part of a larger portfolio of assets.

II

All this may seem a long way from the 1981 Budget. It is therefore now time to bring the discussion back to the contemporary context by discussing the values of income, money, assets and related variables in Britain at the time. The UK's money GDP in 1980 and 1981 were about £215 billion and £233 billion respectively. The gross wealth of the personal sector at the end of 1980 was estimated at £658 billion, split between £461 billion of physical assets (mostly houses) and £283 billion of financial assets, and offset by £86 billion of debt to leave net wealth at £658 billion. Total national wealth – including public sector and corporate assets – was nearer £1100 billion. At the end of 1980 the quantity of money, on the very broad M4 measure which included building society deposits, was worth slightly above £130 billion, while sterling M3 (the subject of the official money targets then in force) was £68.5 billion. The value of all transactions – including all cheque and other clearings between the banks – in 1980 was over £4000 billion.

A number of comments need to be made straight away about these numbers. Two features are striking. First, the value of all transactions was a very high multiple of money GDP (or 'national income'). Roughly speaking, total transactions were about 20 times as large as national income. Secondly, wealth was a high multiple of money GDP. To say that wealth was five times national income would be broadly correct, although the precise multiple depends on the valuation conventions adopted. Most wealth was owned by the personal sector, even though some of it was held indirectly via financial products of various kinds. Housing was the personal sector's principal asset.

It is obvious that the national income and expenditure, the central actors in the naïve Keynesians' circular flow, took bit parts in the wider drama of total transactions. To repeat, national income was somewhat more than £200 billion, while total transactions exceeded £4000 billion. Plainly, the majority of the transactions were not in goods and services, but in assets. In terms of size, the financial circulation dominated the industrial circulation. The preponderance of asset transactions was partly due to the second salient feature, that the value of national wealth was five times that of national income. The value of turnover on the London Stock Exchange in 1980 was £196.3 billion, not much less than GDP, while the value of turnover in gilt-edged securities was over £150 billion. In addition, there were transactions in foreign exchange, in unquoted companies and small businesses, in houses, commercial property and land, and in such items as antiques, second-hand cars and personal chattels.

How does this bear on the debate about the 1981 Budget? The 1980 Budget had proposed a Medium-Term Financial Strategy for both the

budget deficit (defined in terms of the public sector borrowing requirement or PSBR) as a percentage of GDP and money supply growth.
Targets for both these variables had been set for the financial years to
1983/84. The target for the 1981/82 PSBR/GDP ratio in the 1980 Budget
was 3 per cent of GDP. In practice the PSBR in the closing months of
1980 proved much higher than expected and the projections in early 1981
were that, on unchanged policies, the PSBR/GDP ratio in 1981/82 would
be over 5 per cent. The government wanted to restore the credibility of the
MTFS. It therefore announced in the 1981 Budget tax increases and other
measures which would cut the PSBR/GDP ratio in 1981/82 by about 2 per
cent of GDP (that is, about £4 billion). This tightening of fiscal policy at
a time of recession was what provoked the letter to *The Times* from the
364. For economists who believed in naïve Keynesianism and the income-
expenditure model, a demand withdrawal of 2 per cent of GDP implied
that over the year or so from March 1981 national expenditure and
income would be at least 2 per cent lower than would otherwise be the
case. (Some of them might appeal to the multiplier concept, also developed in Keynesian textbooks, to say that the adverse impact on demand
would be 2 per cent plus something extra because of supposed 'multiplier
effects'.)

But hold on. As the past few paragraphs have shown, the total annual
value of transactions in Britain at the time of the 1981 Budget was over
£4000 billion. The £4 billion tax increase might seem quite big relative to
national income and expenditure, but it was a fleabite – a mere 0.1 per cent –
of total transactions. Given that national wealth is about five times national
income, the impact of changes in national wealth on expenditure has to be
brought into the discussion. As it happened, the 1981 Budget was accompanied by a reduction in interest rates, with the Bank of England's
Minimum Lending Rate falling from 14 to 12 per cent. This cut followed
an earlier one, from 16 to 14 per cent, on 25 November 1980. The value of
the UK housing stock and quoted equity market was rising throughout the
period, partly because of rather high money growth and (from the autumn
of 1980) the easing of monetary policy. Over the three years to end-1982
the value of the personal sector's money holdings advanced by over £40
billion and the value of three largest other items in its wealth (dwellings,
equity in life assurance and pension funds, and directly owned 'UK ordinary shares') increased by more than £120 billion and of its net wealth by
almost £200 billion. (See Table 9.1.) These numbers are an order of magni-
tude larger than the £4 billion tax increase in the 1981 Budget. Should
anyone be surprised that the Budget was not followed by a deepening of
'the depression' or by en erosion of 'the industrial base of our economy'
which would 'threaten its social and political stability'?

Table 9.1 Value of the main items in the UK personal sector's wealth, 1979–82 (£ million)

	1979	1980	1981	1982
Notes and coin	7 717	8 307	8 837	9 153
Bank deposits	36 210	43 188	47 662	51 685
Building society deposits	42 442	49 617	56 699	66 993
All monetary assets	86 369	101 112	113 198	127 831
Dwellings	276 600	313 200	323 700	345 900
Equity in life assurance pension funds	37 000	49 000	57 000	75 000
UK ordinary shares	31 389	36 482	38 297	45 035
Three leading assets classes combined	344 989	398 682	418 997	465 935
Net wealth	580 529	657 903	696 909	776 754

Source: February 1984 issue of *Financial Statistics* (London: Her Majesty's Stationery Office), Table S12, p. 140.

With 'exquisite' timing (to use Lawson's word, in *A View from No. 11*), the recovery in the economy began almost immediately after the letter from the 364 appeared in *The Times*. Figure 9.1 shows the annualized growth of domestic demand, in real terms, in two-quarter periods from the start of the Conservative government in mid-1979 to the end of 1984. In every two-quarter period from mid-1979 to the first quarter 1981 domestic demand fell in real terms; in every two-quarter period over the five years from Q1 1981 domestic demand rose in real terms (with two minor exceptions). From mid-1979 to Q1 1981 the compound annualized rate of fall in domestic demand was 3.8 per cent; in the five years from Q1 1981 the compound annual rate of increase in domestic demand was 3.3 per cent. The warnings of a deepening of the depression were not just wrong, but hopelessly so.

III

Of course there is much more to be said about the behaviour of the economy in this period. A naïve Keynesian might ask why – if asset prices were gaining ground in 1980 and 1981 – a recession had occurred at all. While the causes of the 1980 recession are complex, the dominant consideration was plainly the very high level of interest rates. Minimum Lending Rate (then the name for the interest rate on which the Bank of England

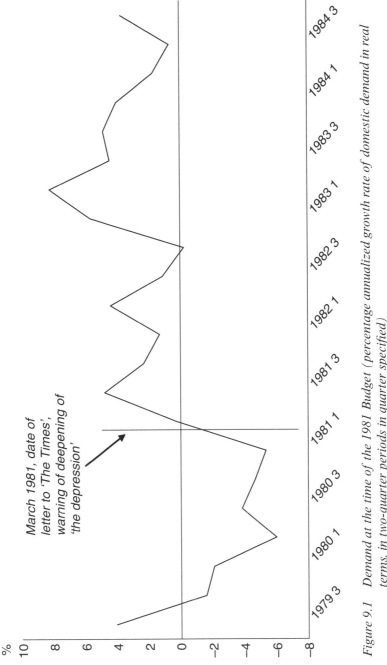

March 1981, date of letter to 'The Times', warning of deepening of 'the depression'

Figure 9.1 Demand at the time of the 1981 Budget (percentage annualized growth rate of domestic demand in real terms, in two-quarter periods in quarter specified)

operated) had been raised to 17 per cent on 30 November 1979 and the average level of clearing bank base rate in 1980 was over 16 per cent. While this had discouraged demand by familiar Keynesian mechanisms (such as the discouragement of investment), monetary forces had also been at work. Dear money had caused money supply growth to be lower than would otherwise have been the case, and encouraged people and companies to hold a higher ratio of interest-bearing money balances to their expenditure. Although money supply growth had been higher than targeted, real money balances had in fact been squeezed. The precise strength of these different 'Keynesian' and 'monetary' influences on demand is difficult to disentangle.

(An appendix derives estimates of the change in the cyclically adjusted public sector financial deficit, as a percentage of GDP, and the change in real broad money balances on an annual basis from 1949 to 2004. The change in the PSFD/GDP ratio is usually regarded as a satisfactory summary measure of fiscal policy. The change in real domestic demand was then regressed on the two variables over four periods, the whole period [that is, 1949–2004] and three sub-periods [1949–64, usually regarded as the 'the Keynesian revolution', 1965–80 and 1981–2004]. The resulting equation for fiscal policy over the whole 1949–2004 period was poor, although not totally disastrous, with a r^2 of 0.11 and a t statistic on the regression coefficient of 2.56, that is, slightly less than the value of three usually thought necessary for a significant relationship. The equation for real broad money was better. It had a r^2 of 0.31 and a t statistic on the regression coefficient of 4.98. However, in the 1981–2004 period no relationship whatever obtained between the change in domestic demand and fiscal policy, whereas monetary policy – as measured by the change in real broad money – still seemed to be working. While this exercise is primitive, it suggests that the naïve Keynesian faith in fiscal policy in 1981 was mistaken. By contrast, the role of the 'real balance effect' – routinely dismissed by Keynesians as virtually irrelevant to the determination of demand – justifies much more investigation. See the appendix to this essay for more details and see Figure 9.2.)

The author of this essay wrote an article in *The Times* on 14 July 1983, under the title 'How 364 economists can be wrong – with the figures to prove it'. It argued that the thinking behind the MTFS was 'that the economy had in-built mechanisms which would sooner or later lead to improved business conditions'. It also pointed out that economies had grown, admittedly with cyclical fluctuations, for centuries before 'the invention of fiscal fine-tuning, demand reflation and the rest of the Keynesian toolkit'. One key sentence was that, 'if we are to understand how the economy might recover without government stimulus today, we should

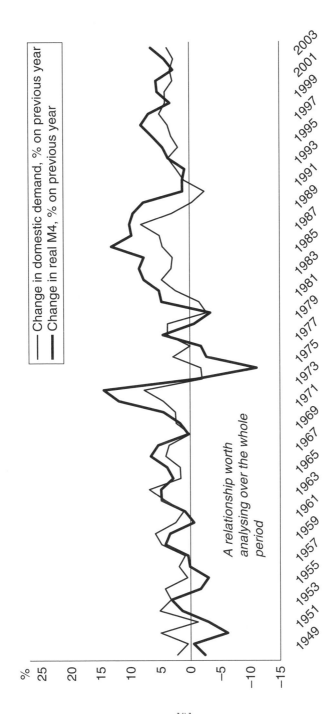

Figure 9.2 *Money growth and demand, 1949–2004*

look at wealth and credit'. Particular attention was paid to the housing market and mortgage credit, since 'borrowing for house purchase is the biggest financial transaction most people undertake'. Data in an accompanying table showed that mortgage credit had more than doubled from £6590 million in 1979 to £13 795 million in 1982.

A reply appeared in the letters column of *The Times* on 29 July from Frank Hahn, one of the two economics professors at the University of Cambridge who had initiated the original letter criticizing the 1981 Budget. Hahn deserves two cheers because he did at least try to defend the 1981 letter, whereas most of the 364 have clammed up. (The author knows a few of them – with later careers of great public prominence – who would prefer not to be reminded that they signed it.) Its opening paragraph was lively and polemical, and may be recalled over 20 years later,

> Suppose 364 doctors stated that there is 'no basis in medical theory or supporting evidence' that a man with an infection will be cured by the administration of toad's liver. Suppose, none the less, that the man is given toad's liver and shows signs of recovery. Mr. Congdon (July 14) wants us to conclude that the doctors were wrong. This is slightly unfair since Mr. Congdon provides a 'theory' of how toad's liver may do good to the patient.

It went on to claim that the recovery in the economy (which Hahn did not dispute) could be explained in 'entirely Keynesian' terms, by the fall in interest rates and its impact on consumer spending.[10]

The trouble here is twofold. First, if Hahn had always believed that a fall in interest rates could rescue the economy, why did he help in organizing the letter from the 364? It is uncontroversial both that a decline in interest rates ought to stimulate demand and that the 1981 Budget was intended to facilitate a reduction in interest rates. Presumably Hahn's concern was about relative magnitudes. He thought that the £4 billion of supposed 'demand withdrawal' announced in the Budget could not be offset by the positive effect on demand of the drop in interest rates and the rise in asset values. If so, he may have shared a characteristic of Cambridge macroeconomic thinking in the immediate post-war decades, that demand is interest-inelastic and that policy-makers should instead rely on fiscal measures.[11] One purpose of the author's article on 14 July 1983 was to show that the housing market was highly responsive to interest rates and that pessimism about the economy's in-built recovery mechanisms was misplaced.[12]

Secondly, and much more fundamentally, Hahn's polemics concealed the deeply unsatisfactory state of Cambridge and indeed British macroeconomics. To simplify greatly but not in a misleading way, part of Keynes's contribution to economic thinking had been to propose a new theory of national income determination. In that theory national income was equal to national expenditure and expenditure was a multiple of so-called 'autonomous expenditure' (that is, investment and government spending). Dow's recapitulation of the circular flow of incomes and expenditure in *Major Recessions* was of course very much in this tradition. But Keynes fully recognized that the new theory was a supplement to an existing theory, 'the monetary theory'. As already explained, when money and assets are introduced into the economy, the equilibrium relationship between them and expenditure has inevitably to be part of the story. Keynes did not intend that the new theory should replace the old theory.

In a celebrated paper written in 1937, as a review article on Keynes's *General Theory*, Hicks had tried to reconcile the two theories in a model (the so-called IS–LM model) where national income was a multiple of investment and investment was equal to savings (that is, the IS curve was defined), and where national income and the interest rate were at levels which equilibrated the demand for money with the supply (that is, the LM curve was also defined). Full equilibrium, with the determination of both interest rates and national income, was achieved by the intersection of the two curves. But in practice most British economists had found the monetary side of the story complicated and confusing, and sidestepped the difficulties by the sort of procedures adopted in Dow's *Major Recessions*. Like Dow, they fixed national income from their income-expenditure model and assumed that the quantity of money adjusted passively (or, in the jargon, 'endogenously'). The quantity of money could then have no causal role in the economy. The LM part of the IS–LM model, and the possibility that asset prices and incomes might have to change to keep the demand to hold money (that is, 'liquidity preferences' or L) in line 'the amount of money created by the banking system' (that is, M), was suppressed. What Keynes deemed in *The General Theory* 'the fundamental proposition of monetary theory' had disappeared from view.[13]

IV

The message of the letter from the 364 was that British academic economists could not see national income determination in monetary terms. They were angry because the Thatcher government had adopted monetary targets to defeat inflation and subordinated fiscal policy to these targets, and because monetary targets made sense only if their pet theory were wrong and the monetary theory of national income determination were correct. In retrospect, it is clear that the 364 had a poor understanding of the forces determining output, employment and the price level. The LM part of the story mattered then (as it matters now), but the 364 could not see the connections between money growth and macroeconomic outcomes. Although policy-making has improved dramatically since the 1970s and 1980s, a fair comment is that British economists are still uncomfortable with monetary analysis. No one knows whether that discomfort will lead through mistaken policy decisions to another boom–bust cycle. But it can be argued that the 1981 letter to *The Times* was part of a wider assault on money supply targeting which led to the abandonment of broad money targets in 1985 and 1986. The sequel was the disastrous Lawson boom and ERM bust of the 1985–92 period. That boom–bust cycle can therefore be blamed on British economists' weak knowledge of monetary economics; it reflected, in other words, 'a great vacuum in intellectual understanding' and may be characterized as 'the revenge of the 364' on the Thatcher government.[14]

At any rate, the 1981 Budget was the end of naïve Keynesianism. It is now over 25 years since British governments renounced the annual adjustment of fiscal policy to manage demand. In that 25-year period fiscal policy has been subordinate either to monetary policy or to rather vague requirements of 'prudence'. In decisions on the size of the budget deficit, governments have respected the aim of keeping public debt under control over a medium-term time frame. The central theme of macroeconomic policy-making today is instead the discretionary adjustment of the short-term interest rate by an independent Bank of England to keep demand growing in such a way that actual output is, as far as possible, equal to trend output (that is, the output gap is zero). Professor Hahn – and as many of the 364 who are still alive and prepared to put their heads above the parapet – might regard the disappearance of fiscal fine-tuning and the apotheosis of interest-rate setting as a diet of 'toad's liver'. Someone should tell them that the patient has lapped it up. The British economy has been more stable over the last 15 years than in any previous period of comparable length. Policy-makers do not pay all that much attention to fiscal policy in their macroeconomic prognoses, although – depressingly – it is still possible to come across textbooks which proclaim the virtues of fiscal policy and its ability to manage demand.[15]

As foreshadowed by the author's article in *The Times* in July 1983, the relationship between interest rates and the housing market has become a more central part of macroeconomic analysis than the supposed impact of changes in the budget deficit in adding to or subtracting from the circular flow of income and expenditure. Nowadays the Bank of England is particularly active in research on the housing market.[16] Much attention is paid to the rate of house price inflation (or deflation), because the change in the price of this asset is thought to have a major influence on consumer spending. But houses are only one asset class. In truth the level and rate of change of all asset prices matter. A key point has now to be reiterated: any plausible theory of money-holding behaviour has to recognize that money is only one part of a larger portfolio of assets. If a number of conditions are met (and over long runs they are met, more or less, in most economies), a 1 per cent increase in the annual rate of money supply growth is associated with a 1 per cent increase in the equilibrium annual growth rates of both nominal national income *and the value of national wealth*. Moreover, national wealth is typically a high multiple of national income. It follows that a sudden acceleration in the rate of money supply growth (of the kind seen in the early phases of the two great boom–bust cycles of the early 1970s and late 1980s) leads to outbreaks of asset price inflation. Big leaps in asset prices cause people and companies to sell assets, and to buy more goods and services, disrupting the smooth flows of incomes and expenditure hypothesized in the naïve Keynesian stories. Because the value of all assets combined is so much higher than the value of national income, the circular income-expenditure flow can become a thoroughly misleading way of thinking about the determination of economic activity.

The macroeconomic effects of the £4 billion tax increase in the 1981 Budget were smothered by the much larger and more powerful macroeconomic effects of changes in monetary policy. No doubt the naïve Keynesian would complain that this is to compare apples and pears, as hypothetical changes in asset values and their impact on expenditure are a long way from the readily quantified and easily forecast impact of budgetary measures. But that would be to duck the main question. As the sequel to the 1981 Budget showed, the naïve Keynesians are kidding themselves if they think either that the economy is adequately described by the income-expenditure model or that the impact of budgetary measures on the economy is easy to forecast.[17] (As the author argued in a series of articles in *The Times* in the mid-1970s on 'crowding-out', the effect of such measures depends heavily on how they are financed and, specifically, on whether they lead to extra money creation.[18] One of these articles is republished here as Essay 8.) Macroeconomics must embrace monetary economics, and integrate the ideas of monetary and portfolio equilibria (and disequilibria) in the theory of national income determination if it is come closer to reality.

It is ironic that the two instigators of the 1981 letter thought themselves to be protecting the 'Keynesian' position in British policy-making and to be attacking 'the monetarists'.[19] As this essay has shown, Keynes's writings – or at any rate his book-length writings – are replete with references to banks, deposits, portfolios, bond prices and such like. No one can say whether he would have approved of the 1981 letter, but it is pretty definite that he would not have based a macroeconomic forecast purely on fiscal variables. The concepts of the industrial and financial circulations were proposed in the

Treatise in 1930. They are building-blocks in a more complete and power-ful theory of national income determination than the simplistic income-expenditure notions advanced in the 'Paying for the war' articles of November 1939. If the Keynesians had paid more attention to what Keynes had said in his great works rather than in his journalism, and if they had been rather more sophisticated in their comments on money and wealth, they might not have been so embarrassingly wrong about the 1981 Budget.

NOTES

1. The articles are reproduced on pp. 41–51 of D. Moggridge (ed.), *The Collected Writings of John Maynard Keynes*, vol. XXII, *Activities 1939–45: Internal War Finance* (London: Macmillan, for the Royal Economic Society, 1978).
2. R.J. Ball, *Money and Employment* (London: Macmillan, 1982), p. 29.
3. J.C.R. (Christopher) Dow, *Major Recessions: Britain and the World 1920–95* (Oxford: Oxford University Press, 1998), p. 38. Dow has a high reputation in some circles. Peter Jay, the former economics editor of the BBC, has referred to 'the learned Dow' and described *Major Recessions* as 'magisterial'. (P. Jay, *The Wealth of Man* [New York: Public Affairs, 2000], p. 238.)
4. The other recognized source of demand injections and withdrawals was the rest of the world, via the balance of payments.
5. As usual in discussions of these concepts, the question of the timing of the receipt of 'income' and the disbursal of 'expenditure' is left a little vague. The income-expenditure story is most plausible if people have nothing (that is, neither money nor assets) at the end of a period, and receive their income at the beginning of a period and have spent it all by the same period's end. In other words, the story is easiest to tell about an economy without private property of any kind.
6. D. Moggridge and E. Johnson (eds), *Collected Writings of Keynes*, vol. V, *A Treatise on Money: 1. The Pure Theory of Money* (Macmillan, 1971, 1st edition 1930), p. 217.
7. Dow, *Major Recessions*, p. 39. Given the context, Dow must have meant 'determinand', not 'determinant'.
8. Moggridge and Johnson (eds), *Collected Writings of Keynes*, vol. VII, *The General Theory*, pp. 84–5. Note that – in this quotation – the word 'prices' referred to the prices *of securities*, not of goods and services.
9. These processes are discussed in more detail in the author's *Money and Asset Prices in Boom and Bust* (London: Institute of Economic Affairs, 2005). It seems that – after a big change in the amount of money – asset prices change with a shorter lag and by larger percentages than the prices of goods and services. The explanation for this undoubted pattern is important to the analysis of real-world business cycles.
10. Hahn made an attempt at self-justification by claiming that 'the monetarists' deny that an injection of newly printed money can boost demand because inflation expectations would deteriorate and 'nothing "real"' will be changed'. But this is to equate 'mon-etarism' with the New Classical Economics of Lucas, Barro, Sargent and others. It is now widely recognized that these are distinct schools of economics. (See, for example, K.D. Hoover, 'Two types of monetarism', *Journal of Economic Literature*, vol. 22, 1984, pp. 58–76.) Hahn's letter ended with a sneer. 'Mr. Congdon's understanding of either side of the argument [by which he presumably mean either the Keynesian or monetarist side] seems very insecure.'
11. 'Elasticity pessimism', that is, a belief that behaviour did not respond to price signals, was common among British economists in the first 20 or 30 years after the Second World War. Investment was thought to be unresponsive to interest rates, while exports and

imports were held to be impervious to changes in the exchange rate. Leijonhufvud has outlined one 'familiar type of argument' as the claim that, 'The interest-elasticity of investment is for various reasons quite low. Hence, monetary policy is not a very useful stabilization instrument'. Hahn and the 364 may have been thinking on these lines. Leijonhufvud says that 'the dogma' of the interest-inelasticity of investment originated in Oxford, with surveys of businessmen carried out in 1938, not in Cambridge. (A. Leijonhufvud, *On Keynesian Economics and the Economics of Keynes* [New York: Oxford University Press, 1968], p. 405.) But it was still widely held in Cambridge and other British universities in the 1970s and even in the 1980s.

12. Before the July 1983 article in *The Times* the author had proposed the concept of 'mortgage equity withdrawal' in a joint paper with Paul Turnbull. (See 'Introducing the concept of "equity withdrawal"', in T. Congdon, *Reflections on Monetarism* [Aldershot, UK and Brookfield, US: Edward Elgar, for the Institute of Economic Affairs, 1992], pp. 274–87, based on a paper of 4 June 1982 for the stockbroking firm of L. Messel & Co., 'The coming boom in housing credit'.) Dozens of articles have subsequently been written about 'mortgage equity withdrawal' and its influence on personal expenditure, and the Bank of England regularly prepares estimates of its size. To economists spoon fed at university on the circular flow of income and the income-expenditure model (in which, as explained, assets do not affect expenditure), mortgage equity withdrawal was a striking idea. It showed how people whose only significant asset was a house (which is of course rather illiquid) could tap into the equity (often boosted in the Britain of the early 1980s by house price inflation) by borrowing.

13. Note that monetary equilibrium could refer to:

     i.   the equivalence of the demand for base money with the supply of base money, or
     ii.   the equivalence of the demand for narrow money with the supply of narrow money, or
     iii. the equivalence of the demand for a broad money measure with the supply of broad money, or
     iv.   the simultaneous equivalence of the demand for all money measures with the supply of all such measures.

     The 'which aggregate?' debate will not go away. The chaos in the subject helps to explain why so many economists have dropped money from their analytical purview.

14. Congdon, *Reflections*, p. 252. The author first used the phrases 'vacuum in intellectual understanding' and 'the revenge of the 364' in an inaugural lecture to Cardiff Business School in November 1990, which now forms the bulk of Essay 3 in this volume.

15. For example, the textbook *Principles of Macroeconomics* (New York: Irwin/McGraw-Hill, 2nd edition, 2003) by Ben Bernanke and Robert Frank contains an account of national income determination and the efficacy of fiscal action which could have been lifted, in its entirety, from a similar textbook of the 1950s. Bernanke was professor of economics at Princeton University, a university widely regarded as in the vanguard of macroeconomic thought, when the textbook was published. Now – as chairman of board of governors of the USA's Federal Reserve – he holds the most important position in monetary policy-making in the world.

16. In the 1970s the Bank of England's *Quarterly Bulletin* did not include a single article on the housing market. In the three years to the summer of 2005 the *Quarterly Bulletin* carried seven articles and two speeches by the members of the Monetary Policy Committee which related specifically to the housing market.

17. But the majority of British economists do not think that the income-expenditure model has been discredited by the sequel to the 1981 Budget. For example, the Bank of England's macro-econometric model remains a large-scale elaboration of an income-expenditure model in which money is, to use the phrase that Dow presumably intended, a 'residuary determinand'. See *The Bank of England Quarterly Model* (London: Bank of England, 2005), *passim*.

18. T. Congdon 'The futility of deficit financing as a cure for recession', *The Times*, 23 October 1975. Some economists had seen in the late 1970s that the impact of fiscal

policy on the economy was not independent of how budget deficits were financed. According to Ball in a book advocating 'practical monetarism', 'if the money supply is chosen as a policy target, the stance of fiscal policy must be consistent with it. [Fiscal and monetary policies] cannot in practice be operated independently in the medium term. For this reason academic debates about the "pure" effects of fiscal policy lose much of their *raison d' etre.*' (Ball, *Money and Employment*, p. 184.) Ball worked closely with T. Burns at the London Business School in the late 1960s and early 1970s, and Burns became the government's Chief Economic Adviser in 1980.

19.		The two instigators were Professor Robert Neild and Professor Frank Hahn. Neild's subsequent interests were in peace studies and corruption in public life. (He has also written a history of the oyster in England and France.) As far as the author can determine, he dropped macroeconomics at some point in the 1980s. Hahn's position is more interesting and, in the author's opinion, more puzzling. He has written numerous academic papers on money (and money-related issues) in general equilibrium theory, brought together in Frank Hahn, *Equilibrium and Macroeconomics* (Oxford: Basil Blackwell, 1984). Most of the papers in the 1984 book were concerned with rarefied topics, such as the existence, stability and optimality of differently specified general equilibria. However, four of the papers (numbered 12 to 15) were more or less directly polemical exercises whose target was 'monetarism' or, at any rate, what Hahn took to be 'monetarism'. They cannot be summarized here for reasons of space, but a salient feature of all the papers was the lack of references to real-world institutions, behaviours and magnitudes. Following Keynes, the author has argued – in the current essay and elsewhere – that a discussion of the determination of national income must be, to a large extent, a discussion of the role of money in portfolios. In a 1980 paper on 'Monetarism and economic theory' Hahn cited a number of recondite papers before seeing in 'recent macroliterature' two elements 'that Keynesians have for long ignored'. One was the portfolio consequences of budget deficits and the other 'wealth effects'. (*Equilibrium and Macroeconomics*, p. 299) Given that, might one ask why Hahn should have been so sarcastic about the author's 1983 article in *The Times*, and its concern with mortgage credit, houses and wealth? And might one also ask whether he really believes (as apparently he did in 1980 and perhaps as he continued to do when he orchestrated the 1981 letter to *The Times*) that the government should make 'the rate of change of the money stock proportional to the difference between actual unemployment and half a million unemployed' (*Equilibrium and Macroeconomics*, p. 305)? Is that the sort of policy which – on a considered analysis – would have led to the macroeconomic stability the UK has enjoyed since 1992?

STATISTICAL APPENDIX: DOES NAÏVE FISCALISM OR NAÏVE MONETARISM FIT THE UK DATA BETTER?

Doubts have been raised about the validity of the monetary theory of national income determination, with some of the sceptics adopting high-powered econometrics to make their point. In 1983 Hendry and Ericsson published a well-known critique of the methodology used in Friedman and Schwartz's *Monetary Trends in the United States and the United Kingdom*.[1] Relatively little work has been directed at assessing the empirical validity of the proposition that changes in domestic demand are heavily, or perhaps even predominantly, influenced by changes in the budget deficit (which might be called 'the fiscalist [or naïve Keynesian] theory of national income determination'). The purpose of this appendix is to compare simple formulations of the fiscal and monetary theories of national income determination. In view of British economists' inclination to downplay or even to dismiss the monetary theory (on the grounds that 'it does not stand up to the facts'), and then to advocate changes in the budget deficit as an appropriate macroeconomic therapy, an exercise on these lines is needed. Series were obtained over the 1948–2004 period for

1. The cyclically adjusted ratio of the public sector financial deficit to GDP, and hence for the change in the ratio from 1949,
2. The change in real broad money, using the M4 measure of money adjusted by the increase in the deflator for GDP at market prices. (The M4 data after 1964 were taken from the official Office for National Statistics website. The M4 data before 1964 used a series prepared at Lombard Street Research, which drew on the data given in F. Capie and A. Webber, *A Monetary History of the United Kingdom, 1870–1982*, vol. 1. (London: Allen and Unwin, 1985).
3. The change in real domestic demand, where the deflator for GDP at market prices was again used to obtain the real-terms numbers.

The cyclical adjustment to the PSFD data was conducted in the same way as in the author's paper 'Did Britain have a Keynesian revolution? Fiscal policy since 1941', pp. 84–115, in J. Maloney (ed.), *Debt and Deficits* (Cheltenham, UK and Lyme, USA: Edward Elgar, 1998), which is reprinted in this collection as Essay 4. (For the years 1963/64 to 1986/87 the author's numbers for the cyclically adjusted PSFD/GDP ratio are virtually identical to those given in HM Treasury's *Occasional Paper No. 4 on Public Finances and the Cycle*, published in September 1995.) The change in the cyclically adjusted public sector financial deficit is usually accepted as a satisfactory summary measure of fiscal policy. (The data are available from timcongdon@btinternet.com.)

The change in real domestic demand was regressed against, first, the change in the cyclically adjusted PSFD/GDP ratio (to test a naïve fiscalist hypothesis) and, secondly, the change in real M4 (to test a naïve monetarist hypothesis) for four periods, 1949–2004 as a whole, 1949–64 (that is, the 'Keynesian revolution', 1965–80 (the period when the Keynesian dominance in policy thinking was being eroded) and 1981–2004 (the period when medium-term fiscal rules were adopted, initially because of 'monetarism', but later because of Mr Gordon Brown's 'prudence'). The results are given in Box 9.1.

BOX 9.1   NAÏVE FISCALISM VS. NAÏVE MONETARISM

1.   The whole 1949–2004 period

Naïve fiscalism

Change in real domestic demand (% p.a.) = 2.61 + 0.56 Change in PSFD/GDP ratio (% of GDP, in year in question)
$R^2 = 0.11$
t statistic on regression coefficient = 2.56

Naïve monetarism

Change in real domestic demand (% p.a.) = 1.74 + 0.28 Change in real M4 (% p.a.)
$R^2 = 0.31$
t statistic on regression coefficient = 4.98

2.   The 1949–1964 sub-period ('the Keynesian revolution')

Change in real domestic demand (% p.a.) = 2.68 + 0.73 Change in PSFD/GDP ratio (% of GDP)
$R^2 = 0.19$
t statistic on regression coefficient = 1.82

Change in real domestic demand (% p.a.) = 2.87 + 0.34 Change in real M4 (% p.a.)
$R^2 = 0.23$
t statistic on regression coefficient = 2.03

3. **The 1965–80 sub-period (the breakdown of the Keynesian consensus)**

Change in real domestic demand (% p.a.) = 1.96 + 0.98 Change in PSFD/GDP ratio (% of GDP)
$R^2 = 0.35$
t statistic on regression coefficient = 2.72

Change in real domestic demand (% p.a.) = 1.16 + 0.37 Change in real M4 (% p.a.)
$R^2 = 0.66$
t statistic on regression coefficient = 5.20

4. **The 1981–2004 sub-period (the period of medium-term fiscal rules)**

Change in real domestic demand (% p.a.) = 2.92 − 0.06 Change in PSFD/GDP ratio (% of GDP)
$R^2 = 0.001$
t statistic on regression coefficient = −0.16

Change in real domestic demand (% p.a.) = 0.64 + 0.38 Change in real M4 (% p.a.)
$R^2 = 0.28$
t statistic on regression coefficient = 2.95

The econometrics in Box 9.1 are primitive, but three comments seem in order. The first is that naïve monetarism works better than naïve fiscalism over both the whole period, and in each of the three sub-periods. (See Figure 9.2 comparing the changes in real M4 and real domestic demand over the whole period.) However, naïve fiscalism was only slightly worse than naïve monetarism in the first sub-period (the period of 'the Keynesian revolution'). The second is that in the final sub-period, when medium-term fiscal rules prevailed, the relationship between changes in the budget deficit and domestic demand disappeared. The results of the naïve fiscalist equation in the 1981–2004 sub-period are atrocious. (See Figure 9.3, with its obvious absence of a relationship. The r^2 is virtually nothing, and the regression coefficient has the wrong sign and is insignificant.) It is not going too far to say that – in these years – naïve Keynesianism was invalid, while the standard prescription of its supporters ('fiscal reflation will boost employment') was bunk. The third is that the 364 were not entirely silly to believe *in 1981* that a reduction in the budget deficit would be deflationary. Although the relationship between the

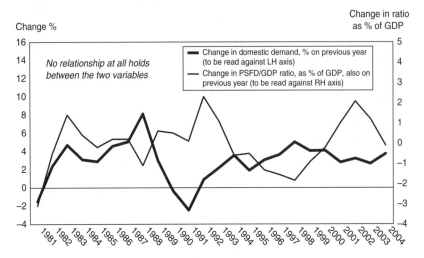

*Figure 9.3   Fiscal policy and demand, 1981–2004 ('the period of medium-
            term fiscal rules')*

changes in the cyclically adjusted budget deficit and domestic demand had
been worse than that between changes in real M4 and domestic demand in
the preceding 15 years, the naïve fiscalist hypothesis had not done all that
badly in the second sub-period. Indeed, by the careful selection of years
one period of 21 years (1953 to 1973 inclusive) could be found with an
impressively strong relationship between fiscal policy and demand outcomes. (See Figure 9.4.)

It was only in the final 25 years of the post-war period that – on the
analysis here – a naïve Keynesian view of national income determination
became indefensible. The extremely poor quality of the fiscal equation in
the final sub-period raises the question, 'was its better performance in the
1949–64 and 1965–80 sub-periods, and particularly in the 1953–73 sub-
period, really because fiscal policy *by itself* was quite powerful or was it
rather because fiscal policy influenced money supply growth and monetary
policy was the relevant, strong influence on demand?'. To answer these
questions, the author regressed the rate of real M4 growth on both the level
and the change in the PSFD/GDP ratio over the whole 1949–2004 period,
and the 1949–64 and 1965–80 sub-periods, and was unable to find a relationship between the variables that met standard criteria of statistical
significance. Much more work should be done, but it seems the apparent
conclusion cannot be denied. To the extent that fiscal policy was effective
between 1949 and 1980, it did not work largely though monetary policy and

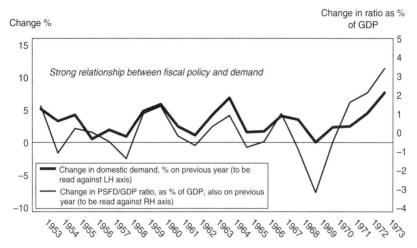

Figure 9.4   Fiscal policy and demand, 1953–73 ('the heyday of Keynesianism')

had some independent effect on the economy. This may solace those (presumably most of the 364) who claim that fiscal policy mattered in these years, even though fiscal policy did not matter after 1980 and monetary policy has always mattered more.

However, a little more investigation raises more questions. The 1953 to 1973 sub-period – the best period for the Keynesian hypothesis – needs to be looked at more carefully. To repeat, fiscal policy ostensibly had a strong effect on domestic demand. (In the equation regressing the change in domestic demand on the change in the PSFD/GDP ratio, the r^2 was 0.62 and the t statistic on the regression coefficient was 5.57. The regression coefficient was remarkably close to unity, at 1.15. In other words, if the Chancellor of the Exchequer were to increase the budget deficit by £500 million over the next fiscal year, he could be expected to increase domestic demand by slightly more than £600 million, just as the textbooks said.) Further, in this sub-period naïve Keynesianism worked better than naïve monetarism. (In the equation regressing the change in domestic demand on the rate of real M4 growth, the r^2 was 0.41 and the t statistic on the regression coefficient was 3.63.) Given that this was how macroeconomic policy operated over such an extended period, were not the Keynesians justified in the mid-1970s in believing in the effectiveness of fiscal policy and in the superiority of fiscal over monetary policy? The answer depends on how one views the relationship between fiscal and monetary policy in those years. When the author regressed the rate of real M4 growth on the level and the

change in the PSFD/GDP ratio over the 1953–73 period, the equation with
the change in the PSFD/GDP ratio was much better than in other sub-
periods and – exceptionally – it was quite good in its own terms. (The r^2 was
0.43 and the t statistic on the regression coefficient was 3.77.) This leaves
open the possibility that fiscal policy 'worked' between 1953 and 1973,
because changes in fiscal policy were accompanied by changes in money
supply growth which operated in the same direction and had powerful
impacts on demand in their own right. Fiscal policy 'mattered' largely via
a monetary channel, because the budget deficit affected the rate of the
growth of the quantity of money.

In his celebrated attack on 'the new monetarism' in the July 1970 issue of
Lloyds Bank Review, Kaldor scorned the role of monetary policy by claiming that changes in money supply growth could be 'explained' by fiscal
policy. In his words: 'I am convinced that the short-run variations in the
"money supply" – in other words, the variation relative to trend – are very
largely explained by the variation in the public sector's borrowing requirement'. He amplified the point in a footnote which read:

> In fact, a simple regression equation of the annual change of the money supply
> on the public sector borrowing requirement for the years 1954–68 shows that the
> money supply increased almost exactly £ for £ with every £1 increase in the
> public sector deficit, with t = 6.1 and R^2 = 0.740, or, in fashionable language,
> 74 per cent of the variation in the money supply is explained by the deficit of the
> public sector alone.[2]

The results of the regression reported in Kaldor's footnote are surprising,
since the PSBR was not introduced as an official statistic until 1963 and
(unless he had access to internal Treasury estimates, which is possible) no
such regression could have been carried out for earlier years. The author
has tried to replicate Kaldor's result by regressing the change in 'the money
supply' (that is, the sum of notes and coin in circulation and clearing bank
deposits) on the public sector financial deficit, for which (to repeat) data are
available back to 1948. The equation was markedly worse than the one
reported by Kaldor (with a regression coefficient of 0.48, a r^2 of 0.38 and a
t statistic of 2.81), but it was not rubbish. It is indeed plausible that – in the
1950s and 1960s, when bank lending to the private sector was officially
restricted for much of the time – a major influence on the growth of banks'
balance sheets was the increase in their holdings of public sector debt.
Fiscal and debt management policies *did* affect money supply growth, as
most economists thought at the time (and despite the rather conflicting
results mentioned in earlier paragraphs).

However, this does not mean – as Kaldor seems to have implied – that in
all circumstances fiscal policy dominated monetary policy and that mon-

etary policy *by itself* was unimportant. In the 1980s and 1990s, after the removal of credit restrictions, bank lending to the private sector became by far the largest credit counterpart of M4 growth, and the change in money and the budget deficit were no longer correlated. But – as this appendix has shown – the influence of money on demand remained identifiable, whereas the influence of fiscal policy on demand vanished.

In retrospect it is clear that Kaldor went too far in his statement about the link between the budget deficit and money growth.[3] However, he did at least recognize that fiscal variables, and not monetary variables alone, needed to be cited as evidence in the debate. British Keynesians have later been much too ready to debunk monetary aggregates. The same standards of proof need to be applied to both monetary *and fiscal* variables.

Notes

1. D. Hendry and N.R. Ericsson, 'Assertion without empirical basis: an econometric appraisal of *Monetary Trends in the United States and United Kingdom*, by Milton Friedman and Anna Schwartz', Bank of England Panel of Economic Consultants, *Monetary Trends in the United Kingdom*, panel paper no. 22, October 1983, pp. 45–101.
2. N. Kaldor, 'The new monetarism', *Lloyds Bank Review*, July 1970, pp. 1–17, reprinted on pp. 261–78 of A. Walters (ed.), *Money and Banking* (Harmondsworth: Penguin Books, 1973). See, in particular, p. 277. In the late 1970s Budd and Burns also argued that the fiscal position had a strong medium-term influence on the rate of monetary growth. See A.P. Budd and T. Burns, 'The relationship between fiscal and monetary policy in the LBS model', *Discussion Paper no. 51* (Econometric Forecasting Unit: London Business School, June 1978).
3. The breakdown of 'Kaldor's rule' was noted in J.H.B. Tew, 'Monetary policy', in F.T. Blackaby (ed.), *British Economic Policy 1960–74* (Cambridge: Cambridge University Press, 1978), ch. 5, pp. 218–303. See, particularly, pp. 277–8. Ironically, for those concerned that excessive money supply growth would lead to inflation, Kaldor's rule justified official action to constrain the budget deficit, as incorporated in the Conservatives' Medium-Term Financial Strategy from 1980.

10. An exchange 25 years later between Professor Stephen Nickell and Tim Congdon

I. 'THE BUDGET OF 1981 WAS OVER THE TOP', BY STEPHEN NICKELL[1] – CONTRIBUTION TO PHILIP BOOTH (ED.), *WERE 364 ECONOMISTS ALL WRONG?* (LONDON: INSTITUTE OF ECONOMIC AFFAIRS, 2006)

After the 1981 Budget, 364 university economists in Britain wrote to *The Times* to complain about the tightness of macroeconomic policy, prompted by the plans in the Budget to cut public sector borrowing by some £3.3 billion, mainly by increasing taxes. It is now a commonplace view that the 364 were wrong to complain because, shortly after publication of the letter, the growth rate of real domestic demand and GDP switched from negative to positive. As it happens, this view is incorrect. As one of the 364, I would say that, wouldn't I? So in what follows I pursue this question by analysing the periods before and after the sending of the letter. I conclude that the 364 economists were perfectly correct to complain about the macroeconomic policy of the day back in 1981.

I signed the letter because, at the time, I had long thought that monetary policy was too tight and tightening fiscal policy in early 1981 was a mistake. While it was true that the letter was not everything I might have wished for, it was the only show in town, and I felt that I should stand up and be counted. In particular, I had always believed that the world was best understood in a NAIRU[2] framework, and indeed at the time I was busy trying to estimate the path of equilibrium unemployment in Britain (see Nickell, 1982). So it is no surprise that I did not find the implicit theoretical analysis underlying points (a) and (d) in the letter entirely to my taste. I approved wholeheartedly, however, of the main points (b) and (c), and still do.[3] So how might they be justified in the light of the fact, already noted, that output growth in Britain turned positive shortly after the letter appeared? Surely, it is typically argued, all this talk of deepening depression must be so much hot air in the light of this fact. Fortunately for me, this argument is just wrong. For the depression to deepen or the output gap to become more negative, output growth does not have to be negative, it merely has to be below trend. So the 364 cannot simply be dismissed out of hand by pointing to the time series of GDP growth. More analysis is required.

When the Thatcher government took office in the spring of 1979, annual inflation (GDP deflator) was close to 11 per cent and had been falling steadily since peaking at over 25 per cent in 1975 after the disaster of the first oil shock. This fall in inflation had been engineered essentially by trying to use an incomes policy to lower the equilibrium rate of unemployment with actual unemployment fairly stable. In the years leading up to 1979, unemployment had been around 6 per cent using the OECD measure and somewhat lower using the Department of Employment (DE) measure (see Layard et al., 1991: table A3). During this period and for many years before, wages tended to respond rapidly to changes in retail price index inflation unless obstructed by incomes policy; inflation expectations were not stable (as far as we know); and there was no belief in the labour market that government macroeconomic policy would respond aggressively to inflationary shocks.

Aside from scrapping incomes policy, the change of government had little impact on these features of the labour market. The rapid response of wages to changes in RPI inflation, now completely unconstrained by incomes policy, was perfectly exemplified by the year following the first Budget of the new administration in June 1979. The main feature of this Budget was the switch from income taxes to VAT (value added tax). This plus the rise in oil prices raised RPI (retail price index) inflation by over five percentage points between the second and third quarters of 1979, so that after a wage–price spiral (see Figure 10.1), by the second quarter of 1980, RPI inflation was 21.5 per cent, wage inflation was 21.3 per cent and the GDP deflator was rising at 22.3 per cent. Wage inflation continued to rise, reaching 22.4 per cent in the third quarter, by which time the rise in VAT had dropped out of the RPI and things started to subside.[4] Monetary policy responded aggressively to this inflationary shock with the interest rates used for monetary policy purposes reaching 17 per cent in November 1979, having been at 12 per cent when Mrs Thatcher took office.

So now the basic problem was to get inflation back down again, preferably to some reasonable level, in a world where, as we have seen, governments had little anti-inflation credibility. There is no option in this situation but to use a tight macroeconomic policy to raise unemployment well above the equilibrium rate and then wait for inflation to subside, before gradually loosening policy. The whole process is tricky, all the more so because if some of the unemployed become detached from the labour market after being unemployed for a long time, they are no longer so useful at exerting downward pressure on pay rises.

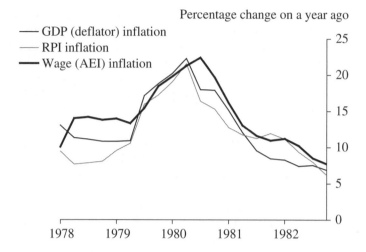

Percentage change on a year ago

——— GDP (deflator) inflation
——— RPI inflation
▬▬ Wage (AEI) inflation

Note: AEI = average earnings index.

Figure 10.1   Inflation, 1978–82

This, in essence, was the policy that was pursued. Of course, the details
of the macroeconomic policy regime were quite complicated with monetary targets, the Medium-Term Financial Strategy and so on. But to get
inflation down, unemployment had to go above the equilibrium rate. In due
course, policies that might reduce the equilibrium rate could be introduced,
but, in the meantime, the current equilibrium rate was probably around 7 or
8 per cent and so macroeconomic policy had to push unemployment above
this level. By the time of the 1981 Budget, unemployment was rising rapidly
thanks to the very tight monetary policy, having increased by some 4.2 percentage points on the DE measure over the previous year.

As we have seen, planned fiscal policy was tightened significantly in the
1981 Budget and, at the same time, interest rates were cut from 14 per cent
to 12 per cent. They were, however, raised back to 14 per cent on
15 September and to 15 per cent on 12 October, so the monetary easing was
temporary. In the complaint of the 364 economists, it was argued that the
depression would deepen. So what happened? Despite positive output
growth, unemployment continued to rise (see Figure 10.2). Unemployment
peaked on the OECD measure at 12.5 per cent in 1983 but did not fall below
11 per cent until 1987. On the DE measure, unemployment continued to
rise, year after year, until it peaked at 11.2 per cent in 1986. Under the not
unreasonable assumption that rising unemployment means that growth is
below trend (there being no reason to believe equilibrium unemployment

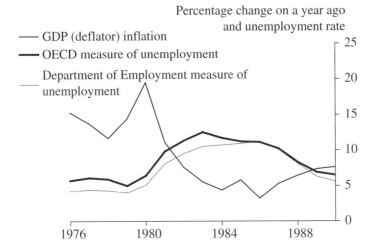

Percentage change on a year ago
and unemployment rate

—— GDP (deflator) inflation

—— OECD measure of unemployment

—— Department of Employment measure of
unemployment

Figure 10.2   Unemployment and inflation, 1976–90

was rising much between 1982 and 1986), the depression deepened until somewhere between 1983 and 1986, as the 364 said it would. Even though unemployment has to be above the equilibrium rate to get inflation down, this strikes me as overkill. By the time of the 1981 Budget, monetary policy was already too tight. It could have been loosened and the fiscal stance need not have been tightened and still unemployment would have been far enough above the equilibrium rate to bring inflation down. Maybe it would not have come down quite so fast, but with the fall in oil prices in 1986, it would almost certainly have been at reasonable levels in 1987. As it happened, of course, by 1987 macroeconomic policy was so gung-ho that by 1990 GDP inflation was back at its 1982 level (7.6 per cent) and the whole business had to be repeated in an only slightly less dramatic fashion.

So is there any excuse for the policy overkill which the 364 economists complained about so bitterly? One possible excuse was that the exceptionally rapid rate of productivity growth from 1982 to 1986 was not expected. During this period, whole economy productivity growth was close to 3 per cent. This was not just a cyclical recovery and was unusually high by recent historical standards (see Nickell et al., 1992, for some explanations). So over this period, trend growth rates would have been especially high, particularly relative to the 1970s. This would make it more likely that macroeconomic policy would be set in such a way as to generate output growth at a rate lower than would be desirable. And this is exactly what happened.

The main complaint of the 364 economists in their 1981 letter was that macroeconomic policy was unnecessarily tight and that it would deepen the depression. By ensuring that subsequent output growth was beneath trend for a number of years, it did indeed deepen the depression just as predicted. Furthermore, it was unnecessarily tight in the sense that a somewhat looser policy would still have raised unemployment far enough above its equilibrium level to bring inflation down over a reasonable period. So in their key comments on the facts of the case, the 364 economists turned out to be completely correct.

Notes

1. I am grateful to Chris Shadforth for his help in the preparation of this paper.
2. Non-accelerating inflation rate of unemployment. Broadly this means the rate below which unemployment cannot fall without inflation rising.
3. The letter is reproduced as an addendum to the introduction to this part of the book, on p. 176, but, in summary, (a) stated that there was no basis or evidence in economic theory that government policies would permanently reduce inflation; (b) stated that the present policies would deepen the depression; (c) stated that there were alternative policies; and (d) stated that the time had come to reject monetarist policies and pursue alternatives.
4. While the report on the Clegg Commission on Public Sector Pay was important for those working in the public sector, its consequences for overall wage inflation were not large. Were Figure 10.1 to be based on private sector wage inflation, it would look very similar. The public sector was not big enough to have a dramatic impact.

References

R. Layard, S. Nickell and R. Jackman, *Unemployment, Macroeconomic Performance and the Labour Market* (Oxford: Oxford University Press, 1991).
Nickell, S.J., 'The determinants of equilibrium unemployment in Britain', *Economic Journal*, vol. 92, September 1982, pp. 555–75.
Nickell S., S. Wadhwani and M. Wall, 'Productivity growth in UK companies, 1975–86', *European Economic Review*, vol. 36, 1992, pp. 1055–91.

II. A COMMENT ON NICKELL'S 'THE 1981 BUDGET WAS OVER THE TOP', BY TIM CONGDON – PUBLISHED IN *ECONOMIC AFFAIRS* (LONDON: IEA), DECEMBER 2006 ISSUE

As is well-known, the large increase in taxation announced in the 1981 Budget provoked 364 economists to write a letter of protest to *The Times*. They predicted that the tax increases would deepen 'the depression' (as they termed it). The consensus view nowadays is that the 364 were wrong, as falls in output in the 18 months to the first quarter of 1981 were succeeded by rising output from the spring of 1981 onwards. In his contribution to the IEA's recent collection of essays on *Were 364 Economists All Wrong?* Professor Stephen Nickell defends the 364, on the grounds that 'For the depression to deepen . . . output growth does not have to be negative, it merely has to be below trend. So the 364 cannot be dismissed out of hand by pointing to the time series of GDP growth. More analysis is needed'. In the key passage he notes that the UK's official measure of unemployment continued to rise until 1986. It follows, in his view, that: 'Under the not unreasonable assumption that rising unemployment means that growth is below trend (there being no reason to believe that equilibrium unemployment was rising much between 1982 and 1986), the depression deepened until somewhere between 1983 and 1986, exactly as the 364 said it would.' The purpose of this note is to refute Nickell's statements and to insist that the 364 were indeed all wrong. Contrary to his claims, it was above-trend growth – and not just growth – that resumed within a few quarters of the 1981 Budget. Nickell's selection of 1986 as the cut-off date to reach his conclusions is somewhat arbitrary and (despite what he says) it has no warrant in the letter from the 364. However, the discussion here relates to Nickell's chosen 1981–86 period.[1]

A condition of above-trend growth can be defined in two ways, either relative to the average rate of growth over the longer run (that is, growth is above trend when it is higher than a long-run average) or by reference to unemployment (that is, growth is above trend when the rate of unemployment, appropriately defined, goes down). Nickell concentrates on unemployment, but it may help to understand the years in question by examining output trends by themselves. An unusual feature of the UK economy is that its long-run growth rate has been stable at about 2¼ per cent a year since 1945. Since the 2¼ per cent figure is generally accepted, a legitimate procedure would be to compare it with actual growth in the 1981–86 period. But purists might object that a calculation should be made of the average growth rates in the cycle concurrent with the events under discussion and in the immediately preceding cycles. The results of this calculation are shown in Table 10.1, which perhaps raises the benchmark to 2½ per cent. (Whether 2¼ or 2½ per cent is the right number seems to the author to be a matter of opinion.)

What, in fact, were the growth rates of output and demand in the five-year period from 1981 to 1986? Were they above, beneath or in line with the critical numbers of 2¼ and 2½ per cent? Table 10.2 gives the answer. (Note that the first one-year period to be reviewed is that to the second quarter *1982*, that is, the first period of a full four quarters following the 1981 Budget. Output is measured by GDP at market prices.)

The evidence in Table 10.2 is clear. Only one of the ten numbers is not *above* 2½ per cent and that is the growth rate of output in the year to Q2 1984, which was hit by the miners' strike. If the Q2 1984 number is put to one side as distorted, the growth rates of output and demand in the five years to the second quarter 1986 were consistently above the 2½ per cent

Table 10.1   What was the 'average' growth rate of the UK economy at the time of the 1981 Budget?

	Growth rates, %, annual, of GDP at market prices	Domestic demand
From Q1 1965 to Q2 1989	2.4	2.6
From Q4 1973 to Q2 1989	2.2	2.3
From Q4 1979 to Q2 1989	2.4	2.9
Average of the three cycles	2.3	2.6

Notes: The previous cyclical peaks had been in Q1 1965, Q4 1973 and Q4 1979. The next cyclical peak was to be in Q2 1989. Peak-to-peak growth rates have to be calculated, as otherwise the average growth rate would be affected too much by changing margins of slack in the economy.

Source: Data in Office for National Statistics website at March 2006 and author's calculations. Calculations made on series in constant prices and seasonally adjusted.

Table 10.2   What were the annual growth rates of demand and output in each of the full five years after the 1981 Budget?

	Growth rates, %, annual, of GDP at market prices	Domestic demand
Year to Q2 1982	2.7	3.3
Year to Q2 1983	2.6	3.9
Year to Q2 1984*	2.5	3.2
Year to Q2 1985*	4.6	2.6
Year to Q2 1986	3.3	4.9

Note: * Affected by miners' strike, downwards in 1984 and upwards (when coal output resumed) in 1985.

Source: Data in ONS website in March 2006 and author's calculations.

threshold.[2] Particularly impressive is that the average annual rate of growth of domestic demand growth was 3.6 per cent, faster than that of output and well above the 2½ per cent number. Since the 364 were Keynesian economists whose policy injunctions ran in terms of demand and who specifically stated in their letter that the then Conservative government's policies involved 'deflating demand', only one verdict makes sense. If the behaviour of the UK economy in the five years from the 1981 Budget is considered in terms of demand and output growth relative to long-run averages, the 364 were hopelessly wrong.

But Nickell instead wants the debate to hinge on developments in the labour market and, particularly, on the change in unemployment. Here he appears to have a significant piece of evidence on his side, that the official measure of the rate of unemployment continued to rise until 1986. As already noted, by invoking what he describes as 'the not unreasonable assumption' that 'rising unemployment means that growth is below trend', he comes to the conclusion that the 364 were 'exactly' (yes, 'exactly') correct. What is to be made of this statement?

Nickell, the immediate past president of the Royal Economic Society, is widely regarded as Britain's leading labour market economist. So any questioning of his conclusions might seem rather foolhardy. However, the statements in his contribution to *Were 364 Economists All Wrong?* are charitably described as careless. They are not only misleading as an account of developments in the UK labour market in the 1980s, but also inconsistent with a much admired book on the subject which has Nickell's name on the front cover.[3] As he says, more analysis is needed.

It has long been understood that the degree of slack in the labour market is not always accurately measured by 'the rate of unemployment' published by official agencies. The unemployment rate can be measured in at least two ways, by adding up the number of claimants of unemployment benefit or by conducting surveys in which people are asked whether they are looking for work. Nickell's comment that unemployment rose until 1986 is based on the claimant-count figure (although he does mention the OECD's survey approach). The claimant-count number must however be treated with caution. Eligibility for unemployment benefit is affected by changes in the rules, while adjustments to the level of benefit (particularly relative to incomes in work) have an impact on both employment decisions and the extent to which genuinely unemployed people register for benefit.

In his celebrated 1967 presidential address to the American Economic Association' Milton Friedman proposed the idea of 'a natural rate of unemployment' at which inflation expectations were fully incorporated in behaviour, the demand for labour matched the supply, and the rate of wage inflation was stable. Although Friedman himself was sceptical that this rate could be identified by statistical methods, economists have subsequently spent much time and effort trying to calculate the natural rate. The concept is sometimes given different names, such as 'the NAIRU' ('the non-accelerating inflation rate of unemployment') or 'the equilibrium rate of unemployment'. In the 2005 second edition of their jointly authored book on *Unemployment* (first published in 1991), the equilibrium rate of unemployment is the phrase favoured by Richard Layard, Stephen Nickell and Richard Jackman (or LNJ). Much of the book is devoted to calculations of the equilibrium rate, which the authors believe is influenced by the unemployment benefit system, employment protection laws, labour taxes and other variables.[4]

A concept closely affiliated to that of the natural or equilibrium rate of unemployment is 'the natural rate of output'. This is the level of output associated with the natural rate of unemployment, and so with stable rates of wage and price inflation. It is often equated with 'trend output', while divergences from trend output are labelled 'the output gap'. In a growing economy the trend level of output is of course increasing over time. The terminology of the output gap has not yet settled down, but the OECD's practice is to define an excess of actual output over trend output 'a positive output gap', with the concept measured as a percentage of trend output. Another usage is to see the output gap as the excess of trend output over actual output, with 'a negative output gap' representing a situation of excess demand or even, in some versions, 'over-full employment'.[5] The author – like LNJ – prefers the OECD practice, which is adopted in the rest of this note.

Two points emerge from the last few paragraphs. First, if the underlying framework is accepted (and it is accepted by both the author and LNJ), statements about the rate of growth relative to trend are equivalent to statements about the output gap. If the level of the output gap was constant in a particular period, growth ran at the economy's trend rate; if a negative output gap became less negative, growth ran at an above-trend rate; and so on. It follows that – if the two sides to the present debate accept a set of estimates of the output gap – then those estimates go a long way to decide the matter at issue. Secondly, the actual rate of unemployment may not always *by itself* give policy-makers a guide to the level of or changes in the output gap. Instead it is necessary to calculate the equilibrium rate of unemployment, and to compare changes in the actual and equilibrium rates. One ostensibly anomalous case needs to be mentioned. *The actual rate of unemployment may be rising, but as long as the rise is less than that in the equilibrium rate, output growth is above trend.*

For many years the author, with his colleagues at Lombard Street Research, prepared a quarterly output gap series and advised clients on its macroeconomic implications. A chart of this series in the period under discussion accompanies the text (Figure 10.3). But this series may not be regarded as authoritative by other economists and the author does not otherwise have access to quarterly numbers. However, an annual series is published in the OECD's *Economic Outlook*. Table 10.3 shows the OECD numbers as they are currently reported by the Ecowin database.[6] The OECD's data generate one conclusion which supports Nickell's side of the argument. This is that growth was still beneath trend in 1982. However, with a mere 0.3 per cent increase in the negative output gap in that year, the

Output as % of trend

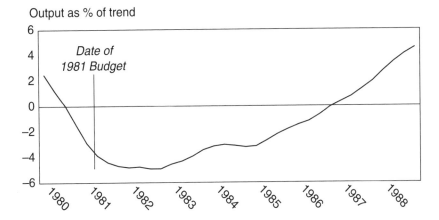

Notes: This output gap series was estimated at Lombard Street Research under the author's direction. After the 1981 Budget two or three quarters of beneath-trend growth were followed by roughly trend growth, with the negative output gap reaching its maximum value in Q4 1982. If the effect of the miners' strike is excluded, growth then ran at an above-trend rate until 1989. Other estimates – including Nickell's – are different.

Figure 10.3   An estimate of the UK output gap, 1980–88

difference from trend was trifling. On the reasonable view that output wobbles all the time around its growth path, a band of growth ½ per cent either side of a 2½ per cent central number could be deemed 'trend'. If so, every year from 1982 to 1988 recorded trend or above trend growth. The 364 were plain wrong – and in his defence of the 364 Nickell remains plain wrong today.

How is trend or above-trend growth reconciled with the increase in claimant-count unemployment? The answer is that the ostensibly anomalous case mentioned above did in fact apply in the 1981–86 period. The actual rate of unemployment rose, but the equilibrium rate of unemployment rose a little more. As a result, the margin of slack in the labour market in 1986 was similar to (or slightly less than) that in 1981. In his contribution to *Were 364 Economists All Wrong?* Nickell noted in parentheses that there was 'no reason to believe equilibrium unemployment was rising much between 1982 and 1986'. He ought to have checked what the excellent book co-authored by himself, Layard and Jackman says about the subject. On page 445 LNJ presents a table with the equilibrium rate of unemployment shown as 7.3 per cent in 1974–80, 8.7 per cent in 1981–87 and 8.7 per cent in 1988–90. The accompanying text comments,

Table 10.3   What do 'output gap' estimates say about growth relative to trend in the 1980s?

	Output gap Difference of actual output from trend output, expressed as a % of trend output, with excess of output over trend as a positive value – %	Implied value of growth relative to trend Above-trend growth indicated by a positive number – %
1980	−3.3	
1981	−6.3	−3.1
1982	−6.0	−0.3
1983	−4.5	1.6
1984	−3.6	0.9
1985	−2.0	1.7
1986	−0.4	1.6
1987	2.0	2.4
1988	4.4	2.4
1989	4.2	−0.2

Source: Ecowin, based on OECD and author's calculations.

The estimates of equilibrium unemployment [in our table] give an impression of remarkable stability in the 1980s. This is perhaps a little misleading, because a more detailed look at the numbers suggests that by the mid-1980s equilibrium unemployment had risen to 10 per cent before falling away. (The estimated value of [the equilibrium rate] for 1984–86 is 9.9 per cent.)[7]

If the equilibrium rate was 8.7 per cent in the seven years 1981–87 inclusive and 9.9 per cent in the three years 1984–86 inclusive, and even if the reader is advised that it was 'falling away' in 1987, the equilibrium rate between 1981 and 1983 must have been *lower* than 8.7 per cent. It may have been little more than 7 per cent in 1981. On this basis, the equilibrium rate must have been rising between 1981 and 1986, perhaps by more than 3 per cent of the work-force. As the increase in the claimant count unemployment rate in the five years to mid-1986 was from 7.9 per cent to 11.2 per cent, the actual rate of unemployment could have risen less than the equilibrium rate (although not by very much). It certainly did not rise by notably more than the equilibrium rate, which is what Nickell requires to establish beneath-trend growth.

Admittedly, the figure work on unemployment in the last paragraph is a weaker part of the refutation of Nickell's statements than the two previous bodies of evidence (that is, the figures comparing output and demand growth in 1981–86 with long-run averages, and the OECD output gap series).[8] The challenge for Nickell is to produce his own quarterly figures for the equilibrium rate of unemployment and the output gap, to argue that the actual rate of unemployment increased more than the equilibrium rate over extended sub-periods within the overall 1981–86 period, and so to rescue something of his position. Enough has been said to demonstrate that his central contention – that growth was beneath trend for five years from the 1981 Budget – is wrong. As one of the 364 economists who signed the letter to *The Times* in March 1981, it is understandable that Nickell should want to assemble the case for their defence. But the consensus view – that the letter from the 364 was mistimed and misjudged, and almost wholly incorrect in its economic prognosis – remains the right one.

Notes

1. Actually the letter was open-ended about the timing of the end of 'the depression'. When Nickell says that the depression ended between 1983 and 1986 'exactly as the 364 said it would', the use of the word 'exactly' is pure invention. Moreover, everyone accepts that the British economy boomed between 1987 and 1989. The return of boom conditions little more than five years from the date of their letter by itself makes a mockery of the 364, but – to keep the discussion alive – it can be limited to the five years from March 1981.
2. Of course there were 20 quarters in the five years to Q2 1986. A few of these had annual growth rates under 2½ per cent. (Others had annual growth rates well above 2½ per cent.) Nickell might jump on the occasional beneath-trend quarters to support his position, but – with one exception – the author regards this as splitting hairs. (Note that in 1984 output was affected by the miners' strike.) The exception is that growth dipped quite sharply in early 1982 after interest rates were raised in autumn 1981, with base rates above 15 per cent for a few weeks. If Nickell views that as monetary 'overkill', the author agrees. In fact he said as much at the time in newspaper articles.
3. R. Layard, S. Nickell and R. Jackman, *Unemployment: Macroeconomic Performance and the Labour Market* (Oxford: Oxford University Press, 2nd edition, 2005).
4. The LNJ volume, of which the first edition appeared in 1991, was at least partly stimulated by Patrick Minford's *Unemployment: Cause and Cure* (Oxford: Martin Robertson), which had been published in 1983. Both Minford and Nickell insisted that the unemployment rate was affected by such factors as trade union power and the generosity of unemployment benefit. In the circumstances of the time (that is, the late 1970s and early 1980s when unemployment was widely attributed solely to demand deficiency) this was a brave and important contribution to the public debate.
5. The terminological muddle about the 'output gap' concept arises because it originated in two different strands of thought. The first is the Keynesian idea of 'Okun's gap', that is, the excess of the *full* employment rate of unemployment over the actual rate; the second is Friedman's 1967 presidential address to the AEA, in which full employment was rejected as a policy goal, and rising wage inflation was attributed to the excess of the actual rate of unemployment over the *natural* rate. The subject is discussed in more detail in the appendix to the Introduction.
6. The 'output gap' can be estimated in different ways and large revisions are not unusual.
7. LNJ, *Unemployment*, 2nd edition, p. 445.
8. Part of the explanation for the divergence between the output gap numbers (which at sharply at variance with Nickell's claims) and the unemployment numbers (which are less decisive in refuting them) is that the LNJ estimates of the equilibrium rate of unemployment use 'a two-period lag on the explanatory variables in order to take some account of the dynamics'. (LNJ, *Unemployment*, 2nd edition, p. 445) These subtleties do not change the main point, that growth was *not* beneath trend in the 1981–86 period.

III. 'AFTER THE 1981 BUDGET: A REPLY TO TIM CONGDON', BY STEPHEN NICKELL[1] – PUBLISHED IN *ECONOMIC AFFAIRS* (LONDON: IEA), DECEMBER 2006 ISSUE

Introduction

Did the depression deepen after the budget in the Spring of 1981? In my contribution to the IEA's recent collection of essays on the 1981 budget (Nickell, 2006), I argued that it did. In Congdon (2006), Tim Congdon proposed a refutation of my arguments. My core argument is set out in one sentence in Nickell (2006): 'Under the not unreasonable assumption that rising unemployment means that growth is below trend (there being no reason to believe that equilibrium unemployment was rising much between 1982 and 1986), the depression deepened until somewhere between 1983 and 1986' (p. 59). In what follows, I expand on this sentence and show that it is indeed correct, contrary to the argument set out in Congdon (2006).[2]

The detail is important. The 364 economists said that the depression would deepen. I said that it did, in fact, deepen from 1981 Q1 to some point in the period from 1983 and 1986. In Congdon (2006) is a figure showing the UK's output gap. Eyeballing this figure reveals that this measure of the output gap reached its lowest point in 1983 Q1. Both the statement of the 364 and my statement are consistent with this fact. I could simply rest my case but it is worth pursuing this issue a little further.

Measuring the Output Gap

A depression deepens if growth is below potential or, more formally, if the output gap becomes more negative. One way of measuring this is simply to work out the average growth rate of the economy over a long period, equate this average to trend growth or the potential growth rate, then compare actual growth to this average. If it is below, the depression deepens, if it is above, it does not. This use of long-run averages is, however, hopeless in periods when the trend of productivity growth is changing. Thus, as in many other countries, trend productivity growth in the UK slowed down in the 1970s. And in the 1980s it speeded up again for reasons which have been much discussed (see Nickell et al., 1992, for example).

So a more precise analysis is required. Let us start with how to measure the output gap. Suppose we have a Cobb–Douglas production function (in logs), namely,

$$y_t = \alpha(n_t + h_t) + (1 - \alpha)k_t + a_t \tag{10.1}$$

y = output, n = employment, h = hours, k = capital, a = total factor productivity (TFP). On trend we have

$$y_t^* = \alpha(n_t^* + h_t^*) + (1 - \alpha)k_t + a_t \tag{10.2}$$

where n_t^* = 'equilibrium' employment, h_t^* = 'equilibrium' hours. Employment, in logs, is given by

$$n_t = pop_t - ia_t - u_t \tag{10.3}$$

where $pop = ln$ (population of working age), ia = inactivity rate, u = unemployment rate.[3]

Inactivity went up very slightly in the early 1980s but assume this was an equilibrium phenomenon. So we have

$$n_t^* = pop_t - ia_t - u_t^* \tag{10.4}$$

where u^* is equilibrium unemployment. Differencing these equations, we have a simple expression for the output gap, namely

$$(y_t - y_t^*) = \alpha[-(u_t - u_t^*) + (h_t - h_t^*)] \tag{10.5}$$

This is based on the assumption that once we control for effort, as captured by hours, the remaining *TFP* fluctuations are equilibrium phenomena. If not, there is little we can do since we have no other readily available data. As we have already noted, an alternative is to use past trends to generate *TFP*. However, when trend *TFP* growth rises, as it did in the 1980s relative to the 1970s, the output gap measure tends to be biased. In order to compute the measure of the output gap defined in (10.5), we need estimates of equilibrium unemployment, u^*. There are two methods of producing such estimates. In the first, u^* is computed by backing it out of a Phillips curve. This method is used in Layard et al. (1991, table 16) and is now used by the OECD and the Bank of England to generate time series of u^*. There is no attempt to explain why u^* changes but it is simply estimated so that it is consistent with upward and downward movements in inflation, given the observed path of u. This method is not reliable for year-on-year changes but only for very long-term trends.

The alternative method of estimating u^* is first to estimate a complete model of the economy including all those factors which influence equilibrium unemployment and then to generate a reduced form equation which explains u^* in terms of these factors. This method is used in Andrews and Nickell (1982, table VII), Minford (1983, pp. 132–3 and table 1.2), and

Table 10.4   *OECD measure of equilibrium unemployment (*u**) (based on
the OECD standardized rate)*

	u*	u	(u − u*)
80	7.0	6.4	−0.6
81i)	7.8	8.8	1.0
81	8.0	9.8	1.8
82	9.0	11.3	2.3
83	9.2	12.4	3.4
84	9.5	11.7	2.2
85	9.5	11.2	1.7
86	9.5	11.2	1.7
87	9.5	10.3	0.8
88	9.5	8.6	−0.9
89	8.8	7.2	−1.6
90	8.5	7.1	−1.4

Source: OECD, method described in Elmeskov et al. (1998).

Layard et al. (1991, table 16). It is superior to the first method
described above but is more difficult to make operational because it is not
possible to obtain data on all the factors which influence equilibrium
unemployment.

In Tables 10.4 and 10.5, we present two sets of estimates of u^* based on
the first method described above. These tend to be rising slowly in the first
half of the 1980s, essentially because given unemployment in 1984–86, the
estimate of u^* has to 'explain' why inflation is not falling very fast.
However, as I noted correctly in my IEA piece, it is hard to see why u^*
should have been rising throughout the first half of the 1980s. The key variables which tend to drive u^* are unions, benefits and taxes. In Layard et al.
(1991), u^* measured this way rose from 6.1 per cent in 1974/80 to 6.6 per
cent in 1981/87 (see table 18), so it was pretty flat in the late 1970s and early
1980s. In Minford (1983) u^* depends on union density, real benefits, payroll
taxes and income taxes (including National Insurance contributions) (see
table 1.2). In Table 10.6, we see what happened to these variables in the early
1980s. From the first quarter of 1981, all the relevant variables were stable
or falling. Indeed, if we use the impact of these variables on u^* set out in
Minford (1983, table 1.2), the fall in union density alone would cut u^* by
around 1.3 million.

So, to summarize, using the first method of computing u^*, $(u − u^*)$ rose
until 1983 Q3. But as we can see, the main factors influencing u^* were all
pointing in the direction of further falls in u^* beyond 1983.

Table 10.5   *Bank of England measure of equilibrium unemployment (*u**)*
(based on the OECD standardized rate)

	u^*	u	$(u-u^*)$		u^*	u	$(u-u^*)$
79i)	6.3	5.1	−1.2	83i)	9.5	12.3	2.8
ii)	6.7	5.0	−1.7	ii)	9.6	12.5	2.9
iii)	7.2	4.9	−2.3	iii)	9.7	12.6	2.9
iv)	7.6	4.9	−2.7	iv)	9.8	12.3	2.5
80i)	7.9	5.3	−2.6	84i)	10.0	11.9	1.9
ii)	8.0	5.9	−3.1	ii)	10.2	11.7	1.5
iii)	8.1	6.8	−1.3	iii)	10.2	11.6	1.4
iv)	8.2	7.9	−0.3	iv)	10.2	11.6	1.4
81i)	8.2	8.8	0.6	85i)	10.3	11.4	1.1
ii)	8.3	9.6	1.3	ii)	10.4	11.2	0.8
iii)	8.4	10.2	1.8	iii)	10.5	11.1	0.6
iv)	8.6	10.6	2.0	iv)	10.6	11.1	0.5
82i)	8.7	10.8	2.1	86i)	10.7	11.1	0.4
ii)	8.8	11.0	2.2	ii)	10.8	11.2	0.4
iii)	9.0	11.5	2.5	iii)	11.0	11.3	0.3
iv)	9.2	11.7	2.5	iv)	11.0	11.0	0.0

Source: Greenslade et al. (2003).

In order to compute the output gap, we see from (10.5) that we need data on working hours relative to their equilibrium value, $h - h^*$. These are available in Larsen et al. (2002) and are reported in Table 10.7. The series is detrended to eliminate the impact of the steady increase in part-time employees. Overall, the series suggests a bottoming out at the end of 1984. The scale of the effect is rather small (that is, a fall of 1.2 per cent from 1981 to the minimum). Looking just at manufacturing hours we see some bigger effects, thus the fall from 1981 Q1 to the minimum in 1983 is over 3 per cent. However, it is probably not surprising that the fall in other sectors of the economy is smaller. Using the data in Tables 10.5 and 10.7, we can compute the output gap from equation (10.5). This is presented in Table 10.8. On the basis of these data, it would appear that the output gap steadily became more negative from 1981 Q1 to 1983 Q3, a period of 2½ years. This indicates a considerable period of below trend growth after the 1981 budget. Furthermore, this is based on a method of computing u^* which relies on a simple specification of the Phillips curve. As we have seen, looking at the standard factors generating u^*, it is not easy to see why u^* should be rising significantly in the first half of the 1980s. However, even if we ignore this point, growth was below trend for a considerable period after the 1981 Budget. Thus the depression did indeed

Table 10.6   Variables influencing u*

Benefits (married couple, 2 kids, combination of unemployment benefit, earnings related supplement and supplementary benefit including child benefit)

	Replacement rate (benefits/wages) (%)	Nominal benefits (£)	Real benefits (Nov. 1980) (£)
Nov. 80	52.6	51.0	51.0
Nov. 81	53.0	54.9	45.6
Nov. 82	51.3	56.7	47.7
Nov. 83	49.2	60.3	48.3
Nov. 84	47.6	63.2	48.3
Nov. 85	47.3	66.6	48.2
July 86	45.4	67.4	47.2

Taxes

	Union density (%)	Total tax wedge (%)	Payroll tax rate (%)	Income tax rate (%)
79	52	49	15.3	14.8
80	51	50	15.6	15.0
81	49	53	16.9	15.6
82	48	53	16.3	15.9
83	47	52	16.5	15.9
84	46	51	16.2	15.5
85	45	50	15.6	15.3
86	44	50	15.1	15.0

Notes:
1. Benefits data are based on the benefit/tax regime along with the average earnings index and the RPI.
2. Union density is from the Centre for Economic Performance (LSE), OECD data set (attached to CEP discussion paper 502).
3. Tax data are those used in Layard et al. (1991).

deepen after 1981 Q1 as predicted in the letter written by the 364. And this process continued until at least 1983 which is in the period 1983–86 as I noted in Nickell (2006).

More General Remarks on the 1981 Budget

Tim Congdon saw the 1981 Budget as a watershed, the end of Keynesian demand management and the beginning of medium-term fiscal rules. I see it as one stop in the process of trying to find a framework for macroeconomic

Table 10.7   Detrended hours worked per quarter

	Hours	$(h - h^*)$ (% index)		Hours	$(h - h^*)$ (% index)
1981i)	440.6	0	1984i)	437.7	−0.7
ii)	441.6	0	ii)	436.9	−0.9
iii)	441.4	0	iii)	436.2	−1.1
iv)	440.7	−0.2	iv)	435.7	−1.2
1982i)	439.7	−0.3	1985i)	435.5	−1.2
ii)	439.1	−0.4	ii)	435.7	−1.2
iii)	438.8	−0.5	iii)	436.1	−0.9
iv)	438.9	−0.4	iv)	436.8	−0.7
1983i)	439.1	−0.4	1986i)	437.3	−0.6
ii)	439.1	−0.4	ii)	437.8	−0.5
iii)	438.9	−0.5	iii)	437.9	−0.5
iv)	438.4	−0.6	iv)	437.8	−0.5

Source: Larsen et al. (2002).

Table 10.8   An 'output gap' index

$-(u_t - u_t^*) + (h_t - h^*)$, (Table 10.2, Table 10.4) (using equation 10.5)			
1981i)	−0.6	1984i)	−2.6
ii)	−1.3	ii)	−2.4
iii)	−1.8	iii)	−2.5
iv)	−2.2	iv)	−2.6
1982i)	−2.4	1985i)	−2.3
ii)	−2.6	ii)	−2.0
iii)	−3.0	iii)	−1.5
iv)	−2.9	iv)	−1.2
1983i)	−3.2	1986i)	−1.0
ii)	−3.3	ii)	−0.9
iii)	−3.4	iii)	−0.8
iv)	−3.1	iv)	−0.5

policy under floating exchange rates which would allow the economy to grow at a rate reasonably close to its potential while having low and stable inflation. Of course, the simple recognition that such a framework was required is a significant achievement. Not surprisingly, a number of strategies were tried during the period from the beginning of the Conservative administration in May 1979 to the fixing of the exchange rate within the European exchange rate mechanism in October 1990. One set of facts is

striking. In mid-June 1979, RPI inflation was 10.6 per cent, Labour Force
Survey (LFS) unemployment was 5.3 per cent, the official interest rate was
14 per cent. In September 1990, RPI inflation was 10.4 per cent, LFS unemployment was 7.1 per cent, the official interest rate was 15 per cent. Little
change there. So a sceptical reader of the data might argue that little had
been achieved in the intervening years. What went wrong during this period
is the subject of considerable controversy. What is clear, however, is that an
agreed, effective and stable structure for macroeconomic policy had not been
found. This is hardly surprising. Given a situation where rapidly responding
wage and price indexation was deeply embedded in both labour and product
markets, operating within a coherent framework for macroeconomic policy
would have been exceptionally difficult. This indexation structure meant that
any relative price shock was going to feed through to general inflation very
rapidly and generate instability in both the nominal and the real economy.
Using an active monetary policy to keep inflation reasonably stable in this
environment is extremely tricky and so it proved. In any event, the 364 economists claimed that the depression would deepen after the 1981 budget, and
so it did.

Notes

1. I am again most greatful to Chris Shadforth for his valuable assistance.
2. Tim Congdon claims in the closing paragraph of Congdon (2006) that I contended that
   growth was beneath trend for five years from the 1981 Budget. I contended no such thing,
   having said that growth was below trend from the 1981 Budget to *some time* during the
   period 1983–86.
3. Note, employment is equal to the population of working age times the product of the
   participation rate and one minus the unemployment rate. Symbolically, we have

$$N = POP\,(1 - ia)\,(1-u) \qquad (10.6)$$

or, in logs,

$$n = pop - ia - u. \qquad (10.7)$$

References

Andrews, M. and Nickell, S., 'Unemployment in the United Kingdom since the
war', *Review of Economic Studies*, vol. 49, 1982, pp. 731–59.
Congdon, T., 'Were the 364 all wrong? – a comment on Stephen Nickell's paper',
Economic Affairs, December 2006.
Elmeskov, J., Martin, J.P. and Scarpetta, S., *Key Lessons for Labour Market
Reforms: Evidence from OECD Countries' Experience* (Paris: OECD, 1998).
Greenslade, J.V., Pierse, R.G. and Saleheen, J., 'A Kalman filter approach to esti-
mating the NAIRU', *Bank of England Working Paper 179*, 2003.
Larsen, J., Neiss, K. and Shorthall, F., 'Factor utilisation and productivity estimates
for the United Kingdom', *Bank of England Working Paper 162*, 2002.

Layard, R., Nickell, S. and Jackman, R., *Unemployment: Macroeconomic Performance and the Labour Market* (Oxford: Oxford University Press, 1991).

Minford, P., *Unemployment Cause and Cure* (Oxford: Martin Robertson, 1983), with D. Davies, M. Peel and A. Sprague.

Nickell, S., 'The Budget of 1981 was over the top', in P. Booth (ed.), *Were 364 Economists All Wrong?* (London: Institute of Economic Affairs, 2006).

Nickell, S., Wadhwani, S. and Wall, M., 'Productivity growth in UK companies, 1975–1986', *European Economic Review*, vol. 36, 1992, pp. 1055–91.

IV. THE 364 WERE OVER THE TOP: A REPLY TO PROFESSOR NICKELL'S REPLY, BY TIM CONGDON – PUBLISHED IN *ECONOMIC AFFAIRS* (LONDON: IEA), DECEMBER 2006 ISSUE

I am grateful to Professor Nickell for his reply, which – if I may say so – is a rigorous and scholarly piece of work. In my opinion, it involves a major climbdown from his original paper. We are now largely in agreement about the key facts in the period. But we remain a long way apart in our interpretations of those facts and in the rhetoric justified by the interpretations.

The letter from the 364 did not predict a date at which the so-called 'depression' would end. The 364 seem to have thought that, if 'monetarist policies' were maintained, falling output or beneath-trend growth would continue indefinitely. The length of the period of falling output and/or beneath-trend growth after the 1981 Budget is therefore the essence of the debate. Since output stopped falling almost immediately after the Budget, the dispute is narrowed down to the length of the period of beneath-trend growth. In his original paper Nickell said that 'the depression deepened until somewhere between 1983 and 1986'. I challenged him to produce 'quarterly figures for the equilibrium rate of unemployment and the output gap' to substantiate his judgement. I must thank him for having done that, as the result is a drastic clarification of the matters under discussion.

In Table 10.9 I compare the quarterly estimates of the output gap prepared at Lombard Street Research, under my direction, with Nickell's in his reply. They are somewhat different in terms of *levels*, possibly because the Lombard Street Research estimates were not adjusted for hours of work in the same way as Nickell's. But – for the purposes of our debate – it is the *changes in the levels* that are critical since it is these that determine whether growth was above or beneath trend. (A negative figure indicates beneath-trend growth and a positive figure above-trend growth.)

Nickell's number and my own are very close together for most of the 1981–86 period. We agree that beneath-trend growth continued for at least

Table 10.9   A comparison of Congdon's and Nickell's views on the output gap and the growth path, 1981–86

		Level of output gap, % of trend output		Change in output gap, as % of trend output*	
		Lombard Street Research estimates, prepared under Congdon's direction	Nickell's May 2006 estimates	Lombard Street Research estimates, prepared under Congdon's direction	Nickell's May 2006 estimates
1981	Q1	−2.9	−0.6		
	Q2	−3.9	−1.3	−1.0	−0.7
	Q3	−4.4	−1.8	−0.5	−0.5
	Q4	−4.7	−2.2	−0.3	−0.4
1982	Q1	−4.8	−2.4	−0.1	−0.2
	Q2	−4.8	−2.6	0.1	−0.2
	Q3	−4.9	−3.0	−0.1	−0.4
	Q4	−4.9	−2.9	0.0	0.1
1983	Q1	−4.5	−3.2	0.4	−0.3
	Q2	−4.3	−3.3	0.2	−0.1
	Q3	−3.9	−3.4	0.4	−0.1
	Q4	−3.4	−3.1	0.5	0.3
1984	Q1	−3.2	−2.6	0.3	0.5
	Q2	−3.0	−2.4	0.1	0.2
	Q3	−3.1	−2.5	−0.1	−0.1
	Q4	−3.2	−2.6	−0.1	−0.1
1985	Q1	−3.2	−2.3	0.1	0.3
	Q2	−2.7	−2.0	0.5	0.3
	Q3	−2.2	−1.5	0.5	0.5
	Q4	−1.8	−1.2	0.4	0.3
1986	Q1	−1.5	−1.0	0.3	0.2
	Q2	−1.2	−0.9	0.3	0.1
	Q3	−0.7	−0.8	0.5	0.1
	Q4	−0.1	−0.5	0.6	0.3

Notes: * These numbers are quarterly changes. They are *not* at annualized rates. So – if the change in the output gap in a quarter was minus 0.2% – the annualized rate of growth was 0.8% beneath trend.

Tim Congdon would like to thank Stewart Robertson, now senior economist at Aviva, and Simon Ward, now chief economist at New Star Asset Management, for their help in preparing the Lombard Street Research output gap series.

three quarters after the first quarter 1981; we also agree that (if the effects of the miners' strike in 1984 are removed) growth was at an above-trend rate from Q4 1983 to the end of 1986. The remaining period of contention is the seven quarters from Q1 1982 to Q3 1983. Nickell believes that the output gap became more negative – by about 1 per cent of trend output – in these seven quarters, whereas the estimates produced by Lombard Street Research suggest that the gap became less negative – also by about 1 per cent of trend output.

I am not going to try to eliminate the residual disagreement. Let us instead suppose – for the sake of discussion – that Nickell's numbers are right. According to them, the rate of growth was on average 0.7 per cent (at an annual rate) beneath trend in the still controversial seven quarters. But how should these quarters be characterized? It is a regrettable fact that output does not rise in a straight line, at a constant rate, in any known economy. There are wiggles and jiggles around the trend, and any sensible person would accept that growth is at trend when it occurs inside a corridor around the exact trend figure. In my comment I proposed: 'On the reasonable view that output wobbles all the time around its growth path, a band of growth ½ per cent either side of a 2½ per cent central number could be deemed "trend".' I then concluded, using my own numbers, that, 'every year from 1982 to 1988 recorded trend or above trend growth. The 364 were plain wrong – and in his defence of the 364 Nickell remains plain wrong today'.

Assuming that Nickell accepts my definition of a trend corridor, we could keep on squabbling. To be precise, we could keep on squabbling about 0.2 per cent of output per quarter![1] I submit that we are pretty much agreed about 'the truth', which is summarized in Box 10.1. No doubt Nickell and I could quibble until kingdom come about the exact words, phrases and decimal points that represent 'this truth', but bluntly – in terms of fact – the debate is over.

As I said at the start, Nickell's numbers involve a major climbdown. In his original paper he said that the depression deepened 'until somewhere between 1983 and 1986'. Despite the second footnote in Nickell's reply, I was therefore justified in reviewing the entire 1981–86 period in my criticism of his claims. In his detailed and specific quarterly numbers it is clear that Nickell has given up three years of the 'depression'. His new position is that 'the depression deepened until the middle of 1983', as the output gap was – on his figures – most negative in Q3 1983. We must remember that the length of the period of beneath-trend growth is the essence of the debate. Given the context, 'somewhere between 1983 and 1986' has a very different connotation from 'the middle of 1983'.

At this stage I want to make two points linking the Congdon–Nickell exchange to the precise contents of the letter from the 364. The first relates to the 364's views on why 'the depression' would 'deepen'. The wording of the letter – with its reference to the 'deflating' of 'demand' – implies that output was expected to be held back because of weakness in demand. So,

---

**BOX 10.1   A SUMMARY OF CONGDON'S AND
NICKELL'S VIEWS ON THE UK
ECONOMY, 1981–86**

Period	Description of economy
1981 Q2 to 1981 Q4	Output stopped falling, but growth was at a beneath-trend rate.
1982 Q1 to 1983 Q3	Trend growth, if growth is accepted as being at trend within a narrow corridor around the exact trend rate, although Nickell believes growth was still significantly beneath trend until 1982 Q3 whereas Congdon's estimates suggest that the negative output gap became smaller in the seven quarters.
1983 Q4 to 1986 Q4	Above-trend growth, if negative effect of miners' strike on output in second half of 1984 is removed.

---

in addition to tracking output (and making estimates of the output gap), it is necessary to check what happened to demand.

Since our disagreement on the length of the 'depression' is now confined to the seven quarters to Q3 1983, the question becomes 'what happened to demand in that seven-quarter period?' Data on the growth of domestic final expenditure in real terms are available in the website of the Office for National Statistics. They show domestic final expenditure (in constant 2002 prices) was £146.4 billion in Q4 1981 and £156.9 billion in Q3 1983, giving an annualized rate of increase of just above 4 per cent. This is undoubtedly an above-trend figure. Nickell may or may not be right that the growth *of output* was significantly beneath trend in the seven quarters. He is plainly wrong if he is claiming – on behalf of the 364 – that the growth *of demand* was beneath trend.

The second point arises because the 364 alleged that official policies 'would erode the industrial base of our economy'. If this remark means anything, it must be that the UK's competitiveness would be undermined by *slow* productivity growth. But – in trying to rescue something of his original debating position – Nickell had to recognize that one of the main reasons for the rise in unemployment until 1986 was not demand weakness, but the unusually *rapid* growth of productivity. In fact, in the six years from Q4 1980 output per filled job in manufacturing climbed at an annual compound rate of 6.0 per cent, whereas in the six years between the cyclical peaks of Q2 1973 and Q2 1979 output per head in manufacturing rose at a compound annual rate of only 1.1 per cent. Productivity growth in UK manufacturing in the early and mid-1980s may have been the fastest ever recorded. Unfortunately, that did lead to heavy job losses in some sectors, but it was vital in restoring the UK's long-run competitiveness. Would the 364 have preferred a continuation of the productivity stagnation of the 1970s?

My last comment is on rhetoric and tone. It turns out that – when we check each other's conceptual frameworks and dig down into the figures – Nickell and I are not a million miles apart. But Nickell keeps on using the exaggerated and emotive word 'depression' to characterize the years from 1981 to 1983, sticks to his bluff that the 364 were right all along, and finally tries to change the subject by making a song and dance about the rise in inflation in the final years of the Thatcher premiership. The explanation for all the huffing and puffing is that – as he knows – the reputation of Keynesian economists in British universities was badly damaged by the sequel to the 1981 Budget. My plea to him, and to as many of the 364 as are still willing to listen, is: 'Dispense with the rhetoric, and be careful with facts and figures. Above all, open your minds to the possibility that you were wrong because your underlying model – the income-expenditure model of the textbooks – is an inadequate representation of a modern economy because it has no meaningful role for monetary influences on asset prices and demand.'

The 364 were over the top, not the 1981 Budget.

Note

1. If this is not immediately apparent, the negative output gap increased on average by 0.17 per cent per quarter (that is, at an annualized rate of 0.7 per cent) in the seven quarters to Q3 1983, according to Nickell. 0.7 per cent is 0.2 per cent more than 0.5 per cent, which (I suggest) would be within a trend corridor.

PART FIVE

Did Monetarism Succeed?

For almost 15 years now (mid-2006) the British economy has enjoyed unparalleled stability. The inflation targeting regime announced by Mr Norman (later Lord) Lamont in October 1992 has worked far better than anyone expected at the time. Not only has the target been met year after year, but also the path of output growth has been remarkably steady. The obvious question is 'why?'

One point is clear. Old-style British Keynesianism – the Keynesianism of incomes policies and fiscal fine-tuning – forms no part of the explanation. Incomes policies and fiscal fine-tuning were dropped by the Conservatives in 1979 and 1980, and New Labour has not brought them back since 1997. Essays 11 and 12 emphasize the importance of monetarism in ending the grip that these two misguided ideas once had on British policy-makers. But that was a largely negative achievement. Monetarism – as it was conceived in the 1970s, with money supply targets as the core of the agenda – cannot claim to have made a major positive contribution to the UK's post-1992 stability. The trend in the equilibrium ratio of money to income changed radically in the early 1980s and invalidated the specific target numbers for money growth envisaged in the Medium-Term Financial Strategy. Essay 12 suggests that there were good reasons for the change in the money/income trend and denies that supposed instabilities in money demand functions justified officialdom's indifference to the explosion in money growth in the late 1980s. The money growth explosion – like that in the early 1970s – resulted in another boom–bust cycle.

However, the continuing validity of the monetary theory of national income did not lead to a restoration of money supply targets. Instead the Bank of England's variation of interest rates became the virtual factotum *of policy. Experience showed that – contrary to the Keynesian orthodoxy of the 1940s and 1950s – aggregate demand was sufficiently interest-elastic for this one instrument to keep demand growth on track and to deliver on-target inflation. Further, the depoliticization of interest rate decisions – which was completed by the granting of operational independence to the Bank of England in 1997 – established accountability in the institutional framework.*

Plainly, money-target monetarism was not responsible for the huge improvement in performance, which is quantified in Essay 13. But the vital intellectual argument for an inflation targeting regime was – and remains – Friedman's 1967 rejection of a long-run trade-off between unemployment and inflation. The Introduction and Essay 13 propose that Friedman's theories foreshadowed the development of the concept of 'the output gap' (as that term is now almost universally used), even if Friedman himself did not really see it. The ideas of the natural rate of unemployment and the output gap led to the emergence of the currently dominant structure of central-bank decision-taking. For these reasons output-gap monetarism does deserve the credit for the macroeconomic stability of the past 15 years, both in the UK and elsewhere.

11. Assessing the Conservatives' record

Control of inflation was the Conservatives' first priority when they were elected in 1979. In the words of *The Right Approach to the Economy*, effectively their statement of intent on economic policy, 'The role of inflation as the great destroyer – of jobs, living standards and a stable order – is now much more widely recognised'. Did the Conservatives – in the end – deliver a worthwhile reduction in inflation? Was inflation much lower in their final years before the 1997 general election than when they came to power?

In the five years to June 1979 the average increase in the retail price index was 15.1 per cent a year, with a peak of 26.9 per cent in August 1975; in the five years to February 1997 the average increase in the retail price index was 2.6 per cent a year, with a peak of 4.3 per cent in May 1992. The facts appear to tell their own story. On the criterion that it regarded as the key measure of performance, the Conservative government of 1979 to 1997 was successful. If an end-of term report were prepared in 1997, the case for an 'alpha' mark might be unconvincing because it did not restore full price stability, but a highly commendable 'beta plus' would be fair. But the facts may be deceptive. Because inflation fell in all the main industrial countries from the 1970s to the 1990s, the Conservatives' achievement was far from unique. Critics might argue that international pressures – such as falling commodity prices and the almost universal adoption of anti-inflationary monetary policies – were the main reasons for the decline in inflation in the UK. The British government could then be portrayed as a bit actor in a drama jointly directed by the American Federal Reserve in Washington and the Bundesbank in Frankfurt.

The question becomes, 'to what extent was the decline in inflation due to the government's own decisions, as it tried to fulfil a predetermined agenda, and not the result of Britain's passive participation in the global trend?' In any answer to this question the word 'monetarism' is inescapable. In June 1979 most members of the newly elected government, including the Prime Minister Mrs (later Lady) Thatcher herself, believed that a distinctive and valuable part of its economic programme was the pledge to combat inflation by reducing the rate of money supply growth. In that sense leading Conservative politicians were 'monetarists', however much they subsequently denied any formal affiliation to a precise set of ideas.

In the British political debate of the late 1970s monetarism was far more than a number of technical propositions about monetary economics. It was, self-consciously, a counter-revolution against the prevalent thought-habits of the time. Indeed, it could be characterized as a rejection of the whole post-war period trend in economic policy. (In his *Who's Who* entry Sir Keith [later Lord] Joseph, perhaps the key figure in the movement, referred to only one pamphlet he wrote for the Centre for Policy Studies, the think tank that he and Thatcher founded in 1974. It was called *Reversing the Trend.*) In particular, monetarism was targeted against two doctrines – which may be labelled corporatism and Keynesianism – whose influence was greatest in the Labour-dominated period from 1964 to 1979.

I

The heart of the first doctrine ('corporatism') was that the state should co-operate with the organized representatives of labour and capital, namely the Trades Union Congress and the Confederation of British Industry, in order to determine both macroeconomic outcomes, such as the inflation rate, and the distribution of income between wages and profits. Annual agreements between the three parties on the rate of wage and dividend increases, also known as 'incomes policies', were the main practical expression of corporatist ideas. Incomes policies enjoyed huge support among the chattering classes, particularly in economics departments at Britain's universities. They were regarded as the correct analytical response to the problem of inflation, as they dealt with hard men like trade union leaders and hard numbers for wage increases. By contrast, monetary control was widely dismissed as a plaything of academic theoreticians. Further, incomes policies were deemed to be particularly appropriate for modern Britain, a nation assumed to suffer – indefinitely into the future – from entrenched trade union power.

One of the monetarists' most important messages in the late 1970s was that excessive monetary growth, not trade union power, was the cause of inflation. It followed that inflation could be controlled by a reduction in money supply growth, whereas over the long run incomes policies would fail. Moreover, the government did not have to rely on trade union co-operation to keep inflation down. On the contrary, the monetarists believed that overmighty trade unions were responsible for serious inefficiencies in some of the most vital parts of Britain's economy, including the car and shipbuilding industries, and the energy utilities. In its battle with corporatism and the trade union movement, the Thatcher government secured a comprehensive victory. In the summer of 1979 it scrapped the machinery of wage and price control. A few months later it re-emphasized its commitment to monetary restraint by raising interest rates to 17 per cent, a move intended to bring money supply growth back into line with the target. By the middle of 1982 inflation was less than 5 per cent. The general election of 1983 was fought with an inflation rate of 4.0 per cent. Even more salient were the heavy defeats inflicted on the trade unions in a sequence of labour disputes. The failure of the coal-miners' strike of 1984 exploded the myth that Britain was ungovernable without the consent of the trade unions.

How important was monetarism in all this? Crucially, it did provide the intellectual rationale for ending the union–government dialogue over prices and incomes. By extension, it made possible the reforms to trade union law which in the 1980s and early 1990s restored managements' ability to manage. One result was that productivity gains in the once heavily union-ized industries of energy supply, steel and cars were spectacular, far higher than in manufacturing industry as a whole. These productivity gains helped to curb inflation, although they did so not by dampening the rate of growth of the quantity of money, but by boosting the rate of growth of the quan-tity of output. More fundamentally, in the early 1980s, the month-by-month movements in the money supply were monitored closely for their future inflationary message. Although this approach to macroeconomic management had been largely (but not entirely) abandoned by the 1990s, it was followed by exactly the decline in inflation that the monetarists wanted.

Corporatism held sway for a relatively brief period in Britain's political economy, roughly from the mid-1960s to 1979, and had never benefited from rigorous intellectual endorsement by an acknowledged leader of thought. The second doctrine of the Labour-dominated era, Keynesianism, was a different matter. Keynes himself undoubtedly had one of the most original and powerful minds ever to have been involved in British policy-making. His thinking was widely credited with the achievement of full employment of the 1950s and 1960s, an achievement which commonly appeared under the banner of 'the Keynesian revolution'. The ascription of full employment to Keynes depends on the claim that macroeconomic policy was transformed by the theoretical novelties in his *General Theory of Employment, Interest and Money*, published in 1936. Before this book Britain's public finances were determined by 'sound finance' and, in particular, the principle that the budget should in normal circumstances be balanced or in small surplus; afterwards the Keynesian wisdom was that the budget deficit could be varied to inject or withdraw demand from the economy, in order to keep output always high enough for full employment. Keynesianism was there-fore associated with the primacy of fiscal policy (that is, variations in the budget deficit) over monetary policy in macroeconomic management, with a permissive attitude towards large budget deficits and with a focus on full employment as the government's pre-eminent economic objective.

Debates about Keynes, Keynesianism and the Keynesian revolution have been endless. Strong evidence can be presented that Keynes himself thought very differently from his disciples about large budget deficits. Moreover, a careful examination of the data shows that fiscal policy in the 20 years from 1945, the heyday of full employment, was not conducted on Keynesian lines.[1] To a large extent the Keynesian revolution was a hoax. Nevertheless, in the late 1970s the monetarists had a hard time battling with a body of thought which was as much myth and make-believe as substance and reality. They insisted on three ideas: first, that monetary policy was more important than fiscal policy in understanding the business cycle; secondly, that over the medium term the budget deficit (on the measure known at the time as 'the public sector borrowing requirement' [PSBR], but relabelled 'the public sector net cash requirement' in 1997) had to be restricted to prevent excessive growth of public debt and to buttress monetary control;[2] and, thirdly, that the reduction of inflation, not full employment, should be the government's foremost macroeconomic aim.

The monetarists pressed these points convincingly in the public debate over the 20 years to 1997 and much of their agenda was implemented in practice.[3] Every projection of fiscal policy in the Conservative years was framed within a medium- or long-term context, with one eye on the implications for the accumulation of public debt and another on the scope for tax cuts if expenditure were kept within proper limits. Apart from Norway, the UK was the only country in the industrial world where the ratio of public debt to national income was lower in 1997 than it had been in 1979. (The New Labour government from 1997 changed the form of the fiscal rules, but retained the medium-term planning context.) The shift towards regarding inflation, not unemployment, as the central concern of macroeconomic policy-making was also surprisingly complete. In part, this shift reflected a new theoretical consensus among economists, that there is no long-run trade-off between unemployment and inflation. In part, it stemmed from a hard-headed recognition that unemployment may be due not to a lack of demand, but to overgenerous social security benefits which leave the unemployed little incentive to seek work.

So – in its intellectual and policy-making struggles with corporatism and Keynesianism – monetarism notched up major victories. Even if it did not force them into unconditional surrender, corporatism and Keynesianism retreated to their university fastnesses, and by the mid-1990s their protagonists declined pitched battle in public debate.[4] By the late 1990s almost no one proposed incomes policy as the most efficient antidote to inflation or aggressive fiscal reflation as the best way to cut unemployment.

II

Sure enough, the number of references to all the 'isms' in the newspapers was drastically lower in the late 1990s than it had been 20 years earlier. Indeed, many of the residual comments on monetarism were derogatory and in the past tense. Such worthies as Will Hutton at the *Observer*, Philip Stephens at the *Financial Times* and Anatole Kaletsky at *The Times*, as well as a host of lesser commentators, poked fun at monetarism from time to time. But none of them were silly enough to suggest that the Trades Union Congress (TUC) determines the inflation rate or that a PSBR of 6 or 7 per cent of national income is financially responsible. They seemed to have forgotten that in the late 1970s the majority of opinion-forms in Britain did believe that the TUC could determine inflation, while fiscal reflation – even with the PSBR already at 6 or 7 per cent of national income – was routinely recommended by the National Institute and leading economists at Cambridge University, such as Professor Wynne Godley of its Department of Economic Affairs.

The question evolves again. If monetarism did achieve in the 1980s and the 1990s much of what its supporters had hoped in the 1970s, why did references to it become so rude and dismissive? A large part of the answer is that, when confronted with real-world monetary policy, the simple messages of late-1970s monetarism were insufficient for the task. Those messages were fine in refuting incomes policies and fiscal reflation, but they were inadequate when they had to be translated into complex and technical decisions about actual policy instruments, such as the setting of interest rates and the management of the public debt. Only a handful of British economists – probably not more than 30 or 40 at the peak – called themselves 'monetarists'. Nevertheless, this small group, far from sharing a cohesive and well-organized body of thought, had radically different views about how the economy worked and about how policy should be conducted. (Their views also differed from those of their counterparts on the other side of the Atlantic, as explained in Essay 7.)[5]

Squabbles between the various denominations broke out early on. Initially the Thatcher government stated its targets for monetary growth in terms of a so-called 'broad aggregate' (that is, one which includes almost any asset that might be called 'money', such as virtually all bank deposits). But this was an embarrassment in the summer of 1980, when overdue measures of financial liberalization caused the target to be exceeded by a wide margin. Professor (later Sir) Alan Walters, who was appointed as Thatcher's economic adviser in early 1981, urged that the targets should instead be expressed in terms of 'narrow money' (equivalent to only notes and coin, or notes and coin plus bank deposits which could be spent without a notice period, such as current accounts). Walters nevertheless favoured a domestic focus for monetary policy and strongly rejected the proposition that a fixed exchange rate system, such as the European Monetary System, was appropriate for the UK.

The debate between broad and narrow monetarists has continued since the early 1980s, and undoubtedly reminds non-participants of medieval scholasticism. As a junior Treasury minister in the early 1980s Mr Nigel (later Lord) Lawson was impatient with all the technicalities. On 15 June 1981 he sent a long note to Sir Geoffrey (later Lord) Howe, the Chancellor of the Exchequer, arguing that the discipline of the European Monetary System (EMS) – and not money supply targets – should become 'the prime determinant' for monetary policy.[6] By the mid-1980s Howe, who had become Foreign Secretary and generally adopted a 'pro-European' stance towards policy issues throughout his career, shared Lawson's enthusiasm for the EMS. It is an ancient principle of monetary economics that a nation cannot simultaneously pursue a money supply target and a fixed exchange rate.[7] EMS membership, focused on a fixed exchange rate between the pound and other European currencies, therefore meant the end of British monetarism, in which money supply targets were an essential ingredient. It was consistent that Lawson – who had succeeded Howe as Chancellor in 1983 – should suspend broad money targets in October 1985, as a prelude to ending them altogether a year later.

But Thatcher – advised by Walters – was against EMS membership. By the late 1980s Thatcher and Walters were engaged in a long-running row with Lawson and Howe about macroeconomic policy, which in its intellectual raucousness and media visibility was comparable to a highbrow Punch and Judy show. Unhappily, none of the four key players in this wonderful piece of political theatre were much interested in what was happening to the money supply on the broad definitions, which back in the late 1970s had been the ark of the monetarist covenant. In the early 1980s the annual rate of broad money growth had been gradually declining and by late 1984 was down to about 10 per cent. But in 1986 and 1987 it accelerated to over 15 per cent a year. In the characteristic manner of such cycles, the first impact on excess money growth was on asset prices which surged forward in 1986 and 1987.[8] A boom in demand and output followed, and it was justly labelled 'the Lawson boom' after the Chancellor who presided over it. As so often, Friedman's 'long and variable lags' between money and inflation confused the interpretation of events. Nevertheless, inflation again exceeded 10 per cent in 1990. Thatcher lost the leadership of the Conservative Party one month after the annual increase in the retail price index (RPI) again went into double digits.[9]

The boom of the late 1980s, and the consequent rise in inflation, proved once again the underlying validity of the monetary theory of inflation. But that was not how Westminster and Whitehall (or indeed Westminster and Whitehall, and Oxford, Cambridge and other universities) saw it. Instead of reinstating the policy framework of 1979, the new administration led by Mr John Major stood by the ERM (exchange rate mechanism). A severe recession ensued, wrecking thousands of small businesses and causing house prices to fall heavily for the first time in two generations. Money supply growth plunged from over 15 per cent a year to under 5 per cent a year, as high interest rates deterred banks' customers from borrowing and undermined banks' ability to lend as asset price falls hit their capital bases.[10] But – because of the ERM commitment – nothing could be done to mitigate the harshness of the monetary contraction.

Finally, in September 1992 the pound sterling was expelled from the ERM by the benign activities of foreign exchange speculators. With the exchange rate no longer the 'prime determinant' of monetary policy (to recall Lawson's own phrase), interest rates tumbled. Clearing bank base rates went down from 10 per cent in early September 1992 to 6 per cent in January 1993. A recovery began and mildly above-trend growth continued, with fits and starts, until the late 1990s. Ironically, the money supply and inflation numbers of the early 1990s were for an extended period rather close to those that might have been prescribed by a high priest of monetarism in the late 1970s. Between mid-1991 and the end of 1994 broad money growth was consistently under 5 per cent a year, and from 1993 to 1997 the annual increase in the retail price index averaged under 3 per cent, with a degree of variation from year to year which was remarkably small compared with the previous 25 years. But – as is evident from the erratic record of official intentions, rationalizations and excuses – this outcome should not be seen as some sort of monetarist nirvana. (It was a fluke.)

In 1995 and 1996 money supply growth again accelerated, and the annual rate of increase in the M4 money measure was to peak at about 12 per cent in the third quarter of 1997. Britain's economists were indifferent to this development. They saw no connection between, on the one hand, the faster rate of money growth and, on the other, the strengthening of asset prices and marked upturn in domestic demand which soon became apparent. They also failed to warn about the risks of a future rise in inflation. This followed a familiar and recurrent pattern. With only a few dozen exceptions, Britain's economists continued to deny that the cyclical turmoil and high inflation of the first 50 post-war years had any relationship with volatile and excessive money supply growth. Fortunately, the Bank of England – which was granted operational independence to set interest rates by the newly elected Labour government in May 1997 – raised interest rates in a sequence of steps to 7½ per cent in June 1998. The effect was to restraint the growth rates of credit and money, and at a further remove to keep the expansion of demand in line with the economy's productive potential.

In terms of their ability to persuade the long-term leaders of British economic thought in the universities and day-to-day opinion-moulders in the press, the monetarists failed almost completely. Keynes's ghost had many occasions to chuckle. The so-called 'Keynesian revolution' contained large elements of fantasy and charade, but the phrase still appears – unadorned with quotation marks – in respectable textbooks. The notion of a 'monetarist counter-revolution' has vanished. Nevertheless, in the late 1970s and early 1980s monetarism was important in shifting the attitudes of Britain's political class away from the quack remedies of the 1960s, namely incomes policy and fiscal activism. At the level of ideas, it refuted both corporatism and the more naïve versions of Keynesianism. Moreover, the reluctant adoption of money supply targets in the late 1970s, and their retention through the early 1980s, did lead to a large fall in inflation, and this achievement makes Lawson's abandonment of broad money targets in 1985 all the more curious.

Looking back, the monetarists' central problem was unexpected. Despite the millions of words written on the subject from a monetary perspective, they did not have an agreed theory of how changes in the quantity of money 'cause' changes in the equilibrium level of money national income. In jargon, they lacked an account of 'the transmission mechanism'. But their problem was also a problem for the Keynesians and, indeed, for any macro-economist who thought seriously about his subject. The sorry truth is that, over 70 years after the publication of Keynes's *General Theory*, economics does not have a definitive theory of the determination of national income. (The standard income-expenditure approach – which has no room for monetary influences on national income – is unsatisfactory, as explained in Essay 9.) British policy-makers' failures to control the business cycle and prevent inflation over the 25 years from the ending of the Bretton Woods system in 1971 should be interpreted as largely due to this theoretical lacuna.

NOTES

1. See Essay 4, on 'Did Britain have a "Keynesian revolution"?', for more discussion.
2. As noted in Essay 7, the emphasis on controlling the PSBR as a key aspect of monetarism seems to have been distinctively British. The author set out the background to British monetarists' concern about high budget deficits in 'The analytical foundations of the Medium-Term Financial Strategy', first published in the May 1984 issue of *Fiscal Studies* and also as pp. 65–77 of T. Congdon, *Reflections on Monetarism* (Aldershot, UK and Brookfield, US: Edward Elgar for the Institute of Economic Affairs, 1992).
3. 'Academic adherents of monetarism were in a small minority in Britain in the 1970s. However, the impact of [their] theories on policy would seem to have been substantial.'

(J. Tomlinson, *Public Policy and the Economy since 1900* [Oxford: Clarendon Press, 1990], p. 297.)

4. Large tax increases led to a big reduction in the cyclically adjusted budget deficit between 1992 and 1995, while the level of output was beneath trend. But – in contrast with the somewhat similar circumstances in 1981 which prompted the letter to *The Times* from the 364 – there was barely a whimper of dissent from the academic Keynesians about the 'tightening' of fiscal policy.

5. Chapter 8 of Lawson's semi-autobiography *The View from No. 11* is on 'the black art of monetary control'. In a footnote on p. 77 he says that the subject matter of the chapter 'is an issue of passionate interest to a small number of people and mind-numbing gobbledygook to many others'. He then remarks, 'The general reader can safely turn straight away to Chapter 9 without losing the thread of this book'. (N. Lawson, *The View from No. 11* [London and New York: Bantam Press, 1992].) But the debates between the 'small number of people' to whom Lawson refers were ultimately fundamental in deciding the macroeconomic outcomes of his period as Chancellor and, later, the reputation of the Conservative Party for competence in managing the economy.

6. Lawson, *The View from No. 11*, p. 111.

7. The author argued that domestically focused money supply targets were incompatible with a fixed exchange rate in an article in *The Times* on 19 January, 1976. (See pp. 18–21 of his *Reflections on Monetarism*, where the article is reprinted.) In view of the disastrous results of the period of ERM membership between 1990 and 1992, two sentences from the 1976 article may be apposite. '[T]o adopt a fixed exchange rate is to abandon the independence of monetary policy. It leaves internal inflation and employment objectives at the mercy of foreign central banks.'

8. The role of asset prices in the transmission mechanism from money to the economy is discussed in more detail in the author's *Money and Asset Prices in Boom and Bust* (London: Institute of Economic Affairs, 2005).

9. In Thatcher's own writings the author has found only one reference to his criticisms of her government's monetary policy. (These criticisms began in early 1986, shortly after the effective ending of broad money targets in October 1985.) The reference is a footnote on p. 710 of the second volume of her memoirs where she says, 'The suggestion that the inflation which began at the end of 1988 and lasted until mid-1991 could be explained by decisions on interest rates and monetary policy in 1985 assumed almost a four-year lag in the effect of monetary expansion on inflation. We know that lags, in Milton Friedman's words, are "long and variable" with an average of about eighteen months. So three to four years is possible, but hardly plausible.' (M. Thatcher, *The Downing Street Years* [London: HarperCollins, 1993].) In fact, the length of the money/inflation lag after the Lawson boom was similar to that after the Heath–Barber boom, which had made 'Thatcherite monetarism' relevant in the late 1970s and so provided the intellectual rationale for the policies the Thatcher government pursued in the early 1980s. (The upturn in money growth in the early 1970s began in the final quarter of 1971, but the peak in inflation came in mid-1975. The money measure under consideration here is a broadly defined one.) The interpretation of both the two major inflationary episodes under the Conservatives is full of misunderstandings. A biography of Keith Joseph by Denham and Garnett notices – over the 1983–88 period – a gap between the 15 per cent annual growth of money and the 5 per cent annual rate of increase in prices. It then remarks, 'Not even the monetarist theory of "time-lags" could explain away this discrepancy.' (A. Denham and M. Garnett, *Keith Joseph* [Chesham: Acumen Publishing, 2001], p. 411.) But the gap between the annual rates of money growth and inflation in the early 1970s was greater than that in the mid and late 1980s, and both periods were followed by sharp upturns in inflation. (In the years to end-1972 and end-1973 M3 rose by 25.5 per cent and 27.4 per cent respectively, while the retail prices index went up by 7.7 per cent and 10.2 per cent respectively. The peak in inflation came in August 1975, when the annual rate of increase in the RPI was 26.9 per cent. Ironically, it was the similarity of the money supply growth rates and the *eventual* inflation outcome that was crucial in persuading Joseph that there was something to the monetary theory of inflation.) A large

short-run divergence between the growth rates of money and prices is not inconsistent with the stability of money demand functions, as the author has explained on many occasions. For a reference, see T. Congdon, 'Monetarism: a rejoinder', *World Economics*, vol. 5, no. 3, July–September 2004, pp. 179–97, particularly pp. 188–94.

10. This sentence invites the misinterpretation that bank lending causes inflation. Note that – in the normal course of events – a new bank loan creates a new bank deposit. So the growth rate of bank lending usually has an important bearing on the growth rate of bank deposits. But bank deposits, not loans, are money. The equilibrium relationships between money and money national income hold, whether the money is created by new bank lending or by banks' purchases of securities.

12. Criticizing the critics of monetarism

By the start of the twenty-first century monetarism – unlike a surprisingly adaptable Keynesianism – was being referred to in the past tense. For some people it was a convenient swearword, used to express their loathing for everything that had gone wrong (as they saw it) since conservative governments in the USA and the UK embraced free-market economics in the 1980s. A more sympathetic author interpreted the rise and fall of monetarism in Britain as a problem in 'social learning'. In his words, writing in the mid-1990s,

> The social learning process since 1979 has been a mixed affair. The 1980s were a time of policy experiments . . . While it would be wrong to see policy as an unqualified success in the 1980s, it would be equally incorrect to conclude that nothing positive has come from the past 16 years.[1]

A particularly interesting discussion by Thomas Mayer and Patrick Minford appeared in the spring 2004 issue of *World Economics*. Their paper on 'Monetarism: a retrospective' concluded that, 'Monetarism as a distinct school is in decline, but monetarist ideas are flourishing and form a major part of the modern synthesis' (p. 184).[2]

The various assessments generally saw monetarism as an outgrowth of theoretical ideas revived by (mostly) American economists in the 1950s and 1960s, and translated into policy across the industrial world to combat the high inflation of the 1970s; and they correctly recognized the strong influence that monetarism had on UK policy-making in the early years of the Thatcher government from 1979. But a common tendency – shared by Mayer and Minford – was to underestimate the success of the monetarist challenge to the styles of policy-making (corporatism and fiscalist Keynesianism) which prevailed, particularly in the UK, before the 1970s. One line of attack on monetarism was technical. In the 1980s a conventional wisdom emerged from a large body of econometric work that demand-for-money functions had become unstable. In some circles the breakdown of money demand stability was thought not only to invalidate the case for money supply targets, but also to argue against the practice of tracking the money supply aggregates for their macroeconomic information. The following discussion is

intended as a critique of the criticisms of monetarism. It will concentrate on
the UK, although the remarks have wider relevance.

I

In their opening remarks and in a section on 'Basic ideas and history',
Mayer and Minford compared monetarism with other schools of macroeconomic thought, particularly Keynesianism. In their view the differences
were hardly fundamental. Whereas the monetarists believed in the importance of money to national income determination in the short and long
runs, the Keynesians accepted the role of money of national income determination in the long run, but questioned it in the short and medium terms;
monetarists such as Milton Friedman regarded the proposition that money
and national income have similar rates of changes as a reasonable working
hypothesis (but acknowledged that the theory of money is an aspect of the
theory of portfolio selection), while Keynesians emphasized that desired
money holdings may change relative to other types of wealth and income,
put questions of portfolio selection first and repudiated a mechanical one-
to-one relationship between money and national income; and so on. In this
ball of economic theory the dancers changed their partners from time to
time, but they all knew the sequence of steps in the Cambridge cash balances equation, the routines of the IS–LM model, and other familiar tunes
and rhythms. Everyone enjoyed everyone else's company, and the gap
between monetarism and other schools of thought arose from differences
of nuance and emphasis. There was no clash of world view and ideology,
and no need for polemics.

But that was not how matters stood in Britain in the mid-1970s or for
many years afterwards. The study of monetary economics in British universities had declined in the 1950s and 1960s, and most university teachers
rejected both a monetary theory of inflation and a role for money in the
determination of national income.[3] Inflation was widely attributed to trade
union greed or 'pushfulness', with one commentator remarking that 'pulp
forests have been consumed' in discussing the role of the trade unions in the
inflationary process.[4] The standard view about the national income was
that both output and income were equal to expenditure, and that expenditure was determined by past income plus or minus demand withdrawals by
the state (that is, by the use of fiscal policy) or from overseas (as the world
economy waxed and waned, or because the exchange rate changed).[5] As a
consequence of these beliefs, mainstream professional opinion favoured
two policy approaches. First, incomes policy (or 'wages and prices policy')
should be used to control inflation, with high-level bargaining between the

government, the trade unions and industry on dividend freezes, pay norms and such like. Secondly, fiscal policy should be used to manage demand, with the annual 'Budget judgement' (that is, the net injection or withdrawal of demand by the state, approximated by the cyclically adjusted change in the budget deficit) being critical. The purpose of demand management was to achieve full employment, in line with an agenda widely attributed to the 1944 White Paper on *Employment Policy*.

Monetary policy – often defined only in terms of interest rates rather than in terms of the quantity of money – was widely considered to be peripheral to the economy, even though interest rates were recognized as having some effect on the exchange rate. According to Goodhart,

> Throughout most of the 1960s . . . interest rates varied mainly in response to external conditions, being raised whenever there was a need to support the fixed exchange rate, which was often under pressure, and lowered – in a spirit of general benevolence towards investment – as each balance-of-payments crisis temporarily receded. With interest rate policy mainly determined by external considerations, the money supply was allowed to vary passively.[6]

Support for incomes policy and active fiscal management, and disdain for monetary policy, had huge political significance. They did not reflect merely technical differences of opinion about the effectiveness of the various economic instruments, but were instead motivated by deeper ideological commitments in British society. The high-level bargaining associated with incomes policy gave the trade unions considerable political power. Comparisons were made between the style of British economic government in the two decades from 1960, as politicians sought economy-wide deals with senior figures in the trade unions and large companies, and the state capitalism or 'corporatism' of several European nations earlier in the twentieth century.[7] Clearly, the greater the reliance on incomes policy to curb inflation, the stronger was the position of the trade unions in key policy debates.

The pre-eminence of fiscal policy also had implications for the UK's social and political structure. In his *General Theory*, published in 1936, Keynes had said that fiscal policy would work best in a nation with 'a somewhat comprehensive socialisation of investment'. He thereby established a persuasive argument for a mixed economy with an extensive state-owned sector. To quote Keynes's words: 'The central controls necessary to ensure full employment will, of course, involve a large extension of the traditional functions of government.'[8] In short, both corporatism and Keynesianism accorded with the interventionist bias of most British writers and thinkers, including most British economists, in the early post-war decades.[9]

A fair comment is that by the early 1970s the macroeconomic thinking of many British economists, and the often rather pugilistic espousal of such

thinking as 'Keynesianism', had become idiosyncratic by international
standards.[10] Nevertheless, a blend of Keynesian and corporatist doctrines
conditioned economic policy-making. Taken to extremes, it prescribed a
policy mix in which incomes policy set a politically determined and admin-
istratively enforced limit on inflation, and fiscal expansionism – justified by
rhetoric about full employment – drove output to its employment-
maximizing level. A policy mix of this kind was indeed favoured by the
National Institute of Economic and Social Research in the 1960s and
1970s, but could not be freely pursued in the 1960s because a fixed exchange
rate constrained UK policy-making.[11] After the breakdown of the Bretton
Woods fixed-exchange-rate system in 1971, the British government was able
for the first time in the post-war period to combine incomes policy with
aggressive fiscal reflation. The external barrier to high money supply
growth was removed, while the increased budget deficit was financed to a
large extent from the banking system. In the two years to the end of 1973
the sterling M3 money supply measure – which consisted mostly of sterling
bank deposits – increased by over 25 per cent a year. A wild boom in 1972
and 1973 was followed by rising inflation in 1974 and a peak inflation rate
(as measured by the annual change in the retail price index) of 26.9 per cent
in August 1975.[12] Well-respected commentators warned of the possible collapse of British democracy.[13]

Monetarism in the UK developed partly under the influence of academic ideas from the USA (such as the quantity theory of money associated with Milton Friedman and the Chicago School), but mostly it was a
response to the economic and political crisis of the mid-1970s. Its central
tenet was that inflation is a monetary phenomenon, in the sense that
inflation is caused by the quantity of money rising too rapidly relative to
the quantity of goods and services. To monetarist participants in the
British public debates at that time the facts supporting this proposition
were compelling. But Friedman's thinking supplemented the education by
events in one very important way. In his presidential address to the
American Economic Association in 1967 he had argued that there is no
long-run trade-off between unemployment and inflation, and that the
pursuit of 'full employment' (meaning a low level of unemployment with
an excess demand for labour) would be accompanied not by a stable high
rate of inflation, but by ever-accelerating inflation. As economists exam-
ined the data, evidence for this 'accelerationist hypothesis' could be found
in the UK and many other countries.

Three vital implications followed. The first was that income policy was
an ineffective answer to inflation and should be dropped; the second was
that fiscal policy should be subordinated to monetary control; and the third
was that policy-making should not try to achieve full employment, but

should instead be focused on the reduction of inflation (and eventual price stability) by lowering the rate of money supply growth. Heavy emphasis must be placed on one point. While the agenda could be presented as largely technical, its wider social and political consequences were far-reaching. Keynesianism and corporatism were ideas that fitted the post-war so-called 'Butskellite' consensus, with a large public sector, extensive state ownership of the nation's capital assets, and close relations (or, at any rate, attempted close relations) between the trade unions and the government.[14] Even into the 1960s many leading figures in British public life saw the mixed economy as a halfway house between the laissez-faire capitalism of the nineteenth century and a communist end-state that was certain to arrive at some future date.[15] Despite bitter controversy the first post-war generation of Labour politicians kept Clause Four (in favour of government ownership of all the means of production) in their party's constitution. In 1979 Tony Benn published a book of *Arguments for Socialism*, which included the proposition that Clause Four had 'growing relevance today as capitalism moves into decline'. In his view, it 'must remain at the core of our work'.[16]

Monetarism represented not just an alternative to Keynesianism and corporatism in technical macroeconomics. More fundamentally, it was an expression of an utterly different world view. Without incomes policy, Cabinet ministers did not need to negotiate with the trade union movement; without an activist fiscal policy, the Keynesian case for a large state sector collapsed; without a full employment commitment, the government could concentrate on the provision of a sound currency to promote the efficiency of a market economy. Monetarism welcomed the liberation of market forces to collect the nation's savings, and their management by private sector companies and financial institutions ('the City', in the UK context) according to profitability. By rejecting the traditional arguments for the state ownership of the so-called 'commanding heights of the economy' (steel mills, nuclear reactors, state-subsidized aluminium smelters and such like), it laid the intellectual foundations for the privatizations of the 1980s. Hundreds of thousands of British people – in the trade unions, in the media, in the universities and indeed in positions of trust as civil servants in government positions – had believed from the 1930s that the inevitable long-run drift in UK policy-making was towards increased state ownership, more planning and intervention, and ever-growing public sector supply of services. It came as a shock to such people to find that in the mid and late 1970s there were advocates of a diametrically opposite point of view. This clash of world views – about which Mayer and Minford said almost nothing in their appraisal of monetarism – must be mentioned if it is to be understood in a British setting.[17]

II

In May 1979 the intellectual jolt to Britain's left-leaning chattering classes became a real-world political trauma. The Conservative Party led by Mrs Margaret (later Lady) Thatcher was elected with a comfortable majority in the House of Commons. It quickly set about implementing an agenda quite different from its Labour predecessor's. Within a few weeks prices and income policies, and the accompanying institutional machinery, were scrapped. In October exchange controls – which had been in force for 40 years – were also abolished. The task of inflation control was to fall exclusively on monetary policy. Thatcher and her ministers were prepared to test the theory that inflation has only monetary causes, and pledged themselves not to commit a U-turn ('the lady's not for turning') and restore incomes policy. In the March 1980 Budget, Sir Geoffrey (later Lord) Howe announced a Medium-Term Financial Strategy, with year-by-year targets for reductions in the rate of money supply growth and in the ratio of the budget deficit (as measured by the 'public sector borrowing requirement') to gross domestic product.

Unhappily, the attempt to curb money supply growth involved very high interest rates, and led to a deep recession in 1980 and early 1981. The severity of the recession undermined tax revenues and increased social security costs, endangering the MTFS target for a lower PSBR/GDP ratio in 1981/82 than in 1980/81. In the 1981 Budget, Howe raised taxes sharply in order to keep the budgetary position under control. This was a direct challenge to Keynesianism, as the cyclically adjusted budget deficit was being cut despite high unemployment and weak demand. The budget deficit was not being varied contra-cyclically (as the textbooks recommended), but in order to facilitate a reduction in money supply growth over the medium term. A letter from 364 economists to *The Times* – undoubtedly representative of mainstream academic opinion in the UK – was categorical in its repudiation of 'monetarist policies'. The 364 threw down the gauntlet and invited the monetarists (who were far fewer in numbers) to a duel of ideas. Implicitly, the duel was to be decided by the future passage of events. (The material in Essays 9 and 10 above, on pp. 181–229, considers the economy's behaviour in the years after the 1981 Budget.)

This is not the place to provide a narrative account, even in a potted version, of the main policy decisions and outcomes of the subsequent 20 years. However, in any meaningful assessment of British monetarism the main features of policy-making after the 1981 letter to *The Times* must be discussed. Mayer and Minford's paper was quite friendly towards monetarism, but it failed to provide such a discussion. Instead their section on 'Monetarism in the United Kingdom' contained an outline of events between the mid-1970s and 1982, implying that – although monetary policy was rather disorganized – 'shock tactics' did get inflation down and eventually 'restored the fortunes of Mrs Thatcher and her supporters'. Almost nothing was said about events after 1982, as if the second Thatcher election victory marked the end of 'the monetarist experiment'. Their implicit view – that, in some sense, British monetarism ended in 1982 or 1983 – may be partly responsible for their judgement that 'as a distinct school' it had fallen into 'decline'. The next few paragraphs will argue that, at the level of real-world policy-making, this conclusion is almost wholly wrong. Far from slipping into decline, monetarism demolished Keynesianism and corporatism.

What has happened in the three crucial areas of incomes policy, fiscal policy and the conduct of monetary policy? Incomes policy may be taken first. If monetarism had really fallen into 'decline', a fair expectation might be that British economists would again be lauding the virtues of incomes policy as a way of curbing inflation. But that is not so. In sharp contrast to 'the pulp forests' consumed in comment about and advocacy of incomes policy in the 1960s and 1970s, it is difficult to think of a single recent book on the topic. Academic articles and historical monographs may still be written about Jack Jones, Vic Feather, Arthur Scargill, the Counter-Inflation Programme, 'the son of £6 a week' and that sort of thing, but incomes policy is no longer a live and relevant option for policy-makers. Trade union membership has fallen heavily, while newspapers no longer feel obliged to report the proceedings of the Trades Union Congress as if the 'union barons' were a major power in the land. In this respect the contrast between Britain today and Britain in the early 1970s could hardly be more total. For all practical purposes incomes policy is dead.

Incomes policy did not become a permanent fixture in standard macro-economics texts and has been easy to forget. Fiscal policy is another matter entirely. Its validity as a stabilization tool has been asserted in most text-books since 1945, and its supposed effectiveness in this role is still widely seen as the explanation for the increased stability of the American and British economies compared with the 1930s. But in fact the textbooks have lost touch with reality. The announcement of the MTFS in 1980 marked the beginning of a period of over 25 years in which fiscal policy decisions would be set within a medium-term framework, with one key objective being to ensure that the ratio of debt to GDP was kept under control. Mayer and Minford implied that a veil was drawn over the MTFS by embarrassed policy-makers in the early 1980s. In their words, 'the MTFS was widely written off as a failure at this time . . . and it came to be seen as a temporary interlude before traditional politics resumed'.[18] On the contrary, a version of the MTFS was retained in all the Budgets until 1997.

Although its contents evolved over the years and the monetary element was downplayed, the MTFS continued to set the context for fiscal policy decisions throughout the long period of Conservative rule. The MTFS undoubtedly had a major effect on public finance outcomes. Whereas in the 1970s the UK was bracketed with Italy as an incorrigible fiscal spendthrift, by the late 1990s the ratio of public debt to GDP was below the average for the industrial world and down to about a third of that in Italy. The British banking system – whose assets had been dominated by claims on the public sector in the 1950s and which therefore was subject to official restraints on its lending to the private sector – held virtually no public sector debt at the start of the twenty-first century.

There may still be a debate about the wisdom of orienting fiscal policy on medium-term debt sustainability rather than short-run demand management. But, if there is such a debate in the UK, it is a very quiet one. When a Labour government replaced the Conservatives in 1997, the MTFS was dropped, but Mr Gordon Brown did not revert to old-style Keynesianism. Instead a commitment to medium-term fiscal stability was a hallmark of Mr Brown's supposedly new policy regime. He announced a 'golden rule' (in which current expenditure was to be covered by taxation) and a 'sustainable investment rule' (which set a limit on the ratio of public debt to GDP). Both these rules had nothing whatever to do with the type of fiscal demand management recommended by British Keynesians in the 1950s and 1960s, and could more plausibly be interpreted as a modern refurbishment of Gladstonian principles of public finance.[19] Again, for all practical purposes Keynesianism – in the sense of short-run changes in the fiscal position to manage demand – is defunct in the UK.

Finally, as far as the conduct of monetary policy is concerned, many years have now passed since it was directed to the maximization of employment. The first half of the Thatcher premiership showed that monetary policy could be used to reduce inflation, without relying on the crutch of incomes policy. (The second half – which saw a marked acceleration in money supply growth in the unfortunate 'Lawson boom' and a subsequent rise in inflation – also demonstrated the validity of the monetary theory of inflation, and is discussed below.) In the 1990s decision-making on interest rates was transferred from politicians to monetary specialists in two steps, first the publication of the minutes of the monthly meetings between the Chancellor of the Exchequer and the Governor of the Bank of England from early 1993, and secondly the granting of operational independence to the Bank of England in 1997. This transfer of power was possible only because informed opinion was quite different from what it had been in the 1960s. The UK's sorry experience of boom and bust had persuaded almost everyone who mattered in policy formation (politicians in all three main parties, their advisers, leading civil servants, the most influential newspaper commentators) of the validity of Friedman's 1967 proposition that no long-run trade-off exists between inflation and unemployment. The phrase 'full employment' had lost its totemic status in public debate.

It was therefore sensible for the setting of interest rates to be taken out of the political domain and given to technicians. Paradoxically, the decade or so from 1994 saw almost uninterrupted increases in employment and falls in unemployment, so that the UK (mid-2006) now has high labour force participation and low unemployment by European standards. These gains can be interpreted as partly due to policy and, in particular, to supply-side reforms to improve labour market flexibility, which date back to the early 1980s. But no one in officialdom had planned them, in the sense of having a quantified target for either employment or unemployment, and no one in the Treasury or the Bank of England would have dreamt at any stage in the 1990s of adjusting interest rates to raise or lower employment. Indeed, the decade from 1992 was characterized by extraordinary macro-economic stability compared with any previous decade in the post-war period, including the years from 1948 to the early 1970s, the heyday of the supposed 'Keynesian revolution'. A case can be made that the vital theor-etical basis for this policy achievement was a generalization of Friedman's ideas on the link between changes in inflation and departures from the so-called 'natural rate of unemployment'.[20] If so, it is monetarism – and cer-tainly not corporatism or Keynesianism – that deserves the accolades for Britain's much improved macroeconomic performance. To say that mon-etarism is 'in decline' is a travesty. It may be in decline in the sense that the number of references to it in newspapers and parliamentary debates has fallen heavily, but the lack of attention is due to the general acceptance of its core recommendations on the structure of policy-making.[21] On a wider canvas, the Labour Party has dropped Clause Four from its constitution and its leaders embrace the market economy, although with reservations.

III

The technical critique of monetarism is directed not against its broad polit-ical and philosophical message, but against the practical value of the style of monetary management with which it was associated in the late 1970s and early 1980s. The centrepiece of this style of monetary management was an annual target for the growth rate of the quantity of money. Superficially, the rationale for such targets was simple. If the quantity of money and the level of nominal national income grew at similar rates in the long run (as evidence from many nations suggested they did), control over monetary growth would deliver control over the growth of nominal national income and, at a further remove, the rise in prices. In the UK context in the early 1980s gradual reductions in money supply growth – of the kind announced in the MTFS from 1980 onwards – ought in due course to achieve lower inflation.

In the more naïve presentations of the argument the velocity of circulation of money (that is, the ratio of national income and expenditure to the quantity of money) was said to be stable and predictable, like some of the constants in nature (such as the freezing and boiling points of water, or the speed of light). The trouble with this line of analysis was that it overlooked that money and banking are human institutions, so that the way in which people use money is always changing. The UK experience with money supply targeting was important to the reputation of monetarism, partly because of the ideological passions aroused by the larger debates over Thatcherism and its challenge to middle-way 'Butskellism'.

Unfortunately for the monetarists, both the radicalism of the supply-side reforms introduced after 1979 and the rigour of anti-inflationary policy disturbed the relationship between money and money national income. The ending of exchange controls in October 1979 was vital to the long-run competitiveness of the City of London as an international financial centre, but it encouraged the location in London of new types of financial institution, and their money balances exploded in the 1980s and 1990s. Financial deregulation – notably the liberalization of mortgage credit from 1982 – led to an intensification of competition and a narrowing of banks' profit margins. This made it less expensive for companies and financial institutions simultaneously to hold bank deposits and to have bank borrowings, and again that raised the desired ratio of money to expenditure. The denationalization of large utility companies after 1984 expanded the private sector and, for the reasons given in Essay 6, that increased the corporate demand to hold money. Finally, the leap in interest rates in late 1979 made it more attractive to keep wealth in the form of interest-bearing deposits (which formed a large part of broad money) than before. Whereas the 1970s were mostly a decade of negative real interest rates, the 1980s saw almost continuously positive real interest rates.

The combined effect of all these developments on the monetary scene was drastic. Whereas from 1945 to the late 1970s money had been growing more slowly than national income, after 1979 its long-run tendency was to increase at an annual rate 2 or 3 per cent a year faster than national income. The targets in the first version of the MTFS made insufficient allowance for this change in behaviour. As a result, the money supply targets were pitched much too low and were routinely exceeded. The overshoots caused the whole machinery of money supply targets, and not just the particular set of target numbers chosen, to be derided by critics as inappropriate and harmful. Far from being a natural constant, the velocity of circulation was shown to vary in the long run, as institutions, technology and regulations evolved. Although its behaviour could still be explained in economic terms, expectations of a stable velocity were shown to be rather naïve.

This experience helps to explain why, according to Mayer and Minford, a stable demand function for money 'disappeared' so that 'monetarism was providing no reliable way of predicting GDP'. Other authors reached a similar conclusion. In the words of a 2003 textbook on *Monetary Economics: Policy and Its Theoretical Basis*, by the mid-1980s 'it was clear both that the authorities' ability to target the broad money stock with any degree of accuracy . . . had been severely undermined, and that the rationale for monetary targets had itself broken down in the face of a sharply falling velocity'.[22] The instability of money demand functions and the inadequacy of money as a forecasting tool became part of the conventional wisdom.[23]

But the critics went much too far. As an analytical matter, a change in the velocity of circulation of money does not imply that the demand for money has become unstable. The velocity of circulation of money may alter because of large shifts in the value of arguments in the money demand function other than national income itself. (For example, the desired ratio of money to income may depend on real interest rates and financial technology. If rises in real interest rates and improvements in financial technology cause agents to want a higher ratio of money to income, their underlying preferences for the quality of 'money-ness' in their portfolios may be stable.) Moreover, the finding of instability in money demand functions was not new in the 1980s. Research at the Bank of England and elsewhere had usually found stable demand functions for broad money in the 1960s, but two papers published by Artis and Lewis in 1974 and 1976 argued that these functions had broken down. The publication of the Artis and Lewis work did not stop, at roughly the same time, the then Labour government announcing a money supply target and the IMF introducing targets for a broadly defined measure of DCE (domestic credit expansion). The government's and IMF's actions relied on the demand for money being *stable enough for policy purposes*, even if it was not *stable enough to meet the criteria of statistical significance required for academic papers*. (The two concepts of 'stability' can be a long way apart.) What had changed by the mid-1980s? Indeed, well before Artis and Lewis, Walters had carried out empirical work on money and incomes spanning the 1880–1962 period, and found sub-periods when the link between money and incomes was weak. But this did not prevent Walters becoming one of the leading advocates of control over the growth of the money supply as a means of curbing inflation.

The critics of monetarism also became sloppy in their use of words and careless in their judgements. It was one thing to show that the quality of an econometric relationship between money and incomes was lower in the 1980s than it had been in the 1960s. That meant that – even if the regression coefficient in a simple two-variable money/income equation were one in both the 1960s and 1980s – any forecast in the 1980s would be made with less confidence than in the 1960s.[24] But it was something else to leap from here to the conclusion that the economy would not be affected at all by a shift from a lower to a higher rate of money supply growth. If the regression coefficient were indeed one in both the 1960s and the 1980s, the correct forecast in both decades was that the most likely outcome of an acceleration in annual money supply growth from 5 per cent to 15 per cent was an acceleration in the annual rate of increase in nominal national income also from 5 per cent to 15 per cent.

There seems little doubt that – when the technicians produced their statistical results for senior officials and their political masters – the message was garbled. In a speech at Loughborough University on 22 October 1986 – given when the annual growth rate of the money supply on the M3 measure had climbed well into the teens – the Governor of the Bank of England, Mr Robin Leigh-Pemberton (later Lord Kingsdown), said that it was 'fair to ask whether a broad money target continues to serve any useful purpose' and perhaps 'we would do better to dispense with monetary targetry altogether'. (One is reminded of Mr Polly, in the H.G. Wells novel, who thought that he could not go bankrupt if he dispensed with an accountant.)[25]

The lower quality of the statistical relationships between money and income in the UK in the 1980s did *not* mean that the behaviour of the quantity of money had no macroeconomic impact whatsoever. (A remarkably large number of people seemed to think that this is what it did mean.) Mayer and Minford – following the conventional wisdom – asserted, in their 2004 paper, that 'monetarism was providing no reliable way of predicting GDP'. But this was to ignore entirely the unhappy sequence of events between 1985 and 1992 in the UK and the relative success of monetarist analysts in their prognostications during the period.

In 1986 and 1987 the growth rate of bank deposits increased markedly, and the consequent excess supply of money led to large asset price increases and a wider economic boom. At the beginning of 1988 the overwhelming majority of forecasting groups were nevertheless afflicted by 'forecasters' droop' and expected 1988 to see a slowdown in the economy.[26] They were hopelessly wrong – and their indifference to money supply developments was the fundamental reason for their misjudgements. In fact, 1988 saw the highest increase in private sector domestic demand (in real terms) in the post-war period. Severe overheating resulted in a widening payments deficit and rising inflation. Policy-makers had to more than double interest rates between the spring of 1988 and the autumn of 1989 to compensate for earlier mistakes. In 1990 the annual rate of inflation reached double-digits, while money supply growth collapsed. The squeeze on real money balances hit asset prices, with real estate (including, for the first time in the post-war period, residential housing) suffering significant price falls. Recovery was delayed until 1993. The Conservative Party was stigmatized for economic mismanagement, with its traditional support among the home-owning middle classes being sharply less in the general elections of 1997, 2001 and 2005 than in those of the 1980s.

The whole boom–bust episode was every bit as incompetent as that between 1971 and 1975, which had developed from the 1971–73 explosion in money growth under Heath (as Prime Minister) and Barber (as Chancellor). Ironically, it was the Heath–Barber boom which had caused Keith Joseph to protest against 'inflation-eering', and so had provided the initial stimulus to the adoption of monetarist ideas by leading figures in the Conservative Party. At any rate, the Lawson boom and the subsequent bust demonstrated yet again the validity of the monetary approach to national income determination. Economists who monitored the behaviour of the money supply (on the broadly defined measures) were the most successful in anticipating the large fluctuations in asset prices, demand and inflation which occurred in the decade from 1985. When Mayer and Minford claimed that monetarism 'was providing no reliable way of predicting GDP', they were being very misleading. It would be closer to the truth to say that – in the more extreme phases of the last major UK boom–bust episode – only the monetarists provided reliable forecasts of GDP.[27]

IV

Whatever one's doctrinal affiliations, there is not much dispute that in the 1970s UK macroeconomic policy-making was in crisis. The monetarists set out an agenda for change which was largely adopted by the Labour government in the late 1970s and, with more commitment, by the Conservatives from 1979. It cannot be emphasized too strongly that in these years the monetarists were heavily outnumbered in the academic debate and that in the early 1980s the monetarist agenda was implemented in defiance of beliefs held by the great majority of British university economists.[28] In March 1981 364 of these economists wrote in protest against 'monetarism' in a letter to *The Times*. The 364 were quite wrong in their forecasts of the economy over the following few years, and in their jeremiads about the UK's 'industrial base' , and 'social and political stability'. (See the exchange between Professor Stephen Nickell and the author reprinted here as Essay 10.)

Nevertheless, they and their students continue to dominate the academic profession in the UK, while like-minded economists are in the majority in the academic profession in other English-speaking nations. There should be no surprise that a conventional wisdom has emerged which is carping and mean towards monetarism, and fails to recognize its contribution to the improvement in the British economy's performance. The technical element in the conventional wisdom (with its aspersions on the instability of velocity, the unreliability of forecasts, and so on) is largely wrong and needs a critical reappraisal. The opponents of monetarism have had it too easy for too long.

NOTES

1. M.J. Oliver, *Whatever Happened to Monetarism?* (Aldershot, UK and Brookfield, USA: Ashgate, 1997), pp. 151–2.
2. T. Mayer and P. Minford, 'Monetarism: a retrospective', *World Economics*, vol. 5, no. 2, April–June 2004, pp. 147–85.
3. M. Ricketts and E. Shoesmith, *British Economic Opinion: A Survey of a Thousand Economists* (London: Institute of Economic Affairs, 1990). A large majority of survey respondents disagreed that the central bank should follow a money supply rule, but agreed – if with reservations – to a wages policy as a means of controlling inflation. See pp. 74–8.
4. The reference to 'pulp forests' was made by Samuel Brittan. (See p. 173 of his paper, 'Inflation and democracy', on pp. 161–85 of F. Hirsch and J.H. Goldthorpe (eds), *The Political Economy of Inflation* [London: Martin Robertson, 1978].) Literally thousands of papers were written in the 1960s and 1970s about the influence of trade union bargaining on inflation. See, for example, J. Johnston and M. Timbrell, 'Empirical tests of a bargaining theory of wage rate determination', in D. Laidler and D. Purdy (eds), *Inflation in Labour Markets* (Manchester: Manchester University Press, 1974), pp. 79–108.
5. An example of strong emphasis on the income-expenditure model of national income determination is provided by the opening pages of Christopher Dow's *Major Recessions: Britain and the World, 1920–1995* (Oxford: Oxford University Press, 2000).
6. C.A.E. Goodhart, *Money Information and Uncertainty* (1st edition, London: Macmillan, 1975), p. 242.
7. The word 'corporatism' was used, for example, by Mr Peter Jay in his Wincott Lecture on 'A general hypothesis of employment, inflation and politics', reproduced on pp. 33–55 of P. Jay, *The Crisis for Western Political Economy* (London: Andre Deutsch, 1984). See p. 47.
8. J.M. Keynes, *The General Theory of Employment, Interest and Money* (London: Macmillan, 1964, paperback reprint of 1936 edition), p. 379.
9. The phrase 'interventionist bias' may seem a little shrill, but opinion surveys of British university economists confirm that the great majority have been and remain supporters of planning and intervention with the price mechanism. See Ricketts and Shoesmith, *British Economic Opinion* and W. Beckerman (ed.), *The Labour Government's Economic Record: 1964–70* (London: Duckworth, 1972), both *passim*. There can also be little

doubt about the bias of elite opinion in the immediate aftermath of the Second World War. According to George Orwell, writing in 1945: 'Among the intelligentsia, it hardly needs saying that the dominant form of nationalism is Communism . . . A Communist, for my purposes here, is one who looks upon the U.S.S.R. as his Fatherland and feels it his duty to justify Russian policy and advance Russian interests at all costs. Obviously, such people abound in England today, and their direct and indirect influence is very great.' S. Orwell and I. Angus (eds), *The Collected Essays, Journalism and Letters of George Orwell*, vol. III (Harmondsworth: Penguin Books in association with Secker and Warburg, 1971, paperback reprint of 1968 hardback original), p. 414.

10. J. Tobin, *Policies for Prosperity* (Brighton: Wheatsheaf Books, 1987), pp. 265–6.
11. R.J. Ball and T. Burns, 'The inflationary mechanism in the UK economy', *American Economic Review*, vol. 66, September 1976, pp. 467–84.
12. In its *Quarterly Review* of May 1973 the National Institute opined – in the middle of the biggest boom in the post-war period – that 'there is no reason why the present boom should either bust or have to be busted'.
13. The alarm was expressed in the weekly columns of Peter Jay in *The Times*, Samuel Brittan in the *Financial Times* and other commentators. On 29 April 1975 *The Wall Street Journal* carried a leading article entitled 'Goodbye, Great Britain'.
14. 'Butskellite' is a corruption of the names of Reginald Butler, Conservative Chancellor of the Exchequer from 1951 to 1955, and Hugh Gaitskell, leader of the Labour Party in the 1950s.
15. The first edition of Karl Popper's polemical *The Poverty of Historicism* (London: Routledge and Kegan Paul), written 'in memory of the countless men and women of all creeds or nations or races who fell victims to the fascist and communist belief in Inexorable Laws of Historical Destiny', was published in 1957 and went through five reprints in the 1960s.
16. T. Benn, *Arguments for Socialism*, ed. C. Mullin (Harmondsworth: Penguin, 1980, originally published in 1979), p. 44.
17. N. Annan, *Our Age: Portrait of a Generation* (London: Weidenfeld and Nicholson, 1990), *passim* but especially chapter 26 'Our vision of life rejected'; and B. Magee, *Confessions of a Philosopher* (London: Weidenfeld and Nicholson, 1997), pp. 413–15.
18. T. Mayer and P. Minford 'Monetarism: a retrospective', *World Economics*, vol. 5, no. 3, April–June 2004, p. 182. For the antecedents to the MTFS, see G. Pepper and M. Oliver, *Monetarism under Thatcher: Lessons for the Future*, Cheltenham, UK and Northampton, MA, USA: Edward Elgar, 2001, especially pp. 8–20.
19. A large part of the rationale for the references to 'prudence' in Mr Gordon Brown's speeches and to the more extended treatment in the 1998 Treasury paper on *Stability and Investment for the Long Term* is to be sought in ideas of inter-generational equity developed in the last 20 years by the American economist, Laurence Kotlikoff, and others. These ideas have nothing whatever to do with Keynes or Keynesianism. New Labour's rules are discussed in Essay 5 in this book. The author proposed that fiscal policy should be organized to achieve medium-term stability in the ratio of public debt to GDP in a paper given the Money Study Group at Brasenose College, Oxford, on 14 September 1976 and reprinted in pp. 39–49 of his 1992 *Reflections on Monetarism* (Aldershot, UK and Brookfield, US). In effect, the 1976 Money Study Group paper anticipated the later announcement of New Labour's 'sustainable investment rule' by over 20 years. Nevertheless, a newspaper report of 23 June 2006 ('Warm tributes paid to economic policy-maker', *Financial Times*, occasioned by the tragically early death of the City economist, David Walton), by Chris Giles and Scheherezade Daneshku, said that 'David Walton's greatest legacy to economic policy was in devising two new rules of thumb – debt sustainability and the golden rule – in November 1993 with Gavyn Davies, the former chief economist of Goldman Sachs'. These rules were apparently 'adopted enthusiastically by Mr. [Gordon] Brown in opposition and subsequently in government'. The author has been unable to track down any papers written by Walton and Davies in which they set out the case for New Labour's rules, although they may well have argued for them in oral presentations to Mr Brown.

20. T. Congdon, 'The UK's achievement of economic stability: how and why did it happen?', *World Economics*, vol. 3, no. 4, October–December 2002, pp. 25–41, and reprinted here as Essay 13.
21. Mayer and Minford did indeed say that 'some of its [monetarism's] basic ideas have become so widely accepted that they are no longer monetarist' (p. 183).
22. K. Bain and P. Howells, *Monetary Economics: Policy and Its Theoretical Basis* (Basingstoke: Palgrave Macmillan, 2003), p. 327.
23. In an important respect the demand for money remained stable throughout the 1980s and 1990s. Of the three non-bank, non-public sectors in the UK (the household, corporate and financial sectors), the largest money-holder from the early 1960s until today has been the household sector. A standard finding in all econometric work is that the household sector's demand-for-money function has remained stable, according to the usual significance tests. (See, for example, L. Drake and K.A. Crystal, 'Personal sector money demand in the UK', *Oxford Economic Papers*, vol. 49, no. 2, April 1997, pp. 188–206, and R.S.J. Thomas, 'The demand for M4: a sectoral analysis. Part I – The personal sector', *Bank of England Working Paper*, no. 61, 1997.) The author first pointed out the stability of household sector money-holding behaviour in a research paper published in May 1986 when he was working for the stockbroking firm, L. Messel & Co., which was then being acquired by (what become) Lehman Brothers. Note that in these years 'the personal sector' became 'the household sector', because of official redefinitions, while the data were often revised. These changes did not alter the key point, that the household/personal sector's demand for money was stable over a period of many decades, despite financial deregulation, macroeconomic upheaval, large changes in interest rates and so on.
24. More precisely, a lower probability value would attach to a specific range of values around, say, the central value of the growth rate of income forecast for a particular value of the growth rate of money.
25. For the Loughborough speech, see 'Financial change and broad money', in the *Bank of England Quarterly Bulletin*, vol. 26, no. 4, December 1986, pp. 499–507. It would be nice to think that Leigh-Pemberton – who had been Thatcher's personal appointee to the governorship – knew what he was talking about. He has written nothing of significance in his own name on monetary theory or policy since leaving the Bank of England. (In his entry in *People of Today*, he lists his recreations as 'country pursuits'.) According to Lawson in *The View from No. 11* (London and New York: Bantam Press, 1992), the 'principal author' (p. 635) of the Loughborough speech was Eddie (later Sir Edward) George, who became the Governor of the Bank of England after Leigh-Pemberton.
26. For an explanation of the phrase 'forecasters' droop', see Essay 3, p. 73.
27. See the three chapters on pp. 50–154 of G. Pepper, *Inside Thatcher's Monetarist Revolution* (London and Basingstoke: Macmillan, 1998) for a comparison of monetarist and non-monetarist forecasts. See also pp. 191–4 of the author's *Reflections on Monetarism*, based on an article in *The Spectator* of 11 March 1989, for an account of the role of monetary data in the largely correct forecast for 1988 made by his forecasting team at L. Messel & Co., and D. Smith, *From Boom to Bust* (Harmondsworth: Penguin, 1992), pp. 69–70. According to Lawson, in the mid-1980s 'nearly all the reputable monetarist gurus – with the exception of the City analyst Tim Congdon – so far from urging broad money targets on me criticized me for giving too much influence to broad money in general and £M3 in particular'. (Lawson, *The View from No. 11*, p. 453.) There is some truth in what Lawson says, but there were in fact a small number of less well-known City economists with similar views to the author's.
28. In view of the lack of support for monetarism among academic economists, it may seem puzzling that monetarism had so much influence on the Conservative Party in the late 1970s and early 1980s. The author's surmise is as follows. The UK has five kinds of economist,

- academics (who are employed by universities),
- officials (who work in the Government Economic Service and the Bank of England),

- business economists (who are mostly attached to companies, but are sometimes consultants),
- City economists (who are employed by banks and broking firms in 'the Square Mile', which is to be understood very loosely in geographical terms), and
- economic journalists.

Most academic economists are left of centre, with a majority voting for the Labour Party. (In the 1987 general election, '43 per cent [of the electorate] voted Conservative; even 25 per cent of unemployed people voted Conservative; but only 17 per cent of academics supported the Conservatives.' [D. Willetts, *Modern Conservatism* (Harmondsworth: Penguin, 1992), p. 21, citing a MORI poll in the *Times Higher Education Supplement* of 5 June, 1987.]) Contacts between officials and Opposition politicians are necessarily limited, and so the Conservatives had no access to officials' advice in the late 1970s (as they have none at the time of writing). The politics of business economists are varied. But City economists are and always have been predominantly in favour of sound money and free markets. They tend to vote for the Conservative Party and indeed to give it financial support. Several City economists (including the author) were strongly attracted to monetarism in the 1970s. Through their involvement with think tanks and contacts with economic journalists, City economists were able to have (what may seem to others) a surprising degree of influence over Conservative Party thinking while it was in Opposition. Gordon Pepper, in particular, had direct personal access to Margaret Thatcher. (G. Pepper and M. Oliver, *Monetarism under Thatcher* [Cheltenham, UK and Northampton, MA, USA: Edward Elgar, 2001], p. 29.) Of course, numerous academic economists – who regarded themselves as intellectually superior to their City and business counterparts – were appalled by these developments. (That was why 364 of them tried to make a fuss in early 1981.) But leading Conservative politicians – and indeed leading Labour politicians – had to look for alternatives to the shambles of macroeconomic policy in the mid-1970s. Adventitiously, the most prominent economic journalists – such as Samuel Brittan and Peter Jay – were at that time also inclined to favour a new approach and wrote at length about monetarist ideas. The longer that the Conservatives were in office after 1979, the less important was the City influence and the more susceptible were the politicians to advice from officials. Officials' careers usually began after graduation from university, but some economists were recruited from outside the Civil Service, largely from academic circles.

13. Has macroeconomic stability since 1992 been due to Keynesianism, monetarism or what?

On Wednesday 16 September 1992 (known at the time as 'Black Wednesday'), heavy selling of the pound on the foreign exchanges forced it out of the European exchange rate mechanism (ERM). The UK's exit from the ERM was regarded at the time as both a failure of economic policy and a national humiliation. As it is now 15 years later, the event can begin to be analysed from a wider historical perspective. The central point is surprising, but clear. The decade following the pound's expulsion from the ERM was a triumph for British economic policy-making. The sterling crisis of September 1992 did not foreshadow increased instability, but instead was followed by greater macroeconomic stability than in any previous phase of the UK's post-war history (and probably than ever before in British history). Black Wednesday became Golden Wednesday.

The paradoxical outcome was highlighted by Sir Alan Budd, Chief Economic Adviser to the Treasury between 1991 and 1997, in the Julian Hodge Institute lecture in April 2002. The lecture, entitled 'The quest for stability', noted that new policy-making arrangements introduced in late 1992 had 'exceeded all expectations'.[1] Not only had the UK had 'remarkably stable growth' in the 1990s, but it had 'survived the recent world recession better than any other major economy'. Budd's lecture was a valuable starting point for discussion, but it prompted two further questions. The first related to quantification. If the decade after September 1992 was better than earlier decades, how much better was it? Without an answer to this question, the impression of greater stability after 1992 remained only an impression. The second and perhaps more fundamental question was one of explanation. On the whole, the UK's record in macroeconomic management between 1945 and 1992 had been mediocre. Indeed, this mediocrity had come to be seen not only as an aspect of a larger economic inadequacy as the UK's share in world output and exports declined year by year, but as inevitable and never-ending. What happened in 1992 which ended (or at any rate interrupted) the unsatisfactory record? (This essay relates to the numbers in the decade from 1992. A brief appendix reviews the period since the third quarter [Q3] of 2002. The improvement in stability certainly now lasts until mid-2006.)

I

Budd argued in his lecture that economic policy-making in the years from September 1992 had a considerable degree of continuity, with a focus on inflation targets and a depoliticization of decision-taking. One way of assessing the stability of the decade after September 1992 is to compare it with previous periods in which economic policy and outcomes also had some sort of unity. In this essay a comparison is made with two earlier periods – a stop–go period from the third quarter Q3 1945 to Q2 1971, and a boom–bust period from Q3 1971 to Q3 1992. In the 26-year period from the end of the Second World War to Q2 1971, the UK participated in the Bretton Woods system of fixed exchange rates. Although the pound suffered a heavy devaluation in 1949, it was then kept within the narrow limits ($2.78–$2.82) set by the Bretton Woods rules until November 1967. This fixity of the exchange rate conditioned all economic policy-making. The world economy was far more stable than it had been in the inter-war period, but the need to defend the pound's exchange rate led to frequent policy changes in the UK and economic activity fluctuated in mild stop–go cycles.

The system of fixed exchange rates came to end with the suspension of the dollar's convertibility into gold in August 1971. Apart from a brief flirtation with the European 'snake' in the spring of 1972, the UK had a floating exchange rate against other major currencies until October 1990, when it joined the ERM. With no explicit external constraint on policy, monetary policy was extremely loose in the 18 months from autumn 1971, and a wild boom developed. Although a degree of order was restored to policy-making by the introduction of money supply targets in 1976, the operation of these targets was widely deemed to be unsatisfactory. With much uncertainty about the best policy regime for the UK, the conduct of policy was often erratic. Big swings in interest rates and inflation were accompanied by two big boom–bust cycles (from 1971 to 1974 and from 1986 to 1992), and one smaller cycle (from 1977 to 1982). The period can be fairly described as 'the boom–bust period'. The analytical task becomes the comparison of macroeconomic stability in three periods – the stop–go period, the boom–bust period, and the decade of stability from September 1992.

The next step is to propose the macroeconomic magnitudes whose variability is to be measured. Macroeconomic instability has at least three dimensions – instability in demand and output, instability in inflation, and instability in interest rates. Of course, other policy goals are relevant. For example, a case could be made that fluctuations in employment have a more meaningful impact on people's welfare than fluctuations in demand and output. Much of the post-war period was indeed characterized by official concern to maintain so-called 'full employment'. However, the labour market saw such extensive structural and legislative changes over the decades that unemployment statistics have a quite different significance in 2002 from what they had in 1945. By contrast, the concept of gross domestic output has remained much the same, despite great changes in its composition and level. Instability in the growth of gross domestic product is therefore chosen as the first indicator. (The growth rate is the annual rate and a quarterly series is analysed.)

Financial instability is measured here by instability in inflation and interest rates, but again there is an alternative. For many companies – particularly manufacturing companies exporting a high proportion of their output – instability in the exchange rate is equally or more important. Despite this, the exchange rate plays no role in the current exercise. One problem is that businesses value stability in the real exchange rate (that is, the exchange rate adjusted for differences in inflation between nations) as well as stability in the nominal exchange rate, but unfortunately there are several ways to measure the real exchange rate. Arguably the omission of the exchange rate handicaps the stop–go period in a comparison with the boom–bust period and the final decade, a point that needs to be remembered in the comparison of the three periods.

A further complication is that the phrase 'the instability of inflation and interest rates' begs the questions 'which inflation rate?' and 'which interest rate?' As the policy target in the final post-ERM decade was expressed in terms of RPIX (that is, the retail price index excluding mortgage interest rates), it might seem logical to use RPIX in the stop–go and boom–bust periods. But there is a difficulty, in that mortgage interest rates were included in the retail price index only from 1976, and the index is not wholly comparable before and after this date. A sensible answer is to regard both the 'headline' RPI and the 'underlying' RPIX as valid inflation measures. Hence the instability of both needs to be measured, and that is what is done here.

The post-war period saw a number of far-reaching changes in the structure of the British financial system. Associated with these changes were shifts in official emphasis on different interest-rate concepts, as well as a few redesignations of interest-rate concepts whose underlying economic meaning was quite stable. Fortunately, one instrument – the three-month Treasury bill – has changed little over the decades. Treasury bill rate has therefore been chosen as the measure of interest rates for current purposes.

So the increase in GDP, the annual rates of RPI and RPIX change, and the Treasury bill rate are taken to be representative of output changes, inflation, and interest rates respectively. Broadly comparable statistical series are available for all three variables over the entire 1945–2002 period under consideration.[2] Their instability is measured here by the standard deviation. (An alternative measure – the coefficient of variation [the standard deviation divided by the mean] – does not add much. It could even be positively misleading with inflation, as successful policy leads to a lower mean inflation rate. For any given value of the standard deviation, that would raise the coefficient of variation.)

The key results are given in the tables below. Table 13.1 shows the variations in output volatility between the three periods. The standard deviation of the output growth rate in the final decade is less than a half that in the two previous periods, plainly a major improvement. One surprise is that the boom–bust period does not appear to be more unstable than the stop–go period, with the two periods having roughly the same standard deviations of the output growth rate. However, this is largely due to extreme output fluctuations in the immediate aftermath of the Second World War. Output fell heavily in 1946 because of demobilization, while the severe winter of 1947 also hit production badly. Conditions returned to normal only in 1948 and 1949, and arguably a more valid alternative period for comparison runs from 1949 Q1 to 1971 Q2. The standard deviation of the output growth rate in this slightly shorter period is appreciably lower, at 1.94.

The effect of excluding the highly disrupted first three post-war years is therefore to make the stop–go period more stable than the boom–bust

Table 13.1   Output volatility in three post-war periods

The figures below relate to the annual (that is, four-quarter) change in gross domestic product (in market prices, with constant 1995 prices). The series analysed is quarterly.

1. *The stop–go period, 1945 Q3–1971 Q2*	
Mean output growth rate	2.5%
Standard deviation of output growth rate	2.80
2. *The boom–bust period, 1971 Q3–1992 Q3*	
Mean output growth rate	2.1%
Standard deviation of output growth rate	2.69
3. *The decade of stability after September 1992*	
Mean output growth rate	2.8%
Standard deviation of output growth rate	1.01

Sources: National Statistics website, and calculations by author and Mr Richard Wild of Cardiff Business School.

period, in accordance with the historical stereotypes. But it is worth noting that the difference between the standard deviations of the output growth rate in the final decade of stability (1.94 minus 1.01, or 0.93), and the post-1949 stop–go period, is greater than the difference between them in the post-1949 stop–go period and the boom–bust period (2.69 minus 1.94, or 0.75). As the stop–go era was commonly regarded by contemporaries as enjoying impressive economic stability compared with the inter-war period, and as it continued to be lionized for this reason during the boom–bust years, the scale of policy-makers' achievement of the 1990s emerges yet more emphatically.[3]

While the output growth comparison demonstrates that the post-September 1992 decade was very good compared with both the stop–go and boom–bust periods, the inflation comparison is even more favourable. Indeed, the stability of inflation in the ten years from September 1992 has to be described as astonishing after all the mishaps and wrong turnings in British macroeconomic policy in the preceding 45 years. Inflation targets were introduced by the Chancellor of the Exchequer, Mr Norman (now Lord) Lamont, in October 1992. The annual increase in RPIX was to be kept within a 1-per-cent-to-4-per-cent band for the rest of the Parliament (which lasted to 1997), with a hope that it would be towards the lower end of the band by the Parliament's end. In 1997 the newly elected Labour government reiterated the 2½ per cent RPIX target as well as announcing the radical institutional change of making the Bank of England independent. The Bank's Monetary Policy Committee was given the job of keeping the annual RPIX increase 1 per cent either side of the 2½ per cent figure. In short, the UK had an inflation target – to be understood as a 2½ per cent annual increase in RPIX – more or less without interruption for a decade.

What happened? The answer – given in Table 13.2 – is that the mean increase in RPIX in the 38 quarters to 2002 Q2 was 2.6 per cent, with a standard deviation of 0.41. So the target was met almost exactly. By contrast, in the boom–bust period the comparable measure of retail price inflation averaged 9.6 per cent with a standard deviation of 5.66. Not only did the UK cut inflation in the post-ERM decade to almost a quarter of the figure seen in the previous 20 years, but it also reduced the volatility of inflation to less than a tenth of the former level! Inflation was not much lower in the final decade than in the 1950s and 1960s, but it was significantly more stable. Overall, the verdict has to be highly complimentary to policy-makers' record in reducing and stabilizing inflation.

The last variable to be considered is the rate of interest. Here, too, the post-ERM decade stands out as by far the most stable phase in the 57 years of post-war experience, with markedly better macroeconomic management than the preceding boom–bust period. Table 13.3 shows that the mean

Table 13.2   Measures of inflation in three post-war periods

I.   Inflation measured by the all-items retail price index
The figures below relate to the annual change in the all-items retail price index.
The series analysed is a quarterly average of the monthly values.

The stop–go period, 1945 Q3–1971 Q2
Mean annual inflation rate   3.84%
Standard deviation of inflation rate   2.66

The boom–bust period, 1971 Q3–1992 Q3
Mean annual inflation rate   9.81%
Standard deviation of inflation rate   5.70

The decade of stability after September 1992
Mean annual inflation rate   2.48%
Standard deviation of inflation rate   0.83

II. Inflation measured by RPIX, that is, retail price index excluding
     mortgage interest payments
The figures below relate to the all-items retail price index until the first
quarter 1976, but to RPIX thereafter. As above, the series analysed is a
quarterly average of the monthly values.

The boom–bust period, 1971 Q3–1992 Q3
Mean annual inflation rate   9.61%
Standard deviation of inflation rate   5.66

The decade of stability after September 1992
Mean annual inflation rate   2.57%
Standard deviation of inflation rate   0.41

Treasury bill rate in the 1992 Q4–2002 Q2 period was 5.83 per cent, with a
standard deviation of 0.70. In the boom–bust period the mean Treasury bill
rate was 10.55 per cent, with a standard deviation of 2.65, and in the stop–go
period it was 3.72 per cent, with a standard deviation of 2.36. So – when measured in this way – the volatility of interest rates in the post-ERM decade was
less than a third that in either the boom–bust or the stop–go period.

The contrast between the UK's macroeconomic performance before and
after September 1992 – between the post-ERM decade and the two previous periods of stop–go and boom–bust – is therefore obvious, easily
quantified and clear. The post-1992 period was far more stable than the
boom–bust period, and it also had a far better record than the generally
acclaimed stop–go period. It is time to move on to the more interesting and
difficult question of explanation. Why was the UK economy so much more
stable after September 1992 than before?

Table 13.3   Measures of interest rate volatility in three post-war periods

The figures below relate to the quarterly average of the Treasury bill rate.	
1. *The stop–go period, 1945 Q3–1971 Q2*	
Mean interest rate	3.72%
Standard deviation of interest rate	2.36
2. *The boom–bust period, 1971 Q3–1992 Q3*	
Mean interest rate	10.55%
Standard deviation of interest rate	2.65
3. *The decade of stability after September 1992*	
Mean interest rate	5.83%
Standard deviation of interest rate	0.70

Sources: National Statistics website, and calculations by author and Mr Richard Wild.

Budd's answer in his lecture was institutional. In his view, the explanation for the greater stability was to be sought in the design of the system,
with 'the establishment of a clearly-defined task', 'the structure of the
Committee' and 'the requirement for transparency in the decision-taking
process'. The clarity of the task's definition stemmed from the technical
nature of the objective. It was to meet the inflation target, with no awkward
political distractions on unemployment, growth or the exchange rate. (Of
course, unemployment, growth and the exchange rate all mattered, but
there were no explicit objectives for any of them.) Transparency was important, because there would be 'no hiding place'. In contrast to the Treasury-
dominated and largely secret system of decision-taking before 1992,
policy-makers' views and voting records would move into the public
domain. If they were wrong, it would be their fault and not that of anyone
else. In short, the big changes in the system of decision-taking after 1992
were that policy became focused on one and only one objective, and that
the people involved were made fully accountable for mistakes.

Budd did not see the change in government in 1997 as a major break. The
Treasury Panel of 'wise men', which started business in early 1993, was not
a decision-taking body. But all its deliberations were on the record and it
therefore played a role in introducing transparency to policy advice. In 1993
the Chancellor of the Exchequer, Mr Kenneth Clarke, announced that the
minutes of the regular meetings between him and the Governor would be
published, and Budd's lecture saw these meetings as foreshadowing the
more complete transfer of power to the Bank in 1997. The Bank of
England's *Inflation Reports* also pre-dated operational independence in
1997, and are evidently considered by Budd to have had an influence on

decision-taking between 1993 and 1997. (The *Inflation Reports* informed the Governor's position in his meetings with the Chancellor.) So, when the Monetary Policy Committee was founded, it continued 'an established system'.[4]

II

Institutions are vital, but an emphasis on a change in institutional structures is surely an incomplete way to explain the radical improvement in policy-making that seems to have occurred. It is also necessary to discuss policy-makers' beliefs and attitudes. The first 45 years of the post-war period were marked by constant intellectual warfare between different tribes of British economists. Indeed, disagreement is popularly seen as a hallmark of modern economics and generates several standard jokes about the profession. But one theme of Budd's lecture was that the excellence of the decisions taken after 1992 reflected the domination of the decision-taking process by economists. This would make sense only if economists shared a consensus view on the determination of inflation, a view that was well known and relatively uncontroversial to them but not familiar to people from other walks of life. (Budd did not say so in as many words, but his lecture implied that politicians, bankers, civil servants, trade unionists and so on should be kept out of monetary policy.)

The question becomes, 'what was the consensus about the determination of inflation that was so extensively shared by the Treasury Panel before 1997, the Monetary Policy Committee after 1997, and by the large numbers of other economist advisers and commentators both within and outside the official machine in these years?' It is important to be clear that the policy achievements of the 1990s were not due to the adoption of the most well-publicized prescriptions of the most well-known schools of thought. In particular, the simpler versions of neither 'Keynesianism' nor 'monetarism' were relevant.

A discussion of these two tribal belief-systems is needed, if only to knock down some of the totem poles in macroeconomic debate. An influential view in Britain until the 1980s is that Keynesianism – in some shape or form – was responsible for the stability and prosperity of the immediate post-war decades. According to Shirley (now Lady) Williams writing in 1981, after the Second World War 'government planning, public finance and government intervention were used to bring about and sustain full employment and economic growth; deficit spending maintained demand during periods of recession . . . The lessons of Maynard Keynes, set out in *The General Theory of Employment, Interest and Money*, had been devotedly learned'.[5] Wynne Godley, a member of the Treasury Panel in the early 1990s, had written in 1983 that the 25 years after 1945 seemed at the time 'a period of remarkable success with regard to all the main objectives of macroeconomic policy' and that this post-war prosperity was 'the consequence of the adoption by governments of "Keynesian" policies'.[6]

This view of the beneficence of the so-called 'Keynesian revolution' is heard less often nowadays, but it continues to lurk behind many debates about the state and the economy. It needs to be remembered that Keynesianism, in the version adopted by the British centre left in the post-war period, is a political doctrine about the optimal size of the state sector as well as a set of economic prescriptions about how to maintain full employment. In the final chapter of *The General Theory*, Keynes claimed that 'a somewhat comprehensive socialisation of investment will prove the only means of securing an approximation to full employment'.[7] This argument was part of the case for nationalization in the late 1940s, and remained central to the defence of the mixed economy until the 1980s. As Crosland recognized in *The Future of Socialism* (first published in 1956): 'Many liberal-minded people, who were instinctively "socialist" in the 1930s . . . have now concluded that "Keynes-plus-modified-capitalism-plus-Welfare-State" works perfectly well.'[8]

The current research exercise throws a different and much more sceptical light on the macroeconomic outcomes of the 1950s and 1960s. Crucially, the UK economy was far more stable in the 1990s than in the apogee of the Keynesian revolution. It has been shown that in the post-ERM decade the standard deviation of output growth was lower than in the years from 1945 to 1971, and it remained more stable when the troublesome 1945–47 period was excluded from the comparison. Further, inflation and interest rates were far less volatile in the 1990s than in the immediate post-war decades. Ironically, the inflation rate was the only variable which was not markedly worse during the period of the supposed Keynesian revolution. (Over the 26 years to 1971 it was just under 4 per cent. Many self-styled Keynesians profess themselves indifferent to inflation.[9])

But it is implausible to claim that the UK's policies were still Keynesian in the 1990s. They certainly were not Keynesian in the Williams' sense of government planning and intervention. On the contrary, the Conservative government from 1979 to 1997 was more committed to the free market than any of its post-war predecessors. In fact, public ownership was in retreat in the early 1990s, with the main energy utilities being privatized and their markets liberalized. But policies were not even Keynesian in the more humdrum sense that government spending and taxation were being varied to influence employment. Instead, fiscal policy was subordinate to the principle that the budget should be balanced over the course of the business cycle. The long-term aim of the budget-balance rule was to prevent excessive growth of the public debt. Not one of the many policy statements from the Treasury in the 1990s envisaged an employment-promoting role for fiscal policy.[10]

So it was not Keynesianism that delivered the macroeconomic stability of the post-ERM decade. What about monetarism? Lamont's announcement of the inflation target in October 1992 was remarkably wide-ranging in its references to variables that policy-makers would have to follow in future. It did mention monitoring ranges for money supply growth, including the concept of 'broad money' which Nigel Lawson had stopped targeting in 1985. But this was a charade. The Treasury itself pretended to be interested in narrow money (particularly as measured by the narrowest possible money measure, M0), but had ignored an overshoot on M0 in the late 1980s, and its officials were not worried about broad money. Most members of the Treasury Panel did not want a discussion of monetary developments to figure in their meetings. It was only after a strong protest by one member of the Panel that a section on money was put on the agenda.[11] From the outset, the Bank of England's *Inflation Report* did include extensive material on the monetary aggregates, but at least one of the Bank's published statements on the transmission mechanism of monetary policy pays scant attention to the quantity of money on any definition.[12] Indeed, when the Bank was given operational independence in 1997, it ended the monitoring range for broad money which had been in place from 1992. According to an article in the Bank's *Quarterly Bulletin*, the justification was that '[o]ver policy-relevant time horizons, the monetary aggregates will be influenced by many factors, such as cyclical shifts in the demand for money and credit, and innovations in financial structure, products and regulation'.[13]

So monetarism – in the sense of money-target monetarism – had almost no relevance to policy-making in the decade after 1992. Like Keynesianism, it cannot take any credit for the improved performance. However, monetarism encompasses a wide range of attitudes and beliefs. While most British economists have never been enthusiasts for money supply targets, a clear professional consensus emerged in the 1980s and 1990s that one element in monetarist thinking was right. This was the view that there is no long-run trade-off between, on the one hand, output and employment and, on the other, inflation. Indeed, the emergence of this consensus was critical to the adoption of a policy-making framework focused on an inflation target. The rationale for the focus on inflation, and so for the demotion of full employment as a policy objective, had first been presented in the late 1960s. The seminal analysis was given by Milton Friedman, the leader of monetarist thought, in his presidential address to the American Economic Association in 1967.[14]

The heart of Friedman's argument was that economic agents were rational. In particular, they could not be deceived by inflationary policy-making. Crucially, pay bargains would be affected by inflationary expectations. If unemployment fell beneath a particular rate (which he called 'the natural rate'), workers and employers would agree a pay rise large enough not only to eliminate the excess demand for labour, but also to compensate for expected inflation. The pay rise would therefore add to next year's inflation and so aggravate inflation expectations further. Next year's pay rise would have to be higher yet again. The logical conclusion was that – while unemployment stayed beneath the natural rate – pay bargains and inflation would rise indefinitely. The only rate of unemployment consistent with stable inflation was the natural rate at which the demand for labour was in balance with the supply.

Government attempts to drive unemployment beneath the natural rate would lead not to high and stable inflation, but to hyper-inflation. Friedman was evasive about certain aspects of his argument. For example, he denied that central banks could measure the natural rate, even though one of his most famous early papers had emphasized the need to develop theories that were testable against data.[15] Other economists were not so cautious. It is, in fact, a simple matter to prepare series for unemployment, the rate of wage increases and the change in the rate of wage increases, and to carry out some econometric tests. Despite many problems of interpretation, economists have been able to derive estimates of the natural rate and to see whether Friedman's 'accelerationist hypothesis' is valid. In country after country the answer has been that – on the whole – it does fit the facts or, when there is some lack of clarity in the data, that Friedman's hypothesis is more convincing than the alternatives.

But labour market institutions – like financial regulation – are evolving all the time. To base monetary policy on an unemployment rate would be not only politically contentious, but also technically difficult. The key to applying Friedman's doctrine to policy-making was a generalization of the natural-rate idea. Instead of emphasizing that there is an unemployment rate at which inflation is stable, economists suggested that there is a level of output ('trend' or 'sustainable output', or even 'the natural rate of output') at which inflation is stable. (At this level of output the demand for labour should be broadly in balance with the supply, with unemployment at the natural rate. But other markets and factors of production are relevant. Ideally, output is at trend when machine capacity is working at a normal utilization level, the office vacancy rate is at a level associated with a stable rate of rent increases, the proportion of the nation's fleet of freight lorries is such as freight charges are increasing at a stable rate, and so on.) When output is above the trend level, there is said to be a positive 'output gap';

when it is beneath the trend level, the output gap is negative. Friedman's insight (that is, the absence of a long-run unemployment/inflation trade-off) is captured, more or less, by the proposition that the *change* in inflation is a positive function of the *level* of the gap.

The implied approach to monetary policy was simple. In late 1992 the UK undoubtedly had a large negative output gap after the recession induced by the ERM. It could therefore enjoy several quarters, perhaps even a few years, of above-trend growth without any serious risk of rising inflation.[16] After a year of very strong growth in 1994 output had returned roughly to its trend level (that is, the output gap was roughly zero) and the annual rate of RPIX inflation was about 2½ per cent. Since then, monetary policy – to be understood almost wholly as changes in short-term interest rates – has been organized to keep the output gap at close to zero. According to the theory, by keeping the output gap at roughly nil, inflation should be stable. In the event, policy has been successful in keeping the output gap at close to zero, and inflation has stayed remarkably steady at about 2½ per cent. Here – in essence – is the explanation for the almost 15 years of stability from 1992.[17]

In his 'Quest for stability' lecture, Budd acknowledged that this theory had motivated the official approach to monetary policy after the UK's exit from the ERM. He noted that British governments had a long record of trying to maximize output and increase employment, and yet the result had been over-full employment, excessive inflation and macroeconomic insta-bility. But the new theory implied that the key to maintaining stability of inflation was to have 'output stability'; and, in his words, 'that is, in effect, what the MPC does. It seeks to keep output as close as it reasonably can to its sustainable level, since that is usually a necessary condition for inflation stability'. Budd did not elaborate the point, but – if the sentences here are to be dignified with a theoretical label – output-gap monetarism seems the most fitting.

III

Output-gap monetarism is hardly complicated. Although its adoption has been particularly successful in the UK, it now provides the dominant the-oretical basis for central banking around the world. It has not eliminated the need for judgement and discretion in policy-making, as there are many difficulties in estimating the output gap and projecting its future course. Nevertheless, it helps to explain why the 1990s were a stable decade not just in the UK but in many other economies too (including, crucially, the USA). The puzzle is, surely, why it took economists in governments, central banks, financial institutions and universities so long to find, develop and accept the key ideas. In the UK the trouble may have stemmed partly from the prestige attached to Keynesian economics, with its very different concepts and emphases, and partly from many politicians' obstinate enthusiasm for basing monetary policy on the exchange rate.[18] (The appendix to the Introduction of this collection argued that the idea of the output gap evolved among practitioners – at the IMF and the OECD, and in broker research departments – in the late 1980s, simply because there was a demand for answers to certain kinds of question.)

But the role of the natural rate of unemployment and the output gap in monetarist economics is also a little uncomfortable. There is no doubt that output-gap monetarism is derived from the accelerationist hypothesis, but Friedman himself failed to see the potential of his 1967 lecture for policy-making. Instead of advertising the positive agenda for stabilization implied by his ideas, he made a needlessly cautious remark about the difficulty of measuring the natural rate, and delivered a vital but entirely negative comment on full employment policies. Further, the apparent triumph of output-gap monetarism does not mean the debates are over. There are still too many muddles about the role of the money in the determination of demand and output, and continued disagreement about the tasks of the central bank and the status of different monetary aggregates in policy-making.

NOTES

1. A. Budd, 'The quest for stability', Julian Hodge Institute of Applied Macroeconomics annual lecture, Cardiff, annual lecture given on 25 April 2002. (Printed as a pamphlet jointly by Cardiff Business School and Julian Hodge Bank.) The lecture was republished in the autumn 2002 issue of *World Economics*, vol. 3, no. 3.
2. The author received help from Mr Richard Wild, then of Cardiff Business School and now at the Office for National Statistics, in the preparation of the data.
3. See pp. 269–70 and notes 5, 6 and 8 below for the belief that the first 25 years were unusually stable because of Keynesian policies.
4. Budd's emphasis on the continuity of policy from 1992 contrasts with claims of a sharp discontinuity in 1997 in *Reforming Britain's Economic and Financial Policy*, a collection of Treasury papers and speeches edited by Ed Balls and Gus O'Donnell. In the foreword to this book, Mr Gordon Brown, the Chancellor of the Exchequer, said, 'My first words from the Treasury . . . were to reaffirm for this government our commitment to the goal set out in 1944 of high and stable levels of growth and employment, and to state that from 1997 onwards the attainment of this goal would require a wholly new monetary and fiscal framework.' A few sentences later Brown talked of 'a new paradigm' in 1997. (E. Balls and G. O'Donnell [eds], *Reforming Britain's Economic and Financial Policy* [Basingstoke and New York: Palgrave, 2002], p. x.)
5. S. Williams, *Politics is for People* (Harmondsworth: Penguin, 1981), p. 17.
6. W. Godley and F. Cripps, *Macroeconomics* (Oxford: Oxford University Press, also in Fontana paperback, 1983), pp. 13–14.

7.   J.M. Keynes, *The General Theory* (London: Macmillan, paperback edition 1964, originally published 1936), p. 378.

8.   C.A.R. Crosland, *The Future of Socialism* (New York: Schocken paperback edition, 1963), p. 79.

9.   See, for example, Hahn's comment in the 1981 Mitsui lectures that 'inflation as such is not an outstanding evil, nor do I believe it to be costly in the sense that economists use that term'. (F. Hahn, *Money and Inflation* [Oxford: Blackwell, 1982], p. 106)

10.   The September 2002 issue of *Euromoney* magazine included a quotation (p. 67) from Joseph Stiglitz, the Nobel-prize-winning economist, to the effect that 'Gordon Brown is a new Keynesian'. The September 2002 issue of *Institutional Investor* magazine carried an interview with Brown where he said, 'We've reduced [public] debt very substantially in Britain, from 44 per cent of national income to 30 per cent . . . So we are fiscal disciplinarians'. If Keynesianism is to be equated with fiscal discipline, then Picasso's *Guernica* was stimulated by T.S. Eliot's poetry and Maoism was heavily indebted to John Stuart Mill. Perhaps – by the phrase 'New Keynesianism' – Stiglitz meant the adjustment of interest rates according to the level of the output gap. But – as explained in the appendix to the Introduction – the label 'New Keynesian' is misapplied to this policy prescription.

11.   At its first meeting in early 1993, five out of the seven members of the Treasury Panel did not want its reports to include a section on monetary developments. The author of this essay wrote two Open Letters to the other members of the Panel, urging that a section on money was needed. (See the March and April 1993 issues of the *Gerrard & National Monthly Economic Review*.) Thereafter, a section on monetary developments did become part of the Treasury Panel's agenda.

12.   See the note on 'The transmission mechanism of monetary policy' delivered to the Treasury Committee of the House of Commons and the House of Lord Select Committee in May 1999. The note is also discussed in note 9 to Essay 14.

13.   A. Hauser and A. Brigden, 'Money and credit in an inflation-targeting regime', autumn 2002, pp. 299–307, *Bank of England Quarterly Bulletin*. The quotation is from p. 299.

14.   The address was republished in Milton Friedman, *The Optimum Quantity of Money* (London: Macmillan, 1969), pp. 95–110.

15.   In a 1952 essay 'The methodology of positive economics', Friedman argued that economic theory generated 'a body of generalizations' whose validity stemmed from 'the accuracy of their predictions'. ('The methodology of positive economics', *Essays in Positive Economics* [Chicago and London: University of Chicago Press, 1953], pp. 3–43.)

16.   '[A]bove-trend growth can be reconciled for several years with low inflation.' (Submission by Professor Tim Congdon of Lombard Street Research in the February 1993 report of the Panel of Independent Forecasters [London: HM Treasury, 1993], p. 25.)

17.   See also pp. 9–11 of the June 1999 issue of Lombard Street Research's *Monthly Economic Review*, with Lord Burns' lecture on Lombard Street Research's tenth birthday. (The lecture was called 'The new consensus on macroeconomic policy: will it prove temporary or permanent?'.)

18.   N. Lawson, *The View from No. 11* (London and New York: Bantam Press, 1992), *passim*. (See also Essay 3 in this collection for British economists' fondness for basing interest rates on the exchange rate.)

APPENDIX: DID STABILITY EXTEND BEYOND Q3 2002?

The paper on which Essay 13 is based was written in September and October of 2002, and published in the October–December 2002 issue of *World Economics*. At the time of writing (mid-2006) a further 14 quarters of data (that is, Q4 2002–Q2 2006) have become available. Do they change the message of the essay?

The short answer is 'no, on the contrary, they enhance it'. Table 13.4 sets out the key numbers. The average growth rate of output in the period after Q4 2002 was a shade lower than in the post-ERM decade, but also with slightly less volatility. The inflation record would be complicated if numbers were given for the consumer price index (CPI), which in 2003 became the measure in which the official target was expressed. However, it is sufficient to keep to the two retail price indices, given the shortness of the experience with the CPI. At any rate, if the RPIX target had been kept at 2.5 per cent, it would have been met on average in the 14 quarters to Q2 2006 and the variability of this inflation rate was even lower than in the post-ERM decade! Finally, interest rates were lower and more stable in the period under review here than in any comparable period in the UK's post-war experience.

Of course, none of the above should be read as a guarantee of continuing stability, but – at the time of writing – the record remains impressive.

Table 13.4   *Measures of volatility in key economic series, in 14 quarters from end of 2002*

	Q4 1992–Q2 2006	Q4 2002–Q2 2006
GDP at constant 2003 prices		
Average growth rate, %	2.9	2.6
Standard deviation of growth rate	0.81	0.61
All-items Retail Price Index		
Average annual increase, %	2.56	2.85
Standard deviation of annual increase	0.74	0.30
RPIX		
Average annual increase, %	2.53	2.45
Standard deviation of annual increase	0.38	0.29
Treasury bill yield		
Average value	5.29	4.28
Standard deviation	1.04	0.47

Source: Office for National website and author's calculations.

PART SIX

How the Economy Works

The current fashions in the theory of macroeconomic policy-making are towards radical simplification and the suppression of references to the quantity of money, where this phrase refers to an aggregate dominated by bank deposits. In a recent book on The New Monetary Policy Arestis and Sawyer outline what they term the New Consensus Monetary Policy (NCMP), which is closely related to the so-called (and in my view misnamed) New Keynesianism of the Introduction. According to Arestis and Sawyer, the context of decision-taking under NCMP can be described with only three equations. Technically, the first is an aggregate demand function (a sort of IS curve, in terms of the familiar IS–LM model), the second is a Phillips curve, in which inflation depends on the output gap, and past and future inflation, and the third is a so-called 'Taylor rule' for the nominal interest rate which is to be set by the central bank according to the output gap, two inflation variables and the 'equilibrium' real interest rate. (See the paper by P. Arestis and M. Sawyer in P. Arestis et al. [eds] The New Monetary Policy [Cheltenham, UK and Northampton, MA, USA: Edward Elgar, 2005], particularly pp. 7–8.)

This approach has no active role for money in the determination of macroeconomic outcomes. It is true that, implicitly, the 'interest rate' in the third rule is a money market rate set by the intersection of the supply and demand 'curves' for high-powered money. But – since the central bank is a monopoly supplier of high-powered money – the way that 'the interest rate' is set has no wider behavioural significance. What matters are how aggregate demand responds to 'the interest rate', how the level of the output gap reacts to the fluctuations in aggregate demand and how the inflation rate varies with the output gap. Clearly, in this framework neither the banking system nor a deposit-dominated quantity of money matters at all. As noted in the Introduction, New Keynesianism shares with the New Classical Economics an aversion to traditional monetary economics, in which bank deposits were crucial in the determination of bond yields (in Keynes's liquidity preference theory of money-holding behaviour), asset prices and national income.

The two final papers in this collection summarize my own experience of over 30 years of interpreting the UK monetary situation and using the data to draw conclusions about the future of the economy. My view is that real interest rates are so volatile that it is almost impossible to use them for forecasting purposes. Instead, careful analysis of the growth of money – both in the aggregate and by sector – yields powerful insights into future spending patterns. Essay 14 presents an analysis of the UK economy in which bank deposits held by companies and financial institution play a critical role in asset *price determination. But constant arbitrage between different types of asset, and between assets and goods, ensures that money is relevant to the* joint *determination of* both *asset prices and national income. As Essay 15 explains, certain key empirical relationships between money and the economy that 'worked' in the 25 years to 1989 continued to 'work' in the following 15 years, when I used them commercially in my forecasting and consultancy business, Lombard Street Research. One aim of my forthcoming* Money in a Modern Economy *will be to argue that banking and money (meaning 'bank deposits') remain fundamental to macroeconomic analysis.*

14. Money, asset prices and economic activity

How does money influence the economy? More exactly, how do changes in the level (or the rate of growth) of the quantity of money affect the values of key macroeconomic variables such as aggregate demand and the price level? As these are straightforward questions which have been asked for over 400 years, economic theory ought by now to have given some reasonably definitive answers. But that is far from the case.

Most economists agree with the proposition that in the long run inflation is 'a monetary phenomenon', in the sense that it is associated with faster increases in the quantity of money than in the quantity of goods and services. But they disagree about almost everything else in monetary economics, with particular uncertainty about the so-called 'transmission mechanism'. The purpose of this essay is to describe key aspects of the transmission mechanism between money and the UK economy in the business cycles between the late 1950s and today, and in particular in the two pronounced boom–bust cycles in the early 1970s and the late 1980s. Heavy emphasis will be placed on the importance of the quantity of money, broadly defined to include most bank deposits, in asset price determination. However, in order better to locate the analysis in the wider debates, a discussion of the origins of certain key motivating ideas is necessary.

I

Irving Fisher of the University of Yale was the first economist to set out, with rigorous statistical techniques, the facts of the relationship between money and the price level in his 1911 study of *The Purchasing Power of Money*. Fisher's aim was to revive and defend the quantity theory of money. In his review of Fisher's book for the *Economic Journal*, John Maynard Keynes was mostly friendly, but expressed some reservations. In his words, 'The most serious defect in Professor Fisher's doctrine is to be found in his account of the mode by which through transitional stages an influx of new money affects prices'.[1] In the preface to the second edition Fisher summarized Keynes' criticism as being the claim that, although his 'book shows *that* changes in the quantity of money do affect the price level', it 'does not show *how* they do so'.[2] In other words, Keynes felt that Fisher had not provided a satisfactory version of the transmission mechanism.

Fisher quickly responded to Keynes. In fact, he used the opportunity of the preface to the second edition of *The Purchasing Power of Money* to direct Keynes to pages 242–7 of another of his works, *Elementary Principles of Economics*, which had been published in 1912 between the first and second editions. In those pages, entitled 'An increase in money does not decrease its velocity', Fisher noted that economic agents have a desired ratio of money to expenditure determined by 'habit' and 'convenience'. If 'some mysterious Santa Claus suddenly doubles the amount [of money] in the possession of each individual', economic agents have excess money balances. They try to get rid of their excess money by increasing their purchases in the shops, which leads to 'a sudden briskness in trade', rising prices and depleting stocks. It might appear that only a few days of high spending should enable people to reduce their money balances to the desired level, but 'we must not forget that the only way in which the individual can get rid of his money is by handing it over to somebody else. Society is not rid of it'. To put it another way, the payments are being made within a closed circuit. It follows that, under Fisher's 'Santa Claus hypothesis', the shopkeepers who receive the surplus cash 'will, in their turn, endeavour to get rid of it by purchasing goods for their business'. Therefore, 'the effort to get rid of it and the consequent effect on prices will continue until prices have reached a sufficiently high level'. The 'sufficiently high level' is attained when prices and expenditure have risen so much that the original desired ratio of money to expenditure has been restored. Prices, as well as the quantity of money, will have doubled.[3]

Three features of Fisher's statement of the transmission mechanism in his *Elementary Principles of Economics* are,

- the emphasis on the stability of the desired ratio of money to expenditure,
- the distinction between 'the individual experiment' (in which every money-holder tries to restore his own desired money/expenditure ratio, given the price level, by changing his money balances) and 'the market experiment' (in which, with the quantity of money held by all individuals being given and hence invariant to the efforts of the individuals to change it, the price level must adjust to take them back to their desired money/expenditure ratios), and
- the lack of references to 'the interest rate' in agents' adjustments of their expenditure to their money holdings.[4]

These are also the hallmarks of several subsequent descriptions of the transmission mechanism. In 1959 Milton Friedman – who became the leading exponent of the quantity theory in the 1960s and 1970s – made a statement to the US Congress about the relationship between money and the economy. He recalled Fisher's themes. After emphasizing the stability of agents' preferences for money, he noted that, 'if individuals as a whole were to try to reduce the number of dollars they held, they could not all do so, they would simply be playing a game of musical chairs'. In response to a sudden increase in the quantity of money, expenditure decisions would keep on being revised until the right balance between money and incomes had returned. While individuals may be 'frustrated in their attempt to reduce the number of dollars they hold, they succeed in achieving an equivalent change in their position, for the rise in money income and in prices reduces the ratio of these balances to their income and also the real value of these balances'.[5] Friedman has also emphasized throughout his career the superiority of monetary aggregates over interest rates as measures of monetary policy.

The claim that, in a long-run equilibrium, the real value of agents' money balances would not be altered by changes in the nominal quantity of money was also a central contention of Patinkin's *Money, Interest and Prices*, the first edition of which was published in 1955. *Money, Interest and Prices* exploited the distinction between the individual and market experiments in a detailed theoretical elaboration of what Patinkin termed 'the real-balance effect'. In his view 'a real-balance effect in the commodity markets is the sine qua non of monetary theory'.[6] The real-balance effect can be viewed as the heart of the transmission mechanism from money to the economy.[7]

II

Despite the lucidity of their descriptions of the transmission mechanism, the impact of Fisher, Friedman and Patinkin on the discussion of macroeconomic policy in the final 40 years of the twentieth century was mixed. In the 1970s Friedman had great success in persuading governments and central banks that curbing the growth of the money supply was vital if they wanted to reduce inflation. However, his theoretical work on money was contested by other leading economists and did not command universal acceptance. By the 1990s the preponderance of academic work on monetary policy focused on interest rates, with the relationship between interest rates and the components of demand in a Keynesian income-expenditure model attracting most attention.[8] When asked by the Treasury Committee of the House of Commons for its views on the transmission mechanism, the Bank of England prepared a paper in which 'official rates' (that is, the short-term interest under the Bank's control) influenced 'market rates', asset prices, expectations and confidence, and the exchange rate, and these four variables then impacted on domestic demand and net external demand. In a 12-page note it reached page 10 before acknowledging that, 'we have discussed how monetary policy changes affect output and inflation, with barely a mention of the quantity of money'.[9] The links between money, in the sense of 'the quantity of money', and the economy were widely neglected or even forgotten.

The relatively simple accounts of the transmission mechanism in Fisher's *Purchasing Power of Money* and some of Friedman's popular work were particularly vulnerable on one score. They concentrated on the relationship between money and expenditure on the goods and services that constitute national income, but neglected the role of financial assets and capital goods in the economy; they analysed the work that money performs in the *flow* of income and expenditure, but did not say how it fits into the numerous individual portfolios which represent a society's *stock* of capital assets. As Keynes had highlighted in his *Treatise on Money* (published in 1931), money is used in two classes of transaction – those in goods, services and tangible capital assets (or 'the industrial circulation', as he called it), and those in financial assets ('the financial circulation').[10] (Keynes's distinction between the two circulations formed part of the argument of Essay 9, on the weakness of the textbook income-expenditure model, above.) The need was therefore to refurbish monetary theory, so that money was located in an economy with capital assets and could affect asset prices as well as the price level of goods and services. Much of Friedman's theoretical work for a professional audience was a response to this requirement. For example, in a 1964 paper written with Meiselman he contrasted a 'credit' view, in which monetary policy 'impinges on a narrow and well-defined range of capital assets and a correspondingly narrow range of associated expenditures' with a 'monetary' view, in which it 'impinges on a much broader range of capital assets and correspondingly broader range of associated expenditures'.[11]

But most macroeconomists have remained more comfortable with the notion that interest rates affect investment (and, at a further remove, the level of national income) than with the claim that the quantity of money has an empirically significant and verifiable role in asset price determination (and that asset prices are fundamental to cyclical fluctuations in national income). The purpose of this essay is to challenge the dominant view; it is to show that in the four closing decades of the twentieth century money was crucial to asset price fluctuations in the UK. It will appeal, in particular, to the first two of the three distinctive features of the naïve transmission mechanism discussed by Fisher in 1912 and Friedman in his 1959 Congressional testimony, namely the stability of the relevant agents' demand for money and the need to differentiate between the individual and market experiments. It will argue that these ideas are useful in the context of the financial markets where asset prices are set, just as they are in the markets for the goods and services which enter consumer price indices.

III

Before relating money to asset prices some remarks on ownership patterns are necessary. Ample official data on the UK's wealth are available. The main constituents of the capital stock throughout the 40 years under consideration here were residential houses, land and infrastructure, commercial property, and plant and equipment, including ships, planes and cars. Ultimately all these assets were owned by people. But often they were in the names of companies and people owned claims on the companies in the form of equities or bonds. Partly to achieve diversity in their asset portfolios and partly to enjoy the advantages of specialized investment management, many households build up their assets through long-term savings products marketed by financial institutions.

The twentieth century saw a rise in the proportion of corporate equity quoted on the stock exchange in tandem with the institutionalization of saving. As a result, financial institutions became the principal holders of UK quoted equities in the closing decades of the century. (See Table 14.1.)[12] They also held substantial portfolios of commercial property and other assets, such as government and corporate bonds. Indeed, over most of the 40 years to the end of the century the institutions were so large that their activities were crucial in the determination of asset prices and particularly of share prices.

Table 14.1   Beneficial ownership of UK shares, 1963–89 (% of total equity owned)

	1963	1975	1989
Insurance companies	10.0	15.9	18.6
Pension funds	6.4	16.8	30.6
Unit trusts	1.3	4.1	5.9
Investment trusts and other financial institutions	11.3	10.5	2.7
Total institutional	29.0	47.3	57.8

Source: Economic Trends, January 1991, article on 'The 1989 Share Register Survey'.

How the economy works

A key question arises from the institutions' heavyweight role in asset markets. What was the significance of money in their portfolio decisions? Is it sensible to view their attitudes towards their holdings of equities, and other assets, as being powerfully influenced by their money balances or not? Fortunately, abundant information has been published on the money supply holdings of the different sectors of the UK economy. Following the Radcliffe Committee's recommendation that more money supply statistics be compiled, the Bank of England and the Office for National Statistics (formerly the Central Statistical Office) have, since 1963, collected information on the bank deposits held by various categories of UK agent. The three types of private sector agent tracked in the data are the personal (or 'household') sector, the corporate sector (known more technically as 'industrial and commercial companies' or 'non-financial companies') and the financial sector (also called 'non-bank [or other] financial institutions'). Separately the Office for National Statistics has collected and published data on the asset holdings of the main types of financial institution in the UK, including their short-term assets such as bank deposits, also from 1963. Together the sector-by-sector money supply numbers and the information on institutions' portfolios represent a rich body of statistical material relevant to the process of asset price determination in the UK.

Some noteworthy facts about the monetary behaviour of the three components of the private sector are presented in Table 14.2. It demonstrates, in a particularly strikingly way, some important differences between the sectors in the 40-year period. The growth rate of financial sector money was almost double that of the personal and corporate sectors. In addition to the long-run institutionalization of saving already mentioned, the period saw radical financial liberalization. The effect of liberalization was to enhance

Table 14.2 *Key facts about different sectors' money holdings in the UK economy, 1964–2003*

	Mean increase (%)	Standard deviation of growth rates
Personal sector	10.9	4.1
Corporate sector (ICCs)	11.0	10.6
Financial sector (OFIs)	18.3	15.7

Note: Table relates to annual changes, quarterly data, with the first rate of change calculated in Q2 1964. Note that the differences in the 'level' series are often very different from the 'changes' series published by National Statistics, because of changes in population and definition.

Source: National Statistics database, updated to 22 February 2004.

the competitiveness of non-bank financial institutions relative to banks and other types of business organization, and to allow them profitably to expand both sides of their balance sheets, and hence their monetary assets, much faster than the quantity of money as a whole. The growth rate of financial sector money was also characterized by more pronounced volatility than that of other sectors' money. The standard deviation of the growth rates (as defined in Table 14.2) of financial sector money was four times that of personal sector money and markedly higher than that of corporate sector money.

The contrast between the different sectors' monetary behaviour is vital in understanding the transmission mechanism from money to the economy. Econometric work on the personal sector's demand-for-money functions in the UK during this period routinely found it to be stable, in the sense that standard tests on the significance of the relationship between personal sector money and a small number of other variables (including nominal incomes) were successful.[13] Similar work on the demand to hold money balances by companies and financial institutions generally failed.[14] However, it would be a serious mistake to believe that companies' and financial institutions' monetary behaviour was entirely erratic and unpredictable.

In fact, the ratio of 'liquid' assets to total assets of life insurance companies and pension funds combined was much the same at the start of the twenty-first century as it had been in the mid-1970s, even though their assets had climbed more than 50 times.[15] (See Figure 14.1. Life insurance companies and pension funds were the two principal types of long-term savings institution in the UK at this period. Assets are 'liquid' if they can be quickly and cheaply converted into other assets. Bank deposits are an example of a liquid asset, but the institutions might from time to time also hold liquidity in assets such as short-dated Treasury or commercial bills which are not money.) Indeed, the long-run stability of the ratios of money and liquidity to the total assets held by the UK institutions in the final three decades of the twentieth century is remarkable, given the wider economic turmoil and institutional upheaval of these years. It is reasonable to propose that the stability of the institutions' desired ratio of money to assets may serve the same purpose in a discussion of asset markets as Fisher's stability of persons' desired ratio of money to expenditure in a discussion of goods markets.

IV

Given the stability of the money/asset ratios in the leading financial institutions, it is easy to sketch – in a simplified way – a link between financial

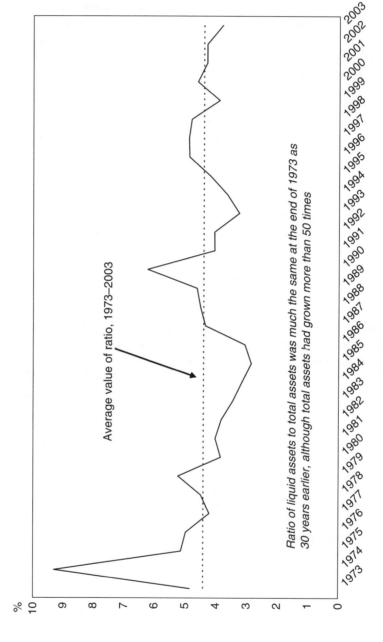

Average value of ratio, 1973–2003

Ratio of liquid assets to total assets was much the same at the end of 1973 as
30 years earlier, although total assets had grown more than 50 times

*Figure 14.1   The institutional 'liquidity ratio' in the UK, 1973–2003 (ratio of liquid assets to total assets at life
assurance companies and pension funds combined)*

sector money and asset prices. As already noted, a crucial feature of Fisher's and Friedman's descriptions of the transmission mechanism was that payments were being made within a closed circuit. As a result, if agents had excess money, individuals' attempts to unload their excess balances by increased expenditure would not change the quantity of money. Spending and national income adjusted to the quantity of money, not the quantity of money to spending and national income. An analogous argument is readily presented in the case of financial institutions in asset markets.

To help in understanding the processes at work, a highly stylized 'asset market' may be assumed. It could be regarded as a naïve characterization of Keynes's 'financial circulation'. Suppose that the UK's financial institutions are the only holders of and traders in UK equities (that is, they operate within a closed circuit), that equities constitute all of their assets and that the stock of equities (that is, the number of shares in issue) never changes. Suppose that – for whatever reason – the financial institutions' money balances jump sharply and that they have excess money. Whereas in the long run they try to keep their ratio of money to total assets at, say, 4 per cent, their money/assets ratio (or 'cash ratio') now stand at 6 per cent. In terms of figures, they might have £60 billion of money and £1000 billion of equities, whereas recently they had £40 billion of money and £1000 billion of equities. Each individual institution tries to get rid of its excess money by buying equities. *But the purchase of equities by one institution is the sale by another. For all the institutions taken together, the assumptions ensure that the flow of purchases and sales cannot change the £60 billion of money in the system.* No matter how frenetic the trading activity and no matter the keenness of particular fund managers to run down their cash, the aggregate £60 billion cannot rise or fall. The value of trading in equities in a year may be an enormous multiple of this £60 billion, but still the £60 billion cannot change.

How, then, is the 4 per cent cash ratio restored? In one round of transactions the excess supply of money causes buyers to be more eager than the sellers and the price of equities edges up, perhaps by 10 per cent, so that the value of the stock of equities is £1100 billion. The cash ratio falls to (£60 billion divided by £1100 billion multiplied by 100) or just under 5½ per cent. This is a movement towards the equilibrium 4 per cent ratio, but it is not enough. The institutions still hold 'too much money'. In the next round of transactions the excess supply of money again causes buyers to be more eager than sellers and the price of equities moves forward again, perhaps by 15 per cent. The value of equities rises to £1265 billion and the cash ratio drops to (£60 billion divided by £1265 billion multiplied by 100) or to about 4¾ per cent. And so on. In every round the value of the money balances stays at £60 billion *It does not change because – within the closed circuit assumed in the exercise – it cannot change.* The return of the institutions' cash ratio to the equilibrium 4 per cent is achieved, after so many rounds of transactions, by a rise in the value of equities to £1500 billion. The institutions' asset values have adjusted to the amount of money they hold. It is a striking, but entirely realistic, feature of the example discussed that a rise in their money balances from £40 billion to £60 billion (that is, of only £20 billion) is associated with ('causes') a rise in equity prices of £500 billion. The argument can be generalized freely. In the advanced economies of today specialized financial institutions are the characteristic holders of assets. It follows that, when they hold excess money, there is likely to be upward pressure on asset prices; conversely, when they have deficient money balances, asset prices tend to fall.

The realism of the analytical sketch above is open to question and will be defended in a later section. By contrast, the claim that asset prices are relevant to spending behaviour should not need extensive discussion. It should be sufficient to emphasize the ubiquity of arbitrage in asset markets and to note two kinds of linkage between asset markets and the rest of the economy. These linkages ensure that asset prices affect spending. Arbitrage is important, because it links the price of equities with the price of the tangible assets and goodwill to which they relate and, at a further remove, to the price of all financial securities and all tangible assets.

An excess supply of money may in the first instance boost the price of existing equities traded on the stock exchange, including – for example – the equities issued by property companies in the past. But that induces new issuance by property companies and the formation of new companies with a view to seeking a quotation. So owners of commercial property package their buildings in a corporate vehicle and try to sell these vehicles to financial institutions. The market price of all property is boosted by the ambitious stock market valuations. In a modern economy similar processes are at work for all assets. Further, arbitrage operates between different assets as well as between different forms of the same asset. If equities rise sharply in price, they may appear overvalued relative to commercial or residential property. The wide variety of wealth-holders found in a modern economy – including rich individuals and companies, as well as the large financial institutions – may then sell equities and use the proceeds to buy property. The excess supply of money – the condition of 'too much money chasing too few assets' – has pervasive effects.

Of course the power of arbitrage to remove asset price anomalies relies on the ability to switch payments between different types of asset market. A key assumption in the analysis – that of a specialized asset market, which constitutes a closed circuit where certain asset prices are set – has to be relaxed. Instead agents compare prices in all asset markets, and sell overvalued assets in one market and buy undervalued assets in another. (Not only do they sell overvalued stocks to buy undervalued stocks and sell small-capitalization stocks to buy big-capitalization stocks and so on, but they also sell houses to buy shares and sell shares to buy houses.) Does that destroy the concept of a closed circuit of payments in which the ability of excess or deficient money to alter asset prices depends on the quantity of money being a given? The short answer, in an economy without international transactions, is 'not at all'. It is true, for example, that – if quoted equities become expensive relative to unquoted companies of the same type – the owners of unquoted companies will float them, which withdraws money from the pool of institutional funds. Conversely, when quoted companies become cheap relative to 'asset value', entrepreneurs organize takeovers, which inject money back into the institutional pool. To the extent that one type of participant has been a net buyer and it has satisfied its purchases by drawing on its bank balances, its bank deposits (that is, its money holdings) must fall. But the money balances of another type of agent must rise. In fact, it is possible to identify particular types of participant in asset markets, and to collect data on their purchases and sales. Table 14.3 gives data on the market in UK quoted ordinary shares in 1994 as an illustration. It needs to be understood that the value of purchases and sales

Table 14.3   An example of an asset market in the UK in 1994 (quoted ordinary shares [equities])

Net sellers of equities	Amount sold (£m.)	Net buyers of equities	Amount bought (£m.)
Banks	393	Life assurance and pension	8 531
Personal sector	679	funds	
Industrial and commercial		Remaining financial	1 097
companies	9 261	institutions	
Public sector	3 646	Overseas sector	4 351
Sum of sales by net sellers	13 979	Sum of purchases by net buyers	13 979
The sum of net sales and purchases was zero.			

Note: Each of the identified types of equity market participant had substantial purchases *and* sales. The gross value of their transactions was a very high multiple of their net purchases and sales. Stock exchange turnover in UK and Irish listed equities was £577 526 million in 1994. (In 1994 the UK's gross domestic product at market prices was about £670 000 million.)

Source: Financial Statistics, June 1998, Tables 8.2A and 6.3A.

in a particular market, and indeed of all asset purchases and sales in economy as a whole, is zero. But the logically necessary *ex post* equivalence of the value of purchases and sales does not mean that the prices of the assets bought and sold cannot change. In particular, prices change when all the agents participating in the numerous asset markets have *ex ante* excess or deficient money holdings. The arena of payments – the closed circuit within which the rounds of transactions take place – becomes the entire economy.[16]

What about the two kinds of influence of asset prices on spending on goods and services? First, investment in new capital items occurs when the market value of assets is above their replacement cost. If the value of an office building were £10 million and it cost only £5 million to purchase the land and build it, it is obviously profitable for an entrepreneur to organize the construction of the new office building. On the other hand, if the value of a building is lower than the replacement cost, no investment takes place. Assets will continue to be bought and sold, and investments will be undertaken or suspended, until the market value of assets is brought into equivalence with their replacement value.[17] Secondly, consumption is affected by changing levels of wealth. When asset price gains increase people's wealth, they are inclined to spend more out of income.[18]

Another way of stating the wider theme is to emphasize that, in the real world, markets in goods and services and markets in assets interact constantly. Keynes's two circulations – the 'industrial circulation' and the 'financial circulation' – are not separate.[19] If excess money in the financial sector causes asset price gains, agents of all kinds will be inclined to sell a portion of their assets and buy more goods and services (that is, to spend a higher proportion of their incomes). On the other hand, if deficient money in the financial sector causes asset price falls, agents will spend a lower proportion of their incomes on goods and services. The adequacy of money balances relative to a desired level, the direction of pressures on asset prices and wealth-influenced changes in the propensity to spend out of income should be seen as an indissoluble whole.

Before reviewing the realism of our account of money's role in asset markets, a polemical note can be injected into the discussion. In none of the above has a reference been made to 'interest rates'. Agents have been adjusting their spending on goods and services, and their asset portfolios, in response to excess or deficient money, and the prices of goods, services and assets have been changing in order to bring agents back into 'monetary equilibrium' (that is, a condition where the demand to hold money balances equals the supply of such balances). The Bank of England's version of the transmission mechanism in its 1999 note to the Treasury Committee – like the innumerable other accounts in which interest rates do all the work – is

far from being the only way of approaching the subject or a definitive statement of the matter.

V

A central motif of the argument has been that spending and asset prices
change in response to the quantity of money, not that the quantity of
money responds to spending and asset prices. However, many economists
dispute this view of the direction of causation. In an early critique of
Friedman's work Kaldor claimed that the quantity of money was determined by national income rather than national income by the quantity of
money.[20] In discussing Friedman's demonstration of the historical stability
of money's velocity of circulation, Kaldor said that stable velocity had been
maintained 'only because . . . the supply of money was unstable'. The
explanation was that 'in one way or another, an increased demand for
money evoked an increase in supply'. The amount of money 'accommo-
dated' to 'the needs of trade', possibly because the official objective of
'financial stabilisation' kept interest rates constant at a particular level or
possibly because the central bank and the government wished to ensure 'an
orderly market for government debt'. Kaldor's remarks begged several new
questions, as the description of money-supply creation was rather unclear.
However, a fair summary is that he thought that – if agents had an excess
supply of or demand for money – banks' customers would talk to their
bank managers, and take the necessary action to reduce or increase the size
of their money balances and so restore it to the desired, equilibrium figure.
If the customers had excess money, they would reduce their bank borrowings and contract the quantity of money; if they had deficient money, they
would increase their bank borrowings and so create more money. The
quantity of money would therefore be 'endogenous'; it would react to 'the
needs of trade' (that is, national income), not the other way round.

Similar statements have also been made about the relationship between
financial sector money and asset prices. It is said that – if agents' money
holdings are out of kilter with the rest of their portfolios – they can easily
change the quantity of money without any effect on asset prices or other
macroeconomic variables. Some of the most forthright such statements
have been written by Minford. One example appeared in a 1996 paper from
the Liverpool Research Group. In Minford's words,

> How much is held on deposit depends on investors; and whether they hold these
> deposits in banks, building societies or other close competitors will depend on
> their relative terms – interest rates and service. However much you change the

definition of money it will be a volatile quantity, as depositors switch from
markets to cash and between institutions inside and outside the definitions.[21]

In short, if agents have excess money, they *as individuals* try to get rid of the
surplus balances by switching into a close alternative asset and the consequence of all these attempts is to reduce the quantity of money *in the aggregate* and thereby eliminate the excess money. Indeed, Minford has made
statements about asset portfolios that imply they can be restructured or reor-
ganized to any extent, and yet still make no difference to macroeconomic
outcomes. In his words, 'There is literally an infinite number of asset-liability
combinations in which the private sector can hold its savings; and each is
good as the other from its viewpoint'. The formation of a new unit trust may
have the result that, again in his words, 'there are more private sector assets
and liabilities; but savings are the same and so are interest rates. As a result
nothing has changed to make people want to spend more or do anything
differently. All that has happened is a reshuffling of balance sheets'.[22]

To summarize, the Minford argument has two parts. The first part says
that, as financial institutions' assets and liabilities must be equal, their net
wealth is always nil and cannot at any time be relevant to expenditure. The
second asserts the infinite plasticity of balance sheets, that any transaction –
any 'reshuffling' to use his terms – may alter the composition of the balance
sheet, but changes in composition are irrelevant to the wider economy. Any
consequences are contained within the financial system, and so have no
bearing on 'savings' and 'the interest rate', two (highly Keynesian) categories
which – in the Minford scheme – evidently do matter.

VI

The causative role of money growth fluctuations in asset price volatility
may be better appreciated by recalling the experience of two particularly
big cycles in the UK, that between late 1971 and 1974 ('the Heath–Barber
boom', and the stock market and property crashes of 1974) and that
between 1985 and 1992 ('the Lawson boom' and the ensuing recession). A
factual and statistical account may also throw light on the validity of the
Kaldorian and Minford arguments, and help to settle the debate about the
direction of causation.

1. Financial Sector Money and Asset Prices in the Heath–Barber Boom

The first of these two episodes is usually named after Mr Edward (later Sir
Edward) Heath, who was Prime Minister at the time, and Mr Anthony

(later Lord) Barber, who was Chancellor of the Exchequer. The starting-point was the liberalization of the financial system in the Competition and Credit Control reforms of September 1971. The reforms were intended to end quantitative restrictions on bank credit, which had been in force for most of the preceding 30 years. Rapid growth in bank credit and, hence, in a broadly defined measure of money followed in 1972 and 1973. In the years to the third quarter 1970 and to Q3 1971 M4 increased by 10.7 per cent and 14.1 per cent respectively. In the following two years M4 advanced by 22.0 per cent and 23.0 per cent respectively.[23] It was shown earlier that the three types of holder of money – personal, corporate and financial – had different behaviours, with the personal money demand being more stable than corporate and financial. The difference in behaviours was particularly clear in the cycle of the early 1970s. In the two years to Q3 1971 personal sector money increased by 11.5 per cent and 13.7 per cent respectively, roughly in line with total M4. But in the next two years personal sector money did not change as much as total M4, and rose by 16.3 per cent and 18.5 per cent respectively.

Logically, the acceleration in the growth rates of corporate and financial sector money had to be extremely sharp. In the years to Q3 1970 and Q3 1971 corporate sector money grew by 2.7 per cent and 22.2 per cent respectively; in the years to Q3 1972 and Q3 1973 it went up by 48.2 per cent and 39.2 per cent respectively. The violence of the change in corporate balance sheets between the two years before the boom and the two years of the boom itself is obvious. However, it was overshadowed by the even more extreme movements in financial sector money. In the year to Q3 1970 financial sector money increased by 22.8 per cent and in the following year it fell slightly, by 1.3 per cent. But in the years to Q3 1972 and to Q3 1973 it jumped by 75.0 per cent and 46.0 per cent respectively! These patterns were reflected in the money holdings of particular types of financial institution. At the end of 1971 the life insurance companies had short-term assets (mostly bank deposits) of £148 million. In 1972 these short-term assets leapt by £115.4 million or by 78.0 per cent and in 1973 by a further £125.7 million or by 47.7 per cent. Again, at the end of 1971 private sector pension funds had short-term assets of £205 million. In 1972 they increased by £158 million (77.1 per cent) and in 1973 by another £287 million (almost 80 per cent!).[24] (See Figure 14.2.)

What happened to asset prices? At the time corporate bonds and government fixed-interest securities (or 'gilts') were a large part of life company and pension fund assets, but some observers were concerned that high money supply growth would lead to inflation and higher interest rates, and that higher interest rates would decimate the value of bonds and gilts. (These observers – such as Professor Alan Day of the London School of

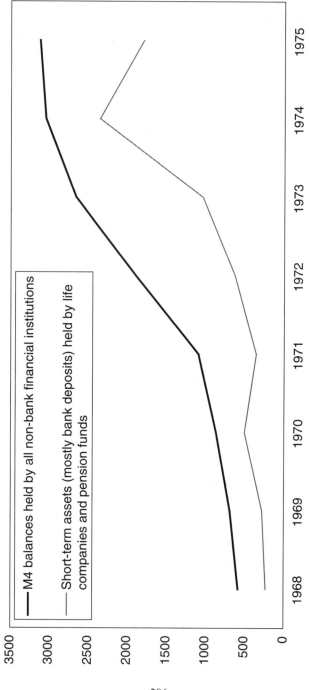

Figure 14.2   The explosion in financial sector money in the Heath–Barber boom

Economics, Peter Jay of *The Times* and Gordon Pepper of W. Greenwell & Co., the stockbrokers – were correct.) The institutions therefore wanted to increase their equity weightings (that is, the proportion of their total assets in equities) while their money balances were exploding at annual rates of between 30 per cent and 80 per cent. As suggested in the analytical sketch above, the individual fund managers wanted to keep their cash ratios down, but – if they bought securities – they would be buying them mostly from other institutions. To use Minford's word, the money would be 'reshuffled' between them. But they would continue to have excess money holdings until share prices had increased. In practice stock exchange turnover soared and share prices rose dramatically. The *Financial Times* (*FT*) index of industrial ordinary shares climbed from 322.8 (1 July 1935 = 100) in May 1971 to 533.7 a year later, an increase of 65.3 per cent.[25]

Unfortunately, that was not the end of the story. The early 1970s were a period of considerable political and social uncertainty, with fears that Britain might become ungovernable because of excessive trade union power. Share prices were constrained by heavy selling by the personal sector. May 1972 was the stock market peak. Asset price buoyancy in the rest of 1972 and during 1973 was instead most marked in property. Both residential and commercial property registered enormous price increases, at a pace never before recorded in the UK's peacetime history. The economy as a whole was profoundly affected. The increase in real domestic demand in 1973 was 7.8 per cent, almost the highest figure in the post-war period. The sequel to the cyclical excesses was a drastic rise in inflation (to over 25 per cent in mid-1975) and the worst recession since the 1930s, as policy-makers struggled to bring inflation down to an internationally acceptable figure.

Once cause of the slide in activity was a severe squeeze on company liquidity in 1974, which was a by-product of a decline in aggregate money supply growth. In the year to the end of 1973 M4 rose by 22.1 per cent, but in the year to end-1974 it increased much more slowly, by only 10.8 per cent. The swing from monetary ease to restraint was more abrupt with an inflation-adjusted rate of money growth, because inflation was higher in 1974 than in 1973. Corporate and financial sector money saw more extreme movements than aggregate money in the downturn, in line with the long-run behaviour patterns and just as they had in the upturn. In the year to Q4 1973 financial sector money advanced by 35.1 per cent; in the first three quarters of 1974 it contracted. Share prices started to fall in late 1973 and plunged in 1974, with the *FT* industrial ordinary index in November at little more than a third of its value in May 1972. Corporate sector money climbed by over a third in the year to Q4 1973, but declined by almost a tenth in the year to Q4 1974. Companies' attempts to protect their balance sheets were responsible for heavy rundowns in stocks and cutbacks in investment, while commercial property values slumped.

2. Financial Sector Money and Asset Prices in the Lawson Boom

After the recession of 1980 and 1981, the early 1980s were a fairly quiet period in which output grew at a slightly above-trend trend, inflation was stable at about 5 per cent a year, employment increased gradually and asset markets were steady. But in late 1985 a drastic change in monetary policy occurred, comparable in its cyclical consequences to Competition and Credit Control in 1971. The growth of the quantity of money had been held back in the early 1980s partly by a technique known as 'over-funding'. This involved sales of government debt to non-banks in excess of the budget deficit, and led to reductions in banks' assets and their deposit liabilities. For technical reasons apparently related to money market management, over-funding was stopped in the autumn of 1985. Broad money targets were suspended and, in due course, they were to be abandoned. An acceleration of money supply growth quickly became clear. Whereas M4 growth averaged 13.0 per cent in the four years to end 1985, it averaged 16.9 per cent in the following four years.[26]

The contrast in monetary conditions before and after autumn 1985 was in fact greater than implied by this 4-per-cent-a-year difference in the annual growth rates. A big fall in oil prices, determined in the global energy market, cut UK inflation in 1986 and dampened inflation expectations. The increase in personal incomes remained fairly steady in 1986 and 1987, and the rise in the personal sector's money holdings was more or less constant – at a little above 11½ per cent a year – from 1983 to 1987. The result – as in the Heath–Barber boom – was that the upturn in aggregate M4 growth led to an explosion in the money holdings of companies and financial institutions. In the four years to 1985 companies' M4 holdings grew on average by 11.6 per cent; in 1986 and 1987 they increased by 30.3 per cent and 19.2 per cent respectively. Financial institutions were in a somewhat different position, because a sequence of liberalization measures had encouraged their rapid growth in the early 1980s, and much of this growth is best interpreted as a benign, once-for-all adjustment in their economic importance. The average growth rate of financial institutions' money holdings in the five years 1980 to 1984 inclusive was a very high 24.8 per cent. Even so in the next five years – the years of the Lawson boom – the average growth rate was about 10 per cent a year more, at 34.4 per cent. (See Figure 14.3.)

The upturn in the growth rate of non-personal money holdings was particularly marked in 1986 and 1987. Indeed, in 1987 financial institutions' money holdings jumped by 58.9 per cent, a figure which was comparable

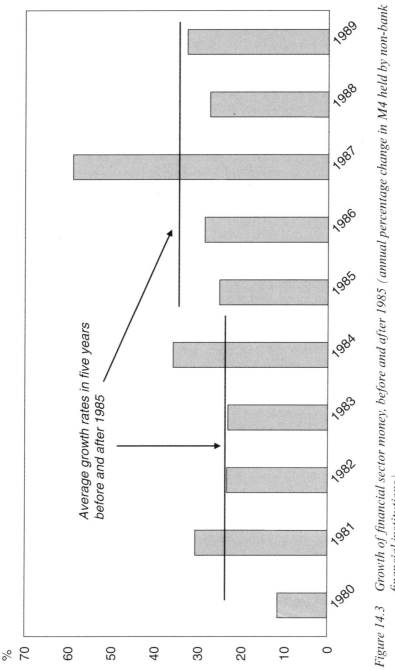

Figure 14.3 Growth of financial sector money; before and after 1985 (annual percentage change in M4 held by non-bank financial institutions)

with their experience in the Heath–Barber boom 15 years earlier. Again it is easy to trace a relationship between the money balances held by the financial sector as a whole and those held by particular types of institution. At the end of 1985 life insurance companies had £3262 million of 'cash and balances with the monetary sector' and £123 million of certificates of deposit (CDs); at the end of 1986 the corresponding figures were £4062 million and £173 million; and at the end of 1987 they were £5975 million and £188 million.[27] At the end of 1985 pension funds had £3970 million of 'cash and balances with banks' and £156 million of CDs; at the end of 1986 the corresponding figures were £5697 million and £229 million; and at the end of 1987 they were £8263 million and £570 million.[28] So the money balances of these two types of institution together advanced from £7511 million at end-1985 to £10161 million at end-1986 (or by 35.3 per cent) and £14996 million at end-1987 (or by 47.6 per cent at end-1986). In two years they almost exactly doubled, while financial sector money in aggregate increased by 104 per cent.

And what happened to asset prices in this cycle? Table 14.1 showed that by the late 1980s insurance companies and pension funds owned about half of all UK equities, while other types of long-term savings institution (unit trust groups and investment trusts) held at least another 10 per cent. It is therefore unsurprising that the surge in these institutions' money holdings should be associated with large stock market gains. In the two years to September 1987 – which, roughly speaking, were the first two years from the end of over-funding and the consequent acceleration in money supply growth – the *Financial Times* all-share index rose from 633.18 to 1174.38. In other words, share prices doubled. They behaved much like financial sector money, and life company and pension fund money, in the same period. It is true that an abrupt fall in share prices in late October 1987 prompted comparisons with the Great Crash in the USA in the late 1920s, with several alarming forecasts being made of an impending slump in economic activity. However, an alternative view – that the stock market fall of October 1987 was due to market participants' anticipation of future inflation trouble – is also tenable. If so, the likely sequel would be attempts to move portfolios away from equities and into property. In fact, the late 1980s were a period of rapid property appreciation, with 1988 seeing the peak of the house price increases and a commercial property bubble.

The response of the economy to asset price gains had many similarities to the events of the Heath–Barber boom. The forecasts of a recession in 1988 were totally wrong. Domestic demand, measured in real terms, grew by 5.0 per cent in 1986 and 5.3 per cent in 1987; it then jumped by 7.9 per cent in 1988, roughly matching the 1973 experience. In mid-1988 particularly large trade deficits were reported. Officialdom began to realize that the boom in spending was out of line with the economy's ability to produce. The boom caused a sharp fall in unemployment, and asset price inflation spread to markets in goods and services. Interest rates were raised sharply in late 1988 and 1989, with clearing bank base rates reaching 15 per cent on 5 October 1989. Higher interest rates dampened the growth of bank credit and money.[29] The monetary data give insights into the balance-sheet strains of the period. As in 1974, money supply growth in 1990 declined while inflation (again affected by international oil prices) was rising. The result was a squeeze on real money balances and a collapse in asset values. M4 growth fell from 18.1 per cent in 1989 to 11.9 per cent in 1990 and 6.0 per cent in 1991. Company sector money – which had been soaring in 1986 and 1987 – contracted in the year to Q1 1991. The change of trend in financial sector money came later, but was more pronounced. Financial sector money dropped by 4.5 per cent (that is, at an annualized rate of almost 9 per cent) in the first half of 1991 and showed little growth from mid-1991 to mid-1993. The imprint of these trends on the pension funds' cash, in particular, was marked. The pension funds had 'cash and balances with banks' of £17492 million at end-1990, but only £9834 million at end-1992.[30]

The main asset classes did not respond in a neat and tidy way to the change in the monetary environment. Nevertheless, the impact of excess money until 1990 and deficient money thereafter is obvious in their general direction of movement. The equity market had reasonable years in 1988 and 1989, but struggled in 1990 and share prices in January 1991 were lower than they had been in September 1987. But a big rally in early 1991 was the start of the long bull market. By contrast, the property market was badly hit by the monetary squeeze and asset price deflation continued until 1993. The fall in house prices in the four years to mid-1993 was the worst in the UK's post-war history and scarred the financial memories of the many millions of people who had been tempted to buy a home in the boom of the late 1980s.

VII

What do the passage of events, and the statistics of money supply change and asset price fluctuations, say about the direction of causation? Do they support or invalidate the Kaldorian and Minford arguments?

1.   A Reply to the Kaldorian Argument

Vital to the Kaldorian argument was the idea that banks and their customers adjusted their money holdings to 'the needs of trade'. Bank borrowing altered to keep the demand for money and the supply of money in balance. However, this argument runs into several difficulties when an attempt is made to relate it to real-world institutions. The greater part of the money supply is held by the members of households (that is, the personal sector) and it is not clear that the phrase 'needs of trade' has any application to them. Indeed, a high proportion of bank and building society deposits is held by people who are retired, and for them the notion of the 'needs of trade' is obviously a misunderstanding. More to the point for the current exercise, the Kaldorian thesis simply does not work in the UK financial sector during the boom–bust cycles. Crucially, neither of the two dominant types of financial institution – the life insurance companies and the pension funds – had any significant bank borrowings.[31]

Even more damaging for Kaldor's thesis is that such modest bank borrowings as they did have did not change in the manner he postulated. It is obvious from Figure 14.4 that life offices and pension funds did not react to the receipt of extra money by repaying bank loans and thereby bringing their money holdings back to the desired level. If Kaldor were right, changes in bank loans and changes in bank deposits would have been inversely related, and the regression equation of changes in bank loans on bank deposits would have had a high correlation coefficient and a regression coefficient close to minus one. An equation relating to these variables accompanies the figure and, very plainly, it does not have these properties. The analytical sketch above comes much closer to describing the task of portfolio management in these large financial organizations. In the periods of rapid money supply growth in the boom–bust cycles the heart of this task was to maintain some sort of equilibrium between their money holdings and their total assets, when money holdings were often exploding by 10 per cent a quarter. Changes in bank borrowing hardly entered the picture. As suggested in the analytical sketch, a realistic assessment is that the senior investment executives tried to keep the money/asset ratios fairly stable. In addition in both the boom–bust cycles they became increasingly, and justifiably, worried that the value of their bond holdings would suffer from rising inflation. As they switched away from bonds, the results were surges in equity prices and commercial property values. These surges seemed inordinate relative to the contemporaneous rates of increase in wages and prices, but they both had an economic explanation and were important for the future behaviour of spending and incomes.

More generally, the problem with the Kaldorian argument is that it is cavalier in its treatment of agents at the individual level. It makes bold assertions about the macroeconomic consequences of certain actions

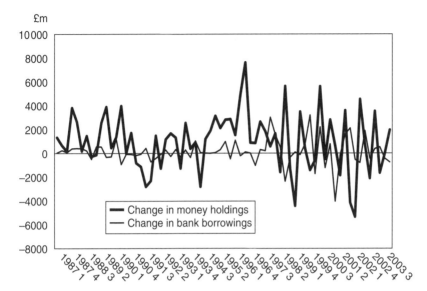

Note: Best-fitting equation for change in bank borrowing (dL) on change in money (dM) is: dL = 641.1 − 0.08 dM, with $r^2 = 0.00$, standard error = 2180, and t statistic on regression coefficient = 0.17.

Figure 14.4   *Does Kaldor's endogeneity thesis work in the UK financial sector? (changes in bank borrowings of life companies and pension funds compared with changes in their money holdings, quarterly data, 1987–2003)*

without taking the trouble to establish a secure microeconomic underpinning for such actions. The primacy of the 'needs of trade' in financial management has obvious applicability only to the corporate sector. But – when interrogated a little – Kaldor's idea does not work even here. If a company is short of money balances, its strained liquidity is typically an aspect of balance-sheet weakness. If so, the banks are unlikely to want to lend to it. At the individual level, bank credit and the quantity of money emphatically do not adjust to 'the needs of trade'. A company on the brink of bankruptcy may need a large bank loan and its managers may plead for 'accommodation' from the local bank manager, but that does not mean it is a deserving supplicant or that it will receive finance.

In two severe corporate liquidity squeezes in our 40-year period – one in 1974, and the other in late 1990 and early 1991 – cash-starved companies could not conjure up new money balances out of thin air or even from easy-going bank managers. The only way they could restore sound balance sheets was to sell more and spend less. If they could not boost their sales revenue, they might try to offload subsidiaries, buildings, spare plots of land and other miscellaneous assets. Obviously, if other companies were also suffering from inadequate liquidity (with corporate sector money balances contracting while general inflation ran at double-digit annual rates), the efforts of numerous companies to offload subsidiaries, buildings, spare plots of land and so on would cause the prices of these assets to fall. The theme recurs, that whereas excess money balances are associated with buoyant asset prices, deficient money balances are accompanied by asset price weakness.

Alternatively, the companies might spend less, by cutting back on investment, and by economizing on holdings of raw materials and components. That would certainly affect aggregate demand. If so, money was driving national expenditure, rather than the other way round. The Kaldorian argument does not fit the facts of the boom–bust cycles. The big fluctuations in aggregate money supply growth – and the associated even larger fluctuations in the money holdings of companies and financial institutions – were in no sense motivated by 'the needs of trade'. Instead they were due to the erratic, foolish and wholly exogenous mismanagement of monetary policy by the government and the Bank of England, and the results were extreme asset price volatility and the destructive boom–bust cycles.[32] (As noted in Essay 12, a speech was given at Loughborough University on 22 October 1986 by the Governor of the Bank of England – although its 'principal author' was apparently his successor – suggesting that it was 'fair to ask whether a broad money target continues to serve any useful purpose' and perhaps 'we would do better to dispense with monetary targetry altogether'. The Loughborough speech was written when the annual growth rate of the money supply on the M3 measure had climbed well into the teens and the impact of excess financial sector money on asset prices was already clear.)

2. A Reply to the Minford Argument

What about the Minford argument? To some extent it is simply a misunderstanding. Of course, the asset and liabilities of financial institutions (and indeed of companies) are equal, and their net wealth is always nil. But the economy's assets must – of course – belong to someone. If a mutually owned life insurance company holds assets in the form of a large portfolio of equities, it may have liabilities to policy-holders equal to these assets and no net wealth. But that does not mean its policy-holders also have no net wealth! On the contrary, the higher the value of the life company's assets because of, say, a soaring stock market, the higher the value of its liabilities and the better-off are the policy-holders. Despite the veil that many layers of financial intermediation may seem to draw over underlying economic realities, and despite the equivalence of financial institutions' assets and liabilities, the value of the assets they hold remains relevant to expenditure decisions.

Further, it is certainly not true that transactions within the financial system leave asset values unchanged. Minford writes as if individual agents can alter the aggregate quantity of money by switching between money balances and close alternative assets. In his discussions such switches can therefore alter the quantity of money, and so eliminate excess or deficient money holdings, without an excess supply of or demand for money affecting asset prices and the economy at large. However, an essential feature of the Fisher and Friedman accounts of the transmission mechanism, and of the sketch of asset price determination given earlier in this essay, is that – when money is in excess supply – individual attempts to reduce the quantity of money do *not* alter the aggregate quantity of money. Indeed, it was precisely this feature of the story – to repeat, the distinction between the individual and market experiments within a closed circuit of payments – that gave the quantity of money the power to determine other variables.

A fundamental feature of the analysis must be emphasized. It is essential to the argument that the quantity of money is an all-inclusive measure (that is, a broadly defined money aggregate, which includes all bank deposits). The point is that an all-inclusive measure of money cannot be changed *in the aggregate* by individual agents' attempts to alter their own money holdings. That is the pivot on which the real balance effect works. But a narrow measure of money does not have the same characteristic. Narrow money – for example, an aggregate measure of money like M1 which includes sight deposits but not time deposits – can be changed by a large number of individual switches between sight and time deposits. Such switches do not lead to any transactions in goods, services or assets, and have no effect on the price level of goods and services or on asset prices.[33]

It is therefore surprising that Minford should prefer narrow money to broad money as a monetary indicator. Indeed, his preference – stated forcefully at the peak of the Lawson boom when asset prices were at their extravagant – was for a particularly limited narrow money measure, M0. M0 consists of notes and coin in circulation outside the Bank of England and banks' operational deposits at the Bank of England; it excludes *all* bank deposits held by private sector agents. According to Minford, 'an implication of financial competition' is that 'money changes its form' and 'in particular the only "pure" money left is currency' (that is, M0).[34] Minford persuaded many economists at the Treasury and the Bank of

England about the importance of M0, and his analysis was one of the inputs into the policy discussion that led to the abandonment of broad money targets in the mid-1980s.

However, an examination of the holders of M0 quickly shows that it cannot have been relevant to the asset price swings seen in the boom–bust cycles. A compelling attribute of modern economies is that companies, financial institutions and wealthy individuals hold negligible amounts of notes. Part of the explanation is that notes cannot be used – without inordinate expense – to conduct the large transactions, notably transactions in substantial assets, in which companies, financial institutions and wealthy individuals are routinely involved. The irrelevance of narrow money to big corporate decisions, to the decisions that determine asset prices and influence company investment, should hardly need to be stated.

In fact, in the 40 years under consideration in this essay no official data were compiled on the currency holdings (that is, notes and coins) of life insurance companies and pension funds, presumably because official statisticians could not see any purpose in the exercise. Since 1987 statistics have been prepared for the currency holdings of non-monetary financial institutions, which include life insurance companies and pension funds. In 1987 they amounted to £55 million and in 2002 to £83 million. It seems likely that the bulk of this is held by minor financial institutions with some retail business involving cash, such as some hire purchase companies and pawnbrokers. For all significant financial institutions, and for all the big institutional players in UK asset markets, note holdings are trifling compared with bank deposits. A sense of perspective is given by comparing the bank deposits held by non-monetary (that is, non-bank, non-building-society) financial institutions with their currency holdings. (See Table 14.4.) At the end of 2002 the deposits – at £279 597 million – were almost 3400 times larger than the amount of currency. For life assurance companies and pension funds by themselves, the multiple would have been considerably higher, but – as noted – official data are not available.

Minford appears to believe that the variations in the growth rate of broad money were unrelated to the extreme asset price movements of the boom–bust cycles. This essay has shown that the broad money growth rates of 20 per cent a year in the boom were associated with both 40 per cent, 50 per cent and 60 per cent annual growth rates of money (that is, which, to repeat, were over 99.9 per cent bank deposits) held by the financial sector as whole, and 40 per cent, 50 per cent and 60 per cent annual growth rates of money held by such leading institutions as life offices and pension funds. Equally, it has shown that the decelerations in broad money growth rates to 10 per cent a year or less during the busts were associated with virtual stagnation in the money holdings of the financial sector and leading

Table 14.4 *The insignificance of financial institutions' currency holdings*

Non-monetary financial institutions' holdings of:			Multiple of deposits held to currency held
	Sterling deposits (£m.)	Currency (£m.)	
1987	40 082	55	729
1988	51 008	59	865
1989	73 142	63	1161
1990	86 210	70	1232
1991	77 117	74	1042
1992	88 140	77	1145
1993	99 866	79	1264
1994	106 180	81	1311
1995	144 709	83	1743
1996	173 317	83	2088
1997	200 529	83	2416
1998	216 459	83	2608
1999	200 617	83	2417
2000	247 853	83	2986
2001	286 958	83	3457
2002	279 597	83	3369

Source: National Statistics website.

financial institutions. It is clear that the periods in which the institutions' money holdings were expanding rapidly were also periods of rising asset prices and that the periods when they were static were periods of falling asset prices. Further, the notion that financial institutions' senior executives cared more about their note holdings (that is, their M0 balances) than about their bank deposits is – to say the least – most implausible, given the quantitative insignificance of the note holdings. Minford wants us to believe that 'monetary forces' are best understood as 'the printing of money' and 'M0', and that such variables 'are still central to our understanding of inflation'. Possibly, but it is difficult to believe that M0 is still central – or has ever been central – to the asset price inflation that was such a notorious element in the boom–bust cycles.[35]

VIII

Nowadays most accounts of the transmission mechanism of monetary policy give pride of place to the level of interest rates or even to only one

interest rate (that is, the central bank rediscount rate) as the economy's factotum. An alternative approach, building on the work of Irving Fisher,
Patinkin and Friedman, sees expenditure decisions as motivated by
individuals' attempts to bring actual money balances into line with the
demand to hold them. Many introductory statements in this tradition focus
on the effect that these attempts have initially on expenditure on goods and
services, and eventually on the price level. They rely for their conclusions
on two features of the adjustment process, the stability of the desired ratio
of money balances to expenditure, and the distinction between the 'individual experiment' and 'market experiment' in a closed circuit of payments
where the quantity of money is kept constant. This essay has shown that
the same sort of story can be told about asset markets, relying on the stability of financial institutions' desired ratio of money balances to asset
totals and the invariance of the pool of institutional money balances as
asset prices are changing. It follows that, when the quantity of money held
by key players in asset markets rises or falls abruptly by a large amount,
powerful forces are at work to increase or lower asset prices.

Of course, the notion of a closed circuit of payments – for either goods
and services or assets – is a simplification. In the real world markets in goods
and services are not separate from asset markets. If excess money leads to a
rise in asset prices, almost certainly the rise in asset prices will influence
expenditure on goods and services. In his 1959 statement to the US Congress
Friedman compared the rounds of payments as agents seek to restore monetary equilibrium (that is, the equivalence of the demand for and supply of
money balances) to a game of musical chairs. In this essay the venue for the
game of musical chairs was the UK economy, including its asset markets.
Moreover, because of the availability of sector-by-sector money supply data
in the UK since 1963, it has become possible to say more about the identity
and behaviour of the main players in the game. Three types of player in the
UK in the 40-year period were individuals as such, companies and financial
institutions. Companies and financial institutions were particularly active in
asset price determination. It has been shown that corporate and financial
sectors' money balances were consistently more volatile than personal
sector money, and the volatility in their money holdings was reflected in
asset prices. The relevant quantity of money here has to be an all-inclusive
or broad money measure, partly because – in modern circumstances –
agents managing large portfolios do not have significant note holdings.

Very high growth rates of broad money were therefore responsible for the
asset price exuberance in the upturn phase of both the Heath–Barber boom
in the early 1970s and the Lawson boom in the late 1980s, and subsequent
very sharp declines in broad money growth were responsible for the asset
price busts which followed. It has been possible to give an account of events

with only an occasional reference to interest rates. Changes to expenditure on goods and services, and decisions to buy and sell assets, could be interpreted as responses to excess or deficient money holdings, not to the putative effect on an interest rate on investment or stock-building. In the same spirit as the 'monetary' view espoused by Friedman and Meiselman back in 1964, the adequacy of agents' money holdings impinged on a very broad 'range of assets' and affected a very wide range of 'associated expenditures'.

The phrase 'too much money chasing too few goods' has been used to characterize an economy suffering from inflationary pressures and it does indeed convey the essence of the transmission mechanism as seen by Fisher, Patinkin and Friedman. The phrase 'too much money chasing too few assets' was used during the Heath–Barber and Lawson booms in the UK, and again captures the spirit of the analytical sketch of asset price determination set out in this essay.[36] But in truth the right phrase is 'too much money chasing too few assets and too few goods', because asset markets are linked with markets in goods and services. One puzzle about the period discussed in the paper is that, while the Heath–Barber boom demonstrated the power of excess money growth to disturb asset markets and cause inflation, an essentially similar sequence of events was played out less than 20 years later with equally disastrous results. The puzzle is heightened by the supposed commitment of the Conservative government from 1979 to 'Thatcherite monetarism', including a Medium-Term Financial Strategy which was intended to outlaw excessive money supply growth. Just as 'monetarism' had developed in the 1970s by the import of largely American ideas, so the abandonment of the monetary element in that strategy reflected the influence of fashionable academic thinking on the other side of the Atlantic.[37] The decline in academic interest in 'the real-balance effect' (or whatever short phase best denotes the genus of transmission mechanism described in this paper) was basic to understanding official decisions and their often catastrophic consequences.

Admittedly, much of the account here has taken narrative form and suffers from the possible risk of being too selective with facts and figures. An econometric exercise was undertaken by Dr Peter Warburton to address this weakness and its results are reported elsewhere.[38] They suggest that non-personal money holdings did have a significant effect on both asset prices and expenditure.[39] In short, the boom–bust cycles in the closing four decades of the twentieth century reflected the UK economy's response to extreme fluctuations in money supply growth. Excess money was accompanied by asset price buoyancy, and provoked both above-trend growth in demand and exchange rate weakness. The eventual result was higher inflation. Similarly, deficient money was associated with asset price declines and slowdowns (or even contractions) in demand. The behaviour of the quantity of money, on the broad definitions, was fundamental to understanding the economy's changing cyclical fortunes over the 40-year period.

NOTES

1. E. Johnson and D. Moggridge (ed.), *The Collected Writings of John Maynard Keynes*, vol. XI, *Economic Articles and Correspondence* (London: Macmillan Press for the Royal Economic Society, 1983), p. 376.
2. W.J. Barber (ed.), *The Works of Irving Fisher*, vol. 4, *The Purchasing Power of Money* (London: Pickering and Chatto, 1997, originally published by Macmillan in New York in 1911), p. 27.
3. Barber (ed.), *Works of Fisher*, vol. 5, *Elementary Principles of Economics* (London: Pickering and Chatto, 1997, originally published by Macmillan in New York in 1912), pp. 242–4.
4. The analysis on pp. 242–7 of *Elementary Principles* is different from that in chapter 4 of *Purchasing Power*, even though chapter 4 had ostensibly been on the same subject of 'the transition period' (that is, the passage of events in the transmission mechanism). Chapter 4 of *Purchasing Power* is highly Wicksellian, with much discussion of the relationship between interest rates and the rate of price change, and then between real interest rates and credit demands. This Wicksellian strand was dropped in pp. 242–7 of *Elementary Principles*.
5. See M. Friedman, 'Statement on monetary theory and policy', given in Congressional hearings in 1959, reprinted on pp. 136–45 of R.J. Ball and P. Boyle (eds), *Inflation* (Harmondsworth: Penguin Books, 1969). The quotations are from p. 141.
6. D. Patinkin, *Money, Interest and Prices* (New York: Harper and Row, 2nd edition, 1965), p. 21. Keynes is sometimes said to be the originator of the idea of 'real balances', as he used the general idea in his 1923 book *A Tract on Monetary Reform* in a discussion of inflation in revolutionary Russia in the early 1920s. Patinkin's view on the importance of the real-balance effect seems to have changed in his later years. In an entry on 'Real balances' in the 1987 Palgrave he said, 'the significance of the real-balance effect is in the real of macroeconomic theory and not policy'. (See P. Newman, M. Milgate and J. Eatwell (eds), *The New Palgrave: Money* [London: Macmillan, 1989, based on 1987 *New Palgrave*], p. 307.)
7. This claim is controversial. Patinkin regarded the real-balance effect as a kind of wealth effect. It was pointed out that, as the banking system's assets and liabilities must be equal, that part of the quantity of money represented by banks' deposit liabilities (so-called 'inside money', from a distinction proposed by Gurley and Shaw in their 1960 *Money in a Theory of Finance* [Washington, DC: Brookings Institution, 1960]) could not represent a nation's net wealth. A logical implication was that the real-balance effect related only to 'outside money', often taken to be equivalent to monetary base assets issued by the central bank. It was then shown that, since the monetary base is modest compared with other elements in a nation's wealth, the real-balance effect is small and cannot have a powerful influence on macroeconomic outcomes. (See, in particular, T. Mayer, 'The empirical significance of the real balance effect', *Quarterly Journal of Economics*, vol. 73, no. 2, 1959, pp. 275–91.) The emphasis in macroeconomic theory moved away from the real-balance effect towards 'the Keynes effect', to be understood as the effect of changes in the quantity of money on interest rates and so on investment. However, an argument can be made that the only concept of money relevant to the real-balance effect is an all-inclusive measure, since agents can eliminate excesses or deficiencies of smaller, less-than-inclusive measures by transfers between money balances (that is, they can switch between sight and time deposits, or between notes and sight deposits). Such 'money

transfers' plainly have no effect on aggregate demand or asset dispositions. (This point is developed in the critique of Minford's views on money on pp. 304–7.) By implication, if the real-balance effect is indeed the *sine qua non* of monetary theory, it must relate to inside money and cannot be exclusively a wealth effect. (See T. Congdon, 'Broad money vs. narrow money', *The Review of Policy Issues*, vol. 1, no. 5, 1995, pp. 13–27, for further discussion.) Laidler has also used the phrase 'the real-balance effect' to mean something more than just a wealth effect and claimed that, in the US economy for the years 1954–78, 'the adjustment of real balances towards the desired long-run values has a pervasive and systematic influence on the macroeconomy'. (D. Laidler, *Money and Macroeconomics* [Cheltenham: Edward Elgar, 1997], p. 172.) Note also that the claim that outside money, that is, the central bank's liabilities, constitutes net wealth to the private sector of the economy is debatable. It would obviously be invalid if the central banks' assets were all claims on the private sector. But, even if government securities were all of the central bank's assets and – in accordance with Barro's doctrine of Ricardian equivalence – government debt were judged not to be net wealth to the private sector, then,

- outside money also cannot be net wealth to the private sector, and
- the private sector's net wealth cannot be increased when the central bank expands its balance sheet.

Yet virtually all macroeconomists accept that something important happens when the central bank shifts the position of the supply curve of the monetary base and changes short-term interest rates. If this effect is not a net wealth effect, how does it change anything and why does it matter? And, if it matters so much even though it is not a wealth effect, why is it that changes in inside money do not matter at all? These are some of the issues to which the author plans to return in his book *Money in a Modern Economy* (forthcoming), to be published by Edward Elgar.

8. In the autumn of 1995 the *Journal of Economic Perspectives* published a number of papers on the transmission mechanism of monetary policy. Not one of the papers focused on the real-balance effect as the heart of this mechanism. Indeed, despite Fisher's and Friedman's clear statements many years earlier, and Friedman's and many others' vast output on the empirical relationship between money and the economy, Bernanke and Gertler opined that 'empirical analysis of the effects of monetary policy has treated the monetary transmission mechanism as a "black box"' (B. Bernanke and M. Gertler, 'Inside the black box: the credit channel of monetary policy transmission', *Journal of Economic Perspectives*, Autumn 1995, pp. 27–48. The quotation is from p. 27.)

9. The Monetary Policy Committee of the Bank of England, *The Transmission Mechanism of Monetary Policy* (London: Bank of England, in response to suggestions by the Treasury Committee of the House of Commons, 1999), p. 10. The note is believed to have been written by John Vickers, the Bank's chief economist at the time. See also S. Dale and A.G. Haldane, 'Interest rates and the channels of monetary transmission: some sectoral estimates', Bank of England, Working Paper Series no. 18, 1993, for a description of the transmission mechanism in which the quantity of money plays no motivating role.

10. Johnson and Moggridge (eds), *Collected Writings of Keynes*, vol. V, *A Treatise on Money: The Pure Theory of Money* (London: Macmillan Press for the Royal Economic Society, 1971, originally published in 1930), ch. 15, 'The industrial circulation and the financial circulation', pp. 217–30. Keynes argued that 'the industrial circulation . . . will vary with . . . the aggregate of money incomes, i.e., with the volume and cost of production of current output' (p. 221), whereas 'the financial circulation is . . . determined by quite a different set of considerations' (p. 222). In his words, 'the amount of business deposits . . . required to look after financial business depends – apart from possible variations in the velocity of these deposits – on the volume of trading X the average value of the instruments traded' (also p. 222). Arguably, these remarks contained the germ of the later distinction between the transactions and speculative motives for holding

money. In the discussion of the financial circulation in *A Treatise of Money* securities (that is, equities and bonds) are the alternative to money; in the discussion of the speculative demand to hold money in *The General Theory* bonds are the alternative to money.

11. M. Friedman and D. Meiselman, 'The relative stability of monetary velocity and the investment multiplier in the United States, 1897–1958' in *Stabilization Policies* (Englewood Cliffs, NJ: Prentice Hall for the Commission on Money and Credit, 1963), pp. 165–268. See, in particular, p. 217.

12. T. Doggett, 'The 1989 Share Register Survey', *Economic Trends*, January 1991, pp. 116–21.

13. R. Thomas, 'The demand for M4: a sectoral analysis, Part I – The personal sector', Bank of England, Working Paper Series no. 61, 1997, and K.A. Chrystal and L. Drake, 'Personal sector money demand in the UK', *Oxford Economic Papers* (Oxford: Clarendon Press, 1967).

14. R. Thomas, 'The demand for M4: a sectoral analysis, Part II – The company sector', Bank of England, Working Paper Series no. 62, 1997 and K.A. Chrystal, 'Company sector money demand: new evidence on the existence of a stable long-run relationship for the UK', *Journal of Money, Credit and Banking*, 1994, vol. 26, pp. 479–94.

15. The author developed his ideas on UK financial institutions' money-holding behaviour over many years as a stockbroking economist and consultant, when such institutions were his principal clients.

16. Of course, every economy has international transactions. Such transactions represent another escape-valve for an excess supply or demand for money balances, in accordance with the monetary approach to the balance of payments. But to discuss the possibilities would take the paper too far. In any case, the incorporation of 'an overseas sector' in data sets on transactions in particular assets is conceptually straightforward. (See Table 14.3.) The overseas sector's transactions become entries in the capital account of the balance of payments. Again, it is conceptually straightforward – although empirically very demanding – to expand the arena of payments, the closed circuit for transactions, so that it becomes the world economy. (The reader may wonder why the essay uses the data for 1994 rather than a later year. The answer is that the Office for National Statistics no longer publishes the data in this form.)

17. The idea that investment adjusts until the market value of a capital equals the replacement cost is associated with James Tobin and 'the Q ratio', that is, the ratio of market value of a firm's capital to its replacement cost. See his article, 'A general equilibrium approach to monetary theory', *Journal of Money, Credit and Banking*, 1969, vol. 1, pp. 15–29. But similar remarks have been made by many economists, including Friedman. See his 'The lag in effect of monetary policy', in M. Friedman, *The Optimum Quantity of Money* (London: Macmillan, 1969), pp. 237–60, reprinted from a paper in 1961 in the *Journal of Political Economy*, and, in particular, pp. 255–6. When an excess supply of money affects asset markets, the result is 'to raise the prices of houses relative to the rents of dwelling units, or the cost of purchasing a car relative to the cost of renting one' and so on. In Friedman's view, 'the process operates through the balance sheet, and it is plausible that balance-sheet adjustments are sluggish in the sense that individuals spread adjustments over a considerable period of time' (p. 256).

18. Numerous studies identify a relationship between wealth and consumption. See, for example, J. Byrne and E.P. Davis, 'Disaggregate wealth and aggregate consumption: an investigation of empirical relationships in the G7', *National Institute of Economic and Social Research Discussion Paper*, no. 180 (London: National Institute, 2001).

19. An implication is that the circular flow of funds – such a familiar part of the undergraduate macroeconomic courses – is misleading and unrealistic when it is taken to imply that national income stays in line with national expenditure unless autonomous injections of demand come from the government or overseas. Any agent can sell any asset, obtain a money balance and use the proceeds to buy a good or service which constitutes part of national output, and the purchase leads to increased national income and expenditure. Similarly, any agent can run down a money balance and buy a good or service, with the same effects. Assets differ from money in that the nominal value of

money is given, whereas the nominal value of assets can vary without limit. The transactions involved in 'mortgage equity withdrawal' from the housing market – at present a topic of much interest – illustrate the merging of asset markets and markets in current goods and services. Much research on this topic has been conducted at the Bank of England. See, for example, M. Davey, 'Mortgage equity withdrawal and consumption', *Bank of England Quarterly Bulletin*, Spring 2001, pp. 100–103. The author introduced the concept of equity withdrawal to the analysis of personal sector spending in a paper written jointly with Paul Turnbull in 1982. (T. Congdon and P. Turnbull, 'The coming boom in housing credit', L. Messel & Co. research paper, June 1982, reprinted in T. Congdon, *Reflections on Monetarism* [Aldershot, UK and Brookfield, US: Edward Elgar for the Institute of Economic Affairs, 1992], pp. 274–87.) (The argument in this note is developed in more length in Essay 9.)

20. N. Kaldor, 'The new monetarism', *Lloyds Bank Review*, July 1970, pp. 1–17, reprinted on pp. 261–78 of A. Walters (ed.), *Money and Banking: Selected Readings* (Harmondsworth: Penguin Education, 1973). See, in particular, p. 268 in the book of papers edited by Walters.
21. Patrick Minford, paper from Liverpool Research Group, summer 1996. The passage was discussed in T. Congdon, 'An open letter to Professor Patrick Minford', *Gerrard & National Monthly Economic Review*, July 1996, pp. 3–12.
22. P. Minford, *The Supply Side Revolution in Britain* (Aldershot, UK and Brookfield, US: Edward Elgar for Institute of Economic Affairs, 1991), p. 70.
23. *Economic Trends: Annual Supplement* (London: National Statistics, 2002 edition), p. 245. The data on changes in the sectors' money balances later in this paragraph and in the next few paragraphs come from the database in the National Statistics website, as it was in the spring of 2004.
24. *Financial Statistics*, September 1972, pp. 88–91, and September 1976, pp. 88–9.
25. The figures for the *FT* industrial ordinary index are monthly averages.
26. *Economic Trends: Annual Supplement* (London: National Statistics, 2002), p. 245.
27. *Financial Statistics*, July 1987 and April 1989, table 7.13 in both issues.
28. *Financial Statistics*, July 1987 and April 1989, table 7.14 in both issues.
29. Note that this is the first occasion that interest rates have been introduced into the narrative. The narrative would undoubtedly have been enriched and been brought closer to reality if they had been introduced earlier, but a perfectly sensible account of events has been given without them.
30. *Financial Statistics*, August 1992, table 7.22, p. 92, and December 1994, table 5.1B, p. 83.
31. This point was noted on p. 11 of D. Chrystal and P. Mizen, 'Other financial corporations: Cinderella or ugly sister?', Bank of England Working Paper Series, no. 151, 2001. In their words, 'Life insurance companies and pension funds, for example, hold money on deposit but they do not take on significant bank borrowings'.
32. Kaldor's own argument is unsustainable. However, another objection to the Fisher/Friedman approach is more difficult to handle. This is that the quantity of money is not a *deus ex machina*; instead it must be endogenous, in that it is determined by processes within the economy. The 'Santa Claus hypothesis' in Fisher's story and the analogous 'helicopter money' idea in Friedman's work are blatantly unrealistic. Money is instead created by governments and central banks, and by banks and their customers, subject to a variety of economic incentives. It is plainly true that, in the real world, money is endogenous in this less ambitious sense. But that does not mean that the real balance effect is not at work. Instead the vital implication of the endogeneity of money is that two types of process need to be distinguished. These are,

● the processes by which money is created, and
● the processes by which the economy adjusts to changes in the quantity of money (i.e., the real-balance effect).

There is no necessity, in any particular quarter or year, either for the quantity of money itself to be in equilibrium (that is, for the banking system's size and deposit liabilities to be stable and unchanging) or for the quantity of money actually in being to be equal to the demand to hold it. Ironically, Kaldor's central claim – that the banking system creates enough money balances to ensure that the demand to hold money equals the supply (and so a real balance effect never unfolds) – prevents discussion of certain problems of macroeconomic instability in a capitalist economy with a banking system. The processes of money supply creation and the processes whereby the economy adjusts to changes in the quantity of money are processes in time. It is possible that the time taken for agents to eliminate excess or deficient money balances is so long that injections or withdrawals of money in the interval are large enough to prevent agents moving back onto their money demand schedules. Agents keep on adjusting their asset dispositions and expenditure on goods and services in order to equate the demand for money with the money supply, but they are constantly frustrated from reaching monetary equilibrium by changes in the money supply. If the changes in the money supply are very rapid (expanding, for example, because of a vast budget deficit, or contracting, for example, because of the effect of debt-deflation on banks' capital and then the quantity of money), they exaggerate the monetary disequilibrium and the economy becomes severely unstable. Examples in one direction are wild hyperinflations and in the other the Great Depression in the USA between 1929 and 1933. The income-expenditure model is useless in understanding such episodes. As Wicksell argued, a modern economy – in which money is created by bank credit – may be inherently unstable, unlike a traditional economy in which all money was a commodity. The suggestions in this note are to be developed in more detail in the author's *Money in a Modern Economy* (forthcoming), to be published by Edward Elgar.

33.	The author has made this point on a number of occasions. See, for example, 'Credit, broad money and economic activity', pp. 171–90, in T. Congdon, *Reflections on Monetarism* (Aldershot, UK and Brookfield, US: Edward Elgar, 1992), particularly pp. 182–3, and T. Congdon, 'Broad money vs. narrow money', in *The Review of Policy Issues* (Sheffield: Sheffield Hallam University, 1995), pp. 13–27. All measures of narrow money are endogenous in that agents' individual attempts to alter their money holdings also change the aggregate quantity of money. An all-inclusive money measure, that is, a broad money measure, is not endogenous in this sense. A broad money measure may nevertheless be endogenous in the sense that it reflects processes within an economy, and particularly processes inside the banking system, subject to price incentives. But the endogeneity of broad money in this sense still leaves it with the ability, when disturbed from an equilibrium level, to change asset dispositions and expenditure patterns, in accordance with the Fisher/Friedman/Patinkin story. See also note 32 above.

34.	P. Minford, *Markets Not Stakes* (London: Orion Business Books, 1998), p. 104.

35.	Minford, *Markets*, p. 105. Milton Friedman in a personal communication with the author complained that this essay's discussion of the irrelevance of the base to financial institutions' behaviour was too long, since the point was obvious. In his reply the author recalled Friedman's own classic 1956 paper restating the quantity theory of money, in which Friedman said 'the theory of the demand for money is a special topic in the theory of capital'. He asked Friedman whether he thought the theory of the demand for *narrow* money was a special topic in the theory of capital, since – on the evidence of UK's financial institutions' behaviour – it plainly was not. Surely – if economists want to assemble *a monetary theory of the joint determination of asset prices and national income* – an all-inclusive measure of money must be put to work. Again, the suggestions here are to be developed in more detail in the author's *Money in a Modern Economy* (forthcoming), to be published by Edward Elgar.

36.	The author used the phrase 'too much money chasing too few assets' in a newspaper article in *The Times* of 9 January 1986, in a reaction on the recent sharp upturn in money supply growth. But it was recognized that inflation was not imminent. Immediately after the mention of money and assets, the comment was, 'But it is nonsense, while unemployment remains above three million, industry has abundant spare capacity and there is scope to increase output, to say that "too much money is chasing too few goods"'.

(The article, 'Why Lawson must repent', was reprinted as 'A forecast of a Lawson min-boom', pp. 123–5, in Congdon's *Reflections on Monetarism.*)

37. Minford attributes his own thinking on money – particularly his view that bank credit, bank deposits and the banking system are irrelevant to macroeconomic outcomes – to an American economist, Eugene Fama, and especially to two papers written by Fama in 1980 and 1983. See Minford, *Supply Side Revolution*, p. 73, and Minford, *Markets not Stakes*, p. 103.

38. See the Annex, by P. Warburton on 'Econometric analysis of one type of real balance effect', pp. 119–21, to T. Congdon, 'Money, asset prices and the boom–bust cycles in the UK: an analysis of the transmission mechanism from money to macroeconomic outcomes', in K. Matthews and P. Booth (eds), *Issues in Monetary Policy* (Chichester: John Wiley and Sons, 2006), pp. 103–22.

39. According to one analyst highly critical of the role of the money supply as a policy guide, the results of his work showed that 'money holdings of OFIs might be the best leading indicator of money income of all the monetary variables', although qualifying this by noting that in Q2 1990 his equation overpredicted the OFIs' money holdings. He appeared not to entertain the possibility that the under-prediction relative to the equation indicated that the OFIs were short of money balances, and that this might affect future asset values and the economy. (G. Young, *The Influence of Financial Intermediaries on the Behaviour of the UK Economy* [London: National Institute of Economic and Social Research, Occasional Papers no. 50, 1996], p. 97.)

15. Some aspects of the transmission mechanism

A common allegation is that monetary economics lacks a theoretically integrated and empirically plausible account of 'the transmission mechanism', where the transmission mechanism is the process (or set of processes) by which changes in the quantity of money lead to changes in national income.[1] As monetarism would be incomplete without a transmission mechanism, this allegation would be serious if it were true. In fact, monetary economics has a simple and persuasive body of ideas which relates the quantity of money to asset prices and national income, and which has been passed down through successive generations of teachers and students at some universities, although certainly not all. (In one case the ideas formed the celebrated 'oral tradition' of Chicago monetary economics.[2]) However, monetary economics is no longer taught with much rigour in most British universities and the transmission mechanism from money to the economy is undoubtedly a mystery to many British economists.

I set up a company, Lombard Street Research, in July 1989. My main aim in establishing the company was to maintain an approach to macroeconomic analysis which I had developed in the 1970s and 1980s as a journalist on *The Times*, and, in much more detail, as an economist at the stockbrokers, L. Messel & Co., and the investment bank, Shearson Lehman (now Lehman Brothers). My ambition was that Lombard Street Research would prove a viable home for a continuing UK macroeconomic forecast with a large role for money. The model contained a transmission mechanism – or rather a number of transmission mechanisms – in which money influenced expenditure on goods and services, both directly and indirectly via asset markets and prices. The purpose of this paper is to outline the development of my thinking on macroeconomic policy, to describe some of the key ideas in the Lombard Street Research approach and to see how well they survived the 15 years to 2004. (I left Lombard Street Research in September 2005.)

I

The two core principles of the approach were not original. They were – and still are – to be found, in one form or another, in virtually every macroeconomics textbook. They are that,

- national income is in equilibrium only when the demand for money is equal to the supply of money (that is, when monetary equilibrium prevails), and,
- the demand to hold money balances (that is, the demand for money) is a stable function of a small number of variables, notably income and the attractiveness of money relative to the nearest alternative asset.

The first principle is integral to a large number of economic models. For example, it is contained in the IS–LM model of national income determination which was devised by Hicks in 1937 as a way of reconciling Keynes's *General Theory* with 'the classics'. The second principle is sometimes deemed to have an ideological tinge, since much of the most influential work in estimating demand-for-money functions was carried out by Professor Milton Friedman, a champion of free market economics. But demand functions can be estimated, as a technical matter, for any product. No one would regard the statement 'the demand for socks (or potatoes or foreign holidays) is a stable function of a small number of variables' as politically contentious.

The two core principles in Lombard Street Research's work have a logically necessary implication. This is that when the supply of money changes, so also does the equilibrium level of nominal national income. Further, when the rate of growth of the money supply increases, so also does the equilibrium rate of growth of nominal national income. Another point follows quickly. It is common sense that nations cannot make themselves rich by the mere printing of money. In the long run real output must depend primarily on real considerations, such as the number of working-age people and their degree of skill. Hence, if the money supply is rising at a faster rate than the trend rate of output growth, an increase in the price level is likely, while an acceleration in money supply growth is likely to lead to a higher rate of inflation.

It has always seemed to me that these ideas ought to be accepted by anyone interested in economics. However, for all of the past 50 years they have been controversial to a greater or lesser degree. In the 1960s and 1970s the preferred style of policy-making in the UK relied on two alternative and quite different sets of ideas, corporatism and Keynesianism.[3] The debates

between monetarism, corporatism and Keynesianism are covered elsewhere in this volume and need not detain us here. At any rate, there is not
much doubt that the late 1970s saw a radical reorientation of British economic policy. In particular, after the 1979 general election the Thatcher
government rejected incomes policy as a method of controlling inflation
and fiscal fine-tuning as an instrument of demand management.

So in the early 1980s it seemed that the monetary theory of the determination of national income and inflation had been adopted by the government, and that in policy-making circles it had become an accepted
orthodoxy. Since money targets were expressed in terms of broad money, a
logical deduction was that the officially favoured theory related to a broadly
defined aggregate. This impression was misleading. In fact, it seems that
none of the key players accorded broad money a prominent position in
their view on national income determination, in so far as they had thought
through the matter at all.[4] The next few years were to see considerable
difficulties in the agenda of monetary control, and the emergence of a far
more eclectic, pragmatic and intellectually confused approach by policy-
makers. It should be emphasized that the new pragmatism did not include
a return to incomes policies and fiscal fine-tuning, and that the UK therefore genuinely did have a 'monetarist counter-revolution'. Corporatism and
Keynesianism were renounced by policy-makers in 1979 and 1980, and
have never come back. Nevertheless, the emphasis on money supply targets
as the centrepiece of policy was heavily diluted. As an economist in the City
in the early 1980s, I commented every week on monetary developments and
spent much of my time writing newspaper articles in defence of the money
supply targets which had been introduced in the late 1970s.

Every quarter I prepared a research document, called *Financial Analysis*,
which considered the financial position and monetary behaviour of the
economy's main sectors. Apart from the banks and the public sector, these
were the personal (or household) sector, the corporate sector (that is, companies as such, or 'industrial and commercial companies') and the financial
sector (that is, 'non-bank financial institutions'). An abundance of data
was available for analysis, because – following the recommendations of the
Radcliffe Report[5] of 1959 – a vast amount of information about the
banking and financial systems has been compiled in the UK since 1963. It
was my work for *Financial Analysis* that led me to organize my ideas about
the so-called 'transmission mechanism' of monetary policy.

One point had seemed obvious to me from the early 1970s, although (as
I gradually realized) it was far from obvious to most other economists. This
point was that – if we want to understand the relationship between the
quantity of money and the spending behaviour of those agents that matter
to the business cycle – only a broadly defined, all-inclusive money supply

measure is of interest. The so-called 'narrow money' measures have some information value, but narrow money measures have little or no causal role in the economy. The reason that narrow money has no causal role in the economy is quite simple, but it may help to elucidate the matter in a few paragraphs.

One of the most compelling theoretical constructs in economics is the notion of a 'general equilibrium'. Simplifying greatly, this is a situation in which the demand and supply functions for all products intersect at their equilibrium points, setting prices and quantities in the economy. As noted in the opening paragraphs to this essay, it is an essential aspect of a general equilibrium that the demand for money should equal the money supply. If the demand for money differs from the money supply, general equilibrium does not prevail. Agents try to eliminate the excess, or shortage, of money by spending above, or beneath, income or by asset re-dispositions. My view – much influenced by the boom–bust cycle of the 1970s, but also by wider reading of economic history – was (and remains) that most cyclical instabilities are the result of such 'monetary disequilibrium'. In other words, fluctuations in asset prices and expenditure are best interpreted as due to mismatches between the demand for money and the money supply, while these mismatches are due to big swings in money supply growth. Such swings arise, typically, from mistakes in interest-rate setting by the central bank, although they can have many other causes. These other causes can include an excessive budget deficit with consequent 'money printing', an inappropriate exchange rate and heavy foreign exchange intervention, and major financial deregulation and associated rapid credit expansion. Plainly, in this story excesses or deficiencies of money balances cause the adjustment of spending plans and asset portfolios, and the two pivotal parts of the process are the decisions taken by agents in their balancing of money against goods, and of money against assets.

In this context the trouble with any measure of narrow money is that it is only a sub-set of money as a whole. For example, in the UK consider the narrow money measure, M0, data for which were published between 1984 and 2006. It consisted mostly of notes and coin, and included no bank deposits. It was less than 5 per cent of the M4 aggregate, which was predominantly bank deposits and included virtually all conceivable money balances. If agents had excess or deficient M0, they could adjust their holding of M0 by transfers of funds between M0 and a non-M0 money balance inside M4. For example, they could transfer cash into or out of bank deposits. Such 'money transfers' restored the equivalence of the demand for M0 with its supply, but they did not affect spending on goods or asset portfolios. Monetary disequilibrium in M0 was therefore irrelevant to the business cycle. (It should also be mentioned that – in both the USA and the UK – the value of transactions in cash is less than 1 per cent of the value of all transactions. The notion that M0 could affect the major investment and portfolio decisions of large companies and financial institutions was particularly silly, since many of them held no cash whatsoever. Their money balances were entirely in the form of bank deposits.)[6]

So an analysis of the relationship between money and the economy must be an analysis of the relationship between an all-inclusive money measure on the one hand, and the spending decisions and asset dispositions of the economy's main sectors on the other. I was amazed that in the early 1980s official policy de-emphasized broad money and paid an increasing amount of attention to M0. This shift of emphasis was partly due to some genuine, although much exaggerated difficulties in the relationship between broad money and expenditure in those years, but also important were criticisms of broad money made by some monetarist economists, notably Sir Alan Walters and Patrick Minford. I disagreed with Walters and Minford (as I still do), and made my disagreement known in various places. Despite the background, I persevered with my work on the UK's flow-of-funds data and sectoral monetary information, and began to notice certain regularities. By the mid-1980s the data series were typically over 20 years long and the number of observations in the key relationships implied acceptable levels of statistical significance. I noticed, in particular, three regularities.

> *Regularity I.* The personal sector's demand-for-money function was more stable than that of the other private sectors' demand-for-money functions (that is, the demand for money function of the corporate and financial sectors, either individually or combined).
>
> *Regularity II.* A key measure of the corporate sector's balance sheet strength was the ratio of companies' money balances to their bank borrowings, which I called 'the corporate liquidity ratio'. This liquidity ratio seemed to be relevant to their investment spending and to private domestic demand as a whole.
>
> *Regularity III.* A key measure of financial institutions' attitude towards their money holdings was the ratio of their monetary assets, or liquid/'short-term' assets, to their total assets. Over long periods this ratio gravitated back to a value of about 4 per cent for the most important UK institutions (that is, the life offices and pension funds [LAPF]). I called this ratio 'the institutional liquidity ratio'.

It needs to be emphasized that none of these regularities had been much disturbed by the turbulence and financial deregulation of the early 1980s. An undoubted implication was that the rate of growth of the money supply, broadly defined, was critical to the economy's behaviour.

In both the Heath–Barber boom of the early 1970s and a milder cyclical episode in the late 1970s (the Healey 'boomlet' of 1978 and 1979) I had noticed a pattern in the growth rates of the different sectors' money balances. This was that an upturn in the growth rate of the money supply was accompanied by only a small change in the growth rate of the personal sector's money, because of *Regularity I*. The upturn in money growth was therefore associated with much more pronounced increases in the growth rate of corporate and financial sector money than in the growth rate of aggregate money. *Regularity II* implied that the consequent sharp rise in the corporate liquidity ratio would lead to more investment spending and buoyant domestic demand, as well as to higher asset prices, in so far as companies tried to eliminate excess money by takeover activity and other asset purchases. Meanwhile *Regularity III* implied unusually large asset price increases. In both the Heath–Barber boom and the Healey boomlet asset price strength became general as companies and people – mostly rich people – bought and sold assets, to bring the valuations of the different assets, and of their monetary and non-monetary assets, into the right relationship with each other. The asset price strength infiltrated the markets for goods and services, and was followed by higher inflation at the retail level.

II

I was therefore astonished when in October 1985 Mr Nigel (later Lord) Lawson, the Chancellor of the Exchequer, suspended (as a prelude to scrapping) broad money targets. The true explanation for this decision was that Lawson had come to regret his commitment to money supply targetry at the very start of the Thatcher government and instead preferred to base monetary policy on the exchange rate, particularly the exchange rate between the pound and the Deutschmark. In the year from October 1985 the annual growth rate of broad money accelerated sharply, by about 5 to 6 per cent on the M3 money measure, which included only bank deposits, and by about 2 or 3 per cent on the M4 measure, which included both bank and building society deposits. The acceleration continued into 1987, when the growth rate of M3 exceeded 20 per cent for the first time since the early 1970s.

Given the work that I had been doing over the previous 15 years, it was obvious to me that the money supply acceleration would lead to a boom and a significant increase in inflation. Moreover, I doubted that a later bust could be avoided if the UK were to restore an internationally respectable inflation rate. From early 1986 I warned about the risks in a sequence of articles in *The Times*, but my warnings were dismissed as lightweight journalism by key policy-makers in the Treasury and the Bank of England.

Their refusal to take the warnings seriously prompted me to ask Peter Warburton – whose econometric expertise had previously been deployed on the highly regarded London Business School model – to join me at Messel/Shearson Lehman. The forecasts we prepared together between late 1986 and mid-1988 were detailed and rigorous, with forward projections of the money holdings of the personal, corporate and financial sectors, and related these agents' asset and expenditure decisions to their money balances. The forecasts were largely correct. The boom of 1987 and 1988 was followed by rising inflation and interest rates in 1989 and 1990, and by a bust between 1990 and 1992.

However, in mid-1988 the outcome of the Lawson boom still lay in the future. After Messel had been bought by Shearson Lehman, my research department became accountable to executives in New York with little interest in British public policy issues, except in so far as they affected 'the bottom line'. My American employers gave me the opportunity to leave, which I was happy to take. In late 1988 I approached Mr Brian (later Sir Brian) Williamson, then a director of Gerrard & National, to see whether his company would like to set up a joint venture with me. The joint venture would be a monetary research company, intended to produce forecasts of the British economy and sell them and other research work, mostly – but not exclusively – to large financial institutions. Mr Williamson persuaded the Gerrard & National board to go along with the proposal. With a capital of £100 and a loan facility of £50 000, Lombard Street Research began trading in July 1989. I was fortunate in my years at Lombard Street Research to enjoy the support and friendship of many excellent colleagues, who worked with me on UK monetary research and macroeconomic forecasting. As a result, the analytical approach I started at Messel was maintained. The first issue of Lombard Street Research's *Quarterly UK Economic Forecast* appeared in December 1989, with the opening sentence: 'Mr Lawson has bungled the electoral business cycle.' Page 9 contained an analysis of 'the sectoral breakdown of monetary growth', on much the same lines as the work done at Messel earlier. Later pages reviewed the money holdings and balance-sheet patterns of the personal, financial and corporate sectors, and related these to expenditure decisions. The format of the *Quarterly UK Economic Forecast* in 2004 was almost exactly as it had been in 1989. Our monthly *Portfolio Strategy* publication also had pages on financial institutions' and companies' liquidity positions, with the purpose of making assessments of likely future movements in asset prices and demand.

Did the linkages between money and the economy in the roughly 25 years of data to 1989 survive into the 15 years to 2004? In particular, did the three regularities continue to apply? In 1993 Simon Ward and I wrote a short econometric research note on the personal sector's demand for money. With a relatively simple specification in which income and the attractiveness of money relative to other assets were the key arguments, it was possible to show that the personal sector's demand for money had been stable, according to the usual statistical significance tests, for 30 years from 1963. Since the personal sector's money balances represented over half of all money, this was a very significant finding. The same equation – with minor amendments – worked fine in the second half of the 1990s, although it did begin to under-predict actual holdings in the opening years of the twenty-first century. Other researchers have also carried out econometric testing on the personal sector's money demand and reached similar results.[7] *Regularity I* seems to have become more widely recognised.

What about *Regularity II*? I had noticed in the late 1970s and 1980s that fluctuations in the corporate liquidity ratio were loosely correlated with fluctuations in gross domestic product, while the ratio itself seemed to average a value slightly above a half. Admittedly, the ratio had been much higher than a half in the early 1960s. But, as the banking system was liberalized and became more competitive in the late 1960s and 1970s, companies seem to have decided that they could manage with lower liquidity. An important watershed was the Competition and Credit Control reforms of September 1971, which were intended to mark the end of quantitative controls on bank lending. In the 25 years from the start of data to the fourth quarter (Q4) of 1988 – that is, in the 25 years before the founding of Lombard Street Research – the average value of the corporate liquidity ratio was 59.4 per cent. Between Q3 1971 and Q4 1988 the average value of the ratio was a shade lower, at 56.6 per cent. The stability of the average value over such long periods led me to expect that the ratio would take much the same value in future. So what did happen in the 15 years to the end of 2003? The answer is that in this period the average value of the liquidity ratio was 57.4 per cent! In other words, UK companies have been operating with much the same notion of a sensible long-run average, or 'equilibrium', ratio of bank deposits to bank borrowings for over 30 years. The tendency of the ratio to revert to the same average value is all the more remarkable, given that in the just over 32 years from Q3 1971 to Q4 2003 their M4 holdings climbed from £4.0 billion to £170.7 billion (or by 42.2 times) and their M4 borrowings increased from £6.9 billion to £270.0 billion (or by 39.3 times).

To say that the ratio has had a tendency to revert to the same equilibrium value does not mean that it has stayed close to the equilibrium value all the time. As Figure 15.1 shows, there were large deviations from the average on the upside in 1972 and in the late 1980s, and on the downside in 1974, 1980 and 1990–91. The two upside deviations were periods of boom, whereas the

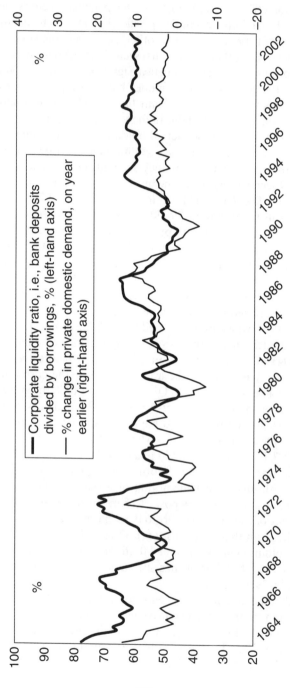

Figure 15.1 Corporate liquidity and domestic demand, 1964–2003 (quarterly data)

three downside deviations saw pronounced demand weakness. The rationale for the relationship is simple. When companies have strong liquidity they are inclined to spend more on capital equipment, recruitment and stock-building, but when liquidity is under pressure they cut back. (The appendix provides some econometric results on the relationship between the corporate liquidity ratio and private sector domestic demand.)

And what about *Regularity III?* In preparing this essay I checked the values of the institutional liquidity ratio over the 31 years to the end of 2003, that is, roughly speaking, the period in which expectations of never-ending inflation had become established and made equities the core asset for most UK savings institutions. In the 16 years to end-1988 the institutional liquidity ratio averaged 4.33 per cent. The ratio saw sharp swings, from a value of over 9 per cent at the end of 1974 to under 3 per cent at the end of 1986. It is interesting that high values generally coincided with stock market weaknesses and low values with stock market strength. Over the 16 years life offices' and pension funds' short-term assets – mostly bank deposits – rose by a multiple of 13.5 times, from £756 million to £20 978 million, while their total assets rose by a multiple of 14.5 times, from £30 224 million to £465 820 million. By contrast, the institutional liquidity ratio changed only slightly, falling by 7 per cent.

When I founded Lombard Street Research I expected that the ratio would vary significantly from year to year, as it had done in the past, but that its long-run average value would be much the same as it had been between 1972 and 1988. By checking the figures I was able to test this hypothesis. It turned out that the ratio in the 15 years to end-2003 averaged 4.37 per cent, astonishingly close to the average of 4.33 per cent in the 16 years to 1988! (See Figure 14.1 on p. 288.) Of course, this result is a fluke. It must be a fluke both because the ratio is volatile from year to year, and because the portfolio preferences of life offices and pension funds are different within the LAPF total. Nevertheless, the similarity of the institutional liquidity ratio in the periods 1972–88 and 1989–2003 is striking, and implies that over a 30-year period senior executives in the UK's long-term savings institutions had a fairly stable notion of the appropriate ratio of monetary, or 'short-term', assets to their total assets. In the 31 years to the end of 2003 the LAPFs' short-term assets rose by 83.6 times and their total assets by 54.8 times, while the liquidity ratio changed by 52 per cent.

III

The conclusion has to be that the three regularities I noticed from the monetary data in the 25 years to 1988 survived to 2004. These regularities related to the monetary behaviour of the entire UK non-bank private sector. My view on these issues remains the same as when I founded Lombard Street Research. I continue to believe that the behaviour of the quantity of money, broadly defined, to include all bank deposits, is fundamental to the cyclical changes in asset prices and investment expenditure observed in the UK economy, and in other economies, and that these changes are in turn critical to demand, employment and inflation. I like to think that my work as a business economist has not only helped my clients, but also improved policy-makers' understanding of how the economy works.

NOTES

1. For an example of scepticism about the monetarist approach to the transmission mechanism, see the criticisms of Friedman made by Goodhart on pp. 190–91 of the 1st edition of his *Money, Information and Uncertainty* (London: Macmillan, 1975). But in the 2nd edition of *Money, Information and Uncertainty* (London: Macmillan, 1989) Goodhart was more sympathetic to the monetarist story, particularly when money was seen as a 'buffer-stock' to even out expenditure. (See pp. 281–5 of the 2nd edition.)
2. Friedman claimed that the University of Chicago had an 'oral tradition' of monetary economics, which explained the distinctiveness of its monetary thought in the 1950s and 1960s. The content of economics course at Chicago in those decades was undoubtedly very different from that in Cambridge, England, or Cambridge, Massachusetts.
3. As this is an autobiographical piece, I thought readers might be interested to know that one of my earliest papers – a critique of the then Conservative government's Counter-Inflation Programme – was published in *The Bankers' Magazine* in 1973. I had written it while at Nuffield College, Oxford, as a postgraduate student. Nigel Lawson was on the same staircase as a Journalist Fellow. He was working (with Jock Bruce-Gardyne) on a book on past blunders in British policy-making, published in 1976 as *The Power Game*. He very kindly took a few hours to read my paper and commented on it favourably.
4. From 1983 – when Nigel Lawson became Chancellor of the Exchequer – the four key individuals close to Treasury policy-making were Lawson himself, Sir Terence (later Lord) Burns, Sir Peter Middleton and Sir Alan Walters. (Burns was Chief Economic Adviser and Middleton Permanent Secretary to the Treasury, and – when he was not away – Walters was Economic Adviser to the Prime Minister, Mrs Thatcher.) Lawson's views on broad money take up barely a sentence or two of his *The View from No. 11* ([London and New York: Bantam Press, 1992] see pp. 78–9) and he was responsible for the introduction of the target for M0 (p. 453); Burns had written on 'international monetarism' and the role of differential monetary growth rates (in different countries) in determining the exchange rate before becoming Chief Economic Adviser in 1980, but he has made no substantial statement on money aggregates and the monetary transmission mechanism since then; Middleton never gave any written justification, in his own name, for whatever views he held in the 1980s on the money aggregates, but he poked fun at monetarists in his 1988 Jubilee Lecture to the National Institute of Economic and Social Research, and that probably represents his true position; Walters shilly-shallied in the course of his career between broad and narrow money, but in the 1980s was committed to narrow money, which he praised on pp. 116–20 of his *Britain's Economic Renaissance* (New York and Oxford: Oxford University Press, 1986). Of this group Walters was plainly the most interested in monetary economics and the transmission mechanism. For a critique of the views on the money aggregates expressed in *Britain's Economic Renaissance*, see T. Congdon, *Money*

and Asset Prices in Boom and Bust (London: Institute of Economic Affairs, 2005), pp. 83–5. For a rather cynical survey of the beliefs of the various players, see G. Pepper and M. Oliver, *Monetarism under Thatcher: Lessons for the Future* (Cheltenham, UK and Northampton, MA, USA: Edward Elgar, 2001).
5. *Report of the Committee on the Working of the Monetary System* (Cmnd. 827) (London: HMSO, 1959).
6. This point is made, in criticism of Minford's views on M0, on pp. 78–83 of T. Congdon, *Money and Asset Prices in Boom and Bust* (London: Institute of Economic Affairs, 2005). See also Essay 14, particularly pp. 304–7.
7. See note 23 to Essay 12.

APPENDIX: THE RELATIONSHIP BETWEEN CORPORATE LIQUIDITY AND PRIVATE SECTOR DOMESTIC DEMAND IN THE UK, 1964–2003

The argument in the text was that – because of the effect of their balance-sheet strength on companies' investment spending (among other things) – the change in private sector domestic demand could be interpreted as heavily influenced by the corporate liquidity ratio (that is, the ratio of industrial and commercial companies' bank deposits to their bank borrowings). Figure 15.1 showed the two series over the 1964–2003 period. (The change in private sector domestic demand was the annual change, that is, the percentage change in the last four quarters, in real terms.)

The following equation relates to the two series over the entire Q1 1964–Q4 2003 period:

Change in real private sector domestic demand (per cent p.a.) = −13.63 + 0.28 Corporate liquidity ratio, %
$R^2 = 0.28$
t statistic on regression coefficient 7.85   (15.1)

The equation for the 25 years from Q1 1964 to Q4 1988 (i.e., the 25 years before the founding of Lombard Street Research) was as follows:

Change in real private sector domestic demand (per cent p.a.) = −12.56 + 0.27 Corporate liquidity ratio, %
$R^2 = 0.23$
t statistic on regression coefficient 5.43   (15.2)

The equation for the 15 years from Q1 1989 to Q4 2003 (that is, the 15 years from the founding of Lombard Street Research) was as follows:

Change in real private sector domestic demand (per cent p.a.) = −16.56 + 0.33 Corporate liquidity ratio, %
$R^2 = 0.48$
t statistic on regression coefficient 7.37   (15.3)

This exercise shows that the relationship between corporate liquidity and the change in private domestic demand – which I had noticed before setting up Lombard Street Research in 1989 – was more well defined in the subsequent 15 years than in the previous 25 years. The corporate liquidity ratio – which is plainly a monetary variable (as it includes bank deposits) – was useful as a forecasting tool. The claim that monetary variables are unhelpful in forecasting (because of 'instabilities', 'the breakdown of relationships', and so on) was wrong, at least in my experience with these particular variables.

Index

Titles of publications are in *italics*.

Index